WORKING WITH AUDIO

Stanley R. Alten

Course Technology PTR

A part of Cengage Learning

COURSE TECHNOLOGY
CENGAGE Learning™

Australia, Brazil, Japan, Korea, Mexico, Singapore, Spain, United Kingdom, United States

COURSE TECHNOLOGY
CENGAGE Learning™

Working with Audio
Stanley R. Alten

Senior Publisher:
Lyn Uhl

Publisher:
Michael Rosenberg

Associate Director of Marketing:
Sarah Panella

Manager of Editorial Services:
Heather Talbot

Marketing Manager:
Mark Hughes

Development Editor:
Megan Garvey

Assistant Editor:
Jillian D'Urso

Editorial Assistant:
Erin Pass

Media Editor:
Jessica Badiner

Project Editors:
Mark Garvey and Karen A. Gill

Interior Layout Tech:
Bill Hartman

Cover Designer:
Luke Fletcher

Indexer:
Valerie Haynes Perry

Proofreader:
Caroline Roop

For product information and technology assistance, contact us at
Cengage Learning Customer & Sales Support, 1-800-354-9706.

For permission to use material from this text or product,
submit all requests online at **cengage.com/permissions**.
Further permissions questions can be e-mailed to
permissionrequest@cengage.com.

All trademarks are the property of their respective owners.

All images © Cengage Learning unless otherwise noted.

Library of Congress Control Number: 2011933248

ISBN-13: 978-1-4354-6055-3

ISBN-10: 1-4354-6055-3

Course Technology, a part of Cengage Learning
20 Channel Center Street
Boston, MA 02210
USA

Cengage Learning is a leading provider of customized learning solutions with office locations around the globe, including Singapore, the United Kingdom, Australia, Mexico, Brazil, and Japan. Locate your local office at: **international.cengage.com/region**.

Cengage Learning products are represented in Canada by Nelson Education, Ltd.

For your lifelong learning solutions, visit **courseptr.com**.

Visit our corporate Web site at **cengage.com**.

Printed in the United States of America
1 2 3 4 5 6 7 15 14 13 12 11

CONTENTS

PREFACE

Learning the fundamentals of any enterprise is a necessary stepping-stone to more advanced study and implementation of skills. This book provides the stepping-stone to the world of audio and audio recording, introducing the basic principles, technology, techniques, and aesthetics of sound.

Structure of the Book

This book's content has been kept as generic as possible, in order to facilitate a general understanding of sound production and to better complement the book's purpose as a basic introduction to the world of audio. Each chapter concludes with a list of its main points. Key terms are identified in **bold italic** and defined in the Glossary. More than two hundred and forty illustrations visually reinforce principles, technical concepts, and production techniques.

Chapter 1, "Behavior of Sound," introduces the physical behavior of sound and its relationship to our psychophysical perception of sound stimuli.

Chapter 2, "The Ear and Hearing," details the characteristics of the human ear; the importance of healthy hearing, especially to the audio professional; and ways to guard against hearing loss.

Chapter 3, "Perception of Sound," develops material in Chapter 1 related to the objective behavior of received sound and its subjective effect on human response.

Chapter 4, "Studio and Control Room Design," discusses the acoustic and psychoacoustic considerations that affect studio and control construction.

Chapter 5, "Monitoring," deals with the relationship between loudspeaker selection and control room monitoring in stereo and surround-sound. A section on headphones is also included.

Chapter 6, "Microphones," introduces their principles, characteristics, types, and accessories.

Chapter 7, "Microphone Techniques," applies how various types of microphones are positioned in relation to speakers, vocalists, musical instruments, and music ensembles. Content includes stereo and surround-sound microphone arrays.

Chapter 8, "Mixers, Consoles, and Control Surfaces," covers their signal flow and design. Patching and console automation are also discussed.

Chapter 9, "Recording," deals with basic digital theory; removable and fixed digital recording systems; Musical Instrument Digital Interface (MIDI); and digital audio networking.

Chapter 10, "Synchronization and Transfers," covers these fundamental aspects of production and postproduction.

Chapter 11, "Signal Processors," addresses the general principles of signal processors—stand-alone and plug-ins—and their effects on sound.

Chapter 12, "Editing," describes the techniques of digital editing. Content includes transitions; general editing guidelines; organizing the edit tracks; and the aesthetic considerations that apply to editing speech, dialogue, music, and sound effects.

Chapter 13, "Mixing," covers its general purposes; aesthetic considerations; mixing for radio, picture, and music; recordkeeping; metering; and evaluation.

Chapter 14, "Internet Audio," deals with sound quality on the Internet, online collaborative recording, podcasting, and producing for mobile media.

Chapter 15, "Influences of Sound on Meaning," brings together the variety of ways in which sound in nonverbal speech, sound effects, and music, and overall sound design, affect meaning.

ACKNOWLEDGMENTS

To the following reviewers, I offer my sincere gratitude for their insightful suggestions that helped direct the content of this book. Steven Buss, California State University at Sacramento; Dan Sheehan, Bergen Community College; Adam Olson, Shenandoah University; Wayne Meals, San Antonio College; Reggie Miles, Howard University; Todd Herreman, Southern Illinois University; Michael Lasater, Indiana University; and Eileen Smitheimer, University of Delaware.

To the legion of industry and academic professionals, too numerous to list here, who contributed to *Audio in Media* over the years and from which much of the material for this book has been adapted, my continuing thanks and appreciation for their contributions.

Special thanks go my colleague, Dr. Douglas Quin, Associate Professor, Syracuse University, for his forward-thinking contributions to several of the chapters and for organizing the art program.

My gratitude to Stuart Provine, sound designer and editor, for his contribution to the Editing chapter.

To Dr. Herbert Zettl, Professor Emeritus, San Francisco State University, goes my appreciation for his counsel.

Thanks to Publisher Michael Rosenberg and Development Editor Megan Garvey for their ongoing help and support.

As anyone familiar with writing a book knows, it is a team effort. I consider myself fortunate to have had such an excellent team involved in this project.

—Stanley R. Alten

1 Behavior of Sound

What is sound? The answer depends on who you ask. A physicist will tell you that sound is both a disturbance of molecules caused by vibrations transmitted through an elastic medium (such as air) and the interaction of these vibrations within an environment. This definition does not mean much to the psychologist, who thinks of sound as a human response.

To put the question another way: If a tree falls in a forest and there is no one to hear it, does the falling tree make a sound? The physicist would say yes because a falling tree causes vibrations, and sound is vibration. The psychologist would probably say no because, without a perceived sensation, there can be no human response; hence, there is no sound. In practical terms, both the physicist and the psychologist are right. Sound is a cause-and-effect phenomenon, and the psychological cannot really be untangled from the physical. Thus, in audio production, you need to understand both the objective and the subjective characteristics of sound. Not to do so is somewhat like arguing about the falling tree in the forest—it is an interesting, but unproductive, exercise.

The Sound Wave

Sound is produced by vibrations that set into motion longitudinal waves of compression and rarefaction propagated through molecular structures such as gases, liquids, and solids. The molecules first set into motion those closest to the vibrating object and then pass on their energy to adjacent molecules, starting a reaction—a *sound wave*—much like the waves that result when a stone is dropped into a pool. The transfer of momentum from one displaced molecule to the next propagates the original vibrations longitudinally from the vibrating object to the hearer. What makes this reaction possible is air or, more precisely, a molecular medium with the property of elasticity. *Elasticity* is the phenomenon in which a displaced molecule tends to pull back to its original position after its initial momentum has caused it to displace nearby molecules.

As a vibrating object moves outward, it compresses molecules closer together, increasing pressure. *Compression* continues away from the object as the momentum of the disturbed molecules displaces the adjacent molecules, producing a crest in the sound wave. When a vibrating object moves inward, it pulls the molecules farther apart and thins them, creating a *rarefaction*. This rarefaction also travels away from the object in a manner similar to compression except that it decreases pressure, thereby producing a trough in the sound wave (see Figure 1-1). As the sound wave moves away from the vibrating object, the individual molecules do not advance with the wave; they vibrate at their average resting place until their motion stills or they are set in motion by another vibration. Inherent in each wave motion are the components that make up a sound wave: frequency, amplitude, velocity, wavelength, and phase (see Figures 1-1, 1-2, and 1-4).

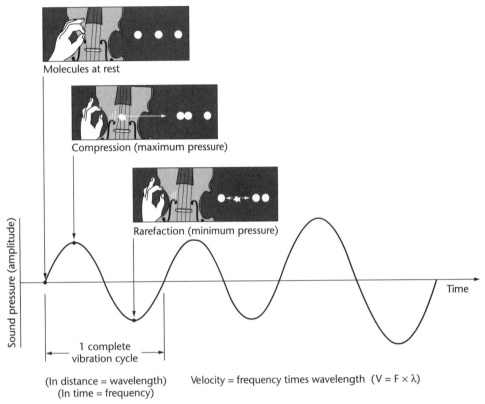

Figure 1-1 Components of a sound wave. The vibrating object causes compression in sound waves when it moves outward (causing molecules to bump into one another). The vibrating object causes rarefaction when it moves inward (pulling the molecules away from one another).

Frequency

When a vibration passes through one complete up-and-down motion, from compression through rarefaction, it has completed one cycle. The number of cycles a vibration completes in one second is expressed as its frequency. If a vibration completes 50 *cycles per second (cps),* its frequency is 50 *hertz (Hz);* if it completes 10,000 cps, its frequency is 10,000 Hz, or 10 *kilohertz (kHz).* Every vibration has a frequency, and humans with excellent hearing may be capable of hearing frequencies from 20 to 20,000 Hz. The limits of low- and high-frequency hearing for most humans, however, are about 35 to

16,000 Hz. Frequencies just below the low end of this range, called *infrasonic*, and those just above the high end of this range, called *ultrasonic*, are sensed more than heard, if they are perceived at all.

These limits change with natural aging, particularly in the higher frequencies. Generally, hearing acuity diminishes to about 15,000 Hz by age 40; to 12,000 Hz by age 50; and to 10,000 Hz or lower beyond age 50. With frequent exposure to loud sound, the audible frequency range can be adversely affected prematurely.

Psychologically, and in musical terms, we perceive frequency as *pitch*—the relative tonal highness or lowness of a sound. Pitch and the frequency spectrum are discussed in Chapter 3.

Amplitude

We noted that vibrations in objects stimulate molecules to move in pressure waves at certain rates of alternation (compression/rarefaction) and that rate determines frequency. Vibrations not only affect the molecules' rate of up-and-down movement but also determine the number of displaced molecules set in motion from equilibrium to a wave's maximum height (crest) and depth (trough). This number depends on the intensity of a vibration; the more intense, the more molecules are displaced.

The greater the number of molecules displaced, the greater the height and the depth of the sound wave. The number of molecules in motion, and therefore the size of a sound-wave, is called *amplitude* (see Figure 1-2). Our subjective impression of amplitude is a sound's loudness or softness. Amplitude is measured in decibels.

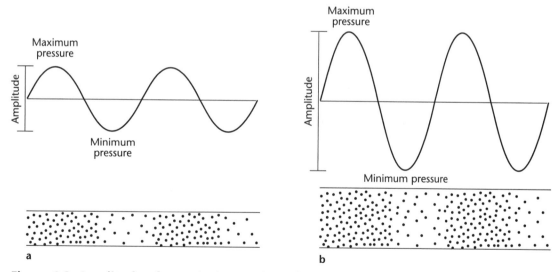

Figure 1-2 Amplitude of sound. The number of molecules displaced by a vibration creates the amplitude, or loudness, of a sound. Because the number of molecules in the sound wave in (b) is greater than the number in the sound wave in (a), the amplitude of the sound wave in (b) is greater.

The Decibel

The *decibel (dB)* is a dimensionless unit and, as such, it has no specifically defined physical quantity. Rather, as a unit of measure, it is used to compare the ratio of two quantities usually in relation to acoustic energy, such as sound pressure, and electric energy, such as power and voltage (see Chapter 8). In mathematical terms, it is 10 times the logarithm to the base 10 of the ratio between the powers of two signals: $dB = 10 \log (P_1 / P_0)$. P_0 is usually a reference power value with which another power value, P_1, is compared. It is abbreviated dB because it stands for one-tenth (deci) of a bel (from Alexander Graham Bell). The bel was the amount a signal dropped in level over a 1-mile distance of telephone wire. Because the amount of level loss was too large to work with as a single unit of measurement, it was divided into tenths for more practical application.

There are other acoustic measurements of human hearing based on the interactive relationship between frequency and amplitude. These are discussed in Chapter 3.

Velocity

Although frequency and amplitude are the most important physical components of a sound wave, another component—*velocity*, or the speed of a sound wave—should be mentioned. Velocity usually has little impact on pitch or loudness and is relatively constant in a controlled environment. Sound travels 1,130 feet per second at sea level when the temperature is 70°F (Fahrenheit). The denser the molecular structure, the greater the vibrational conductivity. Sound travels 4,800 feet per second in water. In solid materials such as wood and steel, sound travels 11,700 and 18,000 feet per second, respectively.

In air, sound velocity changes significantly in very high and very low temperatures, increasing as air warms and decreasing as it cools. For every 1°F change, the speed of sound changes 1.1 feet per second.

Wavelength

Each frequency has a *wavelength*, which is determined by the distance a sound wave travels to complete one cycle of compression and rarefaction; that is, the physical measurement of the length of one cycle is equal to the velocity of sound divided by the frequency of sound ($\lambda = v/f$) (see Figure 1-1). Therefore, frequency and wavelength change inversely with respect to each other. The lower a sound's frequency, the longer its wavelength; the higher a sound's frequency, the shorter its wavelength (see Figure 1-3).

Acoustical Phase

Acoustical phase refers to the time relationship between two or more sound waves at a given point in their cycles.[1] Because sound waves are repetitive, they can be divided into regularly occurring intervals. These intervals are measured in degrees (see Figure 1-4).

---

1. **Polarity** is sometimes used synonymously with **phase**. It is not the same. Polarity refers to values of a signal voltage and is discussed in Chapter 7.

Frequency (Hz)	Wavelength	Frequency (Hz)	Wavelength
20	56.5 feet	1,000	1.1 feet
31.5	35.8	2,000	6.7 inches
63	17.9	4,000	3.3
125	9.0	6,000	2.2
250	4.5	8,000	1.6
440	2.5	10,000	1.3
500	2.2	12,000	1.1
880	1.2	16,000	0.07

Figure 1-3 Selected frequencies and their wavelengths.

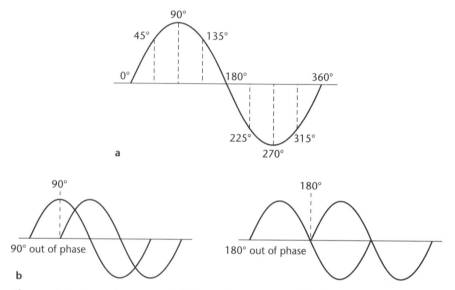

Figure 1-4 Sound waves. (a) Phase is measured in degrees, and one cycle can be divided into 360 degrees. It begins at 0 degrees with 0 amplitude, then increases to a positive maximum at 90 degrees, decreases to 0 at 180 degrees, increases to a negative maximum at 270 degrees, and returns to 0 at 360 degrees. (b) Selected phase relationships of sound waves.

If two identical waves begin their excursions at the same time, their degree intervals will coincide and the waves will be *in phase*. If two identical waves begin their excursions at different times, their degree intervals will not coincide and the waves will be *out of phase*.

Waves in phase reinforce each other, increasing amplitude (see Figure 1-5a); out of phase they weaken each other, decreasing amplitude. When two sound waves are exactly in phase (0-degree phase difference) and have the same frequency, shape, and peak amplitude, the resulting waveform will be twice the original peak amplitude. Two waves exactly out of phase (180-degree phase difference) with the same frequency, shape, and peak amplitude cancel each other (see Figure 1-5b); however, these two conditions rarely occur in the studio.

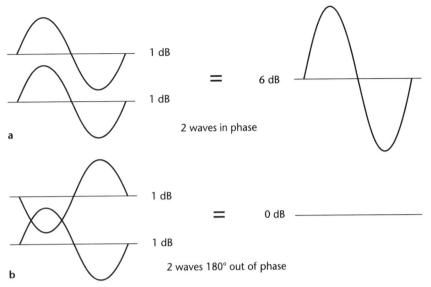

1 dB

1 dB

= 6 dB

2 waves in phase

a

1 dB

1 dB

= 0 dB

2 waves 180° out of phase

b

Figure 1-5 Sound waves in and out of phase. (a) In phase: Their amplitude is additive. Here the sound waves are exactly in phase—a condition that rarely occurs. It should be noted that decibels do not add linearly. As shown, the amplitude here is 6 dB. (b) Out of phase: Their amplitude is subtractive. Sound waves of equal amplitude 180 degrees out of phase cancel each other. This situation also rarely occurs.

It is more likely that sound waves will begin their excursions at different times. If the waves are partially out of phase, there would be *constructive interference*, increasing amplitude, where compression and rarefaction occur at the same time, and *destructive interference*, decreasing amplitude, where compression and rarefaction occur at different times (see Figure 1-6).

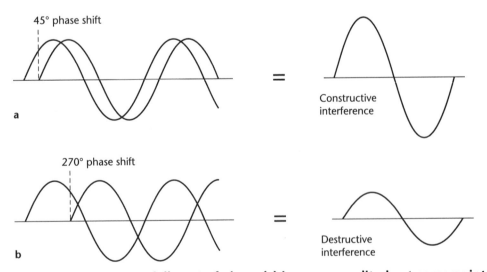

45° phase shift

= Constructive interference

a

270° phase shift

= Destructive interference

b

Figure 1-6 Waves partially out of phase (a) increase amplitude at some points and (b) decrease it at others.

The ability to understand and perceive phase is of considerable importance in, among other things, microphone and loudspeaker placement, mixing, and spatial imaging. If not handled properly, phasing problems can seriously mar sound quality. Phase can also be used as a production tool to create different sonic effects.

Sound Envelope

Another factor that influences the timbre of a sound is its shape, or envelope, which refers to changes in loudness over time. A *sound envelope* has four stages: attack, initial decay, sustain, and release (ADSR). *Attack* is how a sound starts after a sound source has been vibrated. *Initial decay* is the point at which the attack begins to lose amplitude. *Sustain* is the period during which the sound's relative dynamics are maintained after its initial decay. *Release* refers to the time and the manner in which a sound diminishes to inaudibility (see Figure 1-7).

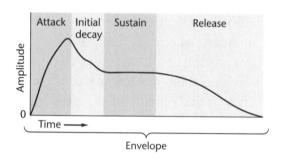

Figure 1-7 Sound envelope.

Two notes with the same frequency and loudness can produce different sounds within different envelopes. A bowed violin string, for example, has a more dynamic sound overall than a plucked violin string. If you take a piano recording and edit out the attacks of the notes, the piano will start to sound like an organ. Do the same with a French horn, and it sounds similar to a saxophone. Edit out the attacks of a trumpet, and it creates an oboe-like sound. The relative differences in frequency spectra and sound envelopes are shown for a piano, violin, flute, and white noise sample in Figure 3-4. In the case of the piano and violin, the fundamental frequency is the same: middle C (261.63 Hz). The flute is played an octave above middle C at C5, or 523.25 Hz. By contrast, noise is unpitched with no fundamental frequency; it comprises all frequencies of the spectrum at the same amplitude.

Direct, Early, and Reverberant Sound

When a sound is emitted in a room, its acoustic "life cycle" can be divided into three phases: direct sound, early reflections, and reverberant sound (see Figure 1-8).

Direct sound reaches the listener first, before it interacts with any other surface. Depending on the distance from the sound source to the listener, the time, T_0, is 20–200 milliseconds (ms). Direct waves provide information about a sound's origin, size, and tonal quality.

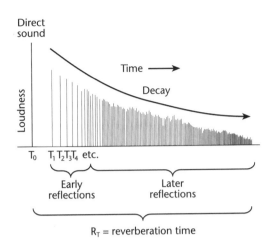

Direct sound

Time →

Decay

Loudness

T_0 $T_1 T_2 T_3 T_4$ etc.

Early reflections   Later reflections

R_T = reverberation time

Figure 1-8 Anatomy of reverberation in an enclosed space. At $time_0$ (T_0) the direct sound is heard. Between T_0 and T_1 is the initial time delay gap—the time between the arrival of the direct sound and the first reflection. At T_2 and T_3, more early reflections of the direct sound arrive as they reflect from nearby surfaces. These early reflections are sensed rather than distinctly heard. At T_4 repetitions of the direct sound spread through the room, reflecting from several surfaces and arriving at the listener so close together that their repetitions are indistinguishable.

The same sound reaching the listener a short time later, after it reflects from various surfaces, is *indirect sound*. Indirect sound is divided into *early reflections*, also known as *early sound* and reverberant sound (see Figure 1-9). Early reflections reaching the ear within 30 ms of when the direct sound is produced are heard as part of the direct sound. *Reverberant sound*, or *reverberation* (*reverb*, for short), is the result of the early reflections becoming smaller and smaller and the time between them decreasing until they combine, making the reflections indistinguishable. They arrive outside of the ear's integration time.

Early sound adds loudness and fullness to the initial sound and helps create our subjective impression of a room's size. Reverb creates acoustical spaciousness and fills out the loudness and the body of a sound. It contains much of a sound's total energy. Also, depending on the *reverberation time*, or *decay time*—the time it takes a sound to decrease 60 dB-sound pressure level (SPL) after its steady-state sound level has stopped—reverb provides information about the absorption and the reflectivity of a room's surfaces as well as about a listener's distance from the sound source. The longer it takes a sound to decay, the larger and more hard-surfaced the room is perceived to be and the farther the listener is or thinks he is from the sound source (see "Sound Pressure-Level" in Chapter 2).

Reverberation and Echo

Reverberation and *echo* are often used synonymously—but incorrectly so. Reverberation is densely spaced reflections created by random, multiple, blended repetitions of a sound. The time between reflections is imperceptible. If a sound is delayed by 35 ms or more, the listener perceives echo—a distinct repeat of the direct sound.

In large rooms, discrete echoes are sometimes perceived. In small rooms, these repetitions, called *flutter echoes*, are short and come in rapid succession. They usually result from reflections between two highly reflective, parallel surfaces. Because echoes usually inhibit sonic clarity, studios and concert halls are designed to eliminate them.

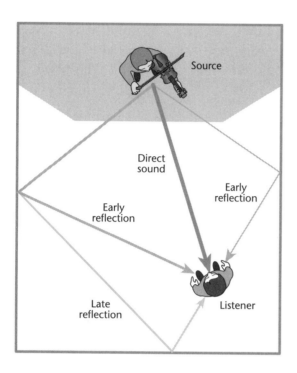

Figure 1-9 Acoustic behavior of sound in an enclosed room. The direct-sound field is all the sound reaching the listener (or the microphone) directly from the sound source without having been reflected off of any of the room's surfaces. The early and later reflections of the indirect sound are all the sound reaching the listener (or the microphone) after being reflected off of one or more of the room's surfaces.

From *Electronic Musician* magazine, March 2002, p. 100. © 2002 Primedia Musician Magazine and Media, Inc. All rights reserved. Reprinted with permission of Prism Business Media, Inc. Copyright © 2005. All rights reserved.

Main Points

- A sound wave is a vibrational disturbance that involves mechanical motion of molecules transmitting energy from one place to another.

- A sound wave is caused when an object vibrates and sets into motion the molecules nearest to it; the initial motion starts a chain reaction. This chain reaction creates pressure waves through the air, which are perceived as sound when they reach the ear and the brain.

- The pressure wave compresses molecules as it moves outward, increasing pressure, and pulls the molecules farther apart as it moves inward, creating a rarefaction by decreasing pressure.

- The components that make up a sound wave are frequency, amplitude, velocity, wavelength, and phase.

- The number of times a sound wave vibrates per second determines its frequency. Humans can hear frequencies between roughly 20 and 20,000 hertz (Hz)—a range of 10 octaves.

- The size of a sound wave determines its amplitude, or loudness. Loudness is measured in decibels.

- The decibel (dB) is a dimensionless unit used to compare the ratio of two quantities usually in relation to acoustic energy, such as sound-pressure level (SPL).

- Velocity, the speed of a sound wave, is 1,130 feet per second at sea level at 70°F. Sound increases or decreases in velocity by 1.1 feet per second for each 1°F change.

- Each frequency has a wavelength, determined by the distance a sound wave travels to complete one cycle of compression and rarefaction. The length of one cycle is equal to the velocity of sound divided by the frequency of sound. The lower a sound's frequency, the longer its wavelength; the higher a sound's frequency, the shorter its wavelength.

- Acoustical phase refers to the time relationship between two or more sound waves at a given point in their cycles. If two waves begin their excursions at the same time, their degree intervals will coincide and the waves will be in phase, reinforcing each other and increasing amplitude. If two waves begin their excursions at different times, their degree intervals will not coincide and the waves will be out of phase, weakening each other and decreasing amplitude.

- A sound's envelope refers to its changes in loudness over time. It has four stages: attack, initial decay, sustain, and release (ADSR).

- The acoustic "life cycle" of a sound can be divided into three phases: direct sound, early reflections, and reverberant sound.

- Direct sound reaches the listener first before it interacts with any other surface. The same sound reaching the listener a short time later, after it reflects from various surfaces, is indirect sound. Indirect sound is divided into early reflections, also known as early sound, and reverberant sound.

- Reverberation is densely spaced reflections created by random, multiple, blended repetitions of a sound. The time between reflections is imperceptible. If a sound is delayed by 35 ms or more, the listener perceives echo, a distinct repeat of the direct sound.

- Reverberation time, or decay time, is the time it takes a sound to decrease 60 dB-SPL after its steady-state sound level has stopped.

- In large rooms, discrete echoes are sometimes perceived. In small rooms, these repetitions—called flutter echoes—are short and come in rapid succession.

2 The Ear and Hearing

To work in sound, aural acuity is all-important. Therefore, before beginning any discussion of the basics of audio, it is essential to understand the ear and hearing. It may belabor the obvious, but if your hearing is impaired, a career in audio production becomes moot. Because we are a nation of the hard-of-hearing, emphasizing the obvious reinforces the importance of ear care and protection against loud sound.

The Auditory System

The human auditory system is one of the body's most complex and delicate systems. In general, when it functions normally, it transforms sound waves into a series of electrical impulses. When these impulses reach the auditory center of the brain, they can be identified as sound. The entire process occurs within a split second.

The human ear is divided into three parts: the *outer ear*, the *middle ear*, and the *inner ear* (see Figure 2-1). Sound waves first reach and are collected by the *pinna* (or *auricle*), the visible part of the outer ear. The sound waves are then focused through the *ear canal*, or *meatus*, to the *eardrum* (*tympanum*) at the beginning of the middle ear.

The tympanic membrane is attached to another membrane, called the *oval window*, by three small bones—the *malleus, incus,* and *stapes*—called *ossicles* and shaped like a hammer, anvil, and stirrup, respectively. The ossicles act as a mechanical lever, changing the small pressure of the sound wave on the eardrum, thereby amplifying the sound vibrations before transmitting them to the inner ear. The combined action of the ossicles and the area of the tympanum allow the middle ear to protect the inner ear from pressure changes (loud sounds) that are too great. It takes about one-tenth of a second to react, however, and therefore provides little protection from sudden loud sounds.

The inner ear contains the *semicircular canals*, which are necessary for balance, and a snail-shaped structure called the *cochlea*. The cochlea is within an area smaller than the diameter of a dime and is filled with a fluid whose total capacity is a fraction of a drop. It is here that sound becomes electricity in the human head. Running through the center of the cochlea is the *basilar membrane*, resting on sensory hair cells attached to nerve fibers composing the *organ of Corti*, the "seat of hearing." These fibers feed the auditory nerve, where the electrical impulses are passed on to the brain. It is estimated that

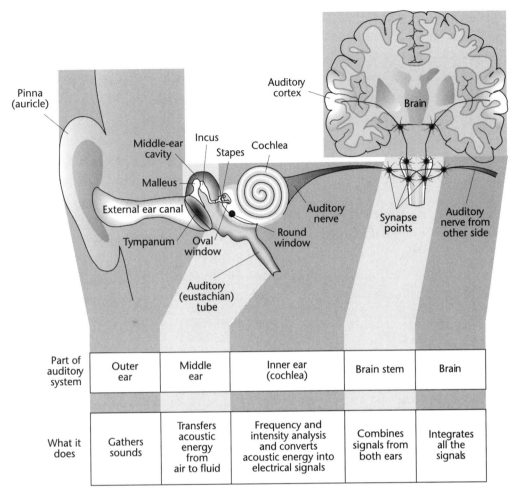

Figure 2-1 Auditory system.

Part of auditory system	Outer ear	Middle ear	Inner ear (cochlea)	Brain stem	Brain
What it does	Gathers sounds	Transfers acoustic energy from air to fluid	Frequency and intensity analysis and converts acoustic energy into electrical signals	Combines signals from both ears	Integrates all the signals

as many as 16,000 sensory hair cells are present at birth. In the upper portion of each cell is a bundle of microscopic hairlike projections called *stereocilia*, or *cilia* for short, which quiver at the approach of sound and begin the process of transforming mechanical vibrations into electrical and chemical signals, which are then sent to the brain. In a symmetrical layout, these sensory hair cells are referred to as "outer" and "inner" sensory hair cells (see Figure 2-2). Approximately 12,000 outer hair cells amplify auditory signals and discriminate frequency. About 140 cilia jut from each cell. The 4,000 inner hair cells are connected to the auditory nerve fibers leading to the brain. About 40 cilia are attached to each inner cell (see Figure 2-3a). Continued exposure to high sound-pressure levels can damage the sensory hair cells, and because they are not naturally repaired or replaced, hearing loss results. The greater the number of damaged hair cells, the greater the loss of hearing (see Figure 2-3b).

Hearing Loss

Every day, the noise around us becomes ever louder—noise from traffic, airplanes, lawn mowers, sirens, vacuum cleaners, hair dryers, air conditioners, blenders, waste disposals, can openers, snow mobiles, and even children's toys. In modern homes with wood floors, cathedral ceilings, brick or stucco walls, and many windows, sound is reflected

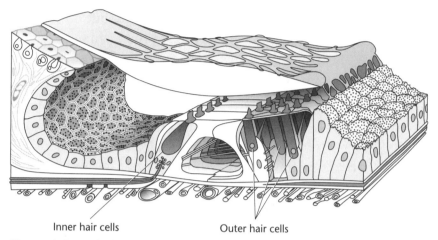

Inner hair cells   Outer hair cells

Figure 2-2 Artistic representation of the organ of Corti, showing the symmetrical layout of the outer and inner sensory hair cells.

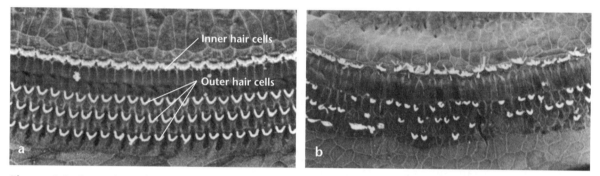

Figure 2-3 Scanning electron micrographs of healthy and damaged stereocilia. (a) In the normal cochlea, the stereocilia of a single row of inner hair cells (top) and three rows of outer hair cells (bottom) are present in an orderly array. (b) In the damaged cochlea, there is disruption of the inner hair cells and loss of the outer hair cells. This damage produced a profound hearing loss after exposure to 90 dBA noise for eight hours six months earlier. Although these micrographs are of the organ of Corti of a lab rat, they serve to demonstrate the severe effects of overexposure to loud sound. (The "A" in the dB value refers to the filter used for measuring frequency response that bears a close resemblance to the response of the human ear.)

and therefore intensified because there is little to absorb it. It is becoming increasingly rare to find a quiet neighborhood.

Parks and campgrounds are inundated with the annoying sounds of RVs, boisterous families, and blaring boom boxes. At beaches, the lap and wash of gentle surf is drowned out by the roar of motorboats and jet skis. Cell phones, MP3 players, and iPods with their ear-mounted headphones or earbuds present an increasing threat to young people, who are showing signs of hearing loss more typical of older adults. At rock concerts, parties, and bars, sound levels are so loud it is necessary to shout to be heard, increasing the din and raising the noise floor even more. More people suffer from hearing loss than from heart disease, cancer, multiple sclerosis, and kidney disease combined. Noise-induced hearing loss affects about one out of every eight children in the United States. Because it is usually not life-threatening, hearing loss is possibly United States's most overlooked physical ailment.

In industrialized societies, some hearing loss is a natural result of aging, but it is not an inevitable consequence. In cultures less technologically advanced than ours, people in their eighties have relatively normal hearing. Short of relocating to such a society, for now the only defense against hearing loss is prevention.

Usually, when hearing loss occurs it does so gradually, typically without warning signs, and it occurs over a lifetime. When there are warning signs, they usually are due to over-stimulation from continuous, prolonged exposure to loud sound. You can tell there has been damage when there is ear discomfort after exposure; it is difficult to hear in noisy surroundings; it is difficult to understand a child's speech or an adult's speech at more than a few feet away; music loses its color; quiet sounds are muffled or inaudible; it is necessary to keep raising the volume on the radio or TV; and your response to a question is usually, "What?" The main problem for most people with hearing loss is not the need for an increase in the level of sound but in the *clarity* of sound.

Two common forms of hearing loss are conductive hearing loss and sensorineural hearing loss.

Conductive Hearing Loss

Conductive hearing loss occurs when the eardrum or middle ear is damaged from disease; infection; excessive ear wax; foreign objects that block the eardrum; trauma to the head or neck; systemic disorders, such as high or low blood pressure, vascular disorders, and thyroid dysfunction; and high doses of certain medications such as sedatives, antidepressants, and anti-inflammatory drugs.

Sensorineural Hearing Loss

Sensorineural hearing loss is nerve-based. It occurs when the microscopic hair cells of the inner ear are compromised or damaged. Once damaged, whatever the degree of hearing loss is permanent and irreversible. Among the causes of sensorineural hearing loss are aging, a genetic disorder, disease, high fever, or overexposure to loud sound, which is the concern here.

Hearing damage caused by exposure to loud sound varies with the exposure time and the individual. Prolonged exposure to loud sound decreases the ear's sensitivity. Decreased sensitivity creates the false perception that sound is not as loud as it actually is. This usually necessitates an increase in levels to compensate for the hearing loss, thus making a bad situation worse.

After exposure to loud sound for a few hours, you may have experienced the sensation that your ears were stuffed with cotton. This is known as ***temporary threshold shift (TTS)***—a reversible desensitization in hearing that disappears in anywhere from a few hours to several days; TTS is also called ***auditory fatigue***. With TTS the ears have, in effect, shut down to protect themselves against very loud sounds. Sometimes intermittent hearing loss can occur in the higher frequencies unrelated to exposure to loud sound. In such instances elevated levels in cholesterol and triglycerides may be the cause. A blood test can determine if this is the case.

Prolonged exposure to loud sounds can bring on *tinnitus*—a ringing, whistling, or buzzing in the ears—even though there is no acoustic stimulus. Although researchers do not know all the specific mechanisms that cause tinnitus, one condition that creates its onset, without question, is inner-ear nerve damage from overexposure to loud noise levels. Tinnitus is a danger signal that the ears may already have suffered—or soon will—*permanent threshold shift* with continued exposure to loud sound.

Sound-Pressure Level

Being aware of sound pressure level is key to understanding the dangers of exposure to loud sound. Acoustic sound pressure is measured in terms of *sound-pressure level (dB-SPL)* because there are periodic variations in atmospheric pressure in a sound wave. Humans have the potential to hear an extremely wide range of these periodic variations, from 0 dB-SPL, the *threshold of hearing*; to 120 dB-SPL, what acousticians call the *threshold of feeling*; to 140 dB-SPL, the *threshold of pain*, and beyond. Figure 2-4 shows the relative loudness of various sounds, many that are common in our everyday lives. The range of the difference in decibels between the loudest and the quietest sound a vibrating object makes is called *dynamic range*. Because this range is so wide, a logarithmic scale is used to compress loudness measurement into more manageable figures. (On a linear scale, a unit of 1 adds an increment of 1. On a logarithmic scale, a unit of 1 multiplies by a factor of 10.)

Humans have the capability to hear loudness at a ratio of 1:10,000,000 and greater. A sound-pressure-level change of 1 dB increases amplitude 12 percent; an increase of 6 dB-SPL doubles amplitude; 20 dB increases amplitude 10 times. Sound at 60 dB-SPL is 1,000 times louder than sound at 0 dB-SPL; at 80 dB-SPL, it is 10 times louder than at 60 dB-SPL. If the amplitude of two similar sounds is 100 dB-SPL each, their amplitude, when added, would be 103 dB-SPL. Nevertheless, most people do not perceive a sound level as doubled until it has increased anywhere from 3 to 10 dB, depending on their aural acuity. There are other acoustic measurements of human hearing based on the interactive relationship between frequency and amplitude (see Chapter 3).

Safeguards Against Hearing Loss

As gradual deterioration of the auditory nerve endings occurs with aging, it usually results in a gradual loss of hearing first in the mid-high-frequency range—at around 3,000 to 6,000 Hz—then in the lower-pitched sounds. The ability to hear in the mid-high-frequency range is important to understanding speech because consonants are mostly composed of high frequencies. Hearing loss in the lower-pitched sounds makes it difficult to understand vowels and lower-pitched voices. Prolonged exposure to loud sounds hastens this deterioration. To avoid premature hearing loss, the remedy is simple: Do not expose your ears to excessively loud sound levels for extended periods of time (see Figures 2-5, 2-6, and 2-7.)

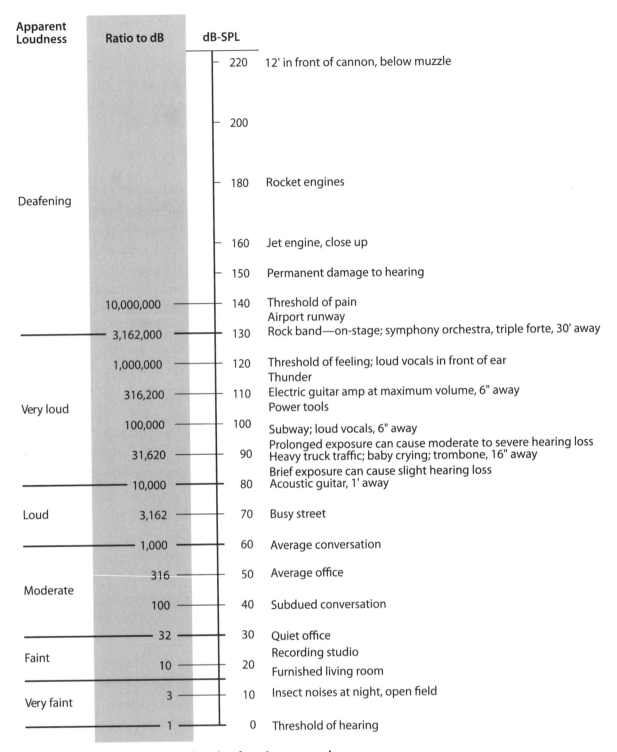

Apparent Loudness	Ratio to dB	dB-SPL	
		220	12' in front of cannon, below muzzle
		200	
Deafening		180	Rocket engines
		160	Jet engine, close up
		150	Permanent damage to hearing
	10,000,000	140	Threshold of pain Airport runway
	3,162,000	130	Rock band—on-stage; symphony orchestra, triple forte, 30' away
	1,000,000	120	Threshold of feeling; loud vocals in front of ear Thunder
Very loud	316,200	110	Electric guitar amp at maximum volume, 6" away Power tools
	100,000	100	Subway; loud vocals, 6" away
	31,620	90	Prolonged exposure can cause moderate to severe hearing loss Heavy truck traffic; baby crying; trombone, 16" away
	10,000	80	Brief exposure can cause slight hearing loss Acoustic guitar, 1' away
Loud	3,162	70	Busy street
	1,000	60	Average conversation
	316	50	Average office
Moderate	100	40	Subdued conversation
	32	30	Quiet office
Faint	10	20	Recording studio Furnished living room
	3	10	Insect noises at night, open field
Very faint	1	0	Threshold of hearing

Figure 2-4 Sound-pressure levels of various sound sources.

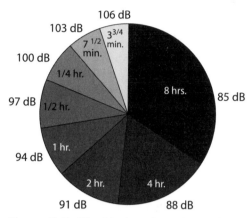

Figure 2-5 The National Institute for Occupational Safety and Health (NIOSH) recommended sound-pressure-level (SPL) exposure guidelines. These guidelines are based on maximum daily safe exposure amounts measured as time-weighted averages (TWAs) over a 40-year period.

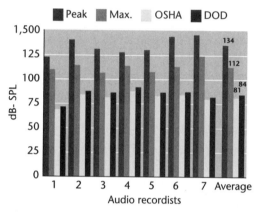

Figure 2-6 Peak, average maximum, and calculated average sound-pressure-level exposures by Occupational Safety and Health Administration (OSHA) and Department of Defense (DOD) standards. These results are in relation to the daily exposure to loudness of seven different audio recordists. It is estimated that recordists work an average of 8 to 10 hours per day.

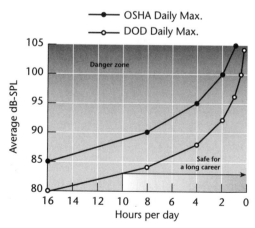

Figure 2-7 Allowable daily exposure of sound-pressure levels plotted in relation to OSHA and DOD-permissible exposure levels.

Hearing impairment is not the only detrimental consequence of loud sound levels. They also produce adverse physiological effects. Sounds transmitted to the brain follow two paths. One path carries sound to the auditory center, where it is perceived and interpreted. The other goes to the brain centers that affect the nervous system. Loud sound taking the latter path can increase heart rate and blood pressure, constrict small blood vessels in the hands and the feet, contract muscles, release stress-related hormones from adrenal glands, disrupt certain stomach and intestinal functions, and create dry mouth, dilated pupils, tension, anxiety, fatigue, and irritability.

When in the presence of loud sound during audio production, including listening to music, wear earplugs designed to reduce loudness without seriously degrading frequency response. Some options among available earplugs are custom-fit earmolds, disposable foam plugs, reusable silicon insert plugs, and industrial headsets. The custom-fit earmold is best to use because, as the term suggests, it is made from a custom mold of your ear canal. It is comfortable and does not give you the stopped-up feeling of foam plugs. It provides balanced sound-level reduction and attenuates all frequencies evenly.

Some custom earplugs can be made with interchangeable inserts that attenuate loudness at different decibel levels. The disposable foam plug is intended for one-time use; it provides noise reduction from 12 to 30 dB, mainly in the high frequencies. The reusable silicon insert plug is a rubberized cushion that covers a tiny metal filtering diaphragm; it reduces sound levels by approximately 17 dB. The silicon insert plug is often used at construction sites and firing ranges. The industrial headset has a cushioned headpad and tight-fitting earseals; it provides maximum sound-level attenuation, often up to 30 dB, and is particularly effective at low frequencies. This is the headset commonly used by personnel around airport runways and in the cabs of heavy-construction equipment (see Figure 2-8).

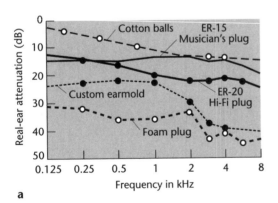

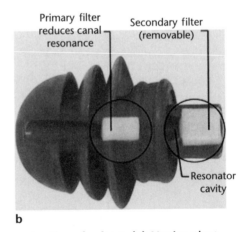

a   b

Figure 2-8 Attenuation effects of selected hearing-protection devices. (a) Notice that compared with a variety of commonly used hearing protectors, the Musician's and Hi-Fi plugs have relatively even attenuation across the frequency spectrum. (The ER-15 and the ER-20 are products of Etymotic Research, which makes a variety of hearing protectors for musicians and hi-fi listeners that attenuate loudness from 9 to 25 dB. (b) The HearPlugz-DF by E.A.R. Inc. provides dual filtering with noise reduction ratings of 12 to 22 dB.)

As a general guideline, hearing protectors are recommended at levels from 87 or 88 db-SPL to 89 dB-SPL; they are necessary from 90 to 97 dB-SPL; and, from 100 dB-SPL and higher, they should be worn with extra care.

The human ear is a very sophisticated electromechanical device. As with any device, regular maintenance is wise, especially for the audio professional. Make at least two visits per year to a qualified ear, nose, and throat (ENT) specialist to have your ears inspected and cleaned. The human ear secretes wax to protect the eardrum and the cochlea from loud sound-pressure levels. Let the doctor clean out the wax. Do not use a cotton swab. You risk the chance of infection and jamming the wax against the eardrum, which obviously exacerbates the situation. If you must clean your ears between visits, ask the ENT doctor about the safest way to do it.

Other safeguards include working with listening levels as low as possible, taking regular breaks in a quiet environment during production sessions, and having an audiologist test your hearing at least once a year. Be aware that most standard hearing tests measure octave bands in only the 125 to 8,000 Hz hearing range, essentially the speech range. There are hearing tests with much wider ranges that are more appropriate for the audio professional.

The implications of all this should be obvious, especially if you are working in audio: not only is your hearing in particular and your physiological well-being in general at risk, but so is your livelihood.

Main Points

- The human auditory system is one of the body's most complex and delicate systems.

- The human ear is divided into three parts: the outer ear, the middle ear, and the inner ear.

- In the basilar membrane of the inner ear, bundles of microscopic hairlike projections called cilia are attached to each sensory hair cell. They quiver at the approach of sound and begin the process of transforming mechanical vibrations into electrical and chemical signals, which are then sent to the brain.

- Conductive hearing loss occurs when the eardrum or middle ear is damaged from disease; infection; excessive ear wax; foreign objects that block the eardrum; trauma to the head or neck; systemic disorders such as high or low blood pressure, vascular disorders, and thyroid dysfunction; and high doses of certain medications such as sedatives, antidepressants, and anti-inflammatory drugs.

- Sensorineural hearing loss is nerve-based. It occurs when the microscopic hair cells of the inner ear are compromised or damaged. The cause of sensorineural hearing loss of concern in audio is overexposure to loud sound.

- Temporary threshold shift (TTS), or auditory fatigue, is a reversible desensitization in hearing caused by exposure to loud sound over a few hours.

- Prolonged exposure to loud sound can bring on tinnitus—a ringing, whistling, or buzzing in the ears—even though there is no acoustic stimulus.

- Exposure to loud sound for extended periods of time can cause permanent threshold shift—a deterioration of the auditory nerve endings in the inner ear.

- Acoustic sound pressure is measured in terms of sound-pressure level (dB-SPL) because there are periodic variations in atmospheric pressure in a sound wave.

- Humans can hear from 0 dB-SPL, the threshold of hearing; to 120 dB-SPL, the threshold of feeling; to 140 dB-SPL, the threshold of pain and beyond. The scale is logarithmic, which means that adding two sounds each with a loudness of 100 dB-SPL would bring it to 103 dB-SPL. The range of difference in decibels between the loudest and the quietest sound a vibrating object makes is called dynamic range.

- In the presence of loud sound during audio production, including listening to music, use an ear filter (hearing protection device) designed to reduce loudness without seriously degrading frequency response.

3 Perception of Sound

You will recall that sound is a cause-and-effect phenomenon. It is one thing to understand the physical, or objective, behavior of sound, but in audio production it is also essential to understand the psychological, or subjective, characteristics of sound.

The Frequency Spectrum

Psychologically, and in musical terms, we perceive frequency as *pitch*—the relative tonal highness or lowness of a sound. The more times per second a sound source vibrates, the higher its pitch. Middle C (C4) on a piano vibrates 261.63 times per second, so its fundamental frequency is 261.63 Hz. The A note above middle C has a frequency of 440 Hz, so the pitch is higher. The fundamental frequency is also called the first harmonic or primary frequency. It is the lowest, or basic, pitch of a musical instrument.

The range of audible frequencies, or the *sound frequency spectrum,* is divided into sections, each with a unique and vital quality. The usual divisions in Western music are called octaves. An *octave* is the interval between any two frequencies that have a tonal ratio of 2:1.

The range of human hearing covers about 10 octaves, which is far greater than the comparable range of the human eye; the visible light frequency spectrum covers less than one octave. The ratio of highest to lowest light frequency visible to humans is barely 2:1, whereas the ratio of the human audible frequency spectrum is 1,000:1.

Starting with 20 Hz, the first octave is 20 to 40 Hz; the second, 40 to 80 Hz; the third, 80 to 160 Hz; and so on. Octaves are grouped into *bass, midrange,* and *treble* and are further subdivided as follows (see Figure 3-1).

- **Low bass**—First and second octaves (20 to 80 Hz). These are the frequencies associated with power, boom, and fullness. There is little musical content in the lower part of this range. In the upper part of the range are the lowest notes of the piano, organ, tuba, and bass and the fundamental of the bass (kick) drum. A *fundamental,* also called the *first harmonic* or *primary frequency,* is the lowest, or basic, pitch of a musical instrument (see "Timbre" later in this chapter). Sounds in these octaves need not occur often to maintain a sense of fullness. If they occur too often, or at too loud a level, the sound can become thick or overly dense. Most loudspeakers are capable of reproducing few, if any, of the first-octave frequencies. Loudspeakers that can reproduce second-octave frequencies often do so with varying loudness levels.

■ **Upper bass**—Third and fourth octaves (80 to 320 Hz). Most of the lower tones generated by rhythm and other support instruments such as drums, piano, bass, cello, and trombone are in this range. They establish balance in a musical structure. Too many frequencies from this range make it sound boomy; too few make it thin. When properly proportioned, pitches in the second, third, and fourth octaves are very satisfying to the ear because we perceive them as giving sound an anchor, that is, fullness or bottom. Too much fourth-octave emphasis, however, can muddy sound. Frequencies in the upper bass range serve an aural structure in the way the horizontal line serves a visual structure—by providing a foundation. Almost all professional loudspeakers can reproduce the frequencies in this range.

■ **Midrange**—Fifth, sixth, and seventh octaves (320 to 2,560 Hz). The midrange gives sound its intensity. It contains the fundamental and the rich lower harmonics and overtones of most sound sources. It is the primary treble octave of musical pitches. The midrange does not necessarily generate pleasant sounds. Although the sixth octave is where the highest fundamental pitches reside, too much emphasis here is heard as a hornlike quality. Too much emphasis of seventh-octave frequencies is heard as a hard, tinny quality. Extended listening to midrange sounds can be annoying and fatiguing.

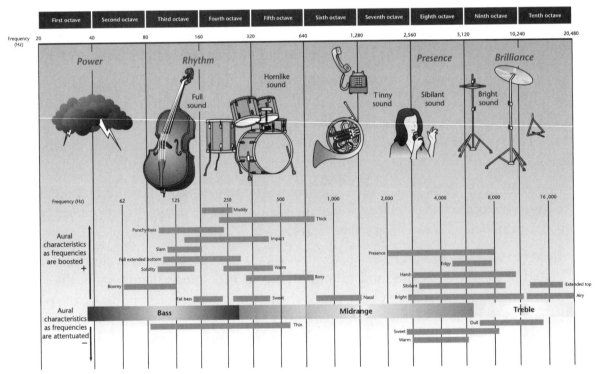

Figure 3-1 Sound frequency spectrum and subjective responses to increases and decreases in various ranges.

- **Upper midrange**—Eighth octave (2,560 to 5,120 Hz). We are most sensitive to frequencies in the eighth octave, a rather curious range. The lower part of the eighth octave (2,560 to 3,500 Hz) contains frequencies that, if properly emphasized, improve the intelligibility of speech and lyrics. These frequencies are roughly 3,000 to 3,500 Hz. If these frequencies are unduly emphasized, however, sound becomes abrasive and unpleasant; vocals, in particular, become harsh and lispy, making some consonants difficult to understand. The upper part of the eighth octave (above 3,500 Hz), on the other hand, contains rich and satisfying pitches that give sound definition, clarity, and realism. Listeners perceive a sound source frequency in this range (and in the lower part of the ninth octave, up to about 6,000 Hz) as being nearby, and for this reason it is also known as the presence range. Increasing loudness at 5,000 Hz, the heart of the presence range, gives the impression that there has been an overall increase in loudness throughout the midrange. Reducing loudness at 5,000 Hz makes a sound seem transparent and farther away.

- **Treble**—Ninth and tenth octaves (5,120 to 20,000 Hz). Although the ninth and tenth octaves generate only 2 percent of the total power output of the sound frequency spectrum, and most human hearing does not extend much beyond 16,000 Hz, they give sound the vital, lifelike qualities of brilliance and sparkle, particularly in the upper-ninth and lower-tenth octaves. Too much emphasis above 6,000 Hz makes sound hissy and brings out electronic noise. Too little emphasis above 6,000 Hz dulls sound.

Understanding the audible frequency spectrum's various sonic qualities is vital to processing spectral balances in audio production. Such processing is called equalization and is discussed at length in Chapters 11 and 13.

Frequency and Loudness

Frequency and amplitude, perceived as loudness, are interdependent. Varying a sound's frequency also affects perception of its loudness; varying a sound's loudness affects perception of its pitch.

Equal Loudness Principle

The response of the human ear is not equally sensitive to all audible frequencies (see Figure 3-2). Depending on loudness, we do not hear low and high frequencies as well as we hear middle frequencies. In fact, the ear is relatively insensitive to low frequencies at low levels. Oddly enough, this is called the *equal loudness principle* (rather than the unequal loudness principle) (see Figure 3-3). As you can see in Figures 3-2 and 3-3, at low frequencies the ear needs about 70 dB more sound level than it does at 3 kHz to be the same loudness. The ear is at its most sensitive at around 3 kHz. At frequencies of 10 kHz and higher, the ear is somewhat more sensitive than it is at low frequencies but not nearly as sensitive as it is at the midrange frequencies.

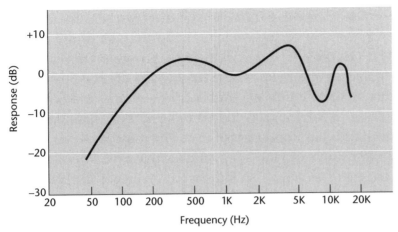

Figure 3-2 Responses to various frequencies by the human ear. This curve shows that the response is not flat and that we hear midrange frequencies better than low and high frequencies.

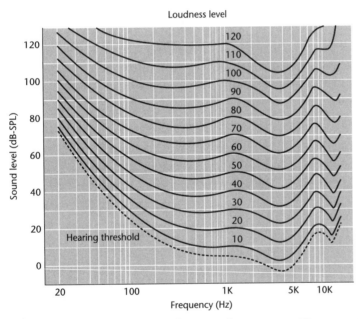

Figure 3-3 Equal loudness curves. These curves illustrate the relationships in Figure 3-2 and our relative lack of sensitivity to low and high frequencies as compared with middle frequencies. A 50 Hz sound would have to be 50 dB louder to seem as loud as a 1,000 Hz sound at 0 dB. To put it another way, at an intensity of, for instance, 40 dB, the level of a 100 Hz sound would have to be 10 times the sound-pressure level of a 1,000 Hz sound for the two sounds to be perceived as equal in loudness. Each curve is identified by the sound-pressure level at 1,000 Hz.

(This graph represents frequencies on a logarithmic scale. The distance from 20 to 200 Hz is the same as from 200 to 2,000 Hz or from 2,000 to 20,000 Hz.) (Based on Robinson-Dadson.)

In other words, if a guitarist, for example, plucks all six strings equally hard, you do not hear each string at the same loudness level. The high E string (328 Hz) sounds louder than the low E string (82 Hz). To make the low string sound as loud, the guitarist would have to pluck it harder. This suggests that the high E string may sound louder because of its higher frequency. But if you sound three tones, say, 50 Hz, 1,000 Hz, and 15,000 Hz, at a fixed loudness level, the 1,000 Hz tone sounds louder than either the 50 Hz or the 15,000 Hz tone.

In a live concert, sound levels are usually louder than they are on a home stereo system. Live music often reaches levels of 100 dB-SPL and higher. At home, levels are as high as 70 to 75 dB-SPL and alas, too often much higher. Sound at 70 dB-SPL requires more bass and treble boost than sound at 100 dB-SPL to obtain equal loudness. Therefore, the frequency balances you hear at 100 dB-SPL will be different when you hear the same sound at 70 dB-SPL.

In a recording or mixdown session, if the loudness level is high during recording and low during playback, both bass and treble frequencies could be considerably reduced in volume and may be virtually inaudible. The converse is also true: If sound level is low during recording and high during playback, the bass and treble frequencies could be too loud relative to the other frequencies and may even overwhelm them.

Masking

Another phenomenon related to the interaction of frequency and loudness is *masking*— the hiding of some sounds by other sounds when each is a different frequency and they are presented together. Generally, loud sounds tend to mask softer ones, and lower-pitched sounds tend to mask higher-pitched ones.

For example, in a noisy environment, you have to raise your voice to be heard. If a 100 Hz tone and 1,000 Hz tone are sounded together at the same level, both tones will be audible but the 1,000 Hz tone will be perceived as louder. Gradually increasing the level of the 100 Hz tone and keeping the amplitude of the 1,000 Hz tone constant will make the 1,000 Hz tone more and more difficult to hear. If an LP (long-playing) record has scratches (high-frequency information), they will probably be masked during loud passages but audible during quiet ones. A symphony orchestra playing full blast may have all its instruments involved at once; flutes and clarinets will probably not be heard over trumpets and trombones, however, because woodwinds are generally higher in frequency and weaker in sound level than the brasses.

Masking has practical uses in audio. In noise-reduction systems, low-level noise can be effectively masked by a high-level signal; and in digital data compression, a desired signal can mask noise from lower resolutions.

Timbre

For the purpose of illustration, sound is often depicted as a single, wavy line (see Figure 1-1). Actually, a wave that generates such a sound is known as a *sine wave*. It is a *pure tone*—a single frequency devoid of harmonics and overtones.

Most sound, though, consists of several different frequencies that produce a complex *waveform*—a graphical representation of a sound's characteristic shape, which can be seen, for example, on test equipment and on digital editing systems (see Figure 12-8) and in spectrographs (see Figure 3-4). Each sound has a unique tonal mix of fundamental and harmonic frequencies that distinguishes it from all other sound, even if the sounds have the same pitch, loudness, and duration. This difference between sounds is what defines their *timbre*—their tonal quality, or tonal color. Harmonics are exact multiples of the fundamental; and its overtones, also known as *inharmonic overtones*, are pitches that are not exact multiples of the fundamental. If a piano sounds a middle C, the fundamental is 261.63 Hz; its harmonics are 523.25 Hz, 1046.5 Hz, and so on; and its overtones are the frequencies in between (see Figure 3-4). Sometimes in usage, harmonics also assume overtones.

Unlike pitch and loudness, which may be considered unidimensional, timbre is multidimensional. The sound frequency spectrum is an objective scale of relative pitches; the table of sound-pressure levels is an objective scale of relative loudness. But there is no objective scale that orders or compares the relative timbres of different sounds. We try to articulate our subjective response to a particular distribution of sonic energy. For example, sound consisting mainly of lower frequencies played by cellos may be perceived as mellow, mournful, or quieting; these same lower frequencies played by a bassoon may be perceived as raspy, honky, or comical. That said, there is evidence to suggest that timbres can be compared objectively because of the two important factors

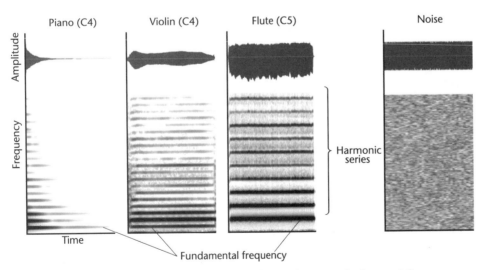

Figure 3-4 Spectrographs of sound envelope characteristics and frequency spectra showing differences between musical sounds and noise. Note that the fundamental and the first few harmonics contain more energy and appear darker in the spectrographs and that the amplitude of the harmonic series diminishes at the higher end of the frequency spectrum.

that help determine timbre: harmonics and how the sound begins—the attack. Along with intuitive response, objective comparisons of timbre serve as a considerable enhancement to professional ears.[1]

Spatial Hearing

Sound is omnidirectional. Our auditory system can hear acoustic space from all around—360 degrees—in any direction, an ability our visual system does not have. More noteworthy is that in an acoustically complex environment, we are able not only to isolate and recognize a particular sound but also to tell from what direction it is coming. To do this, the brain processes differences in both signal *arrival time* and *intensity* at each ear: *interaural time difference (ITD)* and *interaural intensity difference (IID)*, respectively. The ITD and IID occur because the head separates the ears and, depending on which way the head is turned and from what direction the sound is coming, the sound will reach one ear before it reaches the other. The brain compares these differences and tells the listener the sound's location. ITD and IID are frequency dependent, and it is important to bear in mind the particulars of human hearing and the relative sensitivity we have to different frequencies (see Figure 3-2). Furthermore, as measurements, they are most useful in discerning lateral localization, that is, whether a sound is coming from the left or the right. For determining whether a sound is coming from in front, behind, above, or below us, we need to factor in not only the acoustic characteristics of the space but also our physical attributes.

Our ability to localize a sound in space is also affected by our bodies, especially the head, pinnae, and torso. The *head-related transfer function (HRTF)* describes how what we hear is filtered and shaped in establishing its location in three-dimensional space. For example, in addition to serving as passive resonators, pinnae act as filters and tend to reflect frequencies above 4 kHz; whereas sound below 2 kHz is reflected by the torso. The brain's ability to process ITD, IID, and HRTF information makes it possible to hear sound three-dimensionally. This is known as *binaural hearing*, that is, relating to two ears.

Haas and Precedence Effects

When a sound is emitted in a sound-reflectant space, *direct sound* reaches our ears first, before it interacts with any other surface. Indirect sounds, or *reflected sounds*, on the other hand, reach our ears only after bouncing off one or more surfaces. If these small echo delays arrive within a window of 1 to 30 ms of the direct sound, called the *echo threshold*, there are a few perceptual reactions. One, the sound appears louder and fuller because of the addition of energies or summing of the direct and indirect sounds; the listener experience is one of a more lively and natural sound. Two, we do not hear the echoes as distinct and separate unless they exceed the intensity of the direct sound by 10

---

1. William Moylan, *Understanding and Crafting the Mix: The Art of Recording,* 2nd ed. (Boston: Focal Press, 2007).

dB or more. They are suppressed, and the direct and reflected sounds are perceived as one coherent event. This is called the *Haas effect*.

The Haas effect gradually disappears and discrete echoes are heard and as the time interval between direct and reflected sounds increases from roughly 30 to 50 ms. Furthermore, when hearing a sound and its reflections arriving from different directions at short delay intervals, the listener perceives a *temporal fusion* of both sounds as coming from the same direction. The first-arriving sound is dominant when it comes to our ability to localize the source, even if the immediate repetitions coming from another location are louder. Fusion and localization dominance are phenomena associated with what is known as the *precedence effect*.

Binaural Versus Stereo Sound

The term *binaural* is often used synonymously with *stereo*, particularly when it comes to sound reproduction. They are not synonymous. Binaural sound is three-dimensional; its acoustic space is depth, breadth, and height. Stereo is essentially unidimensional sound that creates the illusion of two-dimensional sound—depth and breadth.

Stereo has two static sound sources—the loudspeakers—with nothing but space in between. Although each ear receives the sound at a different time and intensity—the left ear from the left loudspeaker earlier and louder than the right ear and vice versa—the sounds are a composite of the signals from both loudspeakers. Here, the brain adds the two signals together, creating the illusion of a fused auditory image in the middle.

Processing of surround-sound imaging is somewhat different, but its spatial illusion is still not binaural. Basically, this is why recorded sound cannot quite reproduce the definition, fidelity, and dimension of live sound, even with today's technology. The only way a recording can sound similar to live sound is to record and play it back binaurally (see Chapter 6), although some surround-sound techniques can come close (see Chapter 13).

Main Points

- Sound acts according to physical principles, but it also has a psychological effect on humans.

- Psychologically, and in musical terms, we perceive frequency as pitch—the relative tonal highness or lowness of a sound.

- The range of audible frequencies, or the sound frequency spectrum, is divided into octaves, each with a unique and vital quality.

- Generally, the audible frequency spectrum includes the low bass, upper bass, midrange, upper midrange, and treble.

- The ear does not perceive all frequencies at the same loudness even if their amplitudes are the same. This is the equal loudness principle. Humans do not hear lower- and higher-pitched sounds as well as they hear midrange sounds.

- Masking—covering a weaker sound with a stronger sound when each is a different frequency and both vibrate simultaneously—is another perceptual response dependent on the relationship between frequency and loudness.

- Timbre is the tone quality, or tone color, of a sound.

- By processing the time and intensity differences (ITD and IID, respectively) of a sound reaching the ears, and the head-related transfer function (HRTF) that filter the sound, the brain can isolate and recognize the sound and tell from what direction it is coming. This makes it possible to hear sound three-dimensionally and is known as binaural hearing.

- When hearing two sounds arriving from different directions within the Haas fusion zone, we perceive this temporal fusion of both sounds as coming from the same direction as the first-arriving sound, even if the immediate repetitions coming from another location are louder. Fusion and localization dominance phenomena are associated with what is known as the precedence effect.

- Binaural and stereo sound are different. Binaural sound is three-dimensional and stereo has two static sound sources that create the illusion of a fused, multi-dimensional auditory image.

4 Studio and Control Room Design

When a sound wave is emitted in an enclosed space, it bounces off the surfaces of that space. Each surface affects the travels of the wave, depending on its sound-absorbing properties, size, and shape. Some frequencies are absorbed; others are reflected or diffracted. Some waves travel a short distance, bouncing off surfaces once or twice. Waves that travel longer distances arrive later, weaker, and tonally altered.

The science of a sound wave's behavior—that is, its generation, transmission, reception, and effects—is called *acoustics*. The study that deals with the human perception of acoustics is called *psychoacoustics*. The term *acoustics* is used to describe the physical behavior of sound waves in a room; in this context, psychoacoustics is concerned with the relationship of our subjective response to such sound waves.

Differences Between Studios and Control Rooms

The acoustic and psychoacoustic considerations in designing performance studios and control rooms differ because of their primary purposes. Studios are designed for sound suitable for microphone pickup, whereas control rooms are designed for listening to loudspeakers. A home or small project studio may require accommodation for both functions. Appropriate studio acoustics vary with the type of audio produced. Voice-overs and narration, for example, require a relatively dry acoustic environment, whereas orchestral music requires a more reverberant setting. (See "Relationship of Studio Acoustics to Program Material" later in this chapter.) Recordings made in studios in which the acoustics are not quite suitable are provided with the appropriate acoustics artificially in the mixdown (see Chapters 11 and 13).

To accurately assess the reproduced sound in a control room, the main challenge is to reduce the number of unwanted reflections at the stereo and surround-sound monitoring locations so that they are relatively reflection-free zones.

In facilities designed by professional control room architects and acousticians, monitoring environments are less problematic than they are in the burgeoning number of project or home studios that may be housed in a living room, den, basement, or garage. In either case, however, unless the monitoring room is acoustically suitable for its sonic purpose, it seriously inhibits the ability to accurately evaluate the sound quality of audio material. (Control room monitoring is discussed in Chapter 5, "Monitoring.")

The behavior of sound waves in an acoustic environment and how that behavior affects aural perception leads logically to a consideration of the four factors that influence this behavior: sound isolation, room dimensions, room shape, and room acoustics. These factors are directly related to one overriding concern: noise.

Noise

Noise—unwanted sound—is the number one enemy in audio production. As noted in Chapter 2, noise is everywhere. Outside a room, it comes from traffic, airplanes, jack-hammers, thunder, rain, and so on. Inside a room, it is generated by fluorescent lights, heating, ventilation and air conditioning (HVAC) systems, computers, and appliances. And these are only the more obvious examples. A few not-so-obvious examples include the "noise" made by the random motion of molecules, by our nervous and circulatory systems, and by our ears. In short, noise is part of our existence and can never be completely eliminated. (Audio equipment also generates *system noise*.) Even though unwanted sound is always present, when producing audio it must be brought to within tolerable levels so that it does not interfere with the desired sound, particularly with digital recording. Among other things, noise can mask sounds, make speech unintelligible, create distraction, cause annoyance, and reduce if not ruin the aesthetic listening experience.

To this end, acousticians have developed *noise criteria (NC)* that identify, by means of a rating system, background noise levels (see Figure 4-1). From this rating system, NC levels for various types of rooms are derived (see Figure 4-2). This raises the question: Once NC levels for a particular room are known, how is noise control accomplished?

Sound Isolation

Sound studios must be isolated to prevent outside noise from leaking into the room and to keep loud sound levels generated inside the room from disturbing neighbors. This is accomplished in two ways. The first is by determining the loudest outside sound level against the minimum acceptable NC level inside the studio. This is usually between NC 15 and NC 25 (approximately 25 to 35 dBA[1]), depending on the type of sound for which the studio is used. It is also done by determining the loudest sound level inside the studio against a maximum acceptable noise floor outside the studio.

For example, assume that the maximum measured noise outside a studio is 90 dB-SPL and the maximum acceptable noise level inside the studio is 30 dB-SPL at, say, 500 Hz. (These values are always frequency-dependent but are usually based on 500 Hz.) This means the construction of the studio must reduce the loudness of the outside sound level

---

1. The "A" in the dB value refers to the filter used for measuring frequency response that closely resembles the response of the human ear.

by 60 dB. If the loudest sound inside a studio is 110 dB-SPL and the maximum acceptable noise outside the studio is 45 dB-SPL, the studio's construction must reduce the loudness level by 65 dB.

The amount of sound reduction provided by a partition, such as a wall, floor, or ceiling, is referred to as *transmission loss (TL)*. Because TL works both ways, determining partition requirements is equally applicable to sound traveling from inside to outside the studio. Therefore, the partitions constructed to isolate the studio in this example would have to reduce the loudness level by at least 65 dB (500 Hz).

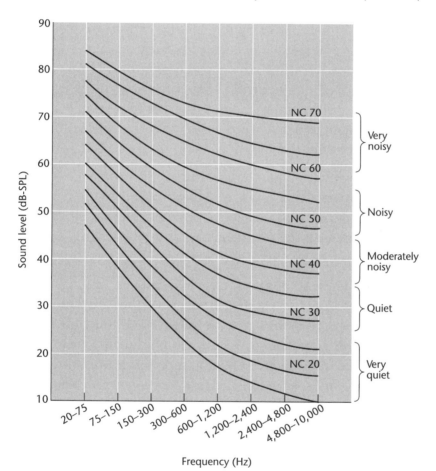

Figure 4-1 Noise criteria (NC) curves.

Type of Room	Recommended NC Curve	dB
Broadcast and recording studios	NC 15–25	25–25
Concert halls	NC 20	30
Drama theaters	NC 20–25	30–35
Motion picture theaters	NC 30	40
Sports arenas	NC 50	60

Figure 4-2 Recommended NC levels for selected rooms.

Just as it is convenient to define a noise spectrum by a single NC rating, it is useful to measure a partition on the basis of its transmission loss; such a measurement is called *sound transmission class (STC)*. Sound transmission class varies with the type and the mass of materials in a partition. If a 4-inch concrete block has an STC of 48, it indicates that sound passing through it will be attenuated by 48 dB. An 8-inch concrete block with an STC of 52 attenuates 4 dB more sound than the 4-inch block. Plastering both sides of the concrete block would add 8 dB more sound attenuation.

Room Dimensions

Sometimes a studio's dimensions accentuate noise by reinforcing certain frequencies, thereby altering, or "coloring," the natural sound. This may also affect the response of a sound's decay (see Figure 4-3). Such coloration affects perception of tonal balance, clarity, and imaging as well. Audio mixed in a control room with these problems will sound markedly different when played in another room. Other factors related to the shape of a studio and the construction materials used therein (discussed in the following two sections) may also affect coloration.

Rooms have particular resonances at which sound will be naturally sustained. These are related to the room's dimensions. *Resonance* results when a vibrating body with the same natural frequencies as another body causes it to vibrate sympathetically and increases the amplitude of both at those frequencies if the vibrations are in acoustical phase.

Resonances occur in a room at frequencies whose wavelengths are the same as or a multiple of one of the room's dimensions. These resonances, called *eigentones*, or more commonly, *room modes*, are increases in loudness at resonant frequencies that are a function of a room's dimensions. When these dimensions are the same as or multiples of a common value, the resonance amplitude is increased. Such a room's dimensions may be 10 × 20 × 30 feet, or 15 × 30 × 45 feet. This creates unequal representation of the frequencies generated by a sound source. In other words, certain frequencies will be reinforced while others will not. To avoid additive resonances, room dimensions should not be the same nor be integer multiples of one another. Dimensions of, say, 9 × 10.1 × 12.5 feet or 15 × 27 × 31.5 feet would be satisfactory. It should be noted, however, that

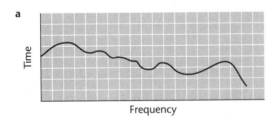

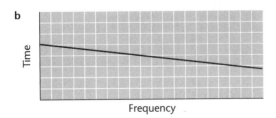

Figure 4-3 Reverberation decay responses. (a) Irregular reverb decay, which is undesirable because it creates unwanted sound coloration. (b) Desirable reverb decay, illustrating no resonant coloration. This acoustic condition is always strived for but in practice is rarely attained.

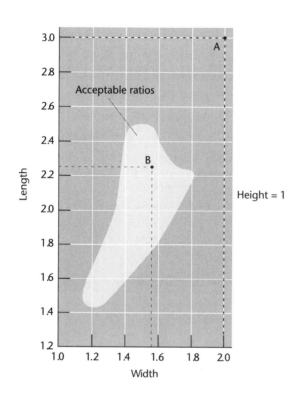

Figure 4-4 Acceptable ratios to control room resonances. Using this pictogram, developed by Newman, Blot, and Baranek in 1957, involves three basic steps: (1) divide all room dimensions by the height (making height equal to 1); (2) plot width and length on the horizontal and vertical scales; and (3) determine acceptability by noting whether the plot is in or out of the "zone."

From *Broadcast Engineering* magazine, February 2003, p.78 © 2003 Mondo Code.

although perfect dimensions are the ideal, they are rarely a reality. Most studios will have some resonant frequencies. Figure 4-4 shows a graph of acceptable room ratios.

Resonance is not always bad, however. The tubing in wind and brass instruments; the pipes in an organ; and the human mouth, nose, chest, and throat are resonators. Air columns passing through them excite resonant frequencies, creating sound. Without resonators such as the "box" of a guitar or violin, weak sound sources would generate little sound. Some studios use this principle to construct resonators that help amplify certain frequencies to enhance the type of sound produced. The section titled "Room Acoustics" later in this chapter explains how resonators are also used to absorb sound.

Room Shape

Acoustics is a science of interacting relationships. Although a studio's walls, floors, and windows may have been properly constructed and their dimensions conform to a set of preferred standards, the room's shape also influences noise reduction and sound dispersion.

Except for bass frequencies, sound behaves like light; *its angle of incidence is equal to its angle of reflectance* (see Figure 4-5). If a studio has reflective parallel walls, sound waves reinforce themselves as they continuously bounce between opposing surfaces (see Figure 4-6). These are called *standing waves*. Another phenomenon associated with parallel walls is *flutter echo* where multiple, short reflections produce a ringing decay of varying duration. If there are concave surfaces, they serve as collecting points, generating unwanted concentrations of sound (see Figure 4-7a). A studio, whether professional or home based, should be designed to break up the paths of sound waves (see Figure 4-7b and Figure 4-7c).

Typical studio designs have adjacent walls at angles other than 90 degrees and different-shaped wall surfaces, such as spherical, cylindrical, serrated, and pyramidal, to help disperse the sound waves (see Figure 4-8). Even the glass between the studio and the control room is angled toward the floor for sound dispersal (and to avoid light reflections), but this is not enough to break up the paths of sound waves; they must be controlled once they hit a surface.

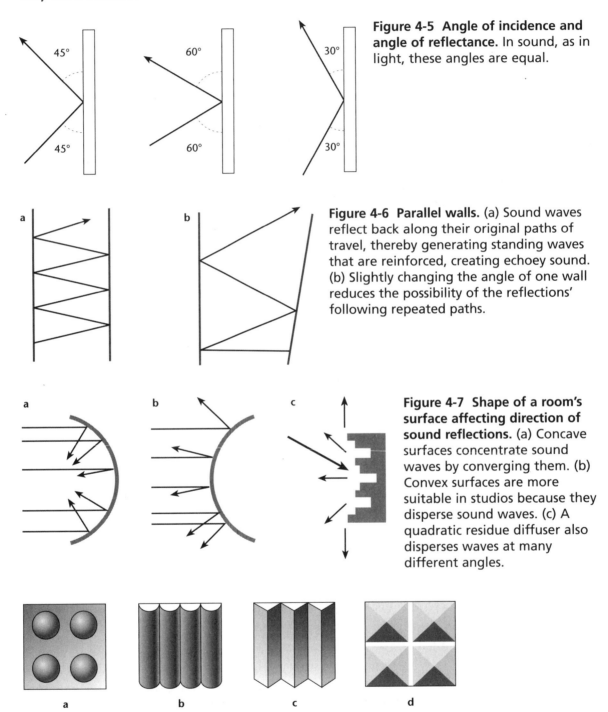

Figure 4-5 Angle of incidence and angle of reflectance. In sound, as in light, these angles are equal.

Figure 4-6 Parallel walls. (a) Sound waves reflect back along their original paths of travel, thereby generating standing waves that are reinforced, creating echoey sound. (b) Slightly changing the angle of one wall reduces the possibility of the reflections' following repeated paths.

Figure 4-7 Shape of a room's surface affecting direction of sound reflections. (a) Concave surfaces concentrate sound waves by converging them. (b) Convex surfaces are more suitable in studios because they disperse sound waves. (c) A quadratic residue diffuser also disperses waves at many different angles.

Figure 4-8 Studio walls with different surface shapes. (a) Spherical, (b) cylindrical, (c) serrated, and (d) pyramidal.

Room Acoustics

When sound hits a surface, one reaction—or a combination of five reactions—happens, depending on the surface's material, mass, and design. Sound is absorbed, reflected, partially absorbed and reflected, diffracted, or diffused.

Absorption and Reflection

When sound hits a surface and is absorbed, it is soaked up: There is little or no reflection, and the sonic result is lifeless, or dry. When sound hits a surface and is reflected, it bounces off the surface and is perceived as reverberation or echo, depending on its interaction with other live surfaces in the vicinity. Conditions under which sound is completely absorbed or reflected are rare. Most materials absorb and reflect sound to some degree (see Figure 4-9).

The amount of indirect sound energy absorbed is given an acoustical rating called a *sound absorption coefficient (SAC)*, also known as a *noise reduction coefficient* (NRC). Theoretically, on a scale from 1.0 to 0.0, material with a sound absorption coefficient of 1.0 completely absorbs sound, whereas material with an NRC of 0.0 is completely sound reflectant. Soft, porous materials absorb more sound than hard, nonporous materials. Drapes, for example, have a higher absorption coefficient than glass. Sound absorption ratings for the same material vary with frequency, however. For example: The sound absorption coefficient of a light, porous concrete block at 125 Hz is 0.36, at 500 Hz it is 0.31, and at 4,000 Hz it is 0.25; heavy plate glass has a SAC of 0.18 at 125 Hz, 0.04 at 500 Hz, and 0.02 at 4,000 Hz; wood parquet's SAC is 0.04 at 125 Hz, 0.07 at 500 Hz, and 0.07 at 4,000 Hz. A list of sound absorption coefficients for many types of materials can be found at acoustic provider websites such as www.acousticalsurfaces.com.

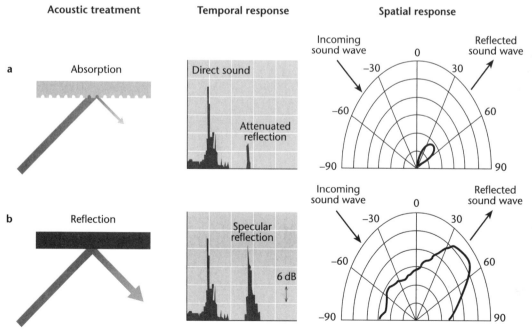

Figure 4-9 Absorption and reflection in relation to temporal and spatial response.

Three types of acoustic absorbers are porous absorbers, diaphragmatic absorbers, and Helmholtz absorbers. ***Porous absorbers*** come in an ever increasing variety of materials, shapes and sizes, including polyurethane and melamine foams (see Figure 4-10), sintered glass, transparent fiber free panels and films, absorptive building materials such as wood and plaster, and metal bass management plate absorbers. Porous absorbers are most effective with high frequencies. Because the wavelengths of high frequencies are short, they tend to get trapped in the tiny air spaces of the porous materials. The thicker and denser the absorbent, the greater the sound absorption—but only to a point. If the material is overly dense, it will act more like a hard wall and reject high-frequency sound. In the middle and lower frequencies, however, an overly dense absorber improves absorption.

Diaphragmatic absorbers are generally flexible panels of wood or pressed wood mounted over an air space. When a sound wave hits the panel, it resonates at a frequency (or frequencies) determined by the stiffness of the panel and the size of the air space. Other sound waves of the same frequency (or frequencies) approaching the panel, therefore, are dampened. Diaphragmatic absorbers are used mainly to absorb low frequencies; for this reason, they are also called ***bass traps*** (see Figure 4-11). This principle can also be applied to absorbing high frequencies.

Figure 4-10 Polyurethane-foam sound absorber. (a) In sheet form, ready to install. (b) Applied to a voice-over room to control unwanted acoustic reflections.

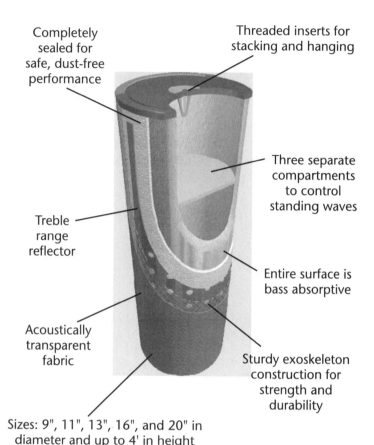

Completely sealed for safe, dust-free performance

Threaded inserts for stacking and hanging

Figure 4-11 Anatomy of a Tube Trap acoustic absorber (bass trap).

Three separate compartments to control standing waves

Treble range reflector

Entire surface is bass absorptive

Acoustically transparent fabric

Sturdy exoskeleton construction for strength and durability

Sizes: 9", 11", 13", 16", and 20" in diameter and up to 4' in height

Because it is difficult to completely dissipate standing waves, especially in small rooms and even with optimal acoustics, bass traps are usually designed to introduce significant absorption for frequencies between 30 Hz and 100 Hz.

A *Helmholtz absorber*, also called a *Helmholtz resonator*, is a tuned absorber designed to remove sound at specific frequencies or within specific frequency ranges, usually the lower-middle frequencies. It functions, in principle, not unlike the action created when blowing into the mouth of a soda bottle. The tone created at the frequency of the bottle's resonance is related to the air mass in the bottle. By filling the bottle with water, the air mass is reduced, so the pitch of the tone is higher.

Diffraction

When sound reaches a surface, in addition to being partially absorbed and reflected, it *diffracts*—spreads around the surface. The amount of *diffraction* depends on the relationship between wavelength and the distances involved. You will recall that each frequency has a wavelength; bass waves are longer, and treble waves are shorter. Hence, the diffraction of bass waves is more difficult to control acoustically than the diffraction of treble waves.

Diffusion

The overriding challenge for the acoustician is controlling the physical behavior of sound waves in a studio. The goal is the uniform distribution of sound energy in a room so that its intensity throughout the room is approximately uniform (see Figure 4-12). This is called *diffusion*.

No matter how weak or strong the sound and regardless of its wavelength, the diffused energy is reduced in amplitude and spread out in time, falling off more or less exponentially. Figure 4-13 displays an example of a combined acoustic treatment.

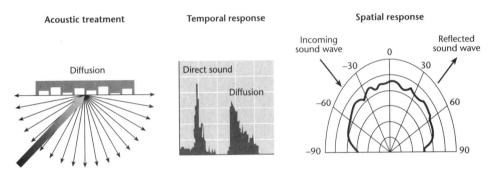

Figure 4-12 Diffusion in relation to temporal and spatial response.

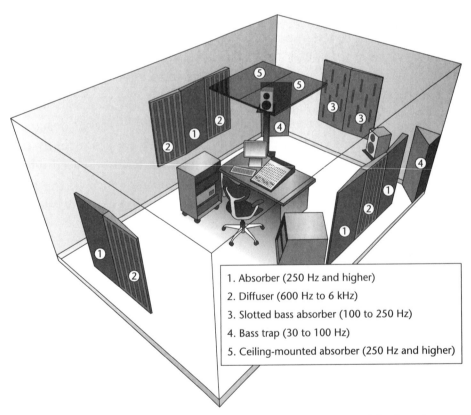

1. Absorber (250 Hz and higher)
2. Diffuser (600 Hz to 6 kHz)
3. Slotted bass absorber (100 to 250 Hz)
4. Bass trap (30 to 100 Hz)
5. Ceiling-mounted absorber (250 Hz and higher)

Figure 4-13 Acoustic treatment system showing a room with absorbers, diffusers, and bass traps.

Variable Acoustics

Basic principles of acoustics apply to any room in which sound is generated. As noted earlier, however, a room's purpose greatly influences how those principles are applied. If a studio is used for rock music and speech, the acoustics must absorb more sound than they diffuse so that there is minimal interference from other sounds and/or from reverberation. On the other hand, studios used for classical music and some types of jazz should diffuse more sound than they absorb to maintain balanced, blended, open sound imaging.

Theoretically, this means that a studio designed to fulfill one sonic purpose is inappropriate for another. In fact, to be more functional, some studios are designed with variable acoustics. They have adjustable panels, louvers, or partitions and portable baffles, or *gobos*, to alter diffusion, absorption, and reverb time (see Figures 4-14, 4-15, and 4-16).

Figure 4-14 Acoustic treatment along walls. (a) Scoring stage with alternating doors and slats that can be opened or closed to vary acoustics. (b) Detail of doors and slats shown in (a).

a

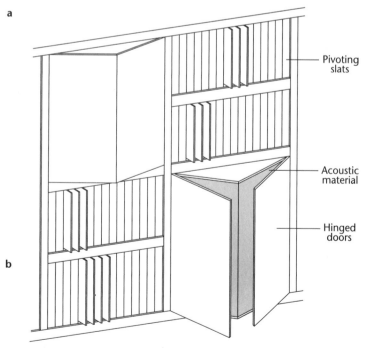

Pivoting slats

Acoustic material

Hinged doors

b

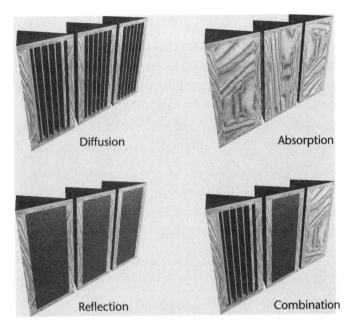

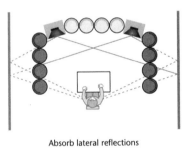

Figure 4-15 Trifussor. Variable equilateral triangle prism acoustic modules can be rotated to expose absorptive, reflective, and diffusive sides in any combination, thereby refining reverb times. For example, in recording an orchestra, the modules adjacent to strings and woodwinds could be turned to their reflective side to enhance these weaker-sounding instruments, and panels nearer brass and tympani could be turned to their absorptive side to help control these strong-sounding instruments.

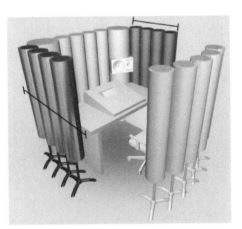

Absorb lateral reflections

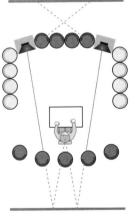

Absorb front/back reflections

Figure 4-16 Acoustic treatment for rooms with less-than-desirable acoustics. One way of handling such a situation is with the Attack Wall, a portable array of reflective/absorptive acoustic traps that can be positioned in various ways around the console and the recordist.

Home and Project Studios

Home and small project recording and postproduction studios are increasingly popular among professionals, audiophiles, and amateur enthusiasts. Although the terms are used interchangeably, the differences between home and project studios usually come down to whether the facility is commercial or not. Project studios typically are; home studios may or may not be. In either case, construction and acoustic considerations are similar. Adapting living space, a basement, or a garage to suit particular needs is often an attractive and affordable alternative to renting studio time. While the general principles and issues of sound isolation, room characteristics, and acoustics are the same as for a professionally designed and built studio, there are a number of considerations particular to working at home or in a small space adapted for audio recording.

In a home or small project studio, sound transmission is a key issue—neighbors don't necessarily want to hear you recording in the middle of the night, and you don't want the sounds of the street on the recording or to be a distraction when editing and mixing. Ideally, situating the studio below ground or in a basement has the advantage of reducing noise transmission. Inner and outer walls may be reinforced acoustically by adding another layer of drywall or acoustically absorbent paneling. If this is built out from an existing wall with additional framing, the space in between forms an important *bass trap* (see Figure 4-11), thereby further reducing unwanted lower frequencies. Carpeting a room and using acoustic carpet underlay—often made of rubber and felt— can reduce the transmission of unwanted sound through the floor.

One of the most challenging aspects of designing a home-based studio involves room dimension and shape with attendant acoustic problems. Where possible, try not to situate the studio in a small, square room. If there is no option, make sure that walls, floor, and ceiling treatments have sufficient absorption to neutralize flutter echoes. Generally, a larger space with a high ceiling offers greater possibilities and better sound for both recording and monitoring.

In a home studio, it is often difficult to avoid perpendicular and parallel walls, whether in a basement, study, or a bedroom. One solution is to position the monitoring location in a corner where there is less risk of standing waves and flutter echo as sound reflects back and forth across a room. But be aware that such positioning may unduly increase bass response (see Figure 5-9). Moveable office partitions with appropriate fabric or other noise-reducing material are also useful in configuring a space for both recording and listening. They have the advantage of coming in various sizes and can be easily stored in a small space.

Consider the acoustic characteristics of the recording and monitoring space(s) and take appropriate measures to control and address problematic issues. Porous absorbers are perhaps the most popular type of acoustic treatment for the home or small project studio. These can often complement surface treatments that are part of a room's décor, where carpeting, curtains, acoustic tile ceilings all contribute to the sonic character of the space. Remember that the walls in most home and small project spaces are drywall (gypsum plaster board), brick, or cinderblock—all highly reflective surfaces. Some treatment will be required to control the interplay of absorption and reflection of sound effectively.

As with any construction project, planning and anticipating the varied uses of a space is essential. So, before knocking out walls, think through the studio design and layout with regard to the kind of audio recording and production projects undertaken. In such planning, be sure to factor in providing easy access to the studio for musicians and additional production personnel and making sure there is sufficient performance and working space (see Figure 4-17).

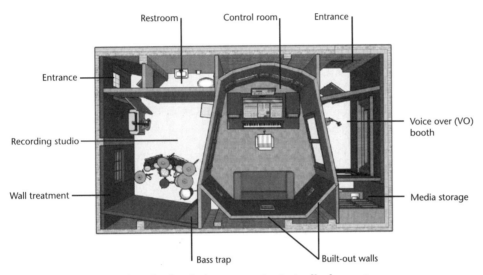

Figure 4-17 Example of a basic home project studio layout.

Relationship of Studio Acoustics to Program Material

Although the science of acoustics is highly developed, there is no such thing as a sound room with perfect acoustics. The sonic requirements of rock-and-roll and classical music, for example, are different, as they are for a radio studio and a studio used for dialogue rerecording in film and television.

A reverberant studio might be suitable for a symphony orchestra because the reflections add needed richness to the music, as they do in a concert hall. The extremely loud music a rock group generates would swim amid too many sound reflections, becoming virtually unintelligible. At the same time, a studio with relatively few reflections, and therefore suitable for rock-and-roll, would render the sound of a symphony orchestra small and lifeless.

A radio studio is relatively quiet but does have some room tone, or atmosphere, so the sound is not too closed down or closet-like. In radio, it is important to maintain the intimate sonic rapport between announcer and listener essential to the personal nature of the medium. Rerecording dialogue in postproduction for a film or TV drama requires a studio virtually devoid of room tone to prevent acoustics from coloring the dialogue so that room tone appropriate to a scene's setting can be added later.

Rooms with reverberation times of one second or more are considered "live." Rooms with reverberation times of one-half second or less are considered "dry," or "dead" (see Figure 4-18). Live rooms reinforce sound, making it relatively louder and more powerful, especially, although not always, in the lower frequencies. They also tend to diffuse detail, smoothing inconsistencies in pitch, tonal quality, and performance.

In dry rooms, sound is reinforced little or not at all, causing it to be concentrated and lifeless. Inconsistencies in pitch, tonal quality, and other aspects of undesirable performance are readily apparent. In instances where dry rooms are required for recording, signal processing is used to provide appropriate reverberation (see Figure 4-19 and Chapter 11). Liveness can be added by increasing the frequencies between roughly 500 and 2,000 Hz and adding reverberation in the range of one to two seconds. Other aspects to consider in the acoustics of a room or recording—depending on the type of program material—are warmth, intimacy, clarity, and auditory source width.

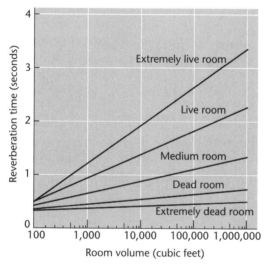

Figure 4-18 Room liveness in relation to reverberation time and room size.

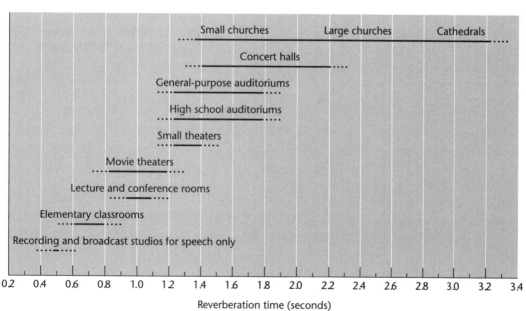

Figure 4-19 Typical reverberation times for various performance spaces.

Warmth is a sonic quality usually associated with the lower frequencies and increased reverberation time—specifically, the frequencies between roughly 125 and 250 Hz—and a high reverb time relative to the midrange frequencies.

Intimacy relates to being a part of the performance and connected with the performers. It results from early reflections that follow the direct sound by no more than 15 to 20 ms.

Clarity refers to the ability to hear sonic detail, such as understanding lyrics or the attack of orchestral sections or a solo instrument. Clarity increases as the direct-to-reverberant sound ratio decreases. Clarity is extremely high in a dry studio, but the sound would not be enjoyable, so clarity must be judged in relation to the amount of reverb in a sound.

Auditory source width (*ASW*) refers to how wide a sound source is perceived to be compared with how wide it actually is. This is a result of both the reverberation values in a room or recording and, in a recording, the microphone and panning techniques by which a spatial illusion is created.

Acousticians have calculated optimum reverb times for various types of audio material that have proved suitable for emulation in the production room (see Figure 4-20). That said, preference for the amount of reverberation and reverb time is a matter of individual taste and perception—and perceptions differ, even among the experts. This is one reason why, for example, concert venues of relatively the same dimensions, or acoustic properties, or both, sound different. One hall may be drier and spare sounding, another more reverberant and rich sounding. Then there are concert venues of such dimensions that they require electronic reinforcement through small loudspeakers throughout the hall to ensure optimal distribution of the direct sound and the early and late reflections.

Generally, it is agreed that certain reverb times for speech, pop and rock music, and orchestral music are desirable. For example, for the intimate clarity of speech in radio,

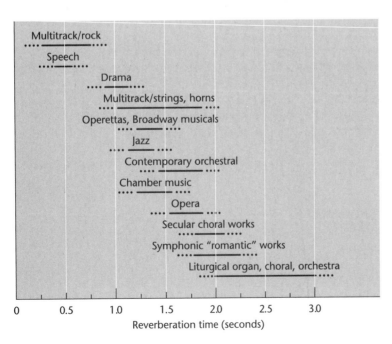

Figure 4-20 Optimal reverberation times for various types of music and speech produced indoors.

a drier reverb time value of 0.4 to 0.6 seconds is considered suitable while 0.5 to 0.7 seconds is acceptable for lecture speech. Too long a reverb time creates a distant, more echoey sound. Too short a reverb time gives speech too dry a quality and is usually uncomfortable for the speaker. Pop and rock require a short reverb time because the music is usually high energy; typically 0.5 to 0.6 seconds is recommended. Longer reverb times would create too many unwanted sound reflections and wash out too much detail. Orchestral music requires longer reverb times to add fullness and body to the sound; depending on the size of the orchestra, 1.5 to 2 seconds is preferred. Shorter reverb times could adversely affect blending and reduce the music's liveness and vitality.

Ergonomics

Sound control is obviously the most important factor in studio and control room design, but human needs should not be ignored. Production is stressful enough without personnel having to endure poor lighting, hard-to-reach equipment, uncomfortable chairs, and so on. Designing an engineering system with the human element in mind is called *ergonomics*.

Among the more important ergonomic considerations are comfortable lighting; sufficient room for personnel and furniture; functional, comfortable furniture; easily accessible equipment; static-free floor covering that facilitates anything on wheels to move about easily; and a computer workstation that reduces back strain and repetitive strain or stress discomfort in the fingers, hands, arms, and shoulders.

Production is demanding enough: *Make it as efficient and easy as possible on the production personnel and yourself.*

Main Points

- When a sound wave is emitted in an enclosed space, it bounces off the surfaces of that space. Each surface affects the travels of the wave, depending on its sound-absorbing properties, size, and shape.

- Acoustics is the science of sound, including its generation, transmission, reception, and effects. Psychoacoustics deals with the human perception of sound. The term acoustics is also used to describe the physical behavior of sound waves in a room. In that context, psychoacoustics is concerned with the relationship of our subjective response to such sound waves.

- The acoustic and psychoacoustic considerations in designing performance studios and control rooms differ because of their primary purposes. Studios are designed for sound suitable for microphone pickup, whereas control rooms are designed for listening to loudspeakers.

- Four factors influence how sound behaves in an acoustic environment: sound isolation, room dimensions, room shape, and room acoustics.

- Noise is any unwanted sound in the audio system, the studio, or the environment.

- Sound isolation in a room is measured in two ways: by determining the loudest outside sound level against the minimum acceptable noise criteria (NC) level inside the room, and by determining the loudest sound level inside the studio against a maximum acceptable noise floor outside the room.

- The NC system rates the level of background noise.

- Transmission loss (TL) is the amount of sound reduction provided by a partition, such as a wall, floor, or ceiling. This value is given a measurement called sound transmission class (STC).

- The dimensions of a sound room—height, width, and length—should not equal nor be exact multiples of one another. Room dimensions create additive resonances, reinforcing certain frequencies and not others and thereby coloring the sound.

- Resonance, another important factor in studio design, results when a vibrating body with the same natural frequencies as another body causes that body to vibrate sympathetically, thereby increasing the amplitude of both at those frequencies if the variables are in acoustical phase.

- The shape of a studio is significant for good noise reduction and sound dispersion.

- When sound hits a surface, one or a combination of five reactions occurs: It is absorbed, reflected, partially absorbed and reflected, diffracted, or diffused.

- The amount of indirect sound energy absorbed is given an acoustical rating called a sound absorption coefficient (SAC), also known as a noise reduction coefficient (NRC).

- Three classifications of acoustic absorbers are porous absorbers, diaphragmatic absorbers, and Helmholtz absorbers or resonators.

- When sound reaches a surface, in addition to being partially absorbed and reflected, it diffracts—or spreads around the surface.

- Diffusion is the uniform distribution of sound energy in a room so that its intensity throughout the room is approximately uniform.

- To be more acoustically functional, many studios are designed with adjustable acoustics—movable panels, louvers, walls, and gobos (portable baffles) to alter diffusion, absorption, and reverb time.

- In designing a home and project studio, the overriding considerations are keeping studio sound from getting outside the room; preventing outside sound from getting into the room; room dimension and shape; acoustic control; equipment positioning; and access.

- Although the science of acoustics is highly developed, there is no such thing as a sound room with perfect acoustics. In designing a studio, the relationship of its acoustics to the program material performed therein is a primary consideration.

- Among the factors in designing an appropriate acoustic recording space are warmth, intimacy, clarity, and auditory source width.

- Ergonomics addresses the design of an engineering system with human comfort and convenience in mind.

5 Monitoring

In audio production, no single item in the sound chain is more important than the reference loudspeakers, and no process in evaluating the product is more important than monitoring. The *sound chain* begins with the microphone, whose signal is sent to a console, mixer, or computer for routing, processing, and recording and heard through a loudspeaker. Although the loudspeaker is last in this signal flow, no matter how good the other components in the audio system, *the quality of every sound evaluated is based on what you hear from a loudspeaker interacting with the room acoustics*. Knowing a loudspeaker's sonic characteristics in relation to the acoustic environment is fundamental to the accurate monitoring and appraisal of audio material.

Performance Requirements of a Monitor Loudspeaker

Loudspeakers are sometimes compared to musical instruments in that they produce sound. But it is more accurate to say that they *reproduce* sound. And, unlike any musical instrument, a loudspeaker has the capability of generating a far wider frequency response and a greater dynamic range.

Loudspeakers are not like purely electronic components such as consoles, which can be objectively tested and rationally evaluated. No two loudspeakers sound quite the same. Comparing the same make and model of loudspeakers in one room tells you only what they sound like in that acoustic environment; in another room, they may sound altogether different. Furthermore, a loudspeaker that satisfies your taste might be unappealing to someone else.

A loudspeaker's specifications can be used only as a reference. No matter how good a speaker looks on paper, keep in mind that the measurements are based on tests made in an *anechoic chamber*—a room with no reflections of any kind.

Another problem in loudspeaker evaluation is that in comparison tests, which are done by switching back and forth between two monitors or switching among more than two monitors, auditory memory is quite short—only a few seconds at best. By the time one listens to a second or third set of monitors, recalling what the comparisons in the first set were or what the first monitor sounded like is unreliable. This is why employing objective testing is an essential part of loudspeaker evaluation.

Even as methods for evaluating loudspeakers improve, it is still difficult to suggest guidelines that will satisfy the general population of audio professionals, though they will agree that monitors used for professional purposes should meet certain performance requirements.

Frequency Response

Evaluating *frequency response* in a loudspeaker involves two considerations: how wide it is and how flat, or linear, it is. Frequency response ideally should be as wide as possible, from at least 40 to 20,000 Hz. But the relationship between the sound produced in the studio and the sound reproduced through the listener's receiver/loudspeaker becomes a factor when selecting a monitor loudspeaker.

For example, TV audio can carry the entire range of audible frequencies. You may have noticed during a televised music program, however, that certain high- and low-pitched instruments are played, but you hear them only faintly or not at all. Overhead cymbals are one example. Generally, their frequency range is between 300 and 12,000 Hz (including overtones), but they usually begin to gain good definition between 4,500 and 8,000 Hz, which is well within the frequency of television transmission. The highest response of many home TV receivers is about 6,000 Hz, however, which is below a good part of the cymbals' range.

Suppose you wish to boost the cymbal frequencies that the home TV receiver can barely reproduce. Unless you listen to the sound over a monitor comparable in output level and response to the average TV speaker, you cannot get a sense of what effect the boost is having. But that monitor will not give you a sense of what viewers with upgraded TV sound systems, such as stereo and surround sound, are hearing (see Figure 5-1). (The audio in *high-definition television*—HDTV—has great potential to level the playing field between the sonic fidelity of the transmission and that of the reception, but it depends on the audio quality of the commercial TV tuner and the willingness of the consumer to purchase an HDTV set.)

Due to the differences between the potential sound response of a medium and its actual response after processing, transmission, and reception, most professional studios use at least two types of studio monitors: one to provide both wide response and sufficient power to reproduce a broad range of sound levels, and the other with response and power that reflect what the average listener hears. Many studios use three sets of monitors to check sound: (1) mediocre-quality loudspeakers with mostly midrange response and limited power output such as those in portable and car radios, portable and desktop TVs, computer-grade speakers, and small playback devices; (2) average-quality loudspeakers with added high and low response such as moderately priced component systems; and (3) high-quality loudspeakers with a very wide response and high output capability.

Device	Typical frequency response
AM radio	80 Hz — 5 kHz
Portable AM/FM radio	80-100 Hz — 10-12 kHz
Table-model standard stereo TV	100 Hz — 5-8 kHz
7-inch portable high-definition TV	300 Hz — 3.5 kHz
Good-quality standard stereo TV	50 Hz — 15 kHz
Large-screen high-definition TV	30 Hz — 20 kHz
Mediocre-quality loudspeaker	150 Hz — 10 kHz
Good-quality small loudspeaker	60 Hz — 20 kHz
Good-quality large loudspeaker	35 Hz — 20 kHz
Good-quality CD/DVD sound system	20 Hz — 20 kHz
Cell phone	300 Hz — 3 kHz

Figure 5-1 Table of frequency responses.

Linearity

The second consideration in evaluating frequency response in a loudspeaker is how linear it is. *Linearity* means that frequencies fed to a loudspeaker at a particular loudness are reproduced at the same loudness. If they are not, it is very difficult to predetermine what listeners will hear. If the level of a 100 Hz sound is 80 dB going in and 55 dB coming out, some—if not most—of the information may be lost. If the level of an 8,000 Hz sound is 80 dB going in and 100 dB coming out, the information loss may be overbearing.

Loudspeaker specifications include a value that indicates how much a monitor deviates from a flat frequency response, by either increasing or decreasing the level. This variance should be no greater than ±3dB.

Amplifier Power

To generate adequately loud sound levels without causing distortion, the loudspeaker amplifier must provide sufficient power. At least 30 W for tweeters (high-frequency loudspeakers) and 100 W for woofers (low-frequency loudspeakers) is generally necessary. Regardless of how good the rest of a loudspeaker's components, if the amp does not have enough power, efficiency suffers considerably.

There is a commonly held and seemingly plausible notion that increasing amplifier power results in a proportional increase in loudness; for example, that a 100 W amplifier can play twice as loud as a 50 W amplifier. In fact, if a 100 W amp and a 50 W amp are playing at top volume, the 100 W amp will sound only slightly louder. What the added wattage gives is clearer and less distorted reproduction in loud sonic peaks.

Distortion

Discussion of amplifier power naturally leads to consideration of *distortion*—appearance of a signal in the reproduced sound that was not in the original sound (see Figure 5-2). Any component in the sound chain can generate distortion. Because distortion is heard at the reproduction (loudspeaker) phase of the sound chain—regardless of where in the system it was generated—and because loudspeakers are the most distortion-prone component in most audio systems, it is appropriate to discuss briefly the various forms of distortion: intermodulation, harmonic, transient, and loudness.

Intermodulation Distortion

The loudspeaker is perhaps most vulnerable to *intermodulation distortion (IM),* which results when two or more frequencies occur at the same time and interact to create combination tones and dissonances unrelated to the original sounds. Audio systems can be most vulnerable to intermodulation distortion when frequencies are far apart, as when a piccolo and a baritone saxophone are playing at the same time. Intermodulation distortion usually occurs in the high frequencies because they are weaker and more delicate than the low frequencies.

Wideness and flatness of frequency response are affected when IM is present. In addition to its obvious effect on perception, even subtle distortion can cause listening fatigue.

Unfortunately, not all specification sheets include percentage of IM, and those that do often list it only for selected frequencies. Nevertheless, knowing the percentage of IM for all frequencies is important to loudspeaker selection. A rating of 0.5 percent IM or less is considered good for a loudspeaker.

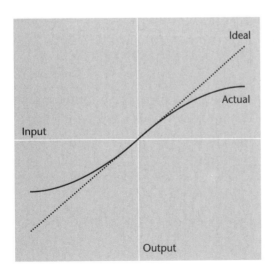

Figure 5-2 Generalized graphic example of distortion. Ideally, a reproduced sound would change in direct proportion to the input. Realistically, the relationship between input and output is rarely linear, resulting in distortion, however slight or significant it may be.

Harmonic Distortion

Harmonic distortion occurs when the audio system introduces harmonics into a recording that were not present originally. Harmonic and IM distortion usually happen when the input and the output of a sound system are *nonlinear*, that is, when they do not change in direct proportion to each other. A loudspeaker's inability to handle amplitude is a common cause of harmonic distortion. This added harmonic content is expressed as a percentage of the total signal or as a component's total harmonic distortion (THD).

Transient Distortion

Transient distortion relates to the inability of an audio component to respond quickly to a rapidly changing signal, such as that produced by percussive sounds. Sometimes transient distortion produces a ringing sound.

Loudness Distortion

Loudness distortion, also called overload distortion, occurs when a signal is recorded or played back at a level of loudness greater than the sound system can handle. The clipping that results from loudness distortion creates a fuzzy, gritty sound.

Dynamic Range

Overly loud signals give a false impression of program quality and balance; nevertheless, a loudspeaker should be capable of reproducing loud sound levels without distorting, blowing fuses, or damaging its components. An output capability of 120 dB-SPL can handle almost all studio work. Even if studio work does not often call for very loud levels, the monitor should be capable of reproducing them because it is sometimes necessary to listen at a loud level to hear subtlety and quiet detail. For soft passages, at least 40 dB-SPL is necessary for most professional recording/mixing situations.

It is worth noting that although monitors in professional facilities have a dynamic range of up to 80 dB (40 dB-SPL to 120 dB-SPL), the dynamic range in consumer loudspeakers is considerably less. Even the better ones may be only 55 dB (50 dB-SPL to 105 dB-SPL).

Sensitivity

Sensitivity is the on-axis sound-pressure level a loudspeaker produces at a given distance when driven at a certain power (about 3.3 feet with 1 W of power). A monitor's sensitivity rating gives you an idea of the system's overall efficiency. Typical ratings range from 84 dB to more than 100 dB.

In real terms, however, a sensitivity rating of, say, 90 dB indicates that the loudspeaker could provide 100 dB from a 10 W input and 110 dB from a 100 W input, depending on the type of driver. It is the combination of sensitivity rating and power rating that indicates whether a monitor loudspeaker will be loud enough to suit your production needs. Generally, a sensitivity rating of 93 dB or louder is required for professional applications.

Polar Response

Polar response indicates how a loudspeaker focuses sound at the monitoring position(s). Because it is important to hear only the sound coming from the studio or the recording, without interacting reflections from the control room walls (vertical surfaces) and ceiling or floor (horizontal surfaces), dispersion must be controlled at the monitoring locations so it is a relatively reflection-free zone (see Figure 5-3).

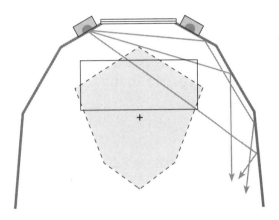

Figure 5-3 The shaded area in this control room design is a reflection-free zone.

This is easier said than done, particularly with bass waves, which are difficult to direct because of their long wavelengths. With bass waves, the room's size, shape, and furnishings have more to do with a speaker's sound than the speaker's inherent design. Therefore, bass traps and other low-frequency absorbers are included in control room design to handle those bass waves not focused at the listening position (see Figures 5-4 and 5-5; see also Figures 4-13 and 4-16).

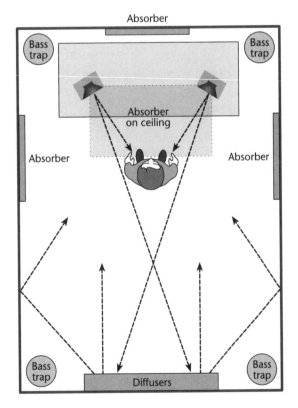

Figure 5-4 Improving control room acoustics. Using strategically placed absorbers, diffusers, and bass traps can help control unwanted room reflections.

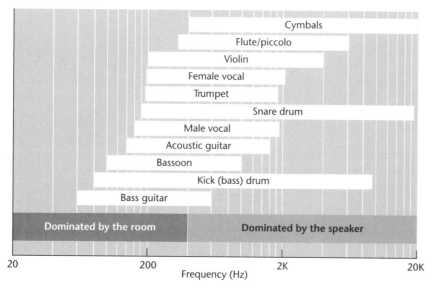

Figure 5-5 Room and loudspeaker influences on the response of selected musical instruments. At frequencies lower than 300 Hz, the room is the dominant factor. Above 300 Hz the inherent loudspeaker characteristics dominate response.

Frequencies from the tweeter(s), on the other hand, are shorter, more directional, and easier to focus. The problem with high frequencies is that as the wavelength shortens, the pattern can narrow and may be off-axis to the listening position. Therefore, the *coverage angle*—defined as the off-axis angle or point at which loudspeaker level is down 6 dB compared with the on-axis output level—may not be wide enough to include the entire listening area.

To help in selecting a loudspeaker with adequate polar response, specifications usually list a monitor's horizontal and vertical coverage angles. These angles should be high enough and wide enough to cover the listening position and still allow the operator or listener some lateral movement without seriously affecting sonic balance (see Figure 5-6).

Figures 5-4, 5-5, and 5-6 display examples of reflection-free zones and coverage angles using conventional two-loudspeaker setups for stereo monitoring. Surround sound presents altogether different acoustic challenges because monitors are located to the front and the rear and/or the sides of the listening position. Theoretically, therefore, for surround monitoring there should be an even distribution of absorbers and diffusers so that the rear-side loudspeakers function in an acoustic environment similar to the frontal speaker array. The problem is that this approach renders mixing rooms designed for stereo unsuitable for surround sound because stereo and surround require different acoustic environments (see "Monitoring Surround Sound" later in this chapter).

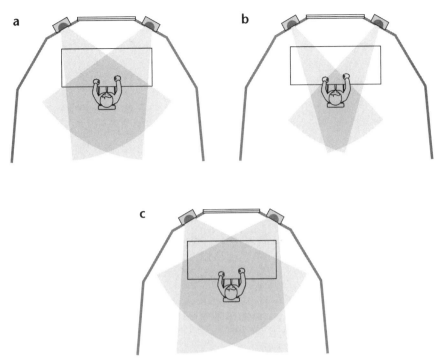

Figure 5-6 Coverage angles of monitor loudspeakers. (a) Desirable coverage angle. Alternative coverage angles include (b) loudspeakers with narrow radiations, which produce a sharp aural image and less envelopment, and (c) loudspeakers that radiate more broadly, which increase envelopment but reduce imaging.

Arrival Time

Even if coverage angles are optimal, unless all reproduced sounds reach the listening position(s) at relatively the same time they were produced, aural perception will be impaired. When you consider the differences in size and power requirements among drivers and the wavelengths they emit, you can see that this is easier said than done.

In two-, three-, and four-way system loudspeakers, the physical separation of each speaker in the system causes the sounds to reach the listener's ears at different times. *Arrival times* that differ by more than 1 ms are not acceptable in professional applications.

Polarity

Sometimes, although dispersal and arrival time are adequate, sound reaching a listener may not be as loud as it should be, or the elements within it may be poorly placed. For example, a rock band may be generating loud levels in the studio, but the sounds in the control room are, in relative terms, not so loud; or an actor is supposed to be situated slightly left in the aural frame but is heard from the right loudspeaker.

These problems may be the result of the loudspeakers' polarity being out of phase: One loudspeaker is pushing sound outward (compression), and the other is pulling sound inward (rarefaction) (see Figure 5-7). *Polarity* problems can occur between woofer and tweeter in the same loudspeaker enclosure or between two separate loudspeakers. In the

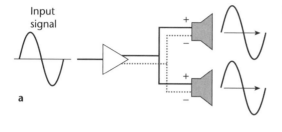

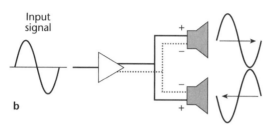

Figure 5-7 Loudspeaker polarity. (a) Cone motions in phase. (b) Cone motions out of phase.

latter case, this usually happens because the connections from loudspeaker to amplifier are improperly wired; that is, the two leads from one loudspeaker may be connected to the amplifier positive-to-negative and negative-to-positive, whereas the other loudspeaker may be connected positive-to-positive and negative-to-negative. If you think sound is out of phase, check the sound-level meters. If they show a similar level and the audio still sounds skewed, the speakers are out of phase; if they show different levels, the phase problem is probably elsewhere.

Another way to test for polarity problems is to use a 9 V battery. Attach the battery's positive lead to the loudspeaker's positive lead and the battery's negative lead to the loudspeaker's negative lead. Touching the battery's positive lead should push the speaker outward. If the speaker moves inward, it is out of polarity. All speakers in a cabinet should move in the same direction.

Monitor Placement

Where you place monitor loudspeakers also affects sound quality, dispersal, and arrival time. Loudspeakers are often designed for a particular room location and are generally positioned in one of four places: well toward the middle of a room, against or flush with a wall, at the intersection of two walls, or in a corner at the ceiling or on the floor. Each position affects the sound's loudness and dispersion differently.

A loudspeaker hanging in the middle of a room radiates sound into what is called a *free-sphere* (or *free-field* or *full space*) where, theoretically, the sound level at any point within a given distance is the same because the loudspeaker can radiate sound with no limiting obstacles or surface (see Figure 5-8). If a loudspeaker is placed against a wall, the wall concentrates the radiations into a *half sphere*, (or *half space*) thereby theoretically increasing the sound level by 3 dB. With loudspeakers mounted at the intersection of two walls, the dispersion is concentrated still more into a *one-quarter sphere*, thus increasing the sound level another 3 dB. Loudspeakers placed in corners at the ceiling or on the floor radiate in a *one-eighth sphere*, generating the most concentrated sound levels in a four-walled room. A significant part of each increase in the overall sound level is due to the loudness increase in the bass (see Figure 5-9). This is particularly the case with frequencies at 300 Hz and below. It is difficult to keep them free of excessive peaks and boominess, thereby inhibiting a coherent, tight bass sound.

For informal listening, one of these monitor positions is not necessarily better than another; placement may depend on a room's layout, furniture position, personal taste, and so on. In professional situations, it is preferable to flush-mount loudspeakers in a wall or soffit (see Figure 5-13). The most important thing in monitor placement is to avoid any appreciable space between the loudspeaker and the wall and any protrusion of the loudspeaker's cabinet edges. Otherwise, the wall or cabinet edges, or both, will act as secondary radiators, degrading frequency response. By flush-mounting loudspeakers, low-frequency response becomes more efficient, back-wall reflections and cancellation are eliminated, and cabinet edge diffraction is reduced.

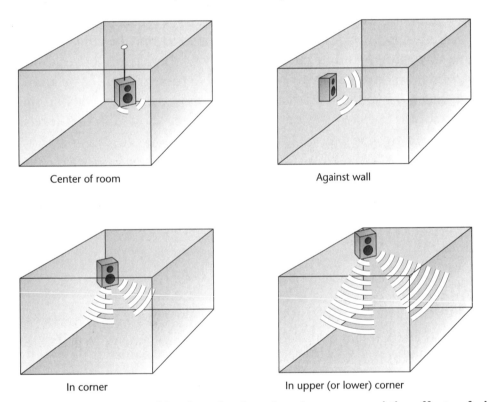

Figure 5-8 Four typical loudspeaker locations in a room and the effects of placement on overall loudness levels.

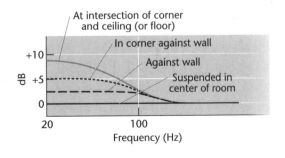

Figure 5-9 Effects of loudspeaker placement on bass response.

Monitoring Stereo

Stereo creates the illusion of two-dimensional sound by imaging depth—front-to-back—and width—side-to-side—in aural space. It requires two discrete loudspeakers each of which, in reality, is producing monaural sound but creating a phantom image between them (see Figure 5-10). In placing these loudspeakers, it is critical that they be positioned to reproduce an accurate and balanced stereo image. The monitoring system should be set up symmetrically within the room. The distance between the speakers should be the same as the distance from each speaker to your ears, forming an equilateral triangle with your head. Also, the center of the equilateral triangle should be equidistant from the room's side walls (see Figure 5-11).

The locations of the front-to-back and side-to-side sound sources are where they should be. If the original material has the vocal in the center (in relation to the two loudspeakers)—the first violins on the left, the bass drum and the bass at the rear-center, the snare drum slightly left or right, and so on—these should be in the same spatial positions when the material is played through the monitor system. If the listener is off the median plane, it skews the stereo imaging (see Figure 5-12). The designated stereo listening position is known as the *sweet spot*.

Far-Field Monitoring

Most professional audio-mixing rooms use at least two sets (or groups) of frontal loudspeakers. One set is for *far-field monitoring*, consisting of large loudspeaker systems that can deliver very wide frequency response at moderate to quite loud levels with relative accuracy. Due to their size and loudness capabilities, these loudspeakers are built into the mixing-room wall above, and at a distance of several feet from, the listening position (see Figure 5-13). Far-field loudspeakers are designed to provide the highest-quality sound reproduction.

Near-Field Monitoring

Even in the best monitor–control room acoustic environments, the distance between wall-mounted loudspeakers and the listening position is often wide enough to generate sonic discontinuities from unwanted control room reflections. To reduce these unwanted reflections, another set of monitors is placed on or near the console's meter bridge (see Figure 5-13).

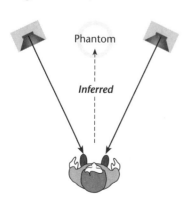

Figure 5-10 Why we perceive a phantom image.
From Dave Moulton, "Median Plane, Sweet Spot, and Phantom Everything," *TV Technology*, November 2007, p. 34.

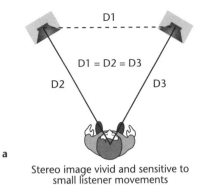

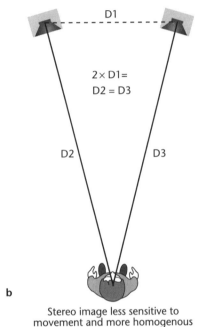

Stereo image vivid and sensitive to
small listener movements

Stereo image less sensitive to
movement and more homogenous

Figure 5-11 To help create an optimal travel path for sound from the loudspeakers to the listening position, carefully measure the loudspeaker separation and the distance between the loudspeakers and the listening position. (a) The distance between the acoustic center (between the loudspeakers) and the listening position is equal. In this arrangement head movement is restricted somewhat and the stereo image will be emphasized or spread out, heightening the sense of where elements in the recording are located. Shortening D2 and D3 will produce a large shift in the stereo image. (b) The distance between the acoustic center and the listening position is about twice as long. With this configuration the movement of the head is less restricted and the stereo image is reduced in width, although it is more homogeneous. The more D2 and D3 are lengthened, the more monaural the stereo image becomes (except for hard-left and hard-right panning).

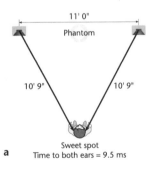

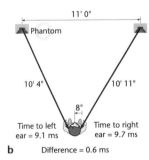

Figure 5-12 Phantom imaging on and off the median plane.

From Dave Moulton, "Median Plane, Sweet Spot, and Phantom Everything," *TV Technology*, November 2007, p. 34.

Figure 5-13 Positions of far-field and near-field monitors.

Near-field monitoring reduces the audibility of control room acoustics by placing loud-speakers close to the listening position. Moreover, near-field monitoring improves source localization because most of the sound reaching the listening position is direct; the early reflections that hinder good source localization are reduced to the point where they are of little consequence. At least that is the theory; in practice, problems with near-field monitoring remain (see Figure 5-14).

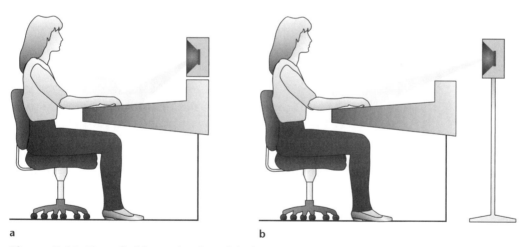

a   b

Figure 5-14 Near-field monitoring. (a) If a meter bridge is too low, early reflections will bounce off the console, degrading the overall monitor sound reaching the operator's ears. (b) One way to minimize this problem is to place the near-field monitors a few inches in back of the console.

Among the requirements for near-field monitors are: loudspeakers small enough to put on or near the console's meter bridge without the sound blowing you away; a uniform frequency response from about 70 to 16,000 Hz, especially smooth response through the midrange; a sensitivity range from 87 to 92 dB; sufficient amplifier power; and good vertical dispersion for more stable stereo imaging.

It is worth remembering that many near-field monitors have a built-in high pass filter to protect the bass unit from overload. The filter is generally set around 50 Hz. Not knowing that the loudspeaker is removing this part of the spectrum can lead to low-frequency balancing problems.

Monitoring Surround Sound

Surround sound differs from stereo by expanding the dimension of depth, thereby placing the listener more in the center of the aural image than in front of it. Accomplishing this requires additional audio channels routed to additional loudspeakers.

The most common surround-sound format (for the time being) uses six discrete audio channels: five full-range and one limited to low frequencies (typically below 125 Hz), called the subwoofer. Hence the format is known as *5.1*. The loudspeakers that correspond to these channels are placed front-left and front-right, like a stereo pair; a center-channel speaker is placed between the stereo pair; and another stereo pair—the surround speakers—are positioned to the left and right sides, or left-rear and right-rear, of the listener. (Unlike stereo, there is no phantom image in surround's frontal loudspeaker arrangement. The center-channel speaker creates a discrete image.) The subwoofer can be placed almost anywhere in the room because low frequencies are relatively omnidirectional, but it is usually situated in the front, between the center and the left or right speaker (see Figure 5-15). Sometimes it is positioned in a corner to reinforce low frequencies.

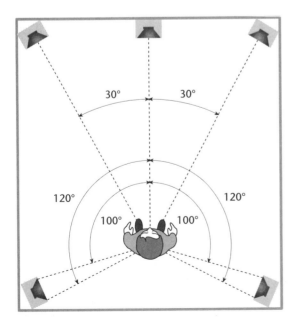

Figure 5-15 International Telecommunications Union guideline for arranging loudspeakers in a surround-sound setup. In a 5.1 system, the front-left and front-right speakers form a 60-degree angle with the listener at the apex; the center-channel speaker is directly in front of the listener. The surround speakers are usually placed at an angle between 100 and 120 degrees from the front-center line.

A problem in positioning the center-channel speaker is the presence of a video monitor if it is situated on the same plane as the loudspeakers. Mounting the center speaker above or below the monitor is not the best location. If it is unavoidable, however, keep the tweeters close to the same plane as the left and right speakers, which may require turning the center speaker upside down. If the image is projected, it becomes possible to mount the center speaker behind a microperforation screen, as they do in movie theaters.

A primary consideration with surround-sound setups is making sure the room is large enough, not only to accommodate the additional equipment and loudspeaker placement specifications, but also to handle the relatively high loudness that is sometimes necessary when monitoring surround sound.

Evaluating the Monitor Loudspeaker[1]

The final test of any monitor loudspeaker is how it sounds. Although the basis for much of the evaluation is subjective, there are guidelines for determining loudspeaker performance.

- Begin with rested ears. Fatigue alters aural perception.

- Sit at the designated stereo listening position—the optimal distance away from and between the loudspeakers. This sweet spot should allow some front-to-back and side-to-side movement without altering perception of loudness, frequency response, and spatial perspective. It is important to know the boundaries of the listening position(s) so that all sound can be monitored on-axis within this area (review Figures 5-6 and 5-11).

- If repositioning near-field monitors is necessary, changes of even a few inches closer or farther or from side to side can make a considerable difference in how the sound is perceived.

- There is no one best listening position with surround sound. Moving around provides different perspectives without significantly changing clarity, dimension, and spatial coherence (see Figure 5-15).

- When evaluating monitors in general and near-field monitors in particular, the tendency is to be drawn to the bass response. The focus should be on overall clarity.

- Use material with which you are intimately familiar for the evaluation, preferably on a high-quality digital disc. Otherwise, if some aspect of the sound is unsatisfactory, you won't know whether the problem is with the original material or the loudspeaker.

---

1. Before evaluating a monitor loudspeaker system, either stereo or surround, it is critical to obtain an objective measure of the correlation between monitor sound and room sound using a calibration system. **Calibration** helps ensure that a system's measurements meet a specified or desired standard. Calibration is usually done by an engineer or technician.

For example, with speech the male voice is a good test to reveal if a loudspeaker is boomy; the female voice helps determine if there is too much high-end reflection from nearby surfaces. With music, consider how the following sonic details would change tonally from speaker to speaker: an overall sound with considerable presence and clarity; the depth and the dynamic range of symphonic music; the separation in the spatial imaging of instruments; a singer whose sound sits in the lower midrange; the sounds of fingers on guitar strings and frets or fingernails plucking the strings; the kiss of the hammers on piano strings; the wisp of brushes on a snare drum; the deep bass response of an organ; the punch of the kick drum; and the upper reaches of a flute's harmonics. Such tests, and there are many others, facilitate the judging of such things as a loudspeaker's bass, midrange, and treble response; dynamic response; imaging; clarity; and presence.

- Keep in mind that as bass response becomes more prominent, midrange clarity suffers due to masking.

- Listen at a comfortable loudness level; 85 dB-SPL is often recommended.

- Listen for sounds you may not have heard before—such as hiss, hum, or buzz. Good monitors may reveal what inferior monitors cover up; or it could indicate that the monitors you are listening to have problems. In either case, you have learned something.

- In listening for spatial balance, make sure the various sounds are positioned in the same places relative to the original material. As an additional test for stereo, put the monitor system into mono and check to make sure the sound appears to be coming from between the two loudspeakers. Move toward the left and right boundaries of the sweet spot. If the sound moves with you before you get near the boundaries, reposition the monitors, then recheck their dispersion in both stereo and mono until you can move within the boundaries of the listening position without the sound following you or skewing the placement of the sound sources. If monitor repositioning is necessary to correct problems with side-to-side sound placement, make sure it does not adversely affect front-to-back sound dispersion to the listening position.

- In evaluating monitor loudspeakers for surround sound, consider the following: Is the imaging of the sound sources cohesive or disjointed? Does the sound emanate from the appropriate loudspeaker location, or does it seem detached from it? In moving around the listening environment, how much of the positional information, or sonic illusion, remains intact? How robust does that illusion remain in another listening environment? If there are motion changes—sound moving left-to-right, right side to right front, and so on—are they smooth? Does any element call unwanted attention to itself?

- In evaluating treble response, listen to the cymbal, triangle, flute, piccolo, and other high-frequency instruments. Are they too bright, crisp, shrill, harsh, or dull? Do you hear their upper harmonics?

- In testing bass response, include such instruments as the tuba and the bass as well as the low end of the organ, piano, bassoon, and cello. Sound should not be thin, boomy, muddy, or grainy. For example, notes of the bass guitar should be uniform in loudness; the piano should not sound metallic.

- Assess the transient response, which is also important in a loudspeaker. Drums, bells, and triangle provide excellent tests, assuming they are properly recorded. Good transient response reproduces a crisp attack with no distortion, breakup, or smearing.

- If you are evaluating a number of different loudspeakers, compare only a few at a time and take notes. Trying to remember, for example, how different speakers color the presence range, their differences in low-end warmth, or their degree of darkness or brightness, is unreliable. Our ability to retain precise auditory information is limited, particularly over time and when comparison testing.

Other important elements to evaluate, such as intermodulation, harmonic, transient, and loudness distortion, were discussed earlier in this chapter.

Monitoring in an Unfamiliar Control Room

When doing a session in a facility you have not worked in before, it is essential to become thoroughly familiar with the interaction between its monitor sound and its room sound. A relatively quick and reliable way to get an objective idea of that interaction is to do a real-time analysis. It is also crucial to put the real-time analysis into perspective with reference recordings and your ears.

Reference recordings on CD, CD-ROM, or DVD can be commercial recordings with which you are entirely familiar or discs specially designed to help assess a listening environment or both. Knowing how a recording sounds in a control room whose monitors and acoustics you are intimately familiar with is a good test in determining the sonic characteristics of, and among, the monitors and the acoustics in a new environment. For example, if you know that a recording has a clear high-end response in your own control room but the high end sounds thinner in another control room, it could indicate, among other things, that the other studio's monitors have inadequate treble response; the presence of harmonic distortion; a phase problem; the room's mediocre sound diffusion; or any combination of these factors.

Digital discs specially produced for referencing are also available. They are variously designed to test monitor and/or room response to a particular instrument, such as a drum set; individual or groups of instruments, such as the voice and clarinet, or strings, brass, and woodwinds; various sizes and types of ensembles, such as orchestras, jazz bands, and rock groups; room acoustics; spatial positioning; and spectral balances.

Headphones

Headphones (also referred to as "cans") are an overlooked but important part of monitoring, especially in field production. The following considerations are basic when using headphones for professional purposes: Although frequency response in headphones is not flat, listen for as wide and uncolored response as possible; you must be thoroughly familiar with their sonic characteristics; they should be ***circumaural*** (around-the-ear), as airtight as possible against the head for acoustical isolation, and comfortable; the fit should stay snug even when you are moving; and, although it may seem obvious, stereo headphones should be used for stereo monitoring, and headphones capable of multichannel reproduction should be used for monitoring surround sound (see Figure 5-16).

Headphones are usually indispensable in field recording because monitor loudspeakers are often unavailable or impractical. In studio control rooms, however, there are pros and cons to using headphones.

The advantages are (1) sound quality will be consistent in different studios; (2) it is easier to hear subtle changes in the recording and the mix; (3) there is no aural smearing due to room reflections; and (4) because so many people listen to portable players through headphones or *earbuds*, you have a reasonably reliable reference to their sonic requirements.

The disadvantages include (1) the sound quality will not be the same as with the monitor loudspeakers; (2) the aural image forms a straight line between your ears and is

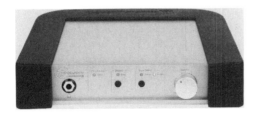

Figure 5-16 Headphone monitoring system. This particular system is called Headzone. It includes stereo headphones and a digital processor that accepts 5.1 signal sources. The processor uses modeling software to reproduce a surround-sound image. It also provides the ability to turn your head while the virtual sound sources stay in the correct spatial positions as they do in control room monitoring through separate loudspeakers. The processor takes various types of connectors, such as a three-pin socket for static ultrasonic receivers, six phono (RCA) sockets for unbalanced 5.1 analog inputs, and a standard sixpin FireWire socket for linking to a computer. The processor can be remotely controlled.

unnaturally wide; (3) in panning signals for stereo, the distance between monitor loudspeakers is greater than the distance between your ears—left and right sounds are directly beside you; (4) no interaction exists between the program material and the acoustics, so the tendency may be to mix in more artificial reverberation than necessary; and (5) in location recording if open-air, or *supra-aural*, headphones are used, bass response will not be as efficient as with circumaural headphones, and outside noise might interfere with listening.

Headphones and Hearing Loss

As we discussed in Chapter 2, high sound levels from everyday sources such as loudspeakers, loud venues, hair dryers, and lawn mowers are detrimental to hearing. Potentially, this is even more the case with headphones because they are mounted directly over the ear or, with earbuds, placed inside the ear. The problem is exacerbated outdoors by the tendency to boost the level so that the program material can be heard above the noise floor. Listening over an extended period of time can also result in cranking up the level to compensate for listening fatigue.

It has been found that listening to headphones at a loud level after only about an hour and a quarter can cause hearing loss. One recommendation is called the *60 percent/60-minute rule*: Limit listening through headphones to no more than one hour per day at levels below 60 percent of maximum volume. You can increase daily listening time by turning down the level even farther.

One development in headphone technology to help reduce the potential of hearing loss is the active *noise-canceling headphone*. Designs differ, but generally the noise-canceling headphone detects ambient noise before it reaches the ears and nullifies it by synthesizing the sound waves. Most noise-canceling headphones act on the more powerful low- to midrange frequencies; the less powerful higher frequencies are not affected. Models may be equipped with a switch to turn the noise-canceling function on or off and may be battery-operated.

Passive noise-canceling can be employed with conventional circumaural headphones. The better the quality of headphones and the tighter the fit, the more effective the reduction of ambient noise.

In-Ear Monitors

The *in-ear monitor (IEM)* was developed for use by musicians in live concerts to replace stage monitors. They allow the performers to hear a mix of the on-stage microphones or instruments, or both, and provide a high level of noise reduction for ear protection. Due to the convenience in adjusting the sound levels and mix of audio sources to personal taste, in-ear monitoring has become increasingly popular with performers in broadcasting and recording. The problem with IEMs is that a performer who prefers loud sound levels or has hearing loss may increase the loudness of the IEM to a harmful level, thereby negating its noise reduction advantage.

A sound level analyzer is available that measures the sound pressure levels reaching the ear canal. Users can determine not only their actual monitoring level, but how long they can safely listen at that volume.

Main Points

- The sound chain begins with the microphone, whose signal is sent to a console, mixer, or computer for routing, processing recording, and heard through a loudspeaker.

- In evaluating a monitor loudspeaker, frequency response, linearity, amplifier power, distortion, dynamic range, sensitivity, polar response, arrival time, and polarity should also be considered.

- Frequency response ideally should be as wide as possible, from at least 40 to 20,000 Hz, especially with digital sound.

- Each medium that records or transmits sound, such as a CD or TV, and each loudspeaker that reproduces sound, such as a studio monitor or home receiver, has certain spectral and amplitude capabilities. For optimal results, audio should be produced with an idea of how the system through which it will be reproduced works.

- Linearity means that frequencies fed to a loudspeaker at a particular loudness are reproduced at the same loudness.

- Amplifier power must be sufficient to drive the loudspeaker system, or distortion, among other things, will result.

- Distortion is the appearance of a signal in the reproduced sound that was not in the original sound.

- Various forms of distortion include intermodulation, harmonic, transient, and loudness.

- Intermodulation (IM) distortion results when two or more frequencies occur at the same time and interact to create combination tones and dissonances unrelated to the original sounds.

- Harmonic distortion occurs when the audio system introduces harmonics into a recording that were not present originally.

- Transient distortion relates to the inability of an audio component to respond quickly to a rapidly changing signal, such as that produced by percussive sounds.

- Loudness distortion, or overload distortion, results when a signal is recorded or played back at an amplitude greater than the sound system can handle.

- To meet most sonic demands, the main studio monitors should have an output-level capability of 120 dB-SPL and a dynamic range of up to 80 dB.

- Sensitivity is the on-axis sound-pressure level a loudspeaker produces at a given distance when driven at a certain power. A monitor's sensitivity rating provides a good overall indication of its efficiency.

- Polar response indicates how a loudspeaker focuses sound at the monitoring position(s).

- The coverage angle is the off-axis angle or point at which loudspeaker level is down 6 dB compared with the on-axis output level.

- A sound's arrival time at the monitoring position(s) should be no more than 1 ms; otherwise, aural perception is impaired.

- Polarity problems can occur between woofer and tweeter in the same loudspeaker enclosure or between two separate loudspeakers.

- Where a loudspeaker is positioned affects sound dispersion and loudness. A loudspeaker in the middle of a room generates the least-concentrated sound; a loudspeaker at the intersection of a ceiling or floor generates the most.

- For professional purposes, it is preferable to flush-mount in a wall or soffit loudspeakers to make low frequency response more efficient and reduce or eliminate back-wall reflections, cancellation, and cabinet edge diffraction.

- Stereo sound is two-dimensional; it has depth and breadth. In placing loudspeakers for monitoring stereo, it is critical that they be positioned symmetrically within a room to reproduce an accurate and balanced front-to-back and side-to-side sonic image.

- Loudspeakers used for far-field monitoring are usually large and can deliver very wide frequency response at moderate to quite loud levels with relative accuracy. They are built into the mixing-room wall above, and at a distance of several feet from, the listening position.

- Near-field monitoring enables the sound engineer to reduce the audibility of control room acoustics, particularly the early reflections, by placing loudspeakers close to the monitoring position.

- Surround sound differs from stereo by expanding the depth dimension, thereby placing the listener more in the center of the aural image than in front of it. Therefore, using the 5.1 surround-sound format, monitors are positioned front-left, center, and front-right, and the surround loudspeakers are placed left and right behind, or to the rear sides of, the console operator. A subwoofer can be positioned in front of, between the center and the left or right speaker, in a front corner, or to the side of the listening position.

- In adjusting and evaluating monitor sound, both objective and subjective measures are necessary.

■ When evaluating the sound of a monitor loudspeaker, it is helpful to, among other things, use material you are intimately familiar with and to test various loudspeaker responses with different types of speech and music.

■ Headphones are an important part of monitoring, particularly on location. The following considerations are basic when using headphones for professional purposes: The frequency response should be wide, flat, and uncolored; you must be thoroughly familiar with their sonic characteristics; they should be circumaural (around-the-ear), as airtight as possible against the head for acoustical isolation, and comfortable; the fit should stay snug even when you are moving; and, although it may seem obvious, stereo headphones should be used for stereo monitoring, and headphones capable of multichannel reproduction should be used for monitoring surround sound.

■ Headphones can be detrimental to hearing because they are mounted directly over the ears or, with earbuds, placed inside the ears. The problem is exacerbated outdoors by the tendency to boost the level so that the program material can be heard above the noise floor.

■ To help reduce the potential of hearing loss is the active noise-canceling headphone, which detects ambient noise before it reaches the ears and nullifies it by synthesizing the sound waves.

■ Passive noise-canceling can be employed using high-quality conventional circumaural headphones that fit snugly over the ears.

■ The in-ear monitor (IEM) allows a performer to hear a mix of on-stage microphones or instruments, or both, and provides a high level of noise reduction for ear protection. Since their development, IEMs are used for other monitoring purposes. A sound level analyzer is available for the specific purpose of measuring in-ear monitoring levels to guard against excessive loudness.

6 Microphones

The analogy can be made that microphones are to audio production what colors are to painting. The more colors and hues available to a painter, the greater the possibilities for coloration on a visual canvas. In recording sound, the more models of microphones, the greater variety of tones on the sonic palette and, hence, the greater the possibilities for coloration in designing an aural canvas.

When choosing a microphone, or mic, consider three basic features: operating principles, directional characteristic(s), and sound response. Appearance may be a fourth feature to consider if the mic is on-camera. Cost and durability may be two other considerations.

Operating Principles

Like the loudspeaker, the microphone is a *transducer*—a device that converts one form of energy into another—but it works in the opposite direction: Instead of changing electric energy into acoustic energy as the loudspeaker does, it changes acoustic energy into electric energy. The electric energy flows through a circuit as voltage.

Impedance

In measuring an electric circuit, a foremost concern is *impedance*—that property of a circuit, or an element, that restricts the flow of alternating current (AC). Impedance is measured in ohms (Ω), a unit of resistance to current flow. The lower the impedance, the better. Microphones used in professional audio are low impedance. Low-impedance microphones and equipment have three advantages over high-impedance mics: They generate less noise, they are much less susceptible to hum and electrical interference such as static from motors and fluorescent lights, and they can be connected to long cables without increasing noise. Professional mics usually range in impedance from 150 to 600 ohms.

Transducing Elements

The device that does the transducing in a microphone is mounted in the mic head and is called the *element*. Each type of mic gets its name from the element it uses. The elements in professional microphones operate on one of two physical principles: magnetic induction and variable capacitance.

Magnetic Induction

Magnetic induction uses a fixed magnet and a movable diaphragm to which a small, lightweight, finely wrapped coil suspended between the poles of a fixed magnet is attached. When it moves through the magnetic field in response to the sound waves hitting the diaphragm, it produces voltage proportional to the sound-pressure level. Such mics are called *moving-coil microphones* (see Figure 6-1).

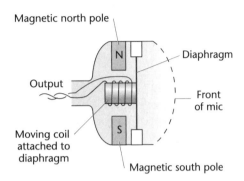

Figure 6-1 The element of a moving-coil microphone.

Another type of mic employing magnetic induction is the *ribbon microphone* (see Figure 6-2). Instead of a moving coil, it uses a metal ribbon attached to a fixed magnet. As the ribbon vibrates from the pressure of the sound waves, voltage is generated. Generally, in the earlier generations of ribbon mics, the ribbon is situated vertically; in many modern ribbon mics, it is positioned horizontally. The longitudinal positioning and the more advanced ribbon design have helped make it possible to house modern ribbon mics in smaller, lighter-weight casings than the older ribbon mics (see Figure 6-3).

Active ribbon microphones use an *amplifier* system, which requires phantom power; *passive microphones* do not require phantom power. *Phantom power* is a method of remotely powering an amplifier or impedance converter by sending voltage along the audio cable (see "Variable Capacitance" later in this chapter). Among the advantages of

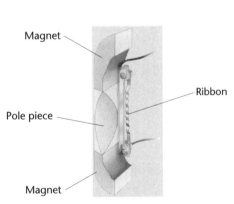

Figure 6-2 The elements of a ribbon microphone.

Figure 6-3 Ribbon microphones. (a) Traditional model with vertical ribbon. (b) Newer model with small, longitudinal ribbon.

the active ribbon microphone over conventional ribbons are higher output and sensitivity, wider and flatter frequency response, and the ability to handle higher sound levels before distortion (see "General Transducer Performance Characteristics" later in this chapter).

Mics that use the magnetic induction principle are classified as **dynamic microphones**. This includes the moving-coil and ribbon transducers. In practice, however, the moving-coil mic is referred to as a *dynamic* mic and the ribbon as a *ribbon* mic; the term moving coil is seldom used when referring to a dynamic mic. To avoid confusion, however, the term moving coil, instead of dynamic, is used throughout this book.

Variable Capacitance

Microphones operating on the variable capacitance principle transduce energy using voltage (electrostatic) variations instead of magnetic (electromagnetic) variations and are called **capacitor microphones**. They are also referred to as **condenser microphones**, a holdover from the past.

The element consists of two parallel plates separated by a small space (see Figure 6-4). The front plate is a thin, metalized plastic diaphragm—the only moving part in the mic head—and the back plate is fixed. Together, these plates or electrodes form a **capacitor**—a device that is capable of holding an electric charge. As acoustic energy moves the diaphragm back and forth in relation to the fixed back plate, the capacitance change causes a voltage change, varying the signal. The signal output is delicate and has a very high impedance, however, and requires a preamplifier (mounted near the mic capsule) to bring it to useable proportions.

Most preamps in capacitor microphones use a transistor circuit, which generally produces a clean sound. But a number of capacitor mics use a tube circuit in the preamp instead. This is due to the particular sonic characteristic that **tube microphones** give to sound, which many perceive as more present, livelier, more detailed, and not as colored as the transistorized capacitors.

Because the capacitor requires polarizing voltage and the preamplifier requires power voltage to operate, capacitor microphones must have a separate power source either from batteries contained inside the mic or from an external, or phantom, power supply. External power eliminates the need for batteries and may be supplied from the console, studio microphone input circuits, or portable units.

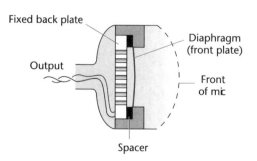

Figure 6-4 Cross-section of the element of a capacitor microphone.

Some capacitor microphones have an electret diaphragm. An *electret* is a material (high-polymer plastic film) that can hold a charge permanently, eliminating the need for external polarizing voltage. Because only a small battery is required to power the preamp, *electret microphones* can be made more compact, which facilitated the design of lavaliere and mini-mics.

General Transducer Performance Characteristics

Each type of microphone is unique. It is not a matter of one microphone being better than another but that one mic may be more suitable for a particular application. Moving-coil microphones are rugged, generate low self-noise, tend to be less susceptible to humidity and wide temperature variations, and handle high sound-pressure levels without distortion. They are usually less expensive than the other professional types and come in a wide variety of makes and models.

The element of a moving-coil mic has more mass than a ribbon or capacitor mic and therefore has greater inertia in responding to sound vibrations. This results in a slower response to *transients*—sounds that begin with a quick attack, such as a drum hit or breaking glass, and then quickly decay. Capacitor microphones have the lowest mass of the three types of professional mics, which makes them best suited to handle transient sounds. The ribbon mic has relatively low mass; its transient response is between that of the moving-coil mic and the capacitor mic. The inertia of the moving-coil element has another effect on pickup: with increased mic-to-source distance, high-frequency response is reduced. At optimal mic-to-source distances, moving-coil microphones typically color sound more than capacitor mics, usually between 5 kHz and 10 kHz. This tends to add presence, clarity, crispness, or edge to sound.

Ribbon microphones are not widely used today except in music recording and for the speaking voice. They are more expensive than many moving-coil mics and have to be handled with care, particularly when it comes to loud sound levels.

Older ribbon mics have mediocre high-frequency response, which can be turned into an advantage because it gives sound a warm, mellow quality. This attribute complements digital recording which can produce an edged, hard sound quality. Modern ribbon mics have a more extended high-frequency response. As pointed out earlier, compared with most ribbon mics, the active ribbon microphone has a higher output and sensitivity, a wider and flatter frequency response, and the ability to handle higher sound levels before distortion. Generally, ribbon mics have low self-noise, but they also have the lowest output level of the three major types. This means a poorer signal-to-noise ratio if the mic is too far from the sound source or if the cable run is too long.

Capacitor microphones are high-performance instruments. They have a wide, smooth frequency response and reproduce clear, airy, detailed sound with the least amount of tonal coloration compared to moving-coil and ribbon mics. They are the choice among professional-quality mics when it is necessary to accurately capture the true sound of a voice, musical instrument, or sound effect. Capacitor mics have high sensitivity, which makes them the preferred choice for distant miking; high-end response is not hampered by extended mic-to-source distances. They also have the highest output level, which gives them a wide signal-to-noise ratio. These advantages come at a cost—capacitors are generally the most expensive type of microphone, although excellent capacitor models are available at lower prices.

Directional Characteristics

A fundamental rule of good microphone technique is that a sound source should be **on-mic**—at an optimal distance from the microphone and directly in its pickup pattern. *Pickup pattern*, formally known as **polar response pattern**, refers to the direction(s) from which a mic hears sound.

Microphones work in a three-dimensional soundfield; sounds arrive at a mic from all directions. Depending on the design, however, a microphone is sensitive only to sound from all around—**omnidirectional**, its front and rear—**bidirectional**, or its front—**unidirectional** (see Figure 6-5a, b, c). Omnidirectional mics are also called *non-directional*; and unidirectional mics are also called *directional*. **Cardioid** is yet another commonly used name for a unidirectional microphone because its pickup pattern is heart-shaped (see Figure 6-5c). Five unidirectional patterns are in common use: **sub-cardioid** (also called **wide-angle cardioid**), **cardioid**, **supercardioid**, **hypercardioid**, and **ultracardioid** (see Figure 6-5c, d, e, f).

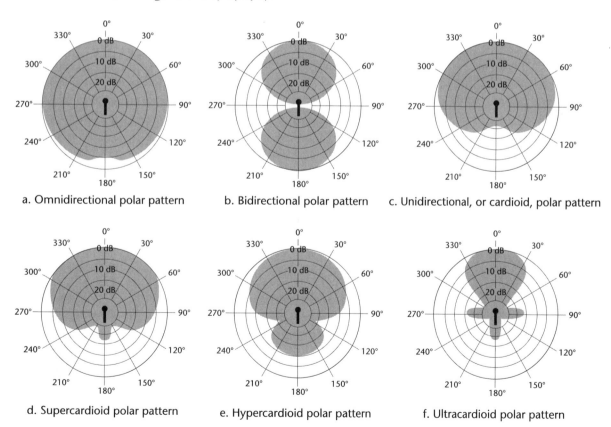

a. Omnidirectional polar pattern   b. Bidirectional polar pattern   c. Unidirectional, or cardioid, polar pattern

d. Supercardioid polar pattern   e. Hypercardioid polar pattern   f. Ultracardioid polar pattern

Figure 6-5 Principal microphone polar patterns.

A microphone's pickup pattern and its transducer classification are unrelated. Moving-coil mics are available in all pickup patterns except bidirectional. Ribbon mics are bidirectional, hypercardioid, or *multidirectional*—providing more than one pickup pattern. Capacitor mics come in all available pickup patterns, including multidirectional. Figure 6-5 displays basic microphone directionalities. The precise pattern varies from mic to mic.

A microphone's unidirectionality is facilitated by ports at the side and/or rear of the mic that cancel sound coming from unwanted directions. For this reason, you should not cover the ports with a hand or with tape. Directional mics are referred to as *single-entry-port microphones*, or *single-D*—having ports in the capsule; or as *multiple-entry-port microphones*, also called *variable-D*—having ports in the capsule and along the handle. In a single-entry directional mic, the rear-entrance port handles all frequencies (see Figure 6-6). A multiple-entry directional mic has several ports, each tuned to a different band of frequencies (see Figure 6-7). The ports closer to the diaphragm process the higher frequencies; the ports farther from the diaphragm process the lower frequencies. Ports also influence a mic's proximity effect, which is discussed later in this chapter.

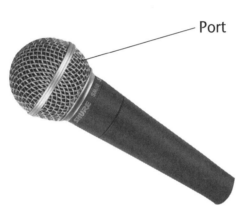

Figure 6-6 Microphone with single entry port. *Note:* This figure and Figure 6-7 indicate the positions of the ports on these mics. The actual ports are concealed by the mic grille.

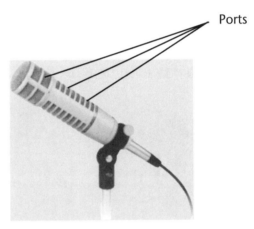

Figure 6-7 Microphone with multiple entry ports.

Polar Response Diagrams

A microphone's directional sensitivity, or polar response pattern, is displayed on a graph. The graph consists of concentric circles, usually divided into segments of 30 degrees. Reading inward, each circle represents a decrease in sound level of 5 dB. The graph depicts response sensitivity in relation to the angle of sound incidence.

The omnidirectional polar pattern shows that sound is picked up almost uniformly from all directions (see Figure 6-5a). The bidirectional polar pattern is most sensitive to sound coming from the front and the rear and least sensitive to sounds entering the sides (see Figure 6-5b).

The cardioid polar pattern illustrates sensitivity to sounds arriving from the front and front-sides (see Figure 6-5c). The subcardioid has a wider front and front-side and therefore a less directional pickup pattern than the cardioid. The supercardioid is more directional at the front than the cardioid (see Figure 6-5d). The hypercardioid polar pattern illustrates its highly directional frontal pickup (see Figure 6-5e).

Here's a brief comparison of the cardioid, supercardioid, hypercardioid, and ultracardioid pickup patterns: The cardioid mic has a wide-angle pickup of sound in front of the mic and maximum sound rejection at its rear. The supercardioid mic has a somewhat narrower on-axis response and less sensitivity at the rear-sides than the cardioid mic. It has maximum difference between its front- and rear-hemisphere pickups. The hypercardioid mic has a far narrower on-axis pickup and has its maximum rejection at the sides compared with the supercardioid mic. Its rear rejection is poorer than the supercardioid mic, however. The ultracardioid microphone has the narrowest on-axis pickup and the widest off-axis sound rejection of the directional mics (see Figure 6-5f).

The polar pattern diagrams shown in Figure 6-5 are ideals. In actual use, a microphone's directional sensitivity varies with frequency. Because treble waves are shorter and bass waves are longer, *the higher the frequency, the more directional a mic becomes; the lower the frequency, the less directional a mic becomes, regardless of pickup pattern.* Even omnidirectional microphones positioned at an angle to the sound source tend not to pick up higher frequencies coming from the sides and the rear, thus making the nondirectional pattern somewhat directional at these frequencies. Figure 6-8 shows an example of a polar pattern indicating the relationship of on- and off-axis pickup to frequency response. It should be noted that a microphone's polar pattern is not an indication of its **reach**—a mic's relative effectiveness in rejecting reverberation (see Figure 6-9).

Although reach is the term commonly used to describe a mic's relative working distance, it is misleading. A microphone does not reach out to pick up sound. A cardioid mic, for

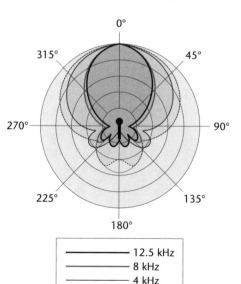

Figure 6-8 Polar pattern indicating differences in directionality at certain frequencies. Notice that the lower the frequency, the less directional the pickup.

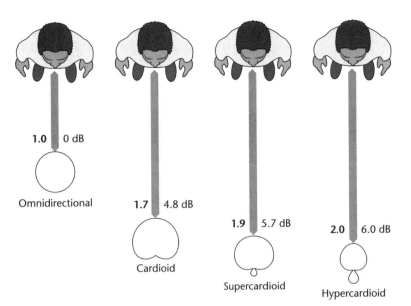

Figure 6-9 Differences in relative working distances among omnidirectional, cardioid, supercardioid, and hypercardioid microphones and their relative effectiveness in rejecting reverberation.

example, appears to have a farther reach than an omnidirectional mic. The difference in their pickup, however, is that the omnidirectional mic hears sound from all directions, whereas the cardioid mic hears sound approaching mainly from the front, rejecting sound in different degrees from the sides and the rear. This creates the perception that the cardioid mic enhances sound waves from the front.

A word of caution about polar patterns: Don't believe everything you read. Looking good on paper is not enough. The microphone has to be put to the test in use to determine its actual response, particularly off-axis.

Sound Response

Clearly, a microphone's operating principle (transducer) and directional characteristics affect the way it sounds. Other sonic features, which are contained in a specification sheet, should also be considered. The specifications are either generalized—giving the response details of a particular line of models for potential buyers—or they are specific to, and included with, the actual mic when it is purchased.

Microphone specifications are useful because they can shortcut the selection process. With the hundreds of professional microphones available, it is difficult to try more than a few of them at any one time. If you are looking for a mic with a particular polar pattern, frequency response, overload limit, and so on, reading a spec sheet can eliminate those mics that do not meet your need. A word of caution, however. Even when a spec sheet suggests that you may have found the "right" mic, regardless of how detailed the specifications are, there is only one ultimate test before selection: *listening and doing what your ears tell you.*

In addition to its type (transducer element) and directional characteristic(s), a microphone's spec sheet includes the following sonic features: frequency response, overload limit, maximum sound-pressure level, sensitivity, self-noise, and signal-to-noise ratio. Proximity effect and humbucking are also considerations when selecting a mic.

Frequency Response

A microphone's *frequency response* is the range of frequencies that it reproduces at an equal level, within a margin of ±3 dB. That is, at a given level, a frequency will not be more or less than 3 dB off.

A microphone's *frequency response curve* is displayed as a graph with the vertical line indicating amplitude (dB) and the horizontal line indicating frequency (Hz) (see Figure 6-10). It shows the tonal balance of the microphone pickup at a designated distance from a sound source, usually 2 or 3 feet.

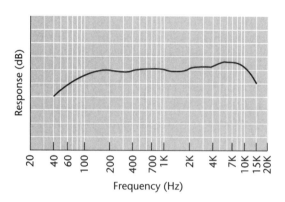

Figure 6-10 Frequency response curve of the Electro-Voice 635A mic.

When the curve is reasonably straight or *flat*, response has little coloration—all frequencies are reproduced at relatively the same level. But flat is not necessarily desirable. In looking at a response curve, it is important to know for what purpose the microphone was developed and what your sonic requirements are. In Figure 6-12, for example, the bass begins rolling off at 150 Hz, there is a boost in the high frequencies between 4,000 and 10,000 Hz, and the high end rolls off beyond 10,000 Hz. Obviously, this particular mic would be unsuitable for instruments such as the bass drum, organ, and cello because it is not very sensitive to the lower frequencies from these instruments. It is also unsuitable for high-frequency sound sources, such as the female singing voice, cymbals, and the piccolo, because it is not that sensitive to their higher frequencies or harmonics. The mic was not designed for these purposes, however; it was designed for the speaking voice, and it is excellent for this purpose. Reproduction of frequencies through the critical upper bass and midrange is flat, the slight boost in the upper midrange adds presence, and the roll-offs in the bass and the treble are beyond the ranges of most speaking voices.

Overload Limit

All microphones will distort if sound levels are too high—a condition known as *overload*—but some mics handle it better than others. Moving-coil and capacitor microphones are not as vulnerable to distortion caused by excessive loudness as ribbon mics. Moving-coil mics can take high levels of loudness without internal damage. Using a ribbon mic when there may be overload risks damaging the element, particularly with older models.

In the capacitor system, although loud sound-pressure levels may not create distortion at the diaphragm, the output signal may be great enough to overload the electronics in the mic. To prevent this, many capacitors contain a built-in pad. Switching the pad into the mic system eliminates overload distortion of the mic's preamp, thereby reducing the output signal so many decibels (see Figure 6-21).

Maximum Sound-Pressure Level

Maximum sound-pressure level is the level at which a microphone's signal begins to distort. If a microphone has a maximum sound-pressure level of 120 dB-SPL, it means the mic will audibly distort when the level of a sound source reaches 120 dB-SPL. A maximum sound-pressure level of 120 dB is good, 135 dB is very good, and 150 dB is excellent.

In a microphone, distortion is measured as *total harmonic distortion (THD)*. THD is a specification that compares the output signal with the input signal and measures the level differences in harmonic frequencies between the two. THD is measured as a percentage. The lower percentage, the better.

Sensitivity

Sensitivity measures the voltage that a microphone produces (dBV) at a certain sound-pressure level. It indicates how loud a microphone is. Capacitor mics are loudest; ribbon mics are quietest. Sensitivity does not affect a mic's sound quality, but it can affect the overall sound quality of a recording. A microphone with high sensitivity has a high voltage output and will not require as much gain as a mic with low sensitivity. Ribbon and small moving-coil mics have low sensitivity (–85 dBV), larger moving-coil mics have medium sensitivity (–75 dBV), and capacitor mics have high sensitivity (–65 dBV).

Self-Noise

Self-noise, also known as *equivalent noise level*, indicates the sound-pressure level that will create the same voltage as the inherent electrical noise, or hiss, that a microphone (or any electronic device) produces. Self-noise is measured in dB-SPL, A-weighted. A fair self-noise rating is around 40 dB-SPL(A), a good rating is around 30 dB-SPL(A), and an excellent rating is 20 dB-SPL(A) or less.

Signal-to-Noise Ratio

Signal-to-noise ratio (S/N) is the ratio of a signal power to the noise power corrupting the signal and is measured in decibels. In relation to microphones, S/N is the difference between sound-pressure level and self-noise. For example, if the microphone's maximum sound-pressure level is 94 dB and the self-noise is 30 dB-SPL, the signal-to-noise ratio is 64 dB. The higher the S/N, the less obtrusive the noise. An S/N of 64 dB is fair, 74 dB is good, and 84 dB and higher is excellent.

Proximity Effect

When any microphone is placed close to a sound source, bass frequencies increase in level relative to midrange and treble frequencies. This response is known as *proximity effect* or *bass tip-up* (see Figure 6-11).

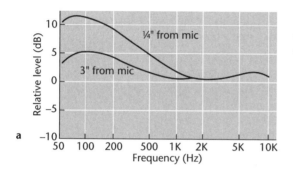

Figure 6-11 Proximity effect. (a) A typical cardioid moving-coil mic and (b) a cardioid capacitor mic.

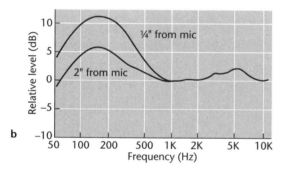

Proximity effect is most pronounced in pressure-gradient (ribbon) microphones—mics in which both sides of the diaphragm are exposed to incident sound. Response is generated by the pressure differential, or gradient, between the sound that reaches the front of the diaphragm relative to the sound that reaches the rear. As mic-to-source distance decreases, acoustic pressure on the diaphragm increases. Because pressure is greater at lower frequencies and the path between the front and the rear of the diaphragm is short, bass response rises.

Response of directional microphones is, in part, pressure-gradient and therefore susceptible to proximity effect but not to the extent of ribbon mics. Omnidirectional microphones are not subject to proximity effect unless the mic is close enough to the sound source to be almost touching it.

Proximity effect can be a blessing or a curse, depending on the situation. For example, in close-miking a bass drum, cello, or thin-sounding voice, proximity effect can add power or solidity to the sound source. Where a singer with a deep bass voice works close to the mic, proximity effect can increase boominess, masking middle and high frequencies.

To neutralize unwanted proximity effect (rumble, or 60-cycle hum), most microphones susceptible to the effect include the feature, called *bass roll-off*, of a limited in-mic equalizer (see Figure 6-21). When turned on, the roll-off attenuates bass frequencies several

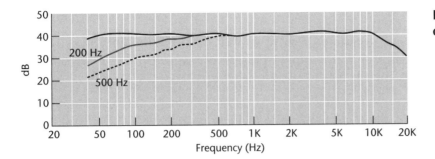

Figure 6-12 Bass roll-off curves.

decibels from a certain point and below, depending on the microphone, thereby canceling or reducing any proximity effect (see Figure 6-12).

Because bass roll-off has so many advantages, it has become a common feature even on mics that have little or no proximity effect. In some models, bass roll-off has been extended to include several different frequency settings at which attenuation can occur, or different levels of attenuation at the same roll-off frequency.

Another way to reduce proximity effect is to use a multiple-entry-port directional microphone because these mics have some distance between the rear-entry low-frequency ports and the sound source. At close mic-to-source distances, however, most multiple-entry-port microphones have some proximity effect.

To avoid proximity effect at close working distances down to a few inches, directional mics have been designed that are frequency independent. One such mic uses two transducers—one to process high frequencies, the other to process low ones. This *two-way system* design also produces a more linear response at the sides of the microphone.

Hum

Hum is an ever-present concern in audio in general and in microphone pickup in particular. In a microphone, hum is typically produced by stray alternating current (AC) magnetic fields at 50 or 60 Hz and is particularly a problem in dynamic mics. One way to minimize hum is to use balanced mic cables and connectors (see "Cables" and "Connectors" later in this chapter). Twisted-pair mic cables with good shield coverage are recommended; the braided shield is particularly effective. Because dynamic microphones are especially susceptible to hum, use one with a humbuck coil.

Humbucking

Humbucking is not so much a response characteristic as it is a feature built into many moving-coil microphones. It is designed to cancel the effect of induced hum by introducing a 50/60 Hz component equal in level and opposite in polarity to the offending hum. Because the original and the introduced hums are opposite in polarity, they cancel each other. Humbucking is affected with a *humbuck coil* that is built into the microphone system and requires no special operation to activate it. The effectiveness of the hum reduction varies with the microphone.

Various Types of Microphones

Certain mics have been designed to meet particular production needs because of their size, pickup characteristics, sound, appearance, or a combination of these features. A number of different types of mics can be considered as special-purpose: lavaliere (minimic), shotgun, parabolic, headset and earset, contact, boundary, noise-canceling, USB, multidirectional, system, stereo, middle-side, infinitely variable pattern, binaural and surround, high definition, and digital.

Lavaliere Microphones (Mini-Mics)

The *lavaliere microphone* was originally hung around the neck, hence the name (*lavaliere* is French for "pendant"). Today, these mics are usually attached to a tie, to the front of a dress in the sternum area or at the neckline, or to a lapel. They are quite small and are known as *miniature microphones*, or *mini-mics* (see Figure 6-13). When they have to be concealed, they are placed in the seam or under clothing, behind the ear, or in the hair.

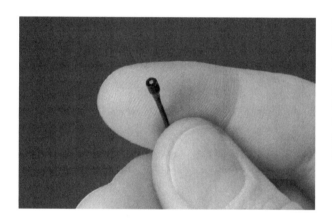

Figure 6-13 Lavaliere miniature microphone. This model measures 1/10 inch in diameter. It features three protective caps that both keep moisture out and alter the mic's color and frequency response to match desired applications. Frequency responses using the three protective caps are flat, +0 dB; bright, +4 dB; and very bright, +8 dB.

Mini-mics designed for use under the chin have two things in common: Most are omnidirectional, although directional minis may be used when background noise is especially loud, and many have a built-in high-frequency boost. The omnidirectional pickup is necessary because, with the mic mounted away from the front of the mouth, a speaker does not talk directly into it but across it. A directional response would not pick up much room presence and would sound too dead. In addition, as a speaker talks, high frequencies, which are directional, travel straight ahead. The chin cuts off many of the less directional high frequencies with longer wavelengths that otherwise would reach the mic. The built-in high-frequency boost compensates for this loss. If you hold in front of your mouth a mini-mic designed for use under the chin, its response will be overly bright and hissy. Their sensitivity to breathing and popping sounds also makes mini-mics unsuitable for use in front of the mouth; they have no pop filter, although windscreens come with many models (see "Windscreens and Pop Filters" later in this chapter).

The mini-mics in common use are electret capacitors. Generally, they fall into two groups: the *proximity oriented mini mic,* which adds presence to close speech while reducing background sound, and the *transparent mini mic,* which picks up more ambience, thereby blending more naturally with the overall sound.

Shotgun Microphones

The *shotgun microphone* is so-called because it resembles a rifle barrel (see Figure 6-38, microphone, far right). The basic principle of the shotgun microphone is that it attenuates sound from all directions except a narrow angle at the front. This creates the perception that it has greater reach. Compared with an omnidirectional microphone, mic-to-source pickup can be 1.7 times greater with a cardioid, 1.9 times greater with a supercardioid, and 2 times greater with a hypercardioid and not affect on-mic presence (see Figure 6-9). Some shotguns are better than others, so be careful when choosing one, especially for use in mediocre acoustic environments. The main consideration should be how well it discriminates sound, front-to-back, in a given situation.

The comparison can be made between a shotgun mic and a telephoto lens on a camera. A telephoto lens compresses front-to-back space. Shot with such a lens, an auditorium, for example, would appear smaller, with the rows of seats closer together than they really are. A shotgun mic does the same thing with acoustic space: It brings the background and the foreground sounds closer together. The extent of this spatial compression depends on the mic's pickup pattern. Of the three types of shotgun pickups—super-, hyper-, and ultracardioid—the supercardioid compresses front-to-rear sound the least and the ultracardioid compresses it the most.

Shotgun mics can sacrifice quality for a more focused pickup. One reason why is because shotguns are usually used for speech, and the frequency ranges of the male and female speaking voices are not very wide. Another reason is that the shotgun becomes less directional at lower frequencies, as do all directional mics, due to its inability to deal well with wavelengths longer than the length of its tube, called the *interference tube.* Interference tubes come in various lengths from 6 inches to 3 feet and longer. The longer the interference tube, the more highly directional the microphone. If the tube of a shotgun mic is 3 feet long, it will maintain directionality for frequencies of 300 Hz and higher—that is, wavelengths of approximately 3 feet and less. For 300 Hz and lower, the mic becomes less and less directional, canceling fewer and fewer of the lower frequencies. Many shotgun mics do have bass roll-off, however.

Most shotgun microphones have monaural pickup. Models with stereo pickup are also available.

Parabolic Microphone System

Another microphone used for long-distance pickup, mainly outdoors at sporting events, film and video shoots, in gathering naturalistic recordings of sounds in the wild, and for surveillance is the *parabolic microphone system.* It consists of either an omni- or a unidirectional mic facing inward and attached to a parabolic reflector. Fine-tuning the pickup is done by moving forward or backward the device that holds the mic. Some parabolic systems enable electronic magnifying of faint or distant sounds by several decibels. Parabolic systems are also available with a built-in recorder.

More than canceling unwanted sound, the parabolic dish, which is concave, concentrates the sound waves from the sound source and directs them to the microphone (see Figure 6-14). As with the shotgun mic, the parabolic mic is most effective within the middle- and high-frequency ranges; its sound quality is not suitable for critical recording.

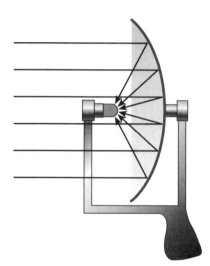

Figure 6-14 Parabolic microphone system. The system uses a concave dish that concentrates the incoming sound waves, based on the principle that a sound wave's angle of incidence is equal to its angle of reflectance (see Chapter 4). The attached microphone can be wired or wireless. With wireless mics the transmitter is usually attached to the parabolic reflector (see "Wireless Microphone System" later in the chapter).

Headset and Earset Microphones

The *headset microphone* is a mic mounted to headphones. The headphones can carry two separate signals: The program feeds through one headphone and the director's feed through the other. The microphone is usually a moving-coil type with a built-in pop filter because of its ability to handle loud sound-pressure levels that sports announcers, in particular, project. It may be omnidirectional for added event ambience or cardioid to keep background sound to a minimum. Hypercardioid models are designed for high rejection of unwanted sounds.

The headset system frees the announcer's hands and frontal working space. Another benefit is that the announcer's distance from the mic does not change once the headset is in place. Small and lightweight headset mics are also available. They are particular popular with singers doing TV, live concerts, and for dance-oriented performances (see Figure 6-15).

The *earset microphone* has no headband. It consists only of an earpiece cable-connected to a microphone, usually omni- or unidirectional. If keeping a mic unobtrusive is important, the earset microphone is far less apparent on-camera than headset models (see Figure 6-16).

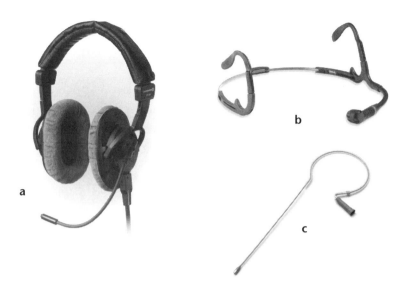

Figure 6-15 Headset microphone systems. (a) Headset microphone system with omnidirectional mic. (b) Small headset microphone system with cardioid mic for vocalists, singing instrumentalists, and radio talk-show hosts. (c) Headset mic with a flexible, telescoping band that fits snugly around the back of the head and is easily concealed under the hair. It has a telescoping boom that can be bent for a custom fit. Headset microphone systems can be wired or wireless.

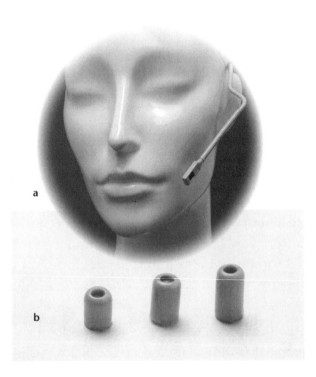

Figure 6-16 Earset microphone. (a) This model comes with protective caps (b) to keep perspiration, makeup, and other foreign materials out of the microphone. The caps also provide different high-frequency responses to control the amount of presence or crispness in the sound. Earset mics can be wired or wireless.

Contact Microphones

Not to quibble about semantics, but some lavalieres, particularly the miniature models, can be classified as *contact microphones*—and vice versa. Essentially, the difference between the two is that a contact mic, also called an *acoustic pickup mic*, has been specially designed to attach to a vibrating surface (see Figure 6-17). Instead of picking up airborne sound waves as conventional mics do, it picks up vibrations through solid materials.

Figure 6-17 Contact microphone designed for attachment to string instruments. Its size is 1 × 0.5 × 0.3 inch. A number of different sizes are available for placement on most musical instruments.

Boundary Microphones

When a conventional microphone is placed on or near a surface, such as a wall, floor, or ceiling, sound waves reach the mic from two directions—directly from the sound source and reflected from the nearby surface. The reflected sound takes longer to reach the microphone than the direct sound because it travels a longer path. This time difference causes phase cancellations at various frequencies, creating a *comb-filter effect*, which gives sound an unnatural, hollow coloration (see Figure 6-18). The *boundary microphone* positions a mini-capacitor mic capsule very close to, but at an optimal distance from, a sound-reflecting plate—the boundary. At this optimal distance, direct and reflected sound travel the same distance and reach the mic at about the same time, thereby eliminating phase cancellations. Any comb filtering occurs out of the range of human hearing.

Boundary microphones have an electret transducer. Their pickup pattern is half omnidirectional or hemispheric, half cardioid, half supercardioid, or stereophonic. Their response is open and, in suitable acoustics, spacious (see Figure 6-19).

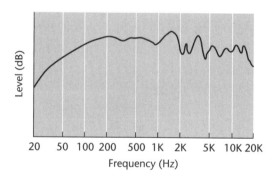

Figure 6-18 Comb-filter effect. Delayed reflected sound combined with direct sound can create this effect.

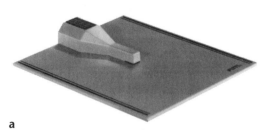

a

b

Figure 6-19 Boundary microphones with (a) hemispheric and (b) stereo pickup patterns.

Noise-Canceling Microphones

As stated earlier, a shotgun mic is designed to pick up at a distance and in so doing focuses sound by reducing unwanted background noise, so long as it is correctly aimed and does not pull in unwanted ambience from behind the primary sound source. The *noise-canceling microphone* is also intended to reject unwanted ambient sound, but it is designed for use close to the mouth. Because of its particular electronics, the noise-canceling mic must be used close to the sound source. If it is held even a short distance away, the performer's sound may be clipped, and the pickup may be *off-mic* entirely.

USB Microphones

The *USB microphone* was developed for those who want to record directly into a computer without an audio interface, such as a console, control surface, or mixer. (USB stands for *Universal Serial Bus*, a protocol used worldwide for data transfer between peripheral devices and computers.)

Like all microphones classified as digital, USB mics have a built-in analog-to-digital (A/D) converter (see "Digital Microphones" later in this chapter). They are available in both moving-coil and capacitor models. With capacitor USB mics, it is important to make sure that, because they use phantom power (which can generate noise) and because USB power can be noisy in the first place, the mic has compensating power conditioning and noise filtering to ensure sound quality that can run from decent to excellent. Another possible source of noise is the quality, or lack thereof, of the A/D converter.

Frequency response among USB mics varies from as narrow as 40 Hz to 14 kHz to as wide as 20 Hz to 20 kHz. Bit depth is generally 16-bit or 18-bit, with sampling rates that range from 8 to 48 kHz (see Chapter 9). Features such as a pad, an internal shock mount, bass roll-off, and variable pickup patterns vary with the mic. It is wise to keep in mind that regardless of how good the USB microphone may be, if problems occur with sound quality, the cause may the programs used or the applications to which the USB mic is connected. One such problem may be *latency*—the period of time it takes data to get from one designated point to another (see Chapter 10).

USB Microphone Converter

Development of the *USB microphone converter* (or *adapter*) makes it possible to connect any dynamic or capacitor XLR mic into a computer via USB (see "Connectors" later in this chapter). Depending on the model, a converter may include a microphone preamp, phantom power, headphone monitoring, and level controls for microphone balancing and playback (see Figure 6-20).

Multidirectional Directional Microphones

Microphones with a single directional response have one fixed diaphragm, or ribbon. By using more than one diaphragm and a switch to select or proportion between them, or by including more than one microphone capsule in a single housing, a mic can be made *multidirectional*, or *polydirectional*, providing two or more ways to pick up sound from various directions (see Figure 6-21).

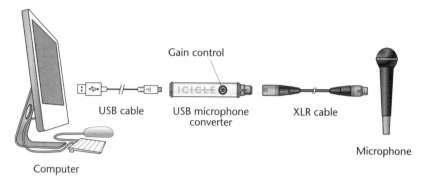

Figure 6-20 USB microphone converter flow chart. This particular converter from Blue Microphones is called Icicle. Shure also manufactures a USB adapter catalogued X2U.

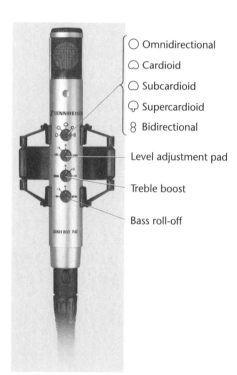

○ Omnidirectional
◌ Cardioid
○ Subcardioid
♀ Supercardioid
8 Bidirectional

Level adjustment pad

Treble boost

Bass roll-off

Figure 6-21 Multidirectional microphone with five pickup patterns: omnidirectional, subcardioid, cardioid, supercardioid, and bidirectional. This microphone also has a three position level adjustment pad (0, –6 dB, and –12 dB; second control from the top), a three-position treble boost at 10 kHz (0, +3 dB, and +6 dB; third control from top), and a bass roll-off at 50 Hz (–3 dB and –6 dB; bottom control). See "Overload Limit" and "Proximity Effect" earlier in this chapter.

System Microphones

One multidirectional mic of sorts is the *system microphone*, which uses interchangeable heads or capsules—each with a particular pickup pattern—that can be mounted onto a common base (see Figure 6-22). Because these systems are capacitors, the power supply and the preamplifier are in the base, and the mic capsule simply screws into the base. Any number of directional capsules—omnidirectional and bidirectional, cardioid, super-cardioid, and hypercardioid—can be interchanged on a single base. Some system mic models may only include two or three directional capsules.

Stereophonic Microphones

Stereophonic microphones are actually microphone capsules with electronically separate systems housed in a single casing. The stereo mic has two distinct elements which, in some models, can be remote-controlled. Generally, stereo mics are configured in one

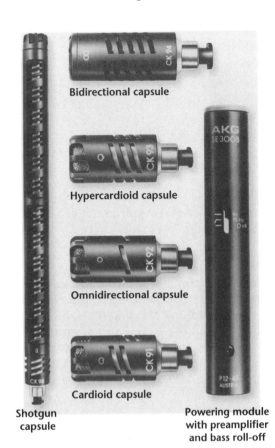

Figure 6-22 System microphone.

Bidirectional capsule

Hypercardioid capsule

Omnidirectional capsule

Cardioid capsule

Shotgun
capsule

Powering module
with preamplifier
and bass roll-off

of three ways: The lower and upper elements are stationary (see Figure 6-23); one element is stationary and the other element rotates 180 to 360 degrees to facilitate several different stereo pickup patterns, depending on the pickup design (see Figure 6-24); both elements rotate (see Figure 6-25).

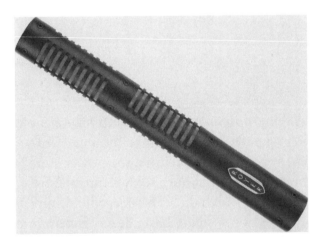

Figure 6-23 A stereo pair of matched ribbon mics mounted one above the other in a single casing. The two ribbons' pickup patterns are 90 degrees off-axis from each other.

Figure 6-24 Stereo microphone with one rotating capsule. The upper capsule in this model can rotate 270 degrees horizontally; the lower capsule is stationary. Two three-way switches control the polar response, high-pass filtering, and –10 dB pad for each capsule.

Figure 6-25 Stereo microphone with two rotating capsules. The angle between the microphone's axes can be adjusted continuously in the range from 0 to 180 degrees.

Figure 6-26 Combined middle-side and stereo microphone. In the stereo mode, this microphone uses its internal matrix to mix the middle and side signals. In the L (low) position, the stereo image spread is small. In the M (medium) position, it is wider. The H (high) position provides the widest stereo spread. In the M-S output mode, the internal stereo matrix is bypassed. The pickup from the front-facing mic capsule is cardioid, and from the side-facing capsule it is bidirectional.

Middle-Side Microphones

Most *middle-side (M-S) microphones* consist of two mic capsules housed in a single casing. One capsule is designated as the midposition microphone aimed at the sound source to pick up mostly direct sound; it is usually cardioid. The other capsule is designated as the side-position microphone; it is usually bidirectional with each lobe oriented 90 degrees laterally to the sides of the sound source to pick up mostly ambient sound. The outputs of the cardioid and bidirectional capsules are combined into a sum-and-difference matrix through a controller that may be external or internal (see Figure 6-26).

Infinitely Variable Pattern Microphones

Instead of having selectable pickup patterns, the infinitely variable pattern microphone allows fine adjustments to any position from omnidirectional through bi- and unidirectional patterns. These microphones typically also include variable controls for bass roll-off and pad.

Binaural Microphone Systems

Binaural microphony picks up sound in three, instead of two, dimensions. The addition of vertical, or height, information to the sonic depth and breadth reproduced by conventional stereo and M-S mics makes sound quite spacious and localization very realistic.

Generally, *binaural microphone systems* consist of an artificial head with a pair of pinnae ear replicas and a matched pair of omnidirectional capacitor microphones or microphone capsules placed in the ear canals. Some go so far as to construct the head and the upper torso based on statistical averaging and variations in real humans. Some even feature felt hair and shoulder padding to simulate the characteristics of hair and clothing.

Surround-Sound Microphone Systems

Surround sound adds greater front-to-rear depth and side-to-side breadth (assuming side placement of the loudspeakers) than stereo but not quite the vertical imaging or sonic envelopment of binaural sound.

Surround-sound microphone systems usually house separate microphones, or microphone capsules, for each pickup in a given surround-sound format and include a controller to adjust spatial imaging. For example, for the 5.1 format there are six microphones for left center, center, right center, left and right surrounds, and low frequency pickup (see Figure 5-15 and Chapter 13). In the 7.1 format, eight separate microphones are delegated for left center, center, right center, left and right side surrounds, left and right rear surrounds, and low-frequency pickup. The arrangement of the microphone elements varies from system to system, however, and a few systems employ fewer mics in a quasi-binaural/surround configuration to reproduce the surround-sound imaging.

High Definition Microphones

The term *high definition microphone* is a trademark of Earthworks, Inc., and refers to its line of these types of mics and its proprietary technology. But so-called high definition microphones, regardless of manufacturer, are generally very high-quality instruments with superior transient response; shorter diaphragm settling time after vibration; extended frequency response; fewer electronic features to reduce signal path; low distortion at high sound-pressure levels; and improved stabilization of the polar response.

High Definition Microphone for Laptop Computers

The mediocre to poor sound quality in laptop computers has long been a bane to users. Upgraded loudspeakers have not helped that much because of the poor quality of available microphones. This problem has been alleviated with the development of a high definition digital microphone for laptop computers and other broadband devices.

One such microphone has wideband frequency response and complies with the audio performance requirement for wideband transmission in applications such as *Voice-over-Internet Protocol (VoIP)* delivering high definition voice quality; is surface-mountable; and provides a L/R user-select function that allows a single device to be configured as either a left or a right microphone.

Digital Microphones

When conventional mics are used in digital recording, the analog signal is converted to a digital signal at some point in the sound chain—but after it leaves the microphone. With the *digital microphone*, the analog signal is converted to digital at the mic capsule, which means the signal going through the sound chain is digital immediately after it is transduced from acoustic energy into electric energy.

Microphone Modeler

A *microphone modeler* is not an actual microphone but a microphone simulator that can be added to a hard-disk recording system as a plug-in (see Figure 6-27). It is designed to emulate the sounds of most professional-grade microphones.

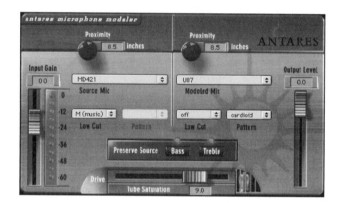

Figure 6-27 Microphone modeler.

Say you have a track recorded with a Sennheiser MD421 and you want to make it sound as though it had been recorded with a Neumann U-87. The mic modeler removes from the audio the characteristics of the original microphone and applies those of the target mic. The microphone modeler can be used either after a track has been recorded or during recording to shape the desired sound. Although the process is not completely accurate in reproducing a particular mic's sound, it does create good virtual similarities of a given microphone's identifying characteristics, thereby providing a much larger mic collection than a recordist might have.

It is useful to note, however, that a microphone modeler cannot make a $30 dynamic mic sound like a $3,000 tube-type capacitor; and because many factors affect a recording, such as a studio's acoustics, the microphone preamplifier, and mic-to-source distance, it cannot make poorly recorded material sound good.

Wireless Microphone System

The *wireless microphone system*, also called a *cordless mic*, an *FM mic*, a *radio mic*, and a *transmitter mic*, consists of three main components (four, if you count the mic): transmitter, antenna, and receiver (see Figure 6-28). Additional system components may include cables and distribution systems. A standard mic is used with the system in one of four ways: lavaliere, handheld, headset, and boom. The lavaliere system typically uses a mini-mic connected to a battery-powered bodypack transmitter, which may be wired or wireless. The handheld wireless mic operates with the transmitter and the microphone

a   b

Figure 6-28 Wireless microphone system. (a) Pocket transmitter. Features include: multiple UHF frequency selection; long-range transmission; illuminated graphic display; auto-lock to avoid accidental change of the selected frequency; mute function; and wireless synchronization of transmitters via infrared interface from the receiver. (b) Receiver. Features include: diversity reception (see "Diversity Reception" later in this section); illuminated graphic display also showing transmitter settings; automatic frequency scan to search for available frequencies; Ethernet port; and integrated equalizer and soundcheck mode.

in a single housing (see Figure 6-29). The headset and earset mics use the bodypack transmitter. The boom microphone's transmitter is usually a plug-on (see Figure 6-30). The plug-on is a wireless transmitter with an XLR connector (discussed later in this chapter) that plugs into the end of the mic.

The microphone's signal is sent to the transmitter, which converts it to a radio signal and relays the signal to a receiver anywhere from several feet to many yards away, depending on the system's power. The receiver converts the radio signal back into an audio

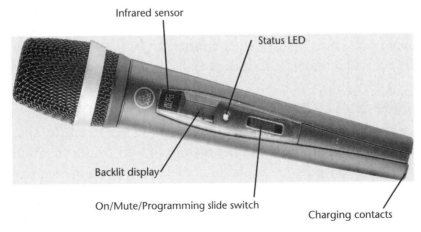

Figure 6-29 Wireless handheld transmitter.

Figure 6-30 Plug-on wireless microphone transmitter.

signal. The transmitter usually includes a flexible wire antenna and controls for on/off power, frequency selection, microphone loudness, and microphone mute. Status lights indicate when the mic is on or off, the battery is low, and the signal is overloading.

The receiver usually includes the antenna(s) and controls for frequency selection (the frequency must match that of the transmitter); the signal level; the squelch-mute threshold control so the receiver picks up the desired signal and mutes when the signal is turned off; and indicator status lights to indicate the level of the incoming signal, the level of the audio sent from the receiver down the signal chain, mute, and diversity operation (see "Diversity Reception" later in this chapter).

Before using a wireless microphone system, consider a few operational and performance criteria: frequency assignment and usage, diversity reception, audio circuitry, sound quality, transmission range, antenna, and power supply.

- **Frequency assignment and usage**—Wireless microphone systems transmit on frequencies in the very high frequency (VHF) and ultra high frequency (UHF) bands. The VHF ranges are: low band—49 to 108 megahertz (MHz); and high band—174 to 216 MHz. The UHF ranges are: low band—470 to 698 MHz; and high band—900 to 952 MHz. The 700 MHz band that was also used for wireless microphone usage was reassigned in 2009 for new commercial services and public safety usage. Most wireless microphone manufacturers anticipating the reallocation by the Federal Communications Commission (FCC) no longer produce wireless systems that transmit in the 700 MHz band.

  The differences between VHF and UHF wireless mic systems relate to bandwidth, flexibility, power, multipath reception, and cost. Because the VHF bandwidth is far narrower than UHF, there is much less room for available frequencies (see Figure 6-31). This limits both its use in large metropolitan areas, where the spectrum is crowded with VHF TV and FM radio stations, and its flexibility in operating a number of wireless systems simultaneously. Therefore, using low-band VHF wireless systems is not recommended because the band is prone to interference from many users. Also, transmitter power is limited, and the required antenna size limits portability.

- **Multipath**—Wireless systems in the higher frequencies, and therefore transmitting shorter wavelengths, are vulnerable to instances of multipath reception. *Multipath* is a physical phenomenon in which more than one radio frequency (RF) signal from the same source arrives at the receiver's front end, creating phase mismatching (see Figure 6-32).

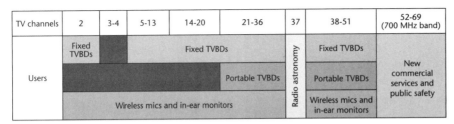

TV channels	2	3-4	5-13	14-20	21-36	37	38-51	52-69 (700 MHz band)

Figure 6-31 New FCC frequency allocations after the digital television (DTV) transition. (TVBD is short for personal and portable TV band devices, previously referred to as white space devices [WSDs]).

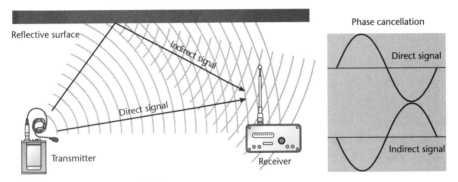

Figure 6-32 Multipath dropout.

- **Fixed- and Variable-Frequency Systems**—Wireless microphones operate on either a fixed frequency or a variable frequency system. *Fixed-frequency wireless microphone systems*, which are less expensive than variable systems, are useful in situations where the mic does not change locations or there are relatively few FM and TV stations in the area or both. These factors make it relatively easy to find an available operating frequency and the wireless system to match it. In large cities, or if the mic is used in different locations, the *variable-frequency wireless microphone system* is necessary. Also known as *frequency-agile systems*, some of these use a technology that automatically selects the best channels at any given time for seamless microphone performance.

- **Diversity reception**—A wireless microphone system transmits radio waves from a transmitter, through the air, to a receiver. Because the waves are transmitted line-of-sight, there is the danger that the radio waves will encounter obstructions en route to the receiver. Another potential hindrance to signal reception could result if the transmitter is out of range. The problem with multipath reception may be a third difficulty. Any of these problems creates a dropout or null in the transmission. *Dropout* is a momentary loss of the signal at the receiver. The technique used to deal with dropout is known as *diversity reception*. Basically, diversity reception ensures that the receiver can satisfactorily process an impeded signal from the transmitter (see Figure 6-33).

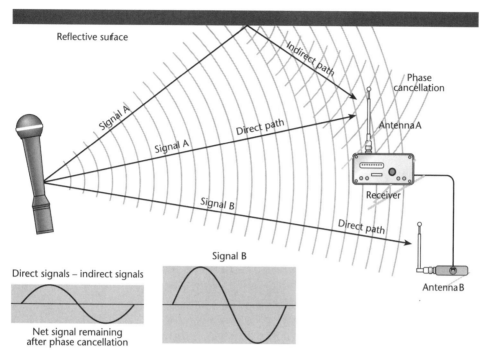

Figure 6-33 Diversity reception.

To check if a wireless system is operating correctly, walk the signal path from the transmitter to the receiver, speaking into the microphone as you go. If you hear dropout, buzzing, or any other sonic anomaly, note the location(s). First check the system to make sure it is in proper working order. If it is, change microphone placement or receiver location, if you can, and retest the signal transmission.

■ **Audio circuitry**—The nature of radio transmission inhibits the quality of the audio signal. To counteract this, the audio signal is processed in two ways, through equalization and companding.

Equalization, in this instance, involves a pre-emphasis and a de-emphasis of the signal to minimize the level of hiss (high-frequency noise) that is unavoidably added during transmission. *Pre-emphasis* boosts the high frequencies in transmission; *de-emphasis* reduces the high-frequency noise at the receiver. The equal but opposite process reduces noise by up to 10 dB.

Companding, a contraction of the words *com*pressing and ex*panding*, compensates for the limited dynamic range of radio transmission. The input signal varies over a range of 80 dB and is compressed at the transmitter to a range of 40 dB, a factor of 2 to 1. At the receiver, the signal is expanded by 40 dB to its original dynamic range, a factor of 1 to 2. Even though companding sometimes creates noise, coloration, and the audible pumping sound caused by compander mistracking, particularly in less expensive systems, a wireless mic is always far better off with companding than without it (see Figure 6-34).

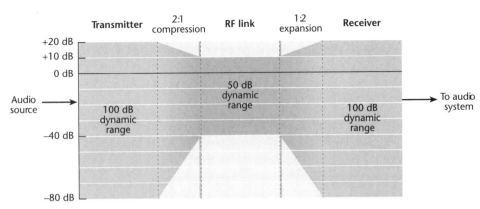

Figure 6-34 Compander action.

Another process important to signal reception at the receiver is called *squelch*. The function of this circuit is to silence or mute the receiver's audio output when there is no radio signal. Otherwise, the "open" receiver could pick up background radio noise or another signal.

■ **Sound quality**—Wireless microphone systems vary widely in quality. Clearly, in professional audio, only a system with wide frequency response and dynamic range should be used. Frequency response should be well beyond the frequency range of the sound recorded. Good wireless systems are now capable of dynamic ranges up to 115 dB. A system with poorer dynamic range needs more compression at the transmitter and more expansion at the receiver, creating an annoying squeezed sound that results from companding loud levels.

■ **Transmission range**—The transmission range of wireless microphone systems varies from as short as 100 feet to as long as 2,500 feet. The range of a given system is provided in its specifications. Transmission range should be based on need. Obviously, a shorter range would suffice in a studio or theater whereas a longer range would be necessary in a stadium or in a long shot for a film.

■ **Antenna**—The antenna should be fully extended and several feet away from any obstruction, including the floor. With transmitters, avoid taping "whip" antennas (and bodypacks) to the skin, as perspiration inhibits signal transmission. Both the transmitter and the receiver antennas should be oriented either vertically or horizontally. If they are not, it hinders reception. Because performers usually stand, the most common antenna position is vertical. Some antennas are more effective than others. To improve system performance, a dipole antenna could increase signal pickup by 3 dB or more.

■ **Power supply**—Wireless mic systems use a variety of battery types, such as AA, 9 V, and VDC (voltage DC). Battery lifetime varies from a few hours to up to 10 hours. Alkaline batteries are good, but lithium batteries last longer. To reduce power supply problems, batteries should be replaced before they have a chance to run down. It is simply not worth holding up a production session to save a few cents, trying to squeeze maximum life out of a battery.

Analog Versus Digital Wireless Microphone Systems

Wireless microphones systems are available in analog and digital formats. By digitizing the signal, the audio gets converted to digital right away at the transmitter. It is then sent to the receiver where the data is received; checked for errors; corrected, if necessary; and converted back to analog. This process has several advantages over analog. Among them are a more robust signal; considerable reduction, if not elimination of interference and overall noise, in RF in the radio path; and the need for squelch.

Microphone Accessories

Microphones come with various accessories. The most common are windscreens and pop filters, shock mounts, cables, connectors, and stands and special-purpose mounts.

Windscreens and Pop Filters

Windscreens and *pop filters* are designed to deal with distortion that results from blowing sounds caused by breathing and wind, the sudden attack of transients, the hiss of sibilant consonants like *s* and *ch*, and the popping plosives of consonants like *p* and *b*. (In practice, the terms *windscreen* and *pop filter* are used interchangeably, but for clarity of discussion here they are given slightly different applications.)

Windscreens are mounted externally and reduce the distortion from blowing and popping but rarely eliminate it from particularly strong sounds (see Figure 6-35). A pop filter is built-in and is most effective against blowing sounds and popping (see Figure 6-36). It allows very close microphone placement to a sound source with little fear of this type of distortion.

Windscreens also slightly affect response, somewhat reducing the crispness of high frequencies (see Figure 6-37). Many directional microphones with pop filters are designed with a high-frequency boost to compensate for reduced treble response.

Pop filters, also known as **blast filters**, are mainly found in moving-coil, newer ribbon, and some capacitor microphones, particularly directional models, because they are more susceptible than omnidirectional mics to breath and popping noise due to their partial pressure-gradient response. They are also more likely to be used closer to a sound source than other microphone types. An omnidirectional mic is about 15 dB less sensitive to wind noise and popping than a unidirectional mic of similar size.

Another way to minimize distortion from sibilance, transients, blowing sounds, and popping is through microphone placement (see Chapter 7).

Shock Mounts

Because solid objects are excellent sound conductors, the danger always exists that unwanted vibrations will travel through the mic stand to the microphone. To reduce noises induced by vibrations, place the microphone in a **shock mount**—a device that suspends and mechanically isolates the mic from the stand (see Figure 6-38). Some microphones are designed with a built-in shock absorber.

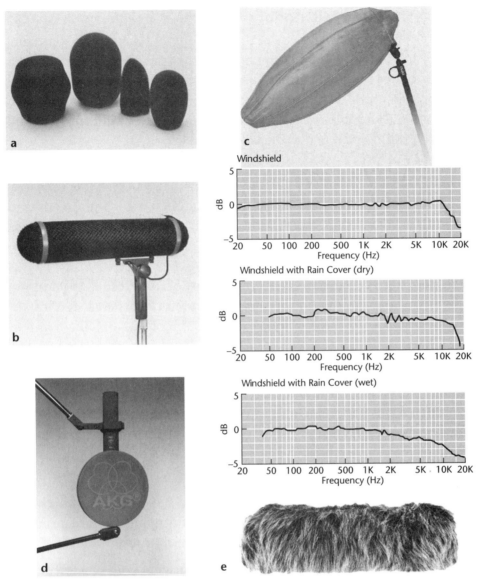

Figure 6-35 Windscreens. (a) Various windscreens for conventional microphones. (b) So-called zeppelin windscreen enclosure for shotgun microphone. (c) Lightweight collapsible windshield consisting of a light metal frame covered with a fine-mesh foam material. The windshield comes with a rain cover. The response curves illustrate the differences in response characteristics without the rain cover, with the rain cover dry, and with the rain cover wet. It should be noted that all windscreens affect frequency response in some way. (d) Stocking (fabric) windscreen designed for use between the sound source and the microphone. This particular model has two layers of mesh material attached to a lightweight wooden ring. (e) Windscreen cover, or windjammer, to cover zeppelin-type windscreens.

Figure 6-36 Built-in pop filter.

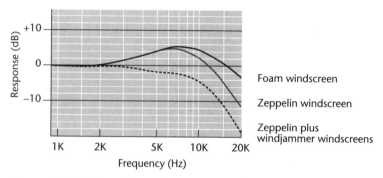

Figure 6-37 The effect of various windscreens on frequency response.

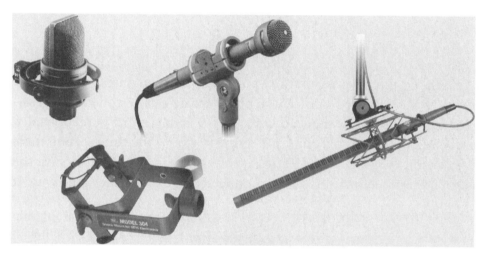

Figure 6-38 Various types of shock mounts.

Cables

A microphone cable is either a **balanced line**—consisting of two conductors and a shield—or an **unbalanced line**—consisting of one conductor with the shield serving as the second conductor. A quad mic cable uses a four-conductor design for added noise control. As with all professional equipment, the balanced line is preferred because it is less susceptible to electrical noise.

When winding mic cable, do not coil it around your arm, and be careful not to make the angle of the wrap too severe or it can damage the internal wires. It is also a good idea to secure the cable with a clasp specially made for this purpose to prevent it from getting tangled (see Figure 6-39).

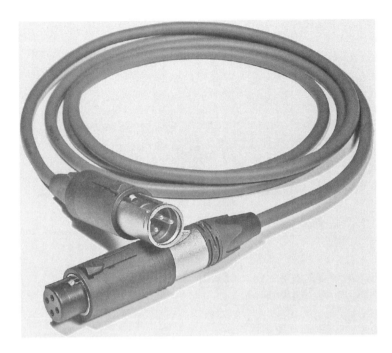

Figure 6-39 Microphone cable. To keep cable intact and avoid damage to internal wires and connections, coil and secure cable when not in use.

Connectors

Most professional mics and mic cables use a three-pin plug that terminates the two conductors and the shield of the balanced line. These plugs are generally called **XLR connectors** (X is the ground or shield, L is the lead wire, and R is the return wire). Usually, the female plug on the microphone cable connects to the mic, and the three-prong male plug connects to the console (see Figure 6-40). It is always important to make sure the three pins in all microphones used in a session are connected in exactly the same way. If

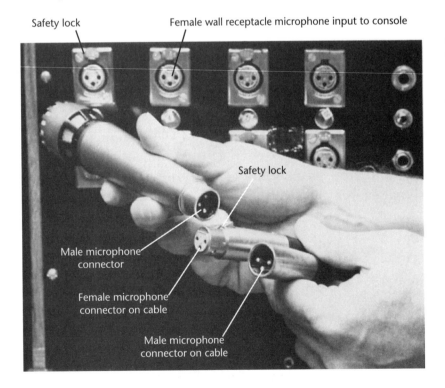

Safety lock

Female wall receptacle microphone input to console

Safety lock

Male microphone connector

Female microphone connector on cable

Male microphone connector on cable

Figure 6-40 Microphone connectors. The female cable connector plugs into the male microphone connector; the male cable connector plugs into the female wall receptacle, which is connected to the microphone input on the console.

pin 1 is ground, pin 2 is positive, and pin 3 is negative, all mics must be wired in the same configuration; otherwise, the mismatched microphones will be electrically out of polarity and reduce or null the audio level.

Microphone Mounts

Just as there are many types of microphones to meet a variety of needs, numerous microphone mounts are available for just about every possible application. Commonly used microphone mounts are shown in Figures 6-41 to 6-49.

Figure 6-41 Gooseneck stand.

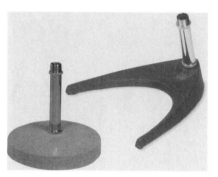

Figure 6-42 Desk stands.

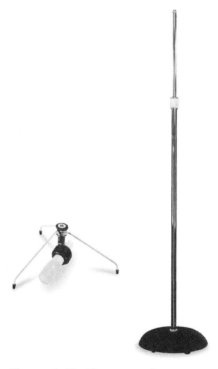

Figure 6-43 Floor stands.

Figure 6-44 Latch Lake micKing 3300 stationary boom with mount.

Figure 6-45 Boom operator with handheld "fishpole."

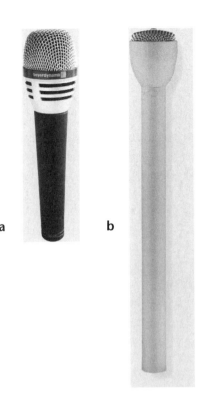

a   b

Figure 6-46 **Handheld microphones.** (a) Microphone with thin tube. It is easily handheld, is shock resistant, and has a pop filter. All are essential in a handheld microphone. (b) Handheld mic with a long handle for added control in broadcast applications and to provide room for a microphone flag.

Figure 6-47 **Hanging microphones.**

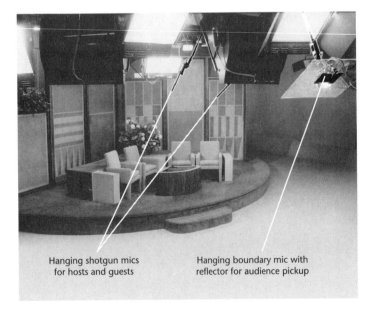

Hanging shotgun mics for hosts and guests

Hanging boundary mic with reflector for audience pickup

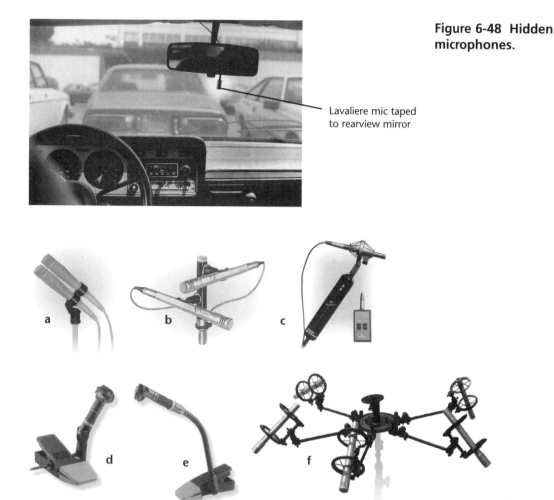

Figure 6-48 Hidden microphones.

Lavaliere mic taped to rearview mirror

Figure 6-49 Special microphone mounts. (a) Redundant mono microphone mount. (b) Stereo microphone mount. (c) Remote panner boom mount and control module. (d) Hypercardioid microphone and mount for attachment to drums. (e) Hypercardioid microphone and mount for attachment to brass and woodwind instruments. (f) Mount for surround-sound miking.

Microphone Care

Poor care of audio equipment adversely affects sound quality—this cannot be stressed enough. Moisture from high humidity or breath can greatly shorten a microphone's life. When moisture is a problem, a windscreen will help protect the microphone element. Avoid blowing into a mic to check if it is on—in addition to the moisture problem, the force can drive particles through the grille and onto the diaphragm.

Ribbon mics are especially sensitive to the force of air pressure from blowing into the grille. Capacitor mics are also sensitive to air turbulence, not only from blowing but from fans and blowers. In fact, a breath blast can perforate a capacitor mic's diaphragm. Be sure to turn off phantom power when a capacitor mic is not in use. The electric charge attracts dust to the mic's diaphragm. While the phantom power is on, do not plug or unplug the mic cable; the abrupt power change could damage the mic's preamp.

Dirt, jarring, cigarette smoke, oil from hands, and pop filters clogged with saliva and/or lipstick also reduce microphone efficiency. Microphones should be cleaned and serviced regularly and kept in carrying cases when not in use. Microphones left on stands between sessions should be covered with a cloth or plastic bag but not so tightly as to create a condensation problem. The working environment should be temperature- and humidity-controlled, kept clean, and vacuumed regularly.

Main Points

- Microphones are transducers that convert acoustic energy into electric energy. The device that does the transducing is called the element.

- Impedance refers to resistance to the flow of voltage in a circuit. The lower the impedance, the better. Professional microphones (and equipment) are low impedance.

- The elements in professional microphones operate on one of two physical principles: magnetic induction and variable capacitance.

- The two types of professional mics that use magnetic induction are the moving-coil mics and the ribbon mics. The type of professional microphone using variable capacitance is the capacitor mic.

- Capacitor microphones require a power supply to operate.

- Each type of microphone is unique. One type is not much better than another as it is more suitable for a particular application.

- Microphones pick up sound from essentially three directions: all around—omnidirectional; front and rear—bidirectional; and front only—unidirectional.

- The unidirectional, or cardioid, design has even narrower pickup patterns. They are supercardioid, hypercardioid, and ultracardioid.

- A microphone's directional sensitivity can be displayed graphically in a polar response diagram.

- A microphone's unidirectionality is facilitated by ports at the side and/or rear of the mic that cancel sound coming from unwanted directions.

- Directional sensitivity in a unidirectional microphone varies with frequency: The higher the frequency, the more directional the pickup; the lower the frequency, the less directional the pickup.

- A microphone's frequency response is the range of frequencies it produces at an equal level, within a margin of ±3 dB. Its frequency response curve can be displayed as a graph.

- All microphones will distort if sound levels are too high—a condition known as overload.

- Maximum sound-pressure level is the level at which a microphone's output signal begins to distort.

- To help protect against loudness distortion, many capacitor mics are equipped with a pad to reduce overloading the mic's electronics.

- Sensitivity measures the voltage a microphone produces (dBV) at a certain sound-pressure level. It indicates how loud a microphone is.

- Self-noise, also known as equivalent noise level, indicates the sound-pressure level that will create the same voltage as the inherent electrical noise, or hiss, a microphone (or any electronic device) produces.

- Signal-to-noise ratio (S/N) is the ratio of a signal power to the noise power corrupting the signal and is measured in decibels. In relation to microphones, S/N is the difference between sound-pressure level and self-noise.

- Bidirectional and most directional microphones are susceptible to proximity effect, or bass tip-up—an increase in the level of bass frequencies relative to midrange and treble frequencies—when they are placed close to a sound source. To neutralize proximity effect, most of these microphones are equipped with bass roll-off.

- Hum is an ever-present concern in microphone pickup. In a mic, it is typically produced by stray alternating current (AC) magnetic fields at 50 or 60 Hz and is particularly a problem in dynamic mics. There are several ways to minimize hum.

- One method used to reduce hum is the humbuck coil built into some dynamic microphones.

- Microphones have been developed for special purposes: for unobtrusiveness, the lavaliere and mini-mics; the shotgun and parabolic mics for long-distance pickup; the headset and earset mics to keep background sound to a minimum by maintaining a close mic-to-source distance; the contact mic for use on a vibrating surface; the boundary mic for use on a boundary (a hard, reflective surface) so that all sound pickup at the microphone is in phase; the noise-canceling mic for use close to the mouth with excellent rejection of ambient sound; the USB mic to record directly to a computer without an audio interface; multidirectional and system microphones, which have more than one pickup pattern; stereophonic, middle-side (M-S), and infinitely variable pattern microphones; the binaural mic for three-dimensional sound imaging; the surround-sound mics for surround-sound pickup; the high-definition mic for extremely high-quality reproduction; and the digital mic, which converts the analog signal to digital when the acoustic energy is transduced to electric energy.

- A microphone modeler is not an actual microphone but a microphone simulator that can be added to a hard-disk recording system as a plug-in. It is designed to emulate the sounds of most professional-grade microphones.

- When using a wireless microphone system, consider the following operational and performance criteria: frequency assignment and usage, diversity reception, audio circuitry, sound quality, transmission range, antenna, and power supply.

■ Windscreens and pop filters are used to reduce distortion caused by wind and transients. An external shock mount, or a built-in shock absorber, is used to prevent unwanted vibrations from reaching the microphone element.

■ Standard accessories used for professional microphones include the following: twin conductor cables called balanced lines, XLR connectors, and various types of stands and clips for microphone mounting.

■ Proper care is very important to the functioning and the sound quality of a microphone.

7 Microphone Techniques

There are probably as many approaches to microphone selection and placement as there are producers of audio. This chapter covers basic, time-tested techniques as they apply to miking the speaking voice in various broadcast and production settings and miking for music recording. They are intended only as guidelines; there is no intention of suggesting that they are the best or only approaches.

Phase and Polarity

Before moving on it is necessary to say a word about phase and polarity. In acoustics *phase* is the time relationship between two or more sound waves at a given point in their cycles (see Chapter 1). In electricity *polarity* is the relative position of two signal leads—high (+) and low (−)—in the same circuit.

Phase

Phase is an important acoustic consideration in microphone placement. If sound sources are not properly placed in relation to mics, sound waves can reach the mics at different times and be out of phase. For example, sound waves from a source slightly off center between two spaced microphones will reach one mic a short time before or after they reach the other mic, causing some cancellation of sound. Perceiving sounds that are considerably out of phase is relatively easy: When you should hear sound, you hear little or none. Perceiving sounds that are only a little out of phase is not so easy.

By changing relative time relationships between given points in the cycles of two waves, a *phase shift* occurs. To detect unwanted phase shift, listen for the following; unequal levels in frequency response, particularly in the bass and the midrange slightly unstable, wishy-washy sound; or a sound source that is slightly out of position in relation to where it should be in the aural frame.

One way to avoid phase problems with microphones is to follow the *three-to-one rule*: Place no two microphones closer together than three times the distance between one of them and its sound source. If one mic is 2 inches from a sound source, for example, the nearest other mic should be no closer to the first mic than 6 inches; if one mic is 3 feet from a sound source, the nearest other mic should be no closer than 9 feet to the first, and so on (see Figure 7-1).

109

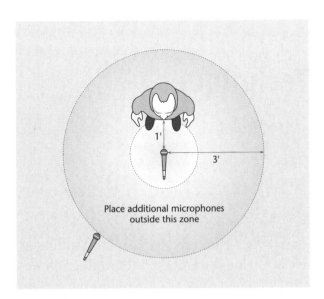

Figure 7-1 Three-to-one rule. Most phasing problems generated by improper microphone placement can be avoided by placing no two mics closer together than three times the distance between one of them and its sound source.

Place additional microphones outside this zone

If a sound source emits loud levels, it might be necessary to increase the ratio between microphones to 4:1 or even 5:1. Quiet levels may facilitate mic placement closer than that prescribed by a ratio of 3:1.

Phasing problems can also be caused by reflections from surfaces close to a microphone bouncing back into the mic's pickup.

Polarity

Signals in a microphone circuit that are electrically out of polarity reduce sound quality or cancel the sound altogether. A common cause of mics being out of polarity is incorrect wiring of the microphone plugs. Male and female XLR connectors used for most mics have three pins: a ground, a positive pin for high output, and a negative pin for low output (see Chapter 6). (XLR five-pin connectors are used for stereo microphones.) Mic cables house three coded wires. All mics in the same facility must have the same-number pin connected to the same-color wire. If they do not and are used simultaneously, they will be electrically out of polarity.

To check the polarity of two mics, first make sure that both are delegated to the same output channel. Adjust the level for a normal reading as someone speaks into a mic. Turn down the fader and repeat the procedure with another mic. Then open both mics to the normal settings. If the meter reading decreases when the levels of both mics are turned up, there is a polarity problem. The obvious way to correct this condition is to rewire the equipment, assuming the problem is not in the mic itself. If there is no time for that, most multichannel consoles and hard-disk recording systems have a polarity reversal control that reverses polarity by 180 degrees (see Chapter 8).

Six Principles

Before getting into specific applications of miking, it will be helpful to keep in mind six principles:

- The closer a microphone is to a sound source, the more detailed, intimate, drier, and, if proximity effect is a factor, bassier the sound. The farther a mic is from a sound source, the more diffused, open, less intimate, and ambient the sound.

- Regardless of a directional microphone's pickup pattern: The higher the frequency, the more directional the sound wave and therefore the mic pickup; the lower the frequency, the more omnidirectional the sound wave and mic pickup.

- When employing a number of microphones, more may not always be better. Each additional mic adds a little more noise to the system, even in digital recording, and means another input to keep track of and control, to say nothing of possible phasing problems.

- With most moving-coil mics, the farther from the sound source they are placed, the more reduced the high-frequency response.

- Generally, large-diaphragm microphones are more suitable in reproducing predominately low-frequency sound sources; small-diaphragm mics are more suitable in reproducing predominately high-frequency sound sources.

- Do not confuse perspective with loudness. Loudness aside, in considering mic-to-source distance, it is hearing more or less of the ambience that helps create perspective.

Microphones for the Speaking Voice

The microphone of choice should be the one that best complements the sound source. That includes the most sonically complex sound source of all: the human voice.

Sound Quality

Sometimes in choosing the "right" microphone, circumstances make the decision for you. For example, if some coloration is desirable, a good moving-coil mic may be the best selection; if mellowness is the primary consideration, a ribbon mic may be most suitable; if detail is important, the capacitor mic may be the likely pick. Remember that each type of microphone has particular attributes (see "General Transducer Performance Characteristics" in Chapter 6).

The evaluation of a mic for speech includes at least four criteria: *clarity*—detail, accuracy, and lack of saturation; *presence*—open yet stands out; *richness*—little or no coloration but full, deep, and warm; and *versatility*—flexibility across different speech applications (important because many of the better microphones are expensive). Other features may also be desirable, such as a built-in pop filter and a shock mount, pad and roll-off controls, variable pickup patterns, and reduced off-axis response.

Directional Pattern

Another common decision in microphone selection is the directional pattern. Usually, the choice is between an omnidirectional and a unidirectional mic. Again, circumstances sometimes make the decision for you. In a noisy environment, a unidirectional mic discriminates against unwanted sound better than an omnidirectional one; to achieve a more open sound, the omnidirectional mic is the better choice. Using a mini-mic almost always means an omnidirectional pickup. If there is an option of choosing either pickup pattern, each has certain advantages and disadvantages, depending on the demands of a given situation (see Figures 7-2 and 7-3).

Bidirectional microphones are rarely used because the audio from two people speaking into the same mic is processed through a single channel and cannot be manipulated without difficulty. Moreover, getting the right level and ambience balances could be time-consuming. At times, a bidirectional pattern is used for a single speaker (or singer) to add some ambient pickup through the open rear lobe of the mic instead of employing an omnidirectional mic, which may add more ambience than desired.

Based on the differences detailed in Figures 7-2 and 7-3, the omnidirectional pickup pattern seems to be the more useful of the two. As with the choice of a mic's transducer type, so it is with deciding on a directional pattern. A microphone's suitability depends on the sonic requirements, not on favoritism.

Microphone-to-Source Distance

Speech is usually close-miked, that is, the distance between the talent and the microphone is about 3 to 6 inches, depending on the force of the delivery and the material performed. Close-miking in-studio produces an intimate sound with little acoustic coloration from ambience. On location, it reduces the chance of unwanted sound from

Advantages	Disadvantages
Does not have to be held directly in front of the mouth to provide adequate pickup	Does not discriminate against unwanted sound
Does not reflect slight changes in the mic-to-source distance	Is difficult to use in noisy environments
Gives a sense of the environment	Presents greater danger of feedback in reverberant locations
Is less susceptible to wind, popping, and handling noises	
Is not subject to the proximity effect	
Is natural sounding in rooms with good acoustics	

Figure 7-2 The omnidirectional microphone.

Advantages	Disadvantages
Discriminates against unwanted sound	Must be angled correctly to the mouth, or the performer will be off-mic
Gives little or no sense of the environment (which could also be a disadvantages)	Will be subject to the proximity effect
Significantly reduces the danger of feedback in reverberant locations	Is susceptible to wind and popping, unless there is a pop filter
	Is more susceptible to handling noises
	Requires care not to cover the ports, if handheld
	Is less natural sounding in rooms with good acoustics

Figure 7-3 The unidirectional microphone.

interfering with or distracting attention from the spoken content, particularly with a directional microphone.

As noted earlier in the chapter, the closer a mic is to a sound source, the warmer, more detailed, denser, more oppressive (if too close) the sound, and the closer the listener perceives the speaker to be. The farther a mic is from the sound source, the less warm, less detailed, thinner (if there is little reverberation) the sound, and the more distant the listener perceives the speaker to be.

In most situations involving speech, the performer must be picked up at close range (1) to ensure that the words are heard clearly and are immediately intelligible, and (2) in-studio, to avoid any interference from ambience, noise, or other unwanted sounds, and on location, to reduce as much as possible these sonic interferences.

Basic Approaches to Miking Speakers

In broadcasting and production, miking speakers usually involves one speaker, such as a disc-jockey, announcer, newscaster, or voice-over performer, two principles as in an interview, or more than two speakers as with a panel program.

Single Speaker: Radio and Television

A microphone positioned for a seated or standing performer in radio is usually mounted on a flexible swivel stand suspended in front of the performer, or sometimes on a table stand (see Figure 7-4). In television, most often a mini-mic is attached to the performer's clothing.

With swivel stand and desk stand mics, it is important to keep excessive sound that is reflected from room surfaces, furniture, and equipment from reaching the mic. This can result in comb filtering, creating a hollow sound quality.

a   b

Figure 7-4 Typical microphone positions for a seated or standing performer in radio. (a) Microphone mounted on a flexible swivel stand. (b) Microphone mounted on a desk stand.

To minimize the sound reflections reaching the microphone, a performer should work at a relatively close mic-to-source distance and use a directional microphone. How directional depends on how much front-to-rear sound rejection is needed. Usually, however, cardioid is the pickup pattern of choice. It gives the performer some flexibility in side-to-side movement without going off-mic and produces the intimate sound essential to creating radio's lip-to-ear rapport with the listener. Keep in mind that with more directional mics, side-to-side movement becomes more restricted.

Because radio studios are acoustically quiet, there is little need for highly directional mics unless more than a few performers are using microphones in close proximity. One problem with using too directional a mic is the usually drier and more closed sound it produces.

It is difficult to suggest an optimal mic-to-source working distance because voice projection and timbre vary from person to person, but here are a few guidelines:

- Always stay within the mic's pickup pattern.

- Maintain voice level between 60 and 100 percent of modulation; some radio stations like it between 80 and 100 percent. With digital sound, level cannot exceed 0 dBFS or the audio will distort. Hence maximum level should ride below 0 dBFS to allow for headroom.

- Working too close to a mic may create oppressive and unnatural sound that is devoid of ambience.

- Working too close to a mic emphasizes tongue movement, lip smacking, and teeth clicks. It could also create proximity effect.

- Working too far from a mic diffuses the sound quality, creating spatial distance between the performer and the listener.

Sometimes a mic is positioned to the side of or under a performer's mouth, with the performer speaking across the mic face (see Figure 7-5). Usually, this is done to reduce the popping and sibilance that often occur when a performer talks directly into a mic.

Speaking across a directional microphone can reduce these unwanted sounds. Unless the mouth-to-mic angle is within the microphone's pickup pattern, however, talking across the mic degrades the response. To eliminate popping and reduce sibilance without overly degrading the response, use a windscreen, use a mic with a built-in pop filter, or point the mic at about a 45-degree angle above, below, or to the side of the performer's mouth, depending on the mic's pickup pattern (see Figure 7-6).

In positioning a mic, make sure its head is not parallel to or facing the tabletop. Remember that the angle of a sound's incidence is equal to its angle of reflectance in midrange and treble frequencies (see Figure 4-5). Therefore, sound waves bouncing from the table will reflect back into the mic's pickup pattern, creating the comb-filter effect. Any hard surface that is close to a mic, such as a table, console, computer monitor, or window, should be angled so that the sound waves do not reflect directly back into the mic (see Figures 7-7 and 7-8).

When changing the mic's angle presents a problem, if possible cover the hard surface with a soft material to absorb most of the unwanted reflections. This reduces popping and sibilance. It is also a good idea to mount the mic in a shock absorber if it does not have one built-in. This reduces or eliminates jarring and handling noises.

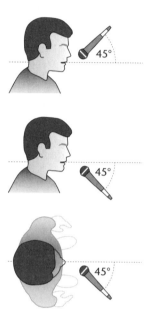

Figure 7-6 Speaking at a 45-degree angle into a directional mic.

Figure 7-5 Directional microphone positioned so that the performer speaks across the mic face. This placement reduces popping and sibilance, but the directional pattern should be wide-angle cardioid, cardioid, or supercardioid so that frequency response is not adversely affected.

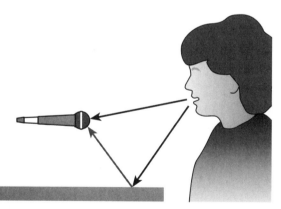

Figure 7-7 Incorrect placement of microphone. Indirect sound waves reflecting back into a mic cause phase cancellations that degrade the response. To avoid this a microphone should not be placed parallel to or more than a few inches from a reflective surface.

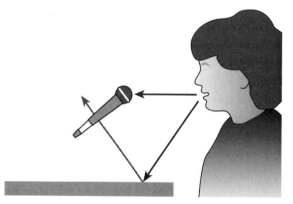

Figure 7-8 Correct placement of microphone. Placing a microphone at an angle to a reflective surface prevents indirect sound from bouncing back into the mic.

Mini-Mic

In television, the advantages of the mini-mic are several:

- It is unobtrusive and tends to disappear on-camera.

- It is easy to mount.

- It is easily adaptable to use with a wireless system, which is how it is mostly employed.

- It keeps the mic-to-source distance constant.

- It reduces the need for frequent loudness adjustments once the levels have been set.

- It requires no special lighting or additional audio operator, as does a boom mic.

- It enables participants to be placed comfortably on a set without concern for maintaining levels and mic-to-source distances, or having them handling the mic, as could happen with desk mics.

- It facilitates using a wireless microphone system, which eliminates cords and cord connections thereby simplifying setups, avoiding entanglements, and eliminating noise from the mic cord rubbing against a participant or surface.

The mini-mic's main disadvantage is that it's a single-purpose microphone. It rarely sounds good used away from the body.

Radio Interview and Panel Setups

When there is more than one speaker, as in interview and panel programs, in radio it is customary to mike each participant with a separate microphone for better sonic control. Directional mics, usually cardioid or supercardioid, are preferred. If the participants are sitting opposite one another, the cardioid is sufficient because it is least sensitive at 180 degrees off-axis. If the participants are sitting side-by-side, facing the host, the supercardioid could be a better choice. Its on-axis response allows sufficient side-to-side head movement, and it is less sensitive at the sides than the cardioid. The hypercardioid mic would also work in the latter situation, but there are the potential problems of restricted head movement due to its quite narrow on-axis pickup and of reduced sound quality because of its poorer rejection at 180 degrees. In any case, microphones are commonly fixed to flexible mic mounts to free frontal working space and to make minor positioning adjustments easier (see Figure 7-9).

When multiple microphones are used, they must have the same directional pattern. Mics with different polar patterns, say, a cardioid mic used with a supercardioid mic, will have perceptible sonic differences. With the cardioid and supercardioid mics, for example, the cardioid will produce a more open sound than the supercardioid; or, to put it another way, the supercardioid will sound tighter than the cardioid.

In choosing a microphone for a guest(s), consider that the person may be unfamiliar with mic technique, be nervous, or speak more softly or loudly than usual. Choosing an end-fed, instead of a side-fed, mic makes it easier for the guest to focus the direction toward

Figure 7-9 Radio talk/interview studio.

which to speak. Also, an end-fed mic is usually smaller than a side-fed mic and therefore less intimidating. (See an example of a side-fed mic in Figure 6-38 top left, and an
end-fed mic, top right.)

The mini-mic is another option. The speaker cannot be off-mic and tends to forget it is
there. The potential problem here is that most mini-mics are omnidirectional and, even
in suitable acoustics, the sound may be too open and airy. Directional lavalieres, on the
other hand, may create a sound that is too dry.

Sometimes headset mics are used. A headset mic facilitates the feeding and the balancing of all program information to each participant, reduces problems of mic placement,
allows host and guests more freedom of head movement, and clears desk space for scripts
and note taking. Because it is radio, appearance is of no concern unless the radio program is televised (simulcast), which is done with some programs on a regular basis. Then
some attention to appearance does become a factor. Whether televised or not, the participants must be comfortably and sensibly arranged for optimal interaction.

Television Panel and Talk Programs

Television panel and talk programs in which the participants are seated invariably use
the wireless mini-mic. The positive attributes of the mini-mic have already been articu-
lated. In some situations, however, other microphone mounts are more appropriate.

For a host moving about a set among guests or going into the audience for questions, the
handheld mic is the popular choice. In situations where the studio is very large and the
audience is seated amphitheater-style, except for overall coverage mics of the audience
sound, handheld mics are the only choice for host, guests, and audience participants.

Hand Mic

The handheld microphone has these advantages:

- It allows the host to control the audience questioning.

- It allows the host to control mic-to-source distances.

- Like the desk mic, it helps the host generate a closer psychological rapport with the television audience. In interview and variety programs, the host sometimes sits behind a mic mounted on a desk stand. Usually the mic is not live. It is being used as a set piece to create a closer psychological rapport between the host and the television audience, to fill the open table space in front of the host, or both. Otherwise, with a few exceptions, desk mics are seldom used. If you do use a live desk mic, select one that is good-looking so it does not call attention to itself; use one with a built-in shock mount to isolate the mic from desk noises; and make sure the mic-to-source angle is on-axis.

The handheld mic should have a built-in pop filter to minimize sibilance and popping and an internal shock mount to eliminate handling noise. Optimal position is 6 to 12 inches from the mouth, pointing upward at about a 45-degree angle (see Figure 7-10).

A disadvantage of the handheld mic is that it ties up one of the host's hands. This is not a problem with the boom mic, and for some situations, it is the mic of choice (see "Boom Mic" later in this chapter).

Hand Mic in the Field

The omnidirectional, moving-coil, handheld microphone is used most often in stand-up news reports from the field. It picks up enough background sound to provide a sense of environment in normal conditions without overwhelming the reporter's sound. It is possible to control the balance of background-to-reporter sound by moving the mic closer to or farther from the speaker (see Figure 7-11). The closer the mic-to-source distance, the greater the reduction in background sound.

What comes into play here is the *inverse square law*: Outdoors, when mic-to-source distance is doubled, the sound-pressure level drops approximately 6 dB, thus reducing loudness to one-fourth. Conversely, cutting the mic-to-source distance in half increases loudness approximately 6 dB (see Figure 7-12). The precise effect of this law depends on the openness of the area and the directionality of the microphone.

Another advantage of the omni mic is that it can be held comfortably below the mouth and in a relatively unobtrusive position on-camera. For interviews, the mic can be situated between reporter and interviewee without necessarily having to move it back and forth for questions and answers (see Figure 7-13).

In noisy environments, an omnidirectional microphone may not discriminate enough against unwanted sound even at a close mic-to-source distance. In such a situation, a directional mic may be suitable. The sound balance between reporter and background can still be maintained by moving the mic closer to or farther from the reporter's mouth.

Figure 7-10 Handheld microphone positioning. Ideally, a handheld mic should be positioned 6 to 12 inches from the user's mouth at an angle of 45 degrees or less. Positioning the mic at an angle of about 90 degrees may result in popping sounds when consonants like *p* and *t* are pronounced.

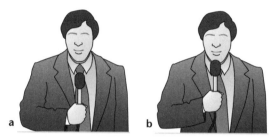

Figure 7-11 Reducing background sound. (a) Holding an omnidirectional microphone at chest level usually creates an optimal mic-to-source distance. (b) If background noise is high, its level can be reduced by decreasing the mic-to-source distance.

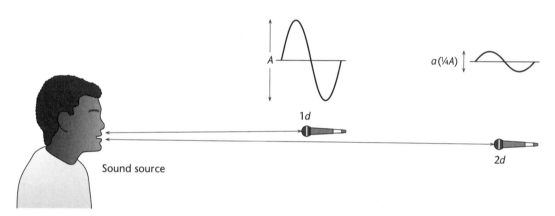

Figure 7-12 Inverse square law. As the distance (d) from a sound source doubles, loudness (A) decreases in proportion to the square of that distance.

Figure 7-13 Using an omnidirectional microphone for on-location interviews. It can be positioned between the principals, usually with little need for repositioning, at least in quiet surroundings.

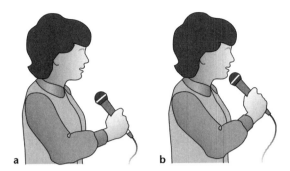

Figure 7-14 Miking when on-location background noise is too loud. Use a directional microphone either (a) several inches from the mouth or (b) close to it, depending on the performer's voice projection. Because the mic is directional, it must be held at the proper angle if the performer is to be on-mic. With cardioids and supercardioids, the angle does not have to be as severe as it would with a hypercardioid mic because of their wider on-axis response compared with the quite narrow on-axis response of the hypercardioid mic.

But remember that directional mics must be held at an appropriate angle to be on-axis to the mouth (see Figure 7-14). Moreover, during interviews, the mic must be moved back and forth between interviewer and interviewee if the sound is to be on-mic. In television, the microphone should not obstruct the mouth.

To provide a stereo feel to the stand-up report, use a middle-side (M-S) microphone. Recall that the M-S mic combines a cardioid and a bidirectional pickup in a single casing (see Figure 6-26). By speaking into the front of the mic, the reporter's audio is monaural and on-mic; the bidirectional sides pick up the ambience, providing expanded sonic imaging to the on-scene story. This technique assumes that the environmental sound is not loud enough to overwhelm the reporter's narrative and that time permits setting up the M-S mic. If, after recording circumstances do not facilitate reproducing the stereo M-S image, the middle, or mono, signal can be separated from the side pickup with no loss in sound and no problem with monaural compatibility.

Boom Mic

When guests are coming and going during the course of a show, for example, the boom mic is often used once they are seated. It is less awkward than having a guest put on and take off a mini-mic on-camera or having a guest hold a mic. Usually, no more than a few guests are seated on the set at any one time, which allows one boom to cover the group adequately. In this type of situation, the host generally uses a live desk mic for several reasons: to set the host apart from the guests; to enhance, psychologically, the rapport with the television audience; and to avoid the lighting and logistical problems that result from having two booms on a set in close proximity.

Whenever one boom covers two or more people in conversation, the boom operator has to make sure that none of the program's content is inaudible or off-mic. A good boom operator must therefore quickly learn the speech rhythms and inflections of the people talking, listen to their conversations, anticipate the nonverbal vocal cues that signal a change in speaker, and, when the change occurs, move the mic from one speaker to another quickly and silently.

Here are a few guidelines to using the boom:

■ Position the boom above and angled in front of the performer's mouth. Remember: Sound comes from the mouth, not from the top of the head.

- Establish mic-to-source operating distance by having the performer raise an arm at a 45-degree angle toward the tip of the mic and extend a finger; the finger should just touch the mic. Appropriate working distances can be planned from there. For example, if the mic-to-source distance in a close-up is 3 feet, in a medium shot it could be about 6 feet, and in a long shot up to 9 feet.

- Directional shotgun microphones compress distance between background and foreground. Aim the mic directly at the performer(s) so as not to increase background sound.

- Hypercardioid shotgun mics have considerable rear sensitivity, so avoid pointing the back end toward a source of unwanted noise, such as ventilators, parabolic lights, and so on.

- Capacitor shotguns are high-output, high-sensitivity instruments and therefore can be used at somewhat longer mic-to-source distances than moving-coil mics without degrading sound quality. Also, high-frequency response in moving-coil mics falls off with increased mic-to-source distance.

- To facilitate learning the shot changes in a multicamera production with drama, provide each boom operator with cue sheets and, if possible, place a TV monitor on the boom (assuming a perambulator boom) or near it. Also provide headphones that feed the program sound to one ear and the director's cues to the other ear. Boom movers should also have access to cue sheets. Rehearse each shot so that the exact mic-to-source distances are established.

- Rehearse all boom operations. Even the slightest movements such as bending down or turning the head while talking can require complicated boom maneuvers. For example, as a head turns while talking, the boom has to be panned and the mic rotated at the same time.

- If a performer has a tendency to do "head whips" while interacting with other guests or because dialogue interaction calls for it, place the mic in front, keeping movement to a minimum so the speech sound and ambience are consistent.

- Have preparatory discussions with the sound recordist or mixer.

- Learn about lighting. A boom operator has to know what side of a set to work from so that the boom does not throw a shadow. Outside it is necessary to be opposite the sun side so that the boom shadow falls away from the performer.

- Anticipate the performer's movements so that the boom leads, rather than follows, the talent.

- Position the boom's base toward the front of the set, not to the side. From the side, it is difficult to judge the microphone's height in relation to the cameras because cameras are usually placed in an arc around the front of the set.

- Indoors or outdoors, it is wise to use a windscreen, especially with a capacitor shotgun because it is particularly susceptible to wind noise. A windscreen permits rapid, abrupt boom movements without distortion from the increased force of air created by such movements.

Due to the size of the perambulator boom, it may be unwieldy in small studios or sets or difficult to maneuver when relatively frequent repositioning is called for, especially if there is no boom mover.

Fishpole Boom

The *fishpole boom* is used in-studio when larger booms cannot negotiate small spaces, but mostly it is the microphone mount of choice in field production in general and dialogue recording in particular. It is more mobile, easier to manage, takes up less space, and requires fewer crew than wheeled booms. A fishpole is handheld and therefore can be moved around a set with relative ease (see Figure 7-15).

Fishpole booms come in various lengths, and most have a telescoping tube that can be extended or retracted (see Figure 7-16). Shorter fishpoles can extend from 16 inches to more than 6 feet and weigh as little as 11 ounces; medium-sized fishpoles can extend from 23 inches to 8 feet and weigh about 14 ounces; longer fishpoles can extend from just under 3 feet to more than 16 feet and weigh a little more than a pound.

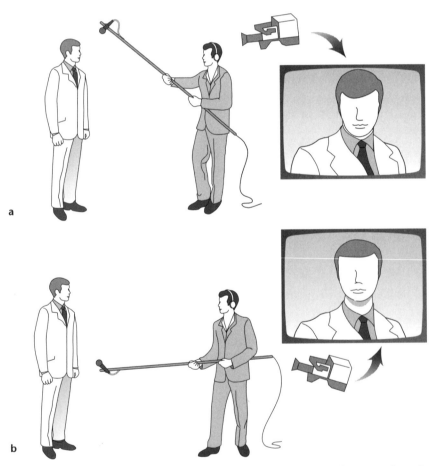

Figure 7-15 Using a fishpole with a directional microphone pointed at the performer's mouth from (a) above and (b) below. The mic's position depends on the focal length and the angle of the shot. Better sound is usually obtained by positioning the mic above the performer because sound rises and the bounce from the floor or ground can brighten the pickup.

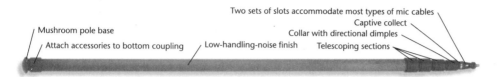

Mushroom pole base
Attach accessories to bottom coupling
Low-handling-noise finish
Two sets of slots accommodate most types of mic cables
Captive collect
Collar with directional dimples
Telescoping sections

Figure 7-16 Fishpole boom and its features.

The fishpole boom does present a few problems. It can get heavy if it has to be carried about the set or held for any length of time, particularly if the mic is weighty. It can be difficult to control precisely, particularly in wider shots when it has to be held high. Furthermore, handling noises can be heard if the fishpole operator is not careful.

- It is politic to remember that in field production, the boom operator is the sound department's eyes and ears on the set.

- Operating a fishpole boom is intense and exhausting work. Be well rested and physically conditioned. Build endurance by holding a fishpole for progressively longer periods of time. If one is not available, practice with a bucket or weights at the end of a broom handle.

- Wear clothing that is comfortable and relatively loose fitting. Dark clothes help avoid reflections. Because fishpole miking often involves being on your feet for extended periods of time, plus a lot of walking and running, forward and backward, sneakers with thick soles are comfortable and quiet.

- Know the script. If one is not available or if last-minute copy changes have been made, learn the body gestures of the performers just before they speak to help anticipate boom movements.

- Always use a windscreen, especially with directional capacitor mics, which are particularly sensitive to even minute air movement.

- Always use a shock mount. High-quality microphones, particularly capacitors with high sensitivity, are apt to pick up sound conductance through the metal tube. It is a good idea to tape foam rubber around the tube a few inches above the handgrip and below the microphone mount to inhibit sound conductance.

- Use high-quality headphones when operating a fishpole boom. Except for the recordist, who may be at some distance, there is no other way to tell what sounds are being picked up or how they are balanced, particularly in relation to the foreground and background sounds.

- Be sure there is enough cable and cleared space on the floor if the fishpole mic must move with the performer(s). To avoid the cable problem altogether, and if it is feasible, boom-mount a wireless mic (see Figure 7-17).

- Remove all jewelry before recording and wear gloves to help dampen handling noise.

- If the fishpole has to be held for any length of time, secure a flag holder around the waist and sit the pole end in its pocket. Some longer fishpoles come with a handle grip on the pole to help support it against the body.

Figure 7-17 Wireless boom mic with mounted transmitter.

The advantage of the boom-mounted microphone on location, as in the studio, is that by varying its distance to the sound source, you can make it reflect the focal length of shots. This advantage applies especially in the field, where there is more likely to be background sound whose relationship to the principal sound source often helps establish the overall sonic environment. This technique is called *perspective miking* because it establishes the audio viewpoint. It is the boom mic's main sonic advantage. Unlike the body-mounted mini-mic whose main sonic disadvantage is that it cannot reflect shot-to-source distances because its perspective is always the same.

Miking Music: Basic Approaches

There are four basic ways to record musical instruments: close miking, distant miking, accent, or off-, miking, and ambient miking. Depending on the music, size of the ensemble, room acoustics, mixer, and software program one or more of these techniques may be employed in a given session.

Close Miking

Close miking places a microphone relatively close to each sound source or group of sound sources in an ensemble—generally at a distance of about an inch to a foot. Close miking is the technique of choice in studio recording for most popular music genres for a number of reasons: Greater control can be achieved in recording the nuances of each musical element; the sound from each instrument, and leakage from other instruments, is better contained; in popular music the difference in loudness between electric and acoustic instruments can be very difficult to balance with distant miking; and much of pop music is played loudly, and in even relatively live acoustics close miking helps prevent the music from being awash in reverberation. Reverberation, spatial positioning, and blend are added in the postproduction *mixdown*.

Generally, directional microphones are used in close miking for better sound control of each instrument and to reduce leakage of one instrument into another instrument's microphone. If acoustics and recording logistics permit, however, there are three good reasons why omnidirectional mics should not be overlooked: (1) the better omni capacitors have an extraordinarily wide, flat response, particularly in the lower frequencies, and little or no off-axis coloration; (2) omnis are not as subject to proximity effect, sibilance, plosives, and breathing sounds as are directional mics; and (3) because of the inverse square law, it is possible to close-mike with an omni and still reduce leakage if the instrument's sound-pressure level is high enough.

Distant Miking

Distant miking places a microphone(s) from about 3 feet to several feet from the sound source. It picks up a fuller range and balance of an instrument, or group of instruments, and captures more of the studio acoustics for a more open and blended sound.

Distant miking is employed when all sounds or voicings, or groups of sounds or voicings, are recorded at the same time and it is important to preserve the ensemble sound, or a sonic sense of it. Orchestral and choral music and certain types of jazz are examples of genres that use distant miking. The technique is also used along with close-miking to enhance a recording by adding natural acoustics.

Accent Miking

Accent miking, also known as *off-miking*, is used to pick up instruments in an ensemble when they solo. It is, in effect, a relatively close-miking technique but used when distant microphones are picking up the ensemble's overall sound and a solo passage needs to stand out.

Ambience Miking

Ambience miking, used along with distant miking, attempts to reproduce the aural experience that audiences receive in a live venue by recording in an acoustically suitable studio or concert hall. Microphones are positioned far enough from the ensemble where the later reflections are more prominent than the direct sound (see Figure 7-18). In the mixdown, the ambient pick up is blended with the pick up from the closer mics, making the natural reverb part of the recording, and not adding it artificially in the mixdown, which may be necessary with distant miking and is definitely necessary with close miking.

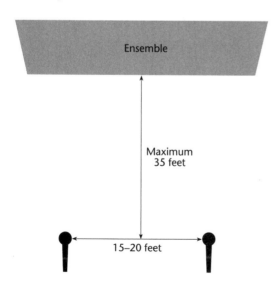

Figure 7-18 Ambience miking. Spaced omnidirectional microphones situated toward the rear of the room. The success of this technique is dependent on a studio or hall with appropriate acoustics. In rooms of some size, to minimize echoes that could result from mixing the direct signal with the signal from the acoustically delayed ambient mics, the distance between the ensemble and the ambient mics should not exceed 35 feet. The distance between the spaced mics should be limited to 15 to 20 feet to minimize comb filtering.

Miking Music: Stereo Arrays

As previously noted, the purpose of distant miking, especially when mixed with sound from close mics, is to add airier, more ambient sound to the overall recording. The microphone arrays used are often stereo arrays. They are mainly coincident, near-coincident, and spaced.

Coincident Miking

Coincident miking, also called *X-Y miking*, employs two matched, directional microphones mounted on a vertical axis—with one mic diaphragm directly over the other—and angled apart to aim approximately toward the left and right sides of the sound source. The degree of angle, the mics' pickup pattern, and the distance from the sound source depend on the width of the stereo image you want to record (see Figure 7-19).

Miking at a distance from the sound source, particularly with classical music, requires high-output, high-sensitivity microphones. Capacitors are the only type of mic that meets this requirement.

Middle-side (*M-S*) miking is another coincident technique (see Figure 6-26). Recall that a MS microphone is housed in a single casing combining a cardioid mic, the mid, with a side-facing bidirectional mic. The middle mic faces the sound source and, depending on the mic-to-source distance, picks up more direct than indirect sound; the null of the bidirectional mic faces the sound source; therefore, it picks up mostly indirect sound from the left and right of the sound source. By increasing the level of the mid, the stereo image narrows; increasing the level of the side widens the stereo image.

Near-Coincident Miking

Near-coincident miking angles two directional microphones, spaced horizontally a few inches apart (see Figure 7-20). It is also referred to as *X-Y miking*. The few inches' difference between the near-coincident and the coincident arrays adds a sense of warmth, depth, and air to sound compared with the coincident array. The mics are close enough

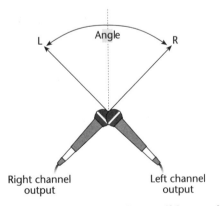

Figure 7-19 Coincident miking technique.

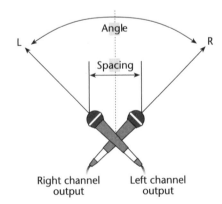

Figure 7-20 Near-coincident miking technique.

to retain intensity differences between channels at low frequencies yet far enough apart to have sufficient time delay between channels for localization at high frequencies. The stereo spread can be increased or decreased with the angle or space between the mics. The time delay between channels creates a problem, however: The greater the delay, the less the chance of stereo-to-mono compatibility.

Spaced Miking

Spaced miking employs two matched microphones at least three to several feet apart, perpendicular to the sound source and symmetrical to each other along a centerline (see Figure 7-21). They reproduce a lusher, more spacious sound than any of the near-coincident arrays—but at a cost. Stereo imaging is more diffused and therefore less detailed. And because so much of the sound reaching the mics derives its directional information from time differences (in addition to intensity differences), stereo-to-mono compatibility is unreliable.

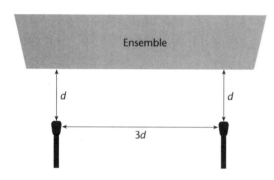

Figure 7-21 Spaced miking technique. This technique positions the mics at a distance (d) of 3 feet or more. It allows the full range and balance of an instrument or ensemble and captures the room sound as well. If the spaced mics are relatively close to the source, to prevent phase anomalies remember the three-to-one rule: The mics should be placed at least three times as far apart as the distance between the sound source and microphone.

If studio acoustics and the music permit, spaced omnidirectional mics are preferred to directional mics because they have less off-axis coloration and flatter overall response, especially in the low frequencies. Capacitors are almost always used. Spacing is determined by the desired width of the stereo image. With omnis, of course, spacing has to be wide enough to reproduce a stereo image. If it is too wide, however, separation may be exaggerated; if spacing is too narrow, the stereo image may lack breadth.

Spaced cardioid mics are arrayed similarly to spaced omnis, but their directionality produces a different sonic outcome. Used with an ensemble, spaced cardioids tend to emphasize the voicings that are most on-axis. They also show the effects of coloration, particularly from any studio ambience. Placement is critical to producing acceptable results with any spaced miking but is even more so with cardioids than with omnis. Spaced cardioids do provide a better chance for mono compatibility, however, because each mic is picking up less common information, reducing the chance of phase cancellations.

Other Types of Stereo Microphone Arrays

There are several variations of the three basic stereo microphone arrays. Figures 7-22 to 7-25 display four of the more commonly employed.

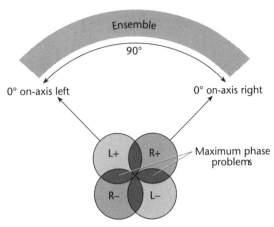

Figure 7-22 Blumlein miking technique. This technique uses two coincident bidirectional mics positioned at a 90-degree angle. It is designed to reproduce accurate representation of the original stereo sound stage, a sense of the ambience surrounding the primary sound source, and the room's reverberance.

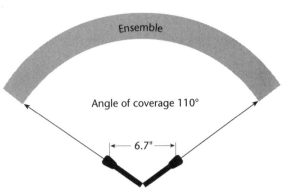

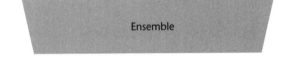

Figure 7-23 ORTF microphone array. The **ORTF array** (named for the Office de Radiodiffusion-Television Française, the French broadcasting system) mounts two cardioid microphones on a single stand spaced just under 7 inches apart at a 110-degree angle, 55 degrees to the left and the right of center. This technique is designed to produce a clean, clear, often bright sound with a sense of openness while still maintaining mono compatibility.

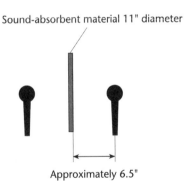

Figure 7-24 Jecklin disk. Also known as the **optimal stereo signal (OSS)**, this technique separates two omnidirectional mics with a sound-absorbing disk or baffle. It is designed to produce a big, spacious sound with good low-frequency response. Localization is adequate but not precise.

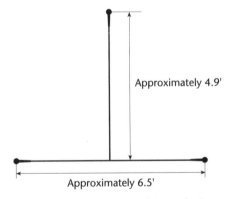

Figure 7-25 Decca Tree. This technique mounts three spaced omni mics at the ends of a T-shaped frame. It is designed to reproduce good stereo imaging with an open, spacious sound. It is favored in recording film scores because it produces a pleasing and stable stereo image that holds up throughout the application of Dolby and other surround-sound matrix systems

Miking Selected Instruments

As noted earlier in this discussion of miking music, close miking is the technique of choice in studio recording for most popular music genres. Among the commonly recorded voicings in those genres are drums, acoustic guitar, electric bass and electric guitar, piano, and vocal. The following sections are designed to provide an idea of typical approaches to close-miking these selected instruments.

Drums[1]

Perhaps no other instrument provides as many possibilities for microphone combinations, and therefore presents as much of a challenge, as the drums. Several different components make up a drum set—at least a bass drum, a floor (low-pitched) tom-tom, medium- and high-pitched tom-toms, a snare drum, a hi-hat cymbal, and two overhead cymbals.

Although the drum kit consists of several different-sounding instruments, it must be miked so that they sound good individually, yet blend as a unit. That said, drums are miked in many ways. The approach to take depends on the desired sound control and the type of music recorded.

Explaining how to deal with sound control is relatively easy: The more components to regulate, the more mics you use (although this can have its drawbacks—possible phasing, for one). Achieving a particular drum sound for a certain type of music involves many variables and is more difficult to explain.

Generally, in rock-and-roll and contemporary pop music, producers like a tight drum sound for added punch and attack. Because this usually requires complete control of the drum sound, they tend to use several microphones for the drums. In jazz, many styles are loose and open, so producers are more likely to use fewer drum mics to achieve an airier sound. Figures 7-26 to 7-28 illustrate three basic approaches to miking the drum kit.

Bass (Kick) Drum

The bass (kick) drum is the foundation of the drum set because it provides the music's downbeat—the primary rhythm pattern with transient punctuations. In much of popular music, it also works along with the bass guitar providing the bottom sound that supports the other musical elements. Because the bass drum also produces high levels of sound pressure and steep transients, large-diaphragm moving-coil microphones usually

---

1. As noted earlier, there are almost as many approaches to miking instruments as there are recordists. This section and the following sections on miking instruments are intended to show some of the basic techniques. Decisions about microphone preference and positioning are personal. Therefore, drawings rather than pictures, are used to avoid showing a specific mic placed in a particular way on an instrument, thereby implicitly suggesting a preference or recommendation. As for the myriad other approaches to microphone selection and placement, the Internet and magazines such as *Mix*, *Electronic Musician*, *EQ*, *Sound on Sound*, and *Recording* abound with examples.

Figure 7-26 Three microphones. Two cardioid capacitor microphones overhead and one directional or nondirectional moving coil in the bass drum. Using two overhead mics helps with the blend and balance and provides a stereo image. The coincident, near-coincident, and spaced arrangements will yield different acoustic results (see "Stereo Arrays" discussed earlier in this chapter). The mic in the bass drum allows separate control of its sound. The directional mic concentrates its impact; the nondirectional mic opens the sound somewhat without picking up much if any of the other drum sounds due to the inverse square law—sound levels increase (or decrease) in inverse proportion to the square of this distance, in this case, from the mic to the drum head. This arrangement produces on open, airy drum sound. Using high-quality microphones is essential, however.

Figure 7-27 Five microphones. Three mics are placed as suggested in Figure 7-26. The fourth is typically placed on the snare drum but sometimes between the snare and hi-hat to obtain a better hi-hat pickup. It can be a moving-coil or capacitor mic depending on the desired sound, and almost always a directional mic (see "Snare Drum" and "Hi-Hat Cymbal" later in this section on "Miking"). The overhead mics, however, may pick up enough of the snare sound so that the sound from the fourth mic can be used only for fill in the mix. The fifth mic is positioned between the medium and high tom-toms for added control of these drums.

Figure 7-28 Miking each drum. For the drum kit in this illustration, eight microphones are required. The advantages of this technique are that it provides the recordist with optimal control of each drum and cymbal sound in the recording and in the mixdown. The disadvantages are that there may be phasing, leakage, or too dense a sound, or some combination of these factors.

work best, although there are a few large-diaphragm capacitor mics that also work well, particularly by adding some midrange coloration.

The common technique for mic placement is to use the hole often cut in the front drumhead or to remove the head entirely and place the mic inside. This gives the sound of the bass drum more punch. Pointing the mic perpendicular to the beater head produces a fuller sound (see Figure 7-29). If the mic is too close to the head, it will pick up more click and attack than fullness and maybe the action of the beater head as well. Pointing it to the side of the drum picks up more of the drum's overtones, creating a rounder sound with more definition but less attack (see Figure 7-30). Placing the mic outside the open head deepens the drum sound but decreases clarity and attack and could pick up leakage from other instruments.

Figure 7-29 A directional microphone pointed at the drumhead produces a fuller sound. Foam rubber padding is placed in the drum to reduce vibrations.

Figure 7-30 A microphone pointed to the side of the drum head produces more of the drum's overtones.

Tom-Toms

Tom-toms come in a variety of sizes and pitches. Typical drum sets have three toms: the low-pitched, fuller-sounding floor tom; the middle-pitched medium tom; and the higher-pitched, sharper-sounding high tom.

Although toms produce loud transients (all drums do), they are not as strong as those the bass drum produces; you can therefore mike them with moving-coil, capacitor, or the more rugged ribbon mics. Placement, as always, depends on the sound you want. Generally, the mic is placed from 1 to 10 inches above the tom and is aimed at the center, or slightly off-center, of the skin. It is usually mounted just over the edge of the rim to avoid interfering with the drummer's sticks (see Figures 7-31 and 7-32).

Figure 7-31 Miking a floor tom.

Figure 7-32 Miking a medium tom (left) and a high tom (right).

Snare Drum

Of all the components in a drum set, the snare usually presents the biggest problem in miking. Most producers prefer a crisp snare drum sound. Miking the snare too closely tends to produce a lifeless sound, whereas miking it too far away tends to pick up annoying overtones, ringing, and leakage from the other drums.

Moving-coil or capacitor mics work well on the snare drum; the moving-coil mic tends to give it a harder edge, and the capacitor mic tends to make it sound richer or crisper. To find the optimal mic position, begin at a point 6 to 10 inches from the drumhead and aim the mic so that its pickup pattern is split between the center and top edge of the drum (see Figure 7-33). This picks up the sounds of the snares and the stick hitting the head.

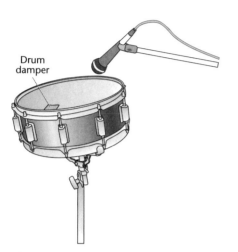

Drum damper

Figure 7-33 Miking a snare drum. The pad on the skin of the drum reduces vibrations.

Figure 7-34 Miking a hi-hat cymbal and a snare drum.

Hi-Hat Cymbal

The hi-hat cymbal produces two sounds: a clap and a shimmer. Depending on how important these accents are to the music, the hi-hat can either share the snare drum's mic or have a mic of its own. If it shares, place the mic between the hi-hat and the snare and adjust the sound balance through mic placement (see Figure 7-34).

If the hi-hat has a separate mic, the two most common positions for it are 4 to 6 inches above the center stem with the mic pointing straight down (see Figure 7-35), and off the edge (see Figure 7-36). Sound is brightest over the edge of the cymbal. Miking too closely off the center produces ringing, and miking off the edge may pick up the rush of air produced each time the two cymbals clap together (see Figure 7-37).

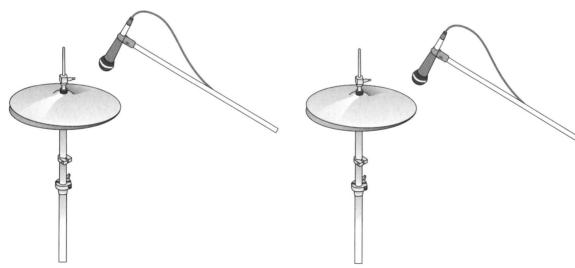

Figure 7-35 Miking over a hi-hat cymbal.

Figure 7-36 Miking at the edge of a hi-hat cymbal.

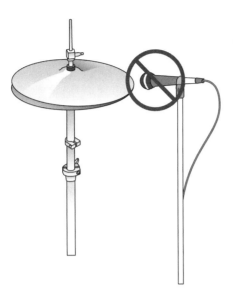

Figure 7-37 A mic aimed at the point where the cymbals clap may pick up the rush of air as they come together.

Overhead Cymbals

To preserve definition, capacitors work best; for stereo pickup, the coincident (see Figure 7-19), near-coincident (see Figure 7-20), or spaced pair can be used (see Figure 7-21). When using the spaced pair, remember to observe the three-to-one rule to avoid phasing problems.

Because the overhead microphones usually blend the sounds of the entire drum set, they must be at least a few feet above the cymbals. If they are too close to the cymbals, the drum blend will be poor and the mics will pick up annoying overtones that sound like ringing or gonging, depending on the narrowness of the mic's pickup pattern. If blending the drum sound is left until the mixdown and it is important to isolate the cymbals, roll off the low frequencies reaching the cymbal microphones from the other drums.

Sometimes, regardless of the miking technique, the sound of the overhead cymbals is disproportionately loud and washes over the drum track. There are two ways to reduce the problem: Have the drummer hit the cymbals with less force and, if the cymbals are thick, use thinner cymbals, which are not so loud.

Acoustic Guitar

Most of the acoustic guitar's sound radiates from the front of the instrument, so centering a microphone off the middle of the sound hole should, theoretically, provide a balanced sound. But the mic has to be at least a foot or more from the instrument to pick up the blend of radiated sound. If a mic is too close to the hole, sound is bassy or boomy. Also, because the sound hole resonates at a low frequency, the mic could pick up those vibrations. If it is moved closer to the bridge, detail is lost. If it is moved closer to the neck, presence is reduced; if it is moved too far away, intimacy is affected and, if other instruments are playing, there could be leakage.

One way to achieve a natural, balanced sound is to position the mic 2 to 3 feet from the sound hole. To set a more high- or low-frequency accent, angle the mic either down

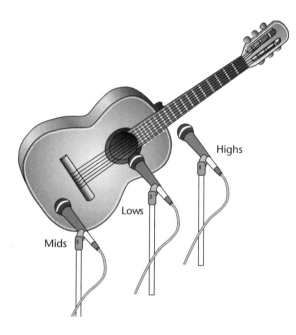

Figure 7-38 The tonal effects of microphone positioning on an acoustic guitar.

Highs

Lows

Mids

toward the high strings or up toward the low strings. Figure 7-38 illustrates general tonal effects of microphone positioning.

Sometimes, two microphones are used on an acoustic guitar to add body or dimension to the sound. Common placements include close-to-far, sound hole/neck, and stereo. In the close-to-far technique, the close mic picks up the essential guitar sound, and the far mic is used to pick up ambience (see Figure 7-39). Placing one mic off the sound hole and another off the neck captures a more detailed low- and high-frequency sound blend (see Figure 7-40). Stereo miking adds size to the guitar sound; be careful, however, not to space the mics too far apart or it will create a hole in the middle of the sound (see Figure 7-41). Stereo imaging can also be achieved using middle-side miking, either with an MS mic or two mics, one cardioid and one bidirectional (see Figure 7-42).

Figure 7-39 Close-to-far miking technique on an acoustic guitar.

Figure 7-40 Sound hole/neck miking technique on an acoustic guitar.

Figure 7-41 Stereo miking technique on an acoustic guitar.

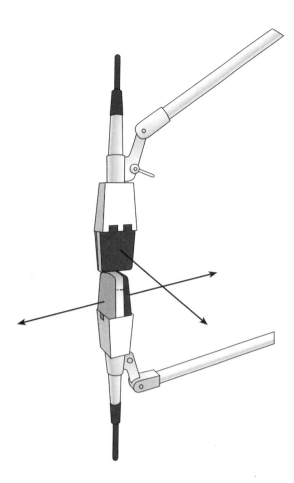

Figure 7-42 Middle-side miking using two multidirectional mics—one set for cardioid pickup and the other set for bidirectional pickup.

Plucking creates quick attacks. Using a dynamic mic, which has slower transient response than a capacitor microphone, can slow the attacks and diminish detail, particularly in the guitar's bass frequencies. But if a capacitor mic brings out too much crispness, a good moving-coil mic can reduce it.

Piano

The piano offers almost unlimited possibilities for sound shaping. More than with many other instruments, the character of the piano sound is dependent on the quality of the piano itself. Smaller grand pianos may have dull, wooden low-end response. Old or abused pianos may ring, thump, or sound dull. Mic technique and signal processing cannot change a piano's voicing from dull to bright, from thin to rich, or from sharp to smooth, but they can alter a piano's existing sound. That said, unless the piano is nicely voiced and well tuned, the most savvy recordist with the best equipment has little chance of producing acceptable sound.

Another factor in piano miking is the music. Classical music and jazz generally require a more open sound, so mic placement and pickup should capture the full sonic radiation of the instrument. Popular music, such as rock and country, usually require a tighter sound, so mic placement and pickup are generally closer.

Regardless of the music, aim the open lid toward the middle of the room, not toward the wall. If you aim the open lid toward the wall, in addition to picking up the piano sound, the mic(s) will also pick up the reflections bouncing back from the wall.

There are many miking techniques for the grand piano. Figures 7-43 to 7-45 display a few of the more common approaches.

Figure 7-43 Middle-side–miking a grand piano. An MS microphone about 12 to 18 inches above the middle strings, 8 inches horizontally from the hammers, produces a natural, balanced sound and a relatively spacious low-end to high-end stereo image (assuming appropriate acoustics). Best results are achieved with the piano lid off. Otherwise the lid should be at full stick. At full stick there will be a more concentrated sound with less ambience pickup.

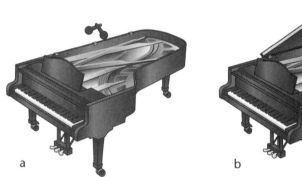

a   b

Figure 7-44 Near-coincident microphone array. (a) This illustration employs an X-Y pair of directional mics about 12 to 18 inches above the middle strings using the ORTF technique (see Figure 7-23). It spaces the array just under 7 inches apart at a 110-degree angle, 55 degrees to the left and the right of center. Stereo imaging is wide and, in good acoustics, spacious, with the mids spread somewhat wider across the aural frame than the low and high ends. Best results are achieved with the lid off. (b) When the piano lid remains attached, it should be at full stick. (At short stick the sound can be too closed and muddy.) Because the pickup usually will be more concentrated and less spacious, use a near-coincident or spaced pair of distant mics to pick up more of the blended radiations and ambience to add openness, regardless of whether close-miking is used over the sound board.

Boundary mic

Figure 7-45 Using boundary microphones. A number of techniques are possible using boundary microphones. Two of the more commonly used are (1) mounting one boundary mic on the piano lid to pick up a blended monaural sound (shown here), or (2) mounting two directional boundary mics on the piano lid, one toward the low strings and the other toward the high strings for a balanced, open stereo pickup.

Electric Instruments

Electric instruments—bass, guitar, and keyboards—generate their sounds through an electric pickup that can be sent to an amplifier or directly to the console. Three techniques are generally used to record an electric instrument: plugging the instrument into an amplifier and placing a mic in front of the amp's loudspeaker; *direct insertion (DI)*, or plugging the instrument directly into the mic input of the mixer through a direct box; or both miking the amp and using DI.

Electric instruments are usually high impedance, whereas professional-quality audio equipment is low impedance. Not surprisingly, high- and low-impedance equipment are incompatible and produce sonic horrors if connected. The direct box matches impedances, making the output of the instrument compatible with the mixer's input (see Figure 7-46).

Figure 7-46 Direct box. This unit converts unbalanced signals from guitar amps, stereo keyboards, CD and tape players, and computer sound cards. There are two sections; each includes an XLR connector, 1/4-inch parallel wired in/out jacks, ground lift switch to help eliminate hum and buzz, and a 20 dB pad switch for connection to inputs with overly loud signal levels.

Miking the Amplifier Loudspeaker

A single amplifier loudspeaker emits directional sound waves whose sonic characteristics change depending on the angle of the microphones and its distance from the amp. A mic on-axis at the center of the speaker tends to produce more bite compared to the mellower sound from a mic positioned off-axis to the center or at the edge of the speaker. An amp cabinet with bass and treble speakers produces a more complex output and usually requires a longer mic-to-source distance to capture a blended sound.

Placement of the cabinet also affects sound. On a carpet, brightness is reduced. On a hard-surfaced floor, depending on the amp, sharpness or brightness is increased. On a riser off the floor, low end is reduced.

When miking an amp loudspeaker, the moving-coil mic is most often used because it can handle loud levels without overloading. With the bass guitar, the directional moving coil is less susceptible to vibration and conductance (especially with a shock mount) caused when the instrument's long, powerful wavelengths are amplified. Due to its powerful low end, the bass is usually recorded direct to obtain a cleaner sound.

Recording Electric Bass

Recording electric bass presents a particular challenge. If there is too much bass, the mix will sound muddy. This could mask the fundamentals of other instruments and result in a thickening and a weighing down of the overall sound. Among the ways to improve clarity are to have the bassist increase treble and reduce bass on the guitar or to equalize in the control room by attenuating around 250 Hz and boosting around 1,500 Hz.

Compression is commonly used in recording the electric bass (see Chapters 11 and 13). It helps reduce noise, smooth variations in attack and loudness, and tighten the sound. Be careful in setting the compressor's release time. If it is too fast in relation to the decay rate of the bass, the sound will be organlike. A slower release time maintains the natural sound of the instrument; too slow a release time muddies the sound.

Recording Electric Guitar

When recording an electric guitar, a directional moving coil adds body to the sound. But if it is necessary to reproduce a subtler, warmer, more detailed sound, try a capacitor or one of the more rugged ribbon mics.

As for placement, the main challenge is understanding the dispersion pattern of the amplifier's loudspeakers (see Figure 7-47). Miking close to the amp and head-on produces a strong central lobe that has considerable high-frequency content within the bandwidth of the instrument itself. Off-axis miking reduces high-frequency content, and backing the mic farther from the amp produces a more blended, balanced sound. Also, the decrease in highs gives the impression of a heavier, bassier sound. Hanging a small mic over the amp emphasizes a guitar's midrange and reduces leakage. If leakage is not a problem, and even if it is, close miking with an omni works well.

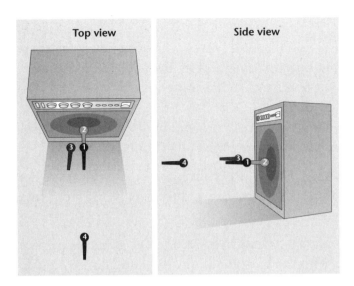

Figure 7-47 Miking an amplifier loudspeaker. (1) Four inches from the amp at the center of the speaker cone produces a natural, balanced sound. (2) One inch from the center of the speaker cone produces a bassy sound but minimizes feedback and leakage. (3) Off-center to the speaker cone produces either a dull or a mellow sound, depending on the acoustics and the microphone, but reduces amplifier noise. (4) Three feet from the center of the speaker cone produces a thinner sound with reduced bass but picks up more ambience and leakage.

An omnidirectional microphone has no proximity effect—its response is uniform. It will therefore pick up various aspects of the loudspeaker dispersion pattern, and the inverse square law takes care of the leakage problem because you are essentially force-feeding the mic from an amp producing a high sound-pressure level at a short mic-to-source distance. Use an omni capacitor or ribbon mic with a fast response.

Producers also record both amp loudspeaker and DI feeds simultaneously. This technique combines the drier, unreverberant but crisp sound of direct insertion with the acoustic coloring of the amplified sound. The amp and DI signals should be recorded on separate tracks. This provides more flexibility in the mixdown when the two sounds are combined or if you decide not to use one of the tracks.

It should be noted that direct recording of guitars does not necessarily guarantee a leakage-free track. If a guitar pickup is near or facing a loud instrument, it will "hear" the vibrations. By turning the musician away from the direct sound waves or by putting a baffle between the instruments, leakage is reduced.

With the electric guitar, special-effect boxes are often used to add to the sonic possibilities. Here too the various signals should be recorded on separate tracks, if possible, to allow flexibility in the mixdown.

Vocal

Although the speaking voice has a comparatively limited frequency range, the singing voice does not, and it can place a severe test on any microphone. The singing voice is capable of subtle and almost unlimited variations in pitch, timbre, and dynamic range. There are also plosives and sibilance—popping and hissing sounds—to deal with.

Timbre

In choosing a vocal mic, the most important consideration is the singer's timbre—how edged, velvety, sharp, mellow, or resonant the voice sounds. The microphone should enhance a voice's attractive qualities and minimize the unattractive. Usually, assuming no serious problems with tone quality, most producers prefer to use capacitor mics for vocals. They are far more sensitive to subtle changes in sound-pressure waves than dynamic mics; they can better handle the complicated pattern of harmonics and overtones in the human voice; and overall sound quality is the most natural.

Dynamic Range

Controlling the dynamic range—the quietest to loudest levels a sound source produces—is another tricky problem. Well-disciplined singers can usually control wide fluctuations in the dynamic range themselves. But many cannot—their voices barely move the peak meter during soft passages and put it in the red during loud ones. In miking these vocalists, a producer has three alternatives: ride the level, adjust the singer's mic position, or use compression. There is a fourth alternative: record the vocal on two tracks.

The preferred methods are to use mic technique to adjust for irregularities in a vocalist's dynamic range, use compression, or use both. In pop music, vocals are often compressed 10 to 13 dB. But to do so requires that a recordist know how to compensate after compression (see Chapters 11 and 13).

One placement method is to situate the vocalist at an average distance from the mic relative to the loudest and softest passages sung; the distance depends on the song, the power of the singer's voice, and the acoustics. From this average distance, you can direct the vocalist how closely to move toward the mic during quiet passages and how far for the loud ones. The success of this method depends on the singer's mic technique—the ability to manage the song and the movements at the same time.

If these approaches don't work, try recording the vocal on two tracks with one track 10 dB down. If there is overload or a problem with the noise floor, the undistorted or less noisy sections of each recording can be intercut during editing.

Breathing, Popping, and Sibilance

The closer to a microphone a performer stands, the greater the chance of picking up unwanted breathing sounds and plosives from *p*'s, *b*'s, *k*'s, and *t*'s and sibilance from *s*'s. If the singer's vocal projection or the type of music permits, increasing the mic-to-source distance significantly reduces these noises. Windscreens also help, but some tend to reduce the higher frequencies, although clearly some high-frequency loss is preferable to sibilance, plosives, or breathiness. If a windscreen is used, the stocking (fabric) windscreen works best (see Figure 6-35d). It is not as dense as most other windscreens and therefore does not inhibit most of the high frequencies from getting through to the mic.

Other ways to reduce popping and sibilance are to have the singer work slightly across mic but within the pickup pattern or to position the mic somewhat above the singer's mouth (see Figure 7-48). If this increases nasality, position the mic at an angle from slightly below the singer's mouth. If leakage is no problem, using an omnidirectional mic permits a closer working distance because it is less susceptible to popping, sibilance, and breathing sounds. The sound may be less intimate, however, because an omni mic picks up more indirect sound waves than a directional mic; but the closeness of the singer should overcome the larger amount of indirect sound picked up.

Figure 7-48 Eliminating unwanted vocal sounds. Positioning the microphone slightly above the performer's mouth is a typical miking technique used to cut down on unwanted popping, sibilance, and breathing sounds.

Although capacitors are almost always the microphone of choice for vocals, they do tend to emphasize sibilance because of the mid- to treble-range response of many models. In such cases, and when other techniques fail to eliminate sibilance, a first-rate moving coil mic, with built-in pop filter, or ribbon mic usually takes care of the problem.

Acoustics

Studios in which high-energy popular music is recorded usually have dry acoustics so the sound does not become awash in reverberation. This can be disconcerting to a singer who is used to hearing a natural acoustic environment as part of the overall vocal sound. To compensate, recordists feed a comfortable amount of reverb through the foldback system so the singer hears the vocal in a more familiar acoustic setting. If there is too much reverb coming through the headphones, however, it can wash out detail and throw off intonation and phrasing. If the reverb is too loud, a singer may tend to lay back in the performance; if it is too soft, a singer may over-project. For these reason, some recordists try to avoid putting any reverb in the foldback so long as it does not inhibit performance.

Reflections

Be aware that when a music stand (or any hard surface) is near the singer's microphone, sound waves reflect off the stand into the mic. This can cause phase cancellations adversely coloring tone quality. Remembering that a sound's angle of incidence is equal to its angle of reflectance, position the music stand so that reflections from it do not reach the mic (see Figure 7-49). Or cover the stand with material to absorb the reflections.

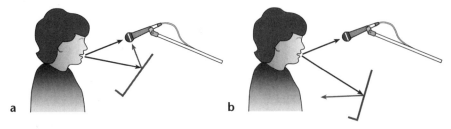

Figure 7-49 Preventing reflections from a music stand from entering a microphone. (a) Problem. (b) Solution.

Mic-to-Source Distance Versus Style

Generally, the style of the music sets the guidelines for mic-to-source distance. In popular music, vocalists usually work close to the mic, from a few inches to a few feet, to create a tight, intimate sound. Classical and jazz vocalists work from a couple feet to several feet from the mic to add room ambience, thereby opening the sound and making it airy.

Isolating the Vocalist

To record as clean a vocal sound as possible, many studios use an isolation booth to prevent leakage from instruments or acoustics from reaching the vocal mic. In the absence of such a booth—or because it may color sound or a vocalist may find it difficult to work in a claustrophobic environment—there are other ways to isolate a microphone (see Figure 7-50).

Figure 7-50 Portable sound filter for recording with reduced room ambience. The filter's main function is to help obtain a dry vocal (or instrumental) recording. It has six main layers, which both absorb and diffuse the sound waves hitting them, so progressively less of the original source's acoustic energy passes through each layer. The filter also helps prevent reflected sound from reaching the back and the sides of the mic.

Surround-Sound Miking

In miking for surround during recording, there are two basic means of handling selection and placement. One is to use direct and ambient miking; the other is to take the direct approach.

Direct/Ambient Surround-Sound Miking

With *direct/ambient surround-sound miking*, either one of two stereo arrays—near-coincident or spaced—will do as a basis for the left-right frontal pickups, then add a center mic for the center channel. Because of the center mic, the angle or space between the stereo mics should be wider than usual. The surround microphones are typically used for ambience and are pointed away from the sound source to the rear or rear-side of the studio or hall.

Figures 7-51 to 7-53 display three examples of surround-sound microphone arrays to provide a sense of the ongoing experimentation with surround miking techniques. None of these examples is intended to suggest that any one approach is preferred to or better than another, nor are they necessarily the most common approaches; there are other workable techniques.

Direct Surround-Sound Miking

The *direct surround-sound miking* approach uses microphone arrays especially designed for surround-sound pickup (see Chapter 6). The array may be used to record individual instruments or groups of instruments or to pick up the sound of an entire ensemble. Direct miking tends to center the listener more "inside" the music by placing the voicings side-to-side across the front and from the front speakers to the surrounds (see Figures 7-54 and 7-55). Or the spatial imaging may be in a horseshoe shape, with the listener centered at or somewhat inside its base.

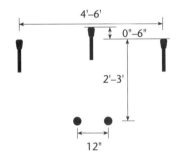

Figure 7-51 A basic approach to direct/ambient surround-sound miking. The mics can be either cardioid or wide-angle cardioid, depending on the breadth of the ensemble. The left, center, and right mics face forward. The left and right surround mics may face toward the ceiling (assuming suitable ceiling height and proper acoustics) or may be angled slightly toward the rear.

From Jason Corey and Geoff Martin, "Surround Sound Miking Techniques," *Broadcast Engineering,* March 2004, p. 42. © 2004 Mondo Code.

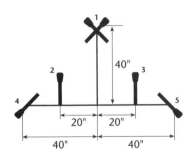

Figure 7-52 Decca Tree surround-sound techniques. Mic 1 is a supercardioid X-Y stereo array, mics 2 and 3 are a near-coincident supercardioid stereo pair, and mics 4 and 5 are a spaced subcardioid stereo pair. For a quasi-traditional Decca Tree, use mics 1, 2, and 3 (the traditional Decca Tree uses three omnis—see Figure 7-25); for an ambient Decca Tree, use mics 1, 4, and 5.

From Ron Streicher and F. Alton Everest, *The New Stereo Soundbook,* 3rd ed. (Pasadena, Calif.: Audio Engineering Associates, 2006), p. 13.

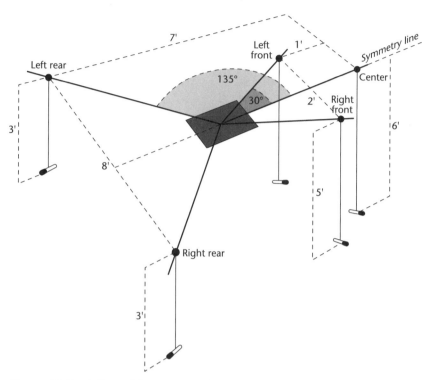

Figure 7-53 Adjustable surround-sound microphone array for small ensembles. This approach uses five capacitor omnidirectional mics positioned horizontally 30 degrees toward the floor. When recording a jazz trio, for example, the array is positioned 6 feet from the ensemble and 12 feet from the floor. For a string quartet, the array is 18 feet from the ensemble and 13 feet high.

From K. K. Profitt, "The Resolution Project," *Mix,* October 2005, p. 74. © 2005 *Mix* magazine.

Figure 7-54 Direct surround-sound miking on drums using the Atmos 5.1 surround-sound microphone.

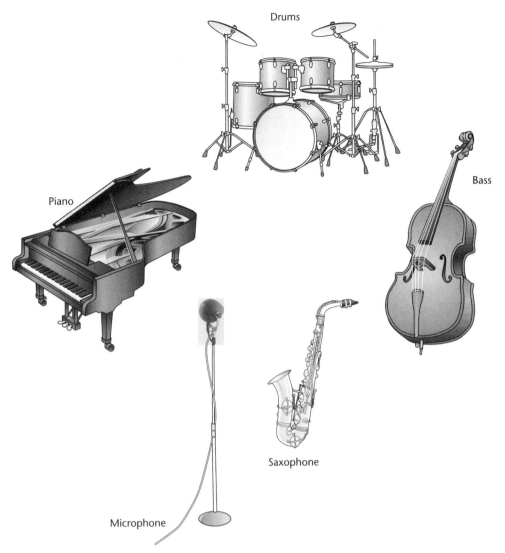

Drums

Piano

Bass

Saxophone

Microphone

Figure 7-55 Direct surround-sound miking of a jazz combo using the Holophone surround-sound microphone.

Main Points

- In acoustics, phase is the time relationship between two or more sound waves at a given point in their cycles.

- In electricity, polarity is the relative position of two signal leads—the high (+) and the low (−)—in the same circuit.

- One way to avoid phase problems with microphones is to follow the three-to-one rule: Place no two microphones closer together than three times the distance between one of them and its sound source.

- With most moving-coil mics, the farther from the sound source they are placed, the more reduced the high-frequency response.

- Generally, large-diaphragm microphones are more suitable in reproducing predominately low-frequency sound sources; small-diaphragm mics are more suitable in reproducing predominately high-frequency sound sources.

- Do not confuse perspective with loudness. Loudness aside, in considering mic-to-source distance, it is hearing more or less of the ambience that helps create perspective.

- Evaluation of a microphone for speech includes at least four criteria: clarity, presence, richness, and versatility.

- Factors that influence a microphone's effect on the sound of the speaking (and singing) voice are its sound quality, directional pattern, and mic-to-source distance.

- In selecting and positioning a mic, keep excessive sound reflected from room surfaces, furniture, and equipment from reaching the mic, or comb filtering can result. Choose a mic and position it to avoid sibilance, plosives, and breath sounds.

- When positioning a microphone in front of a seated or standing performer, it is important to keep excessive sound reflected from surfaces, furniture, and equipment from reaching the mic to preserve sonic intimacy.

- To minimize sound reflections reaching the microphone, a performer should work at a relatively close mic-to-source distance and use a directional microphone.

- In television, for single speakers, interviews, and panel programs, the mini-mic is usually the microphone of choice because of its many advantages. In radio, conventional directional mics are mainly used sometimes mounted on a desk stand but are more commonly mounted on a swivel stand.

- The handheld mic has several advantages, among which are: It allows the host to control the audience questioning; it allows the host to control mic-to-source distances; and it helps the host generate a closer psychological rapport with the viewing audience.

- In the field, when controlling mic-to-source distance, it is useful to keep in mind the inverse square law: When mic-to-source distance is doubled, the sound-pressure level drops approximately 6 dB, thus reducing loudness to one-fourth. Conversely, cutting the mic-to-source distance in half increases loudness approximately 6 dB.

- When operating the large boom or fishpole boom, there are a number of operational factors to bear in mind, depending on whether the performer(s) is seated or moving about a set.

- There are four basic ways to record musical instruments: close miking, distant miking, accent, or off-miking, and ambient miking.

- Close miking places a microphone relatively close to each sound source or group of sound sources in an ensemble—generally at a distance of about an inch to a foot.

- Distant miking places a microphone(s) from about 3 feet to several feet from the sound source. It picks up a fuller range and balance of an instrument, or group of instruments and captures more of the studio acoustics for a more open and blended sound.

- In general, the distant miking stereo arrays are coincident, near-coincident, and spaced.

- Accent miking, also known as off-miking, is used to pick up instruments in an ensemble when they solo.

- Ambience miking, used along with distant miking, attempts to reproduce the aural experience that audiences receive in a live venue by recording in an acoustically suitable studio or concert hall.

- Close miking is the technique of choice in studio recording for most popular music genres. Among the commonly recorded voicings in those genres are drums, acoustic guitar, electric bass and electric guitar, piano, and vocal.

- In miking for surround during recording, there are two basic means of handling selection and placement. One is to use direct and ambient miking; the other is to take the direct approach.

- With direct/ambient surround-sound miking, either one of two stereo arrays—near-coincident or spaced—will do as a basis for the left-right frontal pickups, then add a center mic for the center channel and the two surround mics for rear-side or rear pickup.

- The direct surround-sound miking approach uses microphone arrays especially designed for surround-sound pickup.

8 Mixers, Consoles, and Control Surfaces

Mixers, consoles, and control surfaces perform essentially the same basic operations. They take input signals and route them to output sources such as broadcast, recording, and digital audio workstations.[1] They differ, however, in their complexity and, with a control surface, in the way signals are delegated.

Mixers

Compared to most studio-size consoles, *mixers* are smaller and lighter-weight with limited processing functions that may or may not be computer-assisted.[2] But like consoles, they have three basic control sections: input, output, and monitor.

The *input section* takes the incoming signal from a microphone and, if so equipped, other types of sound sources, such as a CD player, recorder and, if used for broadcast, phone-in caller, in which case each input channel is configured for either low-level or high-level sound sources. A microphone is a low-level sound source; CD players and recorders are high-level sound sources. The loudness level of each channel is regulated by a *fader* (sliding or rotary). For stereo, faders carry either a tandem left/right stereo signal or, stereo pairs, with the left (sliding) fader carrying the left signal and the right (sliding) fader carrying the right signal. Each channel often has a delegation switch that can turn off the signal flow, route it to the output or to the monitor section, which may be designated audition or *cue*. The *output section* is where all input signals are combined for further routing to recording or transmission. Input and output signals are heard as sound through monitor loudspeakers. As they pass through the console, however, they are in the form of voltage. Therefore, meters are necessary to measure the voltages in the input and output sections. By using the fader, these voltages can be kept within

---

1. The different types and models of mixers, consoles, and control surfaces available today are considerable. Their purposes and particular designs differ. To cover the subject with specificity would be unwieldy. Moreover, the details that apply to one mixer, console, or control surface may not apply to another. They do have certain functions in common, however. Therefore, to deal with the topic manageably, the approach in this chapter is generic; the intent is to cover in general the operational features of the main types of mixers, consoles, and control surfaces.
2. The term *mixer* is often used synonymously with *console*. Some mixers include additional features found on consoles, and some small- and medium-format consoles have limited features that could classify them as large mixers.

149

acceptable limits. (Meters are discussed later in this chapter.) The ***monitor section*** provides the means to hear the output signal, which in mixers is usually through headphones. The monitor section makes it possible to listen to program material without it affecting the signal recorded or transmitted.

Although mixers can be used anywhere, their size and compactness make them highly portable, so they are typically used away from the studio, in the field. Some models are equipped with a built-in recorder (see Figures 8-1 and 8-2).

There are two types of microphone mixer: passive and active. A ***passive mic mixer*** combines individual inputs into one output without amplifying the signal. When there are only two on-mic sound sources, such as a reporter and an interviewee, a passive mic mixer with two inputs and one output is easy and convenient to use.

An ***active mic mixer*** allows amplification control of each audio source and usually includes other processing features as well (see Figure 8-1). The format can be mono or stereo, and operation can be manual or automatic. Signal flow is straightforward: Microphones are plugged into the mixer's input channels, where their signals are preamplified and their loudness levels are controlled by faders, usually rotary. The signals are then routed to the output channel, where they are combined, and a master fader controls their overall loudness level before they are sent on to broadcast or recording.

In addition to the features shown in Figure 8-1, more elaborate portable mixers may have additional inputs to accommodate recorders and CD players, and interfaces for direct transmission to the station using a phone line, ISDN, Internet Protocol (IP), and laptop computer.

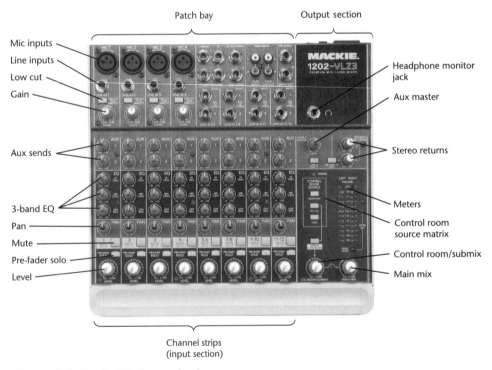

Figure 8-1 Basic 12-channel mixer.

Figure 8-2 Tabletop mixer with iPod recorder.

Consoles

A *console* (also known as a *board*, *mixer*, or, in Europe, *mixing desk*) takes input signals and amplifies, balances, processes, combines, and routes them to broadcast or recording. Many consoles also store operational data. In the majority of modern console systems, many if not most functions are computer-assisted.

Consoles today are available in various configurations; they use different technologies and are designed for specific production purposes. No single system can be used as a generalized example of all the systems out there. They can be grouped into broad categories, however. A console may be analog or digital; appropriate for on-air broadcast, production, or postproduction; and software-based and used as a virtual console with a digital audio workstation.

Analog and Digital Consoles

In an *analog console*, audio signals flow in and out of physical modules through inboard wires and circuits. To add flexibility to the signal flow, large-format and some medium-format consoles usually include an inboard patch bay consisting of jacks wired to the console's components to facilitate the routing and the rerouting of signals within the console and to and from studio outboard equipment. Patch cords plug into the jacks to direct signal flow. (See "Patching" later in this chapter.)

In a *digital console*, incoming analog audio signals are converted to digital information at the inputs, and interfaces handle the routing and the signal processing. If the audio entering the console is already digitized, of course no conversion is necessary. Routing and rerouting signals are also handled by patching, but operations are managed through the console's interfaces, which are inboard. There are no jacks or patch cords needed to effect connections.

Modern analog and digital consoles are capable of data storage, and the operation of many analog models is computer-assisted. Digital consoles almost always incorporate computer-assisted functions.

A virtual console is a simulated console displayed on a computer screen that is part of the software of a digital recording program. Its functions are similar to those of a conventional console and are controlled by a mouse or control surface (see "Control Surfaces" later in this chapter).

On-Air Broadcast Consoles

A console used for on-air broadcasts, including podcasts, is designed to handle audio sources that are immediately distributed to the audience. Whatever is not live has been already produced and packaged and requires only playback. Therefore, an on-air broadcast console needs more controlling elements to manage rapid transitions. In a radio disc jockey program, those transitions are between disc jockey, music, and spot announcements; in an interview or panel program, they are among host, guest(s), call-ins from listeners, and spot announcements. In radio and television news, studio-based anchor(s), field reporters, and recorded segments must be dealt with. Snapshot memory of console parameters enables event storage and recall of a program's baseline settings at the beginning of the program's next broadcast, so operators do not have to take the time to reset those parameters manually.

On-air consoles include a variety of other features such as equalization, compression, and limiting, depending on the complexity of the broadcast and the need for signal processing and programmed functions. A console designed for broadcast may also be able to do double duty and handle off-air production needs as well, as discussed in the following section. Figure 8-3 displays the signal flow of a basic generic broadcast console.

Production Consoles

Production consoles are necessary for producing and postproducing music, film, and video sound tracks, sports, and such live-to-recording programs as parades and variety, talk, and awards shows. They must be capable of handling many sound sources simultaneously and employing the diversity of tasks involved in dynamics processing—equalization, compression, noise gating, reverberation, and delay—necessary for "sweetening" and mixing.

Automation is a necessity. It allows operational data from production sessions to be stored on and retrieved from an in-board memory. In film and television, automated panning facilitates the matching of movement to picture. A production console for music recording often requires a number of **submixers** to **premix** groups of similar voicings such as strings, backup vocals, and the components of a drum set. Network TV news is essentially a one- or two-mic show, yet with recorded music intros, reports from the field, and interviews, it can easily occupy the many inputs of a production console. Specialized, compact consoles with integrated machine interface systems are required to handle the unique requirements of automated dialogue replacement (ADR) and Foley sound-effects recording. Consoles used for music and postproduction mixes in film and television must have sufficient capabilities to handle the many tracks of musical instruments, dialog, and sound effects as well as the stereo and surround-sound processing.

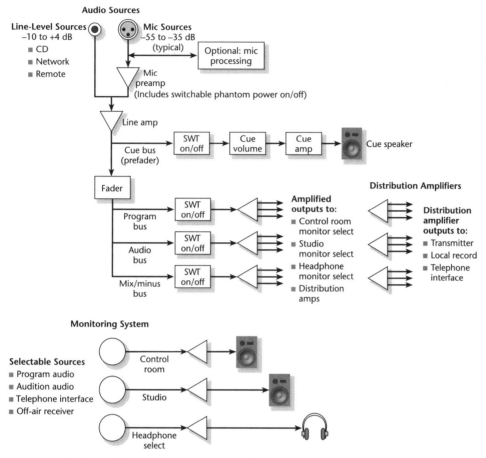

Figure 8-3 Signal flow of a basic generic broadcast console. Typical console found at radio and television stations. It allows for connection of basic playback devices and monitoring and general feeds transmitter(s) for off-air or satellite reception.

Features of the Production Console

The number of features on a production console and how they interface vary with the console's purpose and whether it is analog or digital. Regardless of these factors, however, most production consoles incorporate a number of basic functions (see Figure 8-4).

In the following list, sequence of functions, signal flow, section designations, groupings, and terminology will differ depending on the console architecture and manufacturer. But most of the features are found on the majority of production consoles.

- **Input/output (I/O) channel**—During recording, the *input/output*, or *I/O, channel strip* processes and delegates incoming signals and sends them on for recording (see Figure 8-5). During mixing, the I/O section processes signals from the recorder and routes them to the master section, where they are combined into mono, stereo, or surround channels and routed for the master recording.

- **Input selector control**—You will recall that two types of signal sources feed to input modules: low-level such as microphones and high-level such as recorders and CD players. The *input selector control* delegates which type of signal source enters the input section.

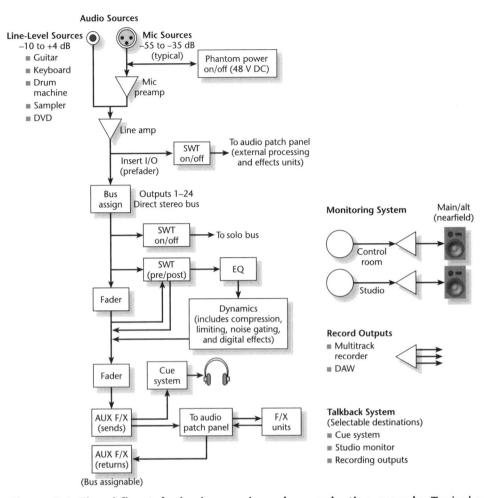

Figure 8-4 Signal flow of a basic generic analog production console. Typical console used for multitrack recording. It allows for connection of external audio processing and effects devices. Found in production studios. Has extended monitoring system for in-studio talent.

- **Phantom power**—When activated, *phantom power* provides voltage (48 V DC, or direct current) for capacitor mics, eliminating the need for batteries.

- **Microphone preamplifier**—A microphone signal entering the console is weak. It requires a mic preamplifier to increase its voltage to a usable level.

  A word about mic preamps in consoles: Whether the audio is analog or digital, each component in the signal flow must be as noise-free as possible. Given the low-noise, high-sensitivity, and high-SPL specifications of many of today's microphones, it is important that the mic preamp be capable of handling a mic's output without strain. If the console's preamp is inadequate to meet this requirement, it is necessary to use an outboard mic preamp (see Figure 8-6).

- **Trim or gain**—The *trim* is a gain control that changes the input sensitivities to accommodate the nominal input levels of various input sources. Trim boosts the lower-level sources to usable proportions and prevents overload distortion in higher-level sources.

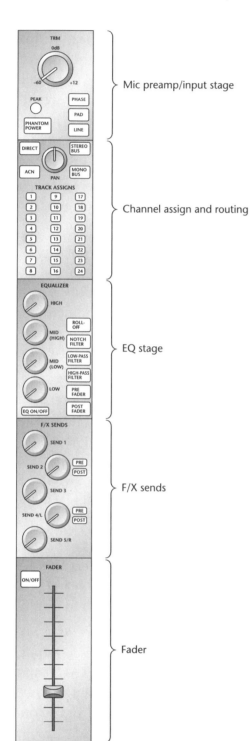

Figure 8-5 Generic input/output channel strip and its features.

Figure 8-6 Microphone preamplifier. This model is portable and battery-powered. Its features include: phantom power; high-pass filter at 80 or 160 Hz; limiter; and 66 dB of gain in 11 discrete steps.

- Pad—A *pad* reduces the power of a signal. On a console, it is placed ahead of the mic input transformer to prevent overload distortion of the transformer and the mic preamplifier. It is used when the trim, by itself, cannot prevent overload in the mic signal. Be cautious about using the pad because in some consoles it reduces signal-to-noise ratio.

- Overload indicator—The *overload indicator*, also called a *peak indicator*, tells you when the input signal is approaching or has reached overload and is clipping. It is usually a *light-emitting diode* (*LED*). In some consoles, the LED flashes green when the input signal is peaking in the safe range and flashes red either to indicate clipping or to warn of impending clipping.

- Polarity (phase) reversal—*Polarity reversal* is a control that inverts the polarity of an input signal 180 degrees. Sometimes called *phase reversal*, it is used to reverse the polarity of miswired equipment, usually microphones, whose signal is out of phase with the signal from a piece of similar equipment correctly wired. Sometimes, intentional polarity reversal is helpful in canceling leakage from adjacent microphones or in creating *electroacoustic* special effects by mixing together out-of-phase signals from mics picking up the same sound source.

- Channel assignment and routing—This is a group of switches on each channel used to direct the signal from that channel to one or more outputs; or several input signals can be combined and sent to one output. For example, assume that three different microphone signals are routed separately to channels 1, 3, and 11 and the recordist wishes to direct them all to channel 18. By pressing assignment switch 18 on channels 1, 3, and 11, the recordist feeds the signals to channel 18's active combining network and then on to recorder track 18.

  An *active combining network* (*ACN*) is an amplifier at which the outputs of two or more signal paths are mixed together to feed a single track of a recorder. To save space, the assignment switches are sometimes paired, either alternately—1 and 3, 2 and 4, and so on—or adjacently—1 and 2, 3 and 4, and so on. In relation to stereo, odd numbers are left channels and even numbers are right channels.

- Direct switch—The *direct switch* connects the channel signal to the channel output, directing the signal to its own track on the recorder, bypassing the channel ACN and thus reducing noise. For example, using the direct switch routes the signal on, say, channel 1 to recorder track 1, the signal on channel 2 to recorder track 2, and so on.

- Pan pot—A *pan pot* (short for *panoramic potentiometer*) is a control that can shift the proportion of sound to any point from left to right between two output buses and, hence, between the two loudspeakers necessary for reproducing a stereo image (see Figure 8-7). Panning is also necessary in surround sound to delegate signals left-to-right, front-to-rear (or to rear-side), and rear side-to-side. To hear a signal louder in one bus than in the other, the pan pot varies the relative levels being fed to the output buses. This facilitates the positioning of a sound source at a particular place in the stereo or surround field between or among the loudspeakers.

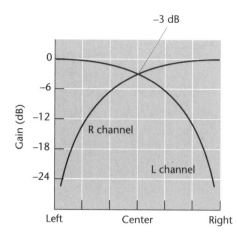

Figure 8-7 Effect of a typical pan pot.

- **Equalizer and filter**—An *equalizer* is an electronic device that alters a signal's frequency response by boosting or attenuating the level of selected portions of the audio spectrum. A *filter* alters frequency response by attenuating frequencies above, below, or at a preset point. Most production consoles have separate equalizer controls for selected frequencies grouped in the bass, midrange, and treble ranges. Filters are usually high-pass and low-pass. Upscale consoles have additional equalizer ranges, such as low and high bass and low and high treble as well as more filter effects. (Equalizers and filters are discussed in Chapter 11.)

  The equalization (EQ) module may also have prefader and postfader controls, that is, any equalization or filtering can be assigned before or after the channel fader. Before, or *prefader*, means the level control at the EQ module is the only one affecting the loudness of the channel's equalization. After, or *postfader*, means the main channel fader also affects the EQ level. In the postfader mode, the level control at the EQ module is still operational but the main channel fader overrides it.

- **Dynamics section**—Production consoles may include a dynamics section in each I/O module or, as is the case with most digital models, in a separate, centralized section to which each channel has access. This adds to a console's signal-processing power and often includes, at least, compression, limiting, and noise gating. Multieffects processing may also include delay, reverb, phasing, and flanging (see Chapter 11).

- **Channel/monitor control**—Some production consoles include a *channel/monitor control* in the EQ and dynamics sections that switches the equalizer, dynamics, and usually selected *send* functions either into the channel signal path for recording or into the monitor signal path for monitoring.

- **Cue and effects sends (pre- or postfader)**—*Cue send* is a monitor function that routes a signal from an input channel to the headphone, or foldback, system. *Foldback* is a monitor system that feeds signals from the console to the headphones. The cue send level control adjusts the loudness of the headphone signal before it is sent to the master cue sends in the monitor module.

At the input channel, the cue send can be assigned before or after the channel fader. Before, or *prefader cue*, means the level control at cue send is the only one affecting the loudness of the channel's cue send. After, or *postfader cue*, means the main channel fader also affects the cue send level. In the postfader mode, the level control at cue send is still operational, but the main channel fader overrides it.

Pre- and postfader controls add flexibility in providing performers with a suitable headphone mix. In music recording, for example, if the musicians were satisfied with their headphone mix and did not want to hear channel fader adjustments made during recording, cue send would be switched to the prefader mode. On the other hand, if the musicians did want to hear changes in level at the channel fader, cue send would be switched to the postfader mode.

The *effects* (*F/X* or *EFX*) send module feeds the input signal to an external (outboard) signal processor such as a reverberation unit, compressor, or harmonizer (see Chapter 11). The effects send module is also called *auxiliary* (*aux*) *send*, *reverb send*, and *echo send*.

Effects send can feed a signal to any external signal processor so long as it is wired to the console's patch bay (see "Patching" later in this chapter). Such a connection is not needed with dynamics processing that is inboard as it is with most modern analog and digital consoles. After the "dry" send signal reaches the outboard signal processor, it returns "wet" to the effects return in the master section for mixing with the main output. The wet signal may also feed to a monitor return system.

The send function also has pre- and postfader controls whereby any signal can be sent before or after the channel fader.

- **Solo and prefader listen**—Feeding different sounds through several channels at once can create an inconvenience if it becomes necessary to hear one of them to check something. Instead of shutting off or turning down all the channels but the one you wish to hear, activating the *solo* control, located in each input module, automatically cuts off all other channels feeding the monitor system; this has no effect on the output system. More than one solo can be pushed to audition several channels at once and still cut off the unwanted channels.

  The solo function is usually prefader. On some consoles, therefore, it is called *prefader listen* (*PFL*). In consoles with both solo and prefader listen functions, PFL is prefader and solo is postfader.

- **Mute (channel on/off)**—The *mute* function, also called *channel on/off*, turns off the signals from the I/O channel. During mixdown, when no sound is feeding through an input channel for the moment, it shuts down the channel or mutes it. This prevents unwanted channel noise from reaching the outputs.

- **Channel and monitor faders**—The *channel and monitor faders* control the channel level of the signal recorded and its monitor level, respectively. During recording, channel levels to the recorder are set for optimal signal-to-noise ratio. Level balances are made during mixdown. To enable the recordist to get a sense of what the balanced levels will sound like, the monitor faders are adjusted to taste, with no effect on the signal recorded.

Meters

For sound (acoustic) energy to be processed through electrical equipment, it must be transduced, or converted, into electric energy. It is a paradox in sound production that the way to determine levels in mixers and consoles is visually—by watching a meter that measures the electric energy passing through an input or output. Audio heard through a monitor system is acoustic, but it passes through the console as voltage, which cannot be heard and therefore must be referenced in another way.

Determining levels with your eyes can be done only to a point. Meters can reflect problems that may not be perceived, or if they are perceived, a meter may identify the problem when you may not be able to. As such, meters can be considered analogous to test equipment. In recording and in mixing in particular, however, it is the ear that should determine audio quality and sonic relationships. After all, it is the sound that matters (see Chapter 13).

VU Meter

The volume-unit meter has been a mainstay for decades and is still found on equipment in use today. But on most new consoles and recording equipment, it is rarely incorporated. The preferred meters today are peak indicators (see "Peak Meters" later in this section).

The *volume-unit (VU) meter* is a voltage meter originally designed to indicate level as it relates to the human ear's perception of loudness. It reflects a signal's perceived volume, but it is not fast enough to track rapid transients. With a complex waveform, the VU meter reads its average loudness level and less than the waveform's peak voltage. Hence, there is headroom built into a console using VU meters so that a signal peaking above 0 level will not distort. (The VU meter uses a linear scale wherein 100 percent of modulation is equal to 0 VU on the volume-unit scale.) *Headroom* is the amount of level equipment can take, above working level, before overload distortion occurs. For these reasons and given that with digital sound, there is no headroom—a level over 100 percent of modulation will distort—the VU meter cannot provide the more exacting measures required for signal processing and recording that peak indicators can.

Two calibrated scales are on the face of the VU meter: a percentage of modulation scale and a volume-unit scale (see Figure 8-8). A needle, the volume indicator, moves back and forth across the scales, pointing out the levels. The needle responds to the electric energy passing through the VU meter. If the energy level is excessively high, the volume indicator will *pin*—hit against the meter's extreme right-hand side. Pinning can damage the VU meter's mechanism, rendering the volume indicator's reading unreliable.

Percentage of modulation is the percentage of an applied signal in relation to the maximum signal a sound system can handle. It is a linear scale wherein 100 percent of modulation is equal to 0 VU on the volume-unit scale. Therefore, 30 percent of modulation is equal to slightly less than –10 VU, 80 percent of modulation is equal to –2 VU, and so on.

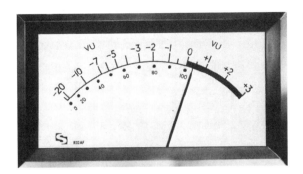

Figure 8-8 Volume-unit (VU) meter.

Any sound below 20 percent of modulation is too quiet, or *in the mud*; and levels above 100 percent of modulation are too loud, or *in the red*. (The scale to the right of 100 percent is red.) As a guideline, the loudness should "kick" between about −5 and +1, although the dynamics of sound make such evenness difficult to accomplish, if not aesthetically undesirable. Usually, the best that can be done is to *ride the gain*—adjust the faders from time to time so that, on average, the level stays out of the mud and the red. Fader movements can also be automated (see "Console Automation" later in this chapter).

When manually operating the faders, ride the gain with a light, fluid hand and do not jerk the faders up and down or make adjustments at the slightest fall or rise in loudness. Changes in level should be smooth and imperceptible because abrupt changes are disconcerting to the listener, unless an abrupt change is called for in, say, a transition from one shot to another.

When the VU meter is in the red, it is a warning to be cautious of loudness distortion. All modern consoles with VU meters are designed with headroom so that a signal peaking a few decibels above 0 VU will not distort.

Because a VU meter is designed to reflect a signal's perceived loudness, it does a poor job of indicating transient peaks, which is a main reason why peak meters are preferred.

Peak Meters

Whereas the VU meter is mechanical, most peak meters are electronic. Their rise time is quite fast because there is no mechanical inertia to overcome. A *peak meter* is able to track peak program levels, thereby making it a more accurate indicator of the signal levels passing through the console and a safer measure when dealing with digital audio. Peak meters read out in bar graphs, using LED or plasma displays.

LED Meters

*LED*s are small light sources (*LED* stands for light-emitting diode). The meters are arranged horizontally or vertically. Usually, green LEDs indicate safe levels and red ones register in the overload region. On professional equipment, the LEDs are about 2 dB apart, so resolution is fair (see Figure 8-9).

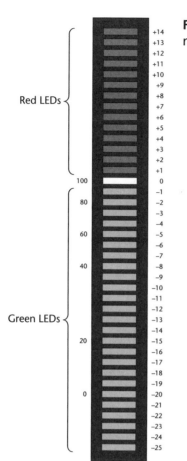

Figure 8-9 LED peak meter. Numbers on the right are peak levels; numbers on the left are their equivalent to VU meter levels.

Plasma Displays

Plasma displays are columns of light that display safe levels in one color, usually green, and overload levels in red. They are more complex than LED meters and have excellent resolution, with an accuracy of 1 dB. One version of a plasma display meter is roughly analogous to a VU meter and peak program meter (see Figure 8-11) combined, thereby establishing a relationship between average and peak levels (see Figure 8-10).

Meter Controls

In modern consoles, meters also have the capability of measuring more than just output signal levels. Controls on the meter panel can be assigned to read bus, cue send, cue return, and monitor mix levels.

Peak Program Meter

Another type of peak indicator is the *peak program meter (ppm)* (see Figure 8-11). With the ppm, as signal levels increase, there is a warning of impending overload distortion. The level indicator makes this easier to notice because its rise time is rapid and its fall-back is slow.

The ppm's scale is linear and in decibels, not volume units. The scale's divisions are 4 dB intervals, except at the extremes of the range; and zero-level is 4, in the middle of the scale.

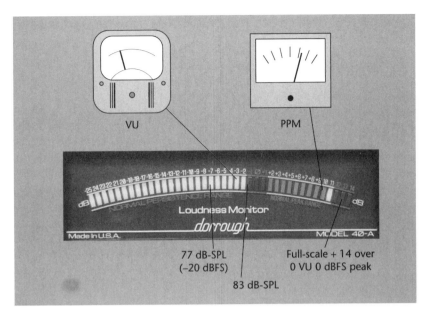

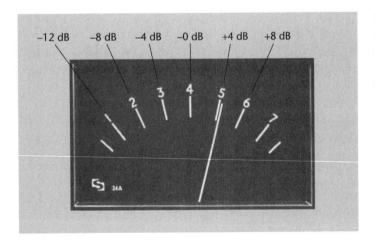

Figure 8-10 Loudness meter. This meter is roughly analogous to a VU meter and a peak program meter combined. It establishes a relationship between the root mean square (RMS) and the peak content of a signal. When riding the gain for balanced loudness, peak should be driven to the brink of the top set of three LEDs (red), while the RMS should be driven to the brink of the center set of three LEDs (red). This is defined as relative loudness, in 1 dB steps. When the signal peaks in the red, the levels should be reduced slightly.

Figure 8-11 Peak program meter with equivalent dB values. Dual-movement ppms with two indicators are for two-channel stereo applications.

Optimizing Digital Levels

One goal in processing audio through the signal chain is to make sure the levels at each stage are optimal. Given the several stages in the sound chain, from microphone to console to recording to mixing to mastering, this is easier said than done. With a console alone, there are a number of reference and overload scales for analog and digital signal levels. They involve a great deal of math that is beyond the scope of this book.

In general, however, there are approaches to optimizing level control in consoles using the available metering. Because just about all production today is handled in the digital domain and there is no headroom with digital signal processing, it makes sense to set the loudest levels below 0 level to avoid *clipping*—distortion. How far below depends on the dynamics of the audio material. Bear in mind that setting levels too low could create signal-to-noise problems with quiet passages.

Meters in digital audio consoles are calibrated in ***decibel full-scale (dBFS)***, a unit of measure for the amplitude of digital audio signals. Zero dBFS occurs when all the binary bits that make up the digital signal are on, that is, are read as 1's (as opposed to 0's, when the digital signal is off). It is the highest digital level that can be encoded, so anything above 0 dBFS will clip. Therefore, setting the digital level at, say, −20 dBFS provides a headroom of 20 dB before overload distortion occurs.

Still another measuring system has been developed and proposed by mastering engineer Bob Katz. Called the ***K-system***, it integrates measures of metering and monitoring to standardize reference loudness.[3] Apparently, many recordists do not find peak meters all that reliable and are using VU meters once again. The K-system is an attempt to establish a reliable, standard 0-level measurement that means the same thing to everyone.

Master Section

The ***master section*** contains the master controls for the master buses, the master fader, the master effects sends and returns, level and mute controls, meters, and other functions (see Figure 8-12).

- **Master buses**—After a signal leaves an input/output module, it travels to its assigned bus(es). In many consoles, these signals may be grouped for premixing at submaster buses before finally combined at the master bus(es). There may be any number of submaster buses, but usually there are only a few master buses because final output signals are mixed down to a few channels such as two-channel stereo and six- (or more) channel surround sound.

- **Master fader**—The ***master fader*** controls the signal level from the master bus to the recorder. Most master faders are configured as a single fader carrying a tandem left/right stereo signal; some are configured as a stereo output pair with the left fader carrying the left signal and the right fader carrying the right signal. A console may have two, four, eight, or more such faders or sets of faders to handle stereo and surround sound. Sometimes there is a mono master fader as well.

- **Master effects sends (aux send, reverb send, and echo send)**—The ***effects sends*** from the I/O channels are first routed to the master effects sends before output to an outboard signal processor.

- **Master effects returns (aux return, reverb return, and echo return)**—Signals routed to an outboard signal processor from the master sends are returned at the master returns and mixed with the main program signal.

- **Level, mute, PFL, solo,** and **pan pot**—Each master aux send and aux return usually has a level control and a mute switch. The master returns also usually have PFL, solo, and pan controls.

---

3. See Bob Katz, *Mastering Audio,* 2nd ed. (Boston: Focal Press, 2007), p. 176.

■ **Meters**—Most modern production consoles provide peak metering for each master fader; a mono meter to indicate the level of a summed stereo signal; a phase meter to show the phase relationship between the left and right stereo signals or among the surround signals; metering to monitor surround-sound levels; and metering to display master send and/or return levels. Some consoles also have meters for the control room monitor outputs.

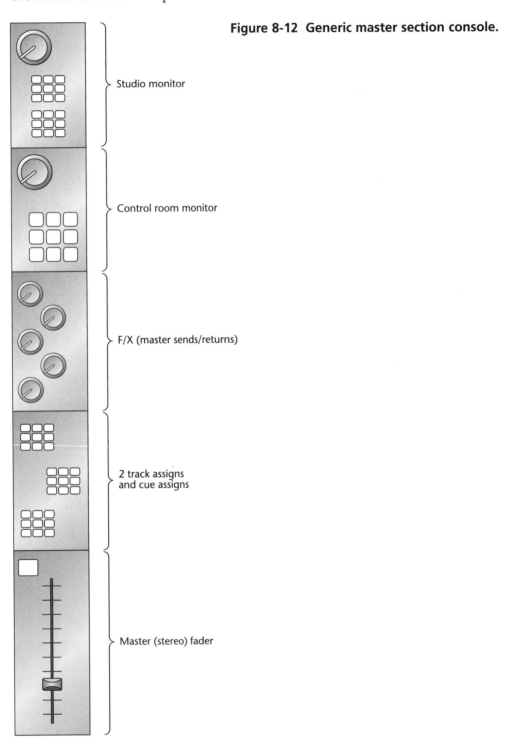

Figure 8-12 Generic master section console.

Studio monitor

Control room monitor

F/X (master sends/returns)

2 track assigns and cue assigns

Master (stereo) fader

Monitor Section

Monitor functions, such as setting monitor level and panning for each channel, may be performed by the I/O module. The **monitor section**, among other things, allows monitoring of the line or recorder input, selects various inputs to the control room and studio monitors, and controls their levels.

- **Recorder select switches**—These switches select a recorder for direct feed to the monitor system, bypassing the I/O controls. There may also be aux in switches for direct feeds to the monitor system from other sound sources such as a CD player or a recorder.

- **Send switches**—These route signals from the sends to the input of the control room or studio monitors or both.

- **Mix switches**—These select the mix input (i.e., stereo or surround sound) for the monitor system.

- **Speaker select switches**—These select the control room or studio loudspeakers for monitoring. There is a level control for each set of loudspeakers. Monitor sections also have a *dim* switch for the control room monitors. Instead of having to turn the monitor level down and up during control room conversation, the dim function reduces monitor level by several decibels or more at the touch of a button.

A monitor section may also have a pan pot, mutes for the left- and right-channel signals to the control room, and a phase coherence switch. The *phase coherence* switch inverts the left-channel signal before it combines with the right-channel signal. If the stereo signals are in phase, sound quality should suffer and, in particular, the sonic images in the center (between the two loudspeakers) should be severely attenuated. If the phase coherence check improves the mono signal, there is a problem with the stereo signal's mono compatibility.

Additional Features

Additional features found on most consoles include talkback, slate, and oscillator.

- **Talkback**—The *talkback* permits the recordist in the control room to speak to the studio performers or music conductor or both via a console microphone. The talkback may be directed through the studio monitor, headphones, or a slate system.

- **Slate/talkback**—Many multichannel consoles also have a *slate* feature that automatically feeds to a recording anything said through the talkback. It is a convenient way to transcribe information about the name of the recording, the artist, the take number, and so on.

- *Oscillator*—An *oscillator* is a signal generator that produces pure tones or sine waves (sound waves with no harmonics or overtones) at selected frequencies. On a console, it is used both to calibrate the console with the recorder so that their levels are the same and to put reference tone levels on analog recordings.

Channel Strips

In general a *channel strip* refers to one channel (usually input) of a console. In the past, the sound quality of some console channel strips have been so highly regarded that they were ordered separately from the console manufacturer and rigged to a power supply and input/output connections for stand-alone use. A microphone could be plugged directly into the channel strip and the signal sent directly to a recorder, thereby producing a purer and far less complex signal path while eliminating the need to deal with a larger console.

Today, stand-alone and plug-in channel strips are so popular that they have become a separate product category. They may include some or most of the functions usually found in most conventional and virtual console channel strips, such as a microphone preamp, equalization, compression, limiting, de-essing, and noise-gating (see Figures 8-13 and 8-14).

Figure 8-13 Stand-alone channel strip. This rack-mountable model is designed to reproduce the sound from vintage Neve console models. It includes a mic preamp, a three-band equalizer, high- and low-frequency shelving, high-pass filters, and phantom power. The *silk* control is designed to reduce negative feedback and adjust the frequency spectrum to provide a more musical sound.

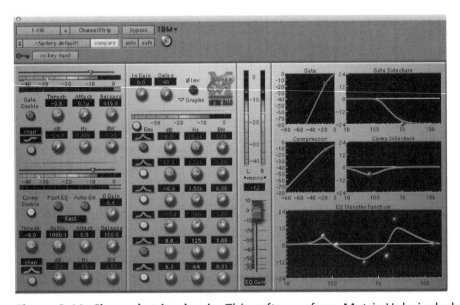

Figure 8-14 Channel strip plug-in. This software from Metric Halo includes input gain and trim, polarity reversal, a six-band parametric equalizer, high- and low-frequency shelving, expander/gate, compressor, delay, and time alignment; it also displays detailed visual feedback about the effects of the processing applied.

Patching

Audio facilities require flexibility in sending signals to various components within the console and to and from outboard equipment in the control room.[4] In studios where active components are not wired directly to one another but to the console or outboard gear, or both, one or more patch bays are required. A *patch bay* is a central terminal that facilitates the routing of sound through pathways not provided in the normal console design. Each hole in the patch bay (or *patch panel*), called a *jack*, becomes the connecting point to the input or output of each electronic component in the sound studio (see Figure 8-15). Patching is the interconnecting of these inputs and outputs using a *patch cord* (see Figures 8-16 and 8-17). In this context, a patch bay is more like an old-fashioned telephone switchboard.

In digital consoles, there is no separate patch bay. Patching is handled internally without the need for special wiring or patch cords (see "Digital Consoles" later in this chapter). Control surfaces can handle signal routing using network routers (see "Control Surfaces" later in this chapter).

In a well-equipped and active analog facility, the patch bay could become a confusing jungle of patch cords. In all studios, regardless of size and activity, a signal travels some paths more often than others. For example, it is more likely that a signal in a console will travel from mic (or line) input to pan pot to equalizer to assignment control to fader,

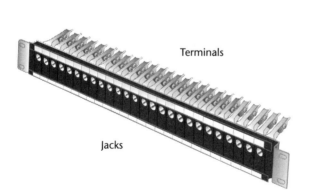

Figure 8-15 Patch bay with a row of jacks.

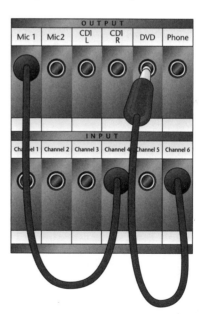

Figure 8-16 Use of patch bay. Any sound source wired to the patch panel can be connected to any other one with a patch cord plugged into the appropriate jack.

4. Although patching operations are handled internally in many of the consoles produced today, there are a sufficient number of facilities with equipment that requires patching to warrant coverage here.

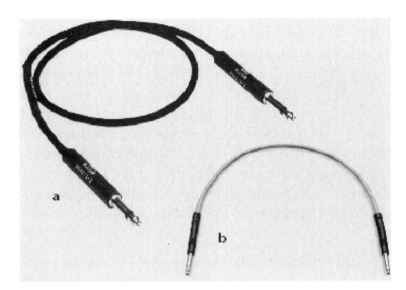

Figure 8-17 Patch cords with (a) 1/4-inch phone plugs and (b) bantam (mini or tiny telephone) phone plugs.

rather than directly from mic (or line) input to output bus. It is also more likely that a signal will travel from mic to console to recorder rather than directly from a mic to a recorder.

As a way of both reducing the clutter of patch cords at the patch bay and simplifying production, terminals wired to certain equipment can also be wired, or normaled, to one another. A *normal* connection is one that permits a signal to flow freely among components without any patching. To route a signal through components that have terminals not normaled or wired to one another, patch cords are put in the appropriate jacks to *break normal*—that is, to interrupt the normal signal flow—thus rerouting the signal. In some patch bays, normaling can be done manually, without the need for rewiring.

The ability to reroute a signal is also advantageous when equipment fails. Suppose a microphone is plugged into studio mic input 1, which connects directly to console channel 1, and channel 1 becomes defective. With all inputs and outputs connected at the patch bay, the defective console channel 1 can be bypassed by patching the output from studio mic input 1 to any other working console channel.

Here are some other features of patch bays:

■ **Input/output**—Patch bays are usually wired so that a row of input jacks is directly below a row of output jacks. By reading a patch bay downward, it is possible to get a good idea of the console's (or studio's) signal flow.

■ **Full-normal and half-normal**—Input jacks are wired so that a patch cord always interrupts the normal connection. These connections are called *full-normal*. Output jacks may be wired as either full-normal or *half-normal*—connections that continue rather than interrupt signal flow. Hence, a half-normal connection becomes a junction rather than a switch.

■ **Multiple**—Most patch bays include jacks called *multiples*, or *mults*, that are wired to one another instead of to any electronic component. Multiples provide the flexibility to feed the same signal to several different sources at once.

■ **Tie line**—When the only patch bay in a control room is located in the console, the other control room equipment, such as CD and DVD players and signal processors, must be wired to it to maintain flexibility in signal routing. *Tie lines* in the patch bay facilitate the interconnecting of outboard devices in the control room. When a control room has two patch bays, one in the console and one for the other control room equipment, tie lines can interconnect them. The tie line is also used to interconnect separate studios, control rooms, or any devices in different locations.

General Guidelines for Patching

■ Do not patch mic-level signals into line-level jacks and vice versa. The signal will be barely audible in the first instance and will distort in the latter one.

■ Do not patch input to input or output to output.

■ Unless jacks are half-normaled, do not patch the output of a component back into its input, or feedback will occur.

■ When patching microphones, make sure the fader controls are turned down. Otherwise, the loud popping sound that occurs when patch cords are inserted into jacks with the faders turned up could damage the microphone or loudspeaker element.

Plugs

The patch-cord plugs most commonly used in professional facilities are the *1/4-inch phone plug* and the *bantam phone plug*. The bantam (also called *mini* and *tiny telephone*) plug, and the smaller patch panel with which it is used, has all but replaced the larger 1/4-inch phone plug and its patch panel (see Figure 8-17).

These plugs are either *unbalanced*—tip and sleeve—or *balanced*—tip, ring, and sleeve (see Figure 8-18). An unbalanced audio cable has two conductors: a center wire and a braided shield surrounding it. A balanced audio cable has three conductors: two center wires and a braided shield. The balanced line is preferred for professional use because it is not so susceptible to electrical interference and can be used in long cable runs without undue loss in signal-to-noise ratio.

Computer Patching

Instead of hardware-based patch panels, many modern consoles in general and most digital consoles in particular handle patching using computer programming. Routing signals via patching does not require a physical patch bay or cords. At the touch of a few keys, routing information is entered into a programmer that tells the electronic patch panel to connect the selected signal source to the desired console channel. All patching commands can be stored for future use. Computer patching is convenient, flexible, and tidy. It is worth emphasizing, however, the importance of keeping track of all the patching assignments. Otherwise, it could lead to confusion in managing the signal flows.

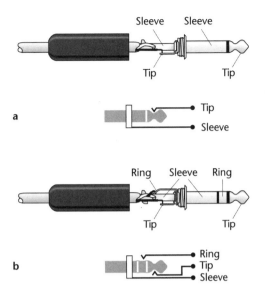

Figure 8-18

Mono unbalanced phone plug and (b) stereo balanced phone plug.

Console Automation

Given today's complex production consoles and the myriad procedures involved in mixing many tracks to a few, console automation has become indispensable. It greatly facilitates operations by automatically keeping track of the various mixer settings and by storing the information for recall at any time.

Operating Modes

Console automation systems have at least three basic operating modes: write, read, and update. All functions may be used independently on any or all channels.

- **Write mode**—The *write mode* is used to create an automated mix. In the write mode, the automation system monitors and stores data from the faders. Only current fader movements are stored in the write mode.

- **Read mode**—The *read mode* plays back or recalls the stored automation data. In the read mode, also called the *safe mode*, the console's faders are inoperative. They take their control voltage information only from the stored data on the disk to reproduce the "recorded" fader movements in real time.

- **Update mode**—The *update mode* allows the operator to read the stored information at any time and make changes simply by moving the appropriate fader. A new data track is generated from the original data track with the changes that have been made.

Snapshot and Continuous Automation

In general, two methods are used to handle data changes in console automation: snapshot control and continuous control. With *snapshot control,* the automation system takes an instant reading of the console settings for recall from storage. The reading reflects the state of the console at a particular moment. With *continuous*, or *dynamic*, *control,* the motion of the mixer controls is recorded. Gradual changes of parameters, from small adjustments in level to larger changes such as fades, are stored as they are made over time.

Advantages of Console Automation

Mixing various sounds once they are recorded can be exacting and tedious. It requires dozens, maybe hundreds, of replays and myriad adjustments to get the right equalization, reverberation, blend, spatial balance, timing of inserts, and so on. Comparing one mix with another is difficult unless settings are written down (which is time-consuming) so that controls can be returned to previous positions if necessary. It is not uncommon to discard a mix because someone forgot to adjust one control or decided after a few days to change a few settings without noting the original positions. Then the controls have to be set up all over again. Mixing one song can take many hours or even days; a production can take months.

Console automation greatly facilitates the recordkeeping and the accuracy of mixing; it makes the engineer's arms "longer." Many productions are so involved that they would be nearly impossible without automation.

Disadvantages of Console Automation

As necessary as automation is in so much of audio production, it also has some disadvantages. It tends to be confusing, even to experienced operators. Some systems are so complex that it is easy to lose track of the many operations necessary to perform a mix, which defeats the purpose of automation. Some systems may not play back exactly what the operator wrote. If the mix is complex, a difference of a few decibels overall may not be perceptible. That would not be the case, however, in more subtle mixes.

Automation systems, like all computer systems, are vulnerable to crashing. Getting the system operational again, even assuming you had the forethought to make a backup copy of the mix before completion, often involves a frustrating loss of production time and continuity, to say nothing of the financial cost.

An aesthetic concern with automation is "sameness." Unless an automated mix is done with skill, its dynamics can sound the same from beginning to end.

The disadvantages of console automation notwithstanding, most audio production today would be difficult without it.

Digital Consoles

Aside from their differences in technologies, the main innovation in digital consoles compared with analog consoles is the divorcing of circuitry from panel controls. The control surface still comprises the familiar controls—faders, equalizer, input selectors, sends, returns, and so on—but there is no physical connection between the controls on the console surface and the audio circuit elements nor are specific controls necessarily dedicated to particular channels.

With an analog console, the controls in one input/output channel strip must be duplicated for each channel strip in the console. With digital consoles, many of these functions pass through a central processor, eliminating the need for duplication and making it possible to increase the number of operations in a smaller surface area. Operational commands are recorded in the system's memory for recall at any time and are assignable.

For example, instead of having an EQ module in each channel strip, the console is designed into a central control panel to which all channels have access. Select, say, channel 1 and pass its signal through the equalizer in the central control panel; make the desired EQ adjustments, which are recorded in the console's memory; then move on to, say, channel 2 and pass its signal through the equalizer; make the desired EQ adjustments, which are recorded in the console's memory; and so on. With most digital consoles today, the same can be done with other dynamic effects that are part of the central control panel such as compression, limiting, noise gating, and delay as well as effects sends, monitor levels, and panning. (A pan control may also be included in each channel strip.)

The *assignable console* design has several advantages over conventional production consoles. In addition to making many more operations possible in a more compact chassis, signals can be handled more quickly and easily because functions are grouped and, with fewer controls, there are fewer operations to perform; and patching can be accomplished at the touch of a few keys, inboard, without the need for a patch bay and patch cords (see Figure 8-19).

Digital consoles are available in three basic configurations. One configuration is actually an analog console that is digitally controlled. The signal path is distributed and processed in analog form, but the console's control parameters are maintained digitally.

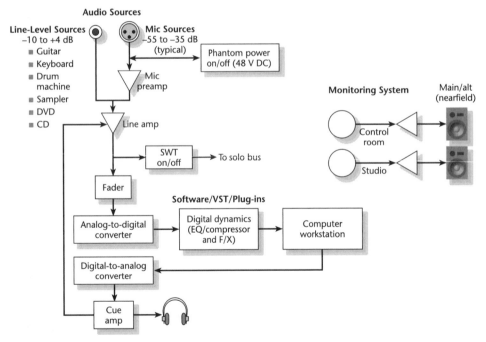

Figure 8-19 Signal flow of a basic generic assignable digital console. Console is used in typical digital audio workstation (DAW) applications. It provides a connection point for input sources to a computer-based audio recording software program, such as Pro Tools and SONAR. It can also be used as a control surface. Each channel strip is separate and houses a number of functions similar to channel strips on most consoles. In an assignable console, however, functions such as EQ, compression, noise gating, and delay are located in a central processing unit and can be individually custom-assigned to each channel strip and retained in the console's memory.

The second configuration is the all-digital console, which uses two approaches. The analog input signal is first encoded into a digital signal, or it is directly accepted as digital information. In either case, the data are distributed and processed digitally. The output might be decoded back into analog or may remain in digital form, depending on its destination.

A third type of digital mixer is actually a virtual console. As the term suggests, a virtual console is not a console per se but an integrated system that combines a hard-disk computer and specialized software to record and process audio directly to disk. Instead of feeding a sound source to a conventional console, it is fed directly to the computer. The controls are displayed on the computer monitor and look like those of a typical analog console—faders, EQ, panning, sends, returns, and so on (see Figure 8-20). Operations and functions are manipulated using some type of *human interface device* (**HID**) such as a mouse, keyboard, joystick, or touch screen, although these tools are not always suited to the hands-on control associated with various aspects of audio production. Mixing with a mouse and keyboard can be cumbersome and awkward, at best. An increasingly diverse range of HIDs called *control surfaces*, or *work surfaces*, provide more tactile means of control across a spectrum of digital audio systems, devices, and software applications.

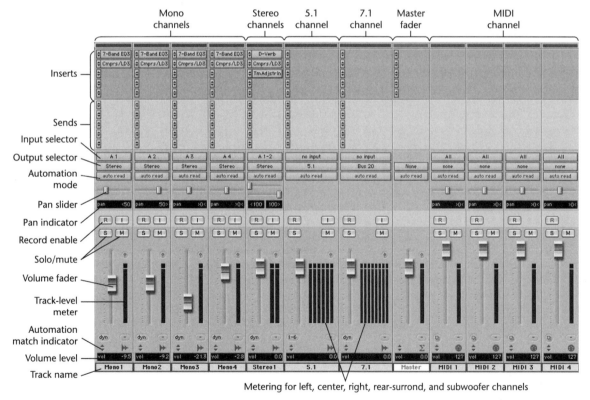

Figure 8-20 Virtual console, shown in what is referred to in recording/editing software programs as the mix window.

Control Surfaces

In much the same way that digital tablet and pen technology liberated graphic artists from the limitations of creating with a keyboard and a mouse, an audio *control surface* provides a tactual means of controlling the various elements of sound production. Also called a *work surface*, the design, features, and appearance of a given control surface vary according to its function: from a dedicated virtual instrument or digital signal processing (DSP) plug-in controller, to universal and hybrid work surfaces (see Figures 8-21 and 8-22). Generally, there are no actual audio signals present inside a simple control surface—only control circuitry that sends digital instructions to the device doing the actual audio signal processing.

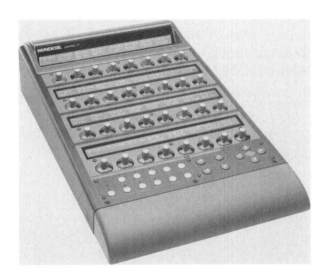

Figure 8-21 Control surface designed to facilitate editing of DSP and virtual instrument plug-ins with a variety of different software. This controller may be used as a stand-alone solution or in tandem with other control surface components for analog-style control over tracks and plug-ins.

Figure 8-22 Universal control surface. This model provides transport, automation, and DSP functions without the need for a mouse or keyboard. Used primarily for mixing, it resembles an analog mixing console. Controls include record, play, stop, fast-forward, rewind, and other frequently used editing functions. A jog/shuttle wheel facilitates positioning and scrub-editing.

Depending on the digital audio workstation environment and the technology employed, control surfaces may function or be configured in different ways. The most popular means of connecting a control surface to a host computer or other peripheral device is via the MIDI standard (see Chapter 9). Other equipment may support a number of connections: a proprietary interface; a Universal Serial Bus (USB) port; FireWire cable, which generally provides more rapid data and media transfer and access speeds than USB; or an Ethernet connection. Universal and hybrid control surfaces often integrate analog and digital audio signals and paths with DSP control capability across a complement of compatible programs. Control surfaces can be used in most types of audio production: in performance from dedicated control over MIDI devices including virtual instruments, synthesizers, samplers and sequencing software applications; and in recording, mixing, DSP, and automation.

Another use for a control surface is via router connectivity, thereby enabling access to a broadcast station's or production facility's entire network of audio sources and assets.

Digital consoles and control surfaces have several advantages over their all-analog counterparts, especially as more and more facets of audio production move into the digital domain. They are virtually distortion- and noise-free; every control move, manual or preprogrammed, is stored and retrieved digitally with a greater degree of accuracy. For example, manipulating a knob—or in the parlance of the control surface—a *rotary encoder* sends a set of precise, digital instructions to a device. This is far more efficient than manually modulating voltage control through a potentiometer, with all its associated system noise, artifact, and margin of user error from one move to the next. Control parameters may be combined or matrixed in such a way that one control instruction can direct several preprogrammed functions to occur simultaneously. Physical inboard and outboard patch bays are unnecessary, although limited in control surfaces compared with the routing flexibility in digital consoles; a compact chassis preserves valuable control room space; and, given the variety and the efficiency of operational potential and capacities, compared with their analog cousins, whether the console or control surface is modest or upscale, there are enough models available to suit any budget and production requirement.

Main Points

- Mixers, consoles, and control surfaces perform essentially the same basic operations. They take input signals and route them to output sources such as broadcast, recording, and digital audio workstations.

- The differences between a mixer and a console are that a mixer is small, highly portable, and performs limited processing functions whereas a console is larger and performs numerous processing functions. In most modern consoles, these functions are computer-assisted.

- The term mixer is often used synonymously with console. Some mixers include additional features found on consoles and some small- and medium-format consoles have limited features that could classify them as large mixers.

- Mixers and consoles have three basic control sections: input, output, and monitor.

- The input section takes incoming signals and routes them to the output section. The output section routes signals to broadcast, recording, or to a router. The monitor section enables signals to be heard.

- There are two types of microphone mixer: passive and active. A passive mic mixer combines individual inputs into one output without amplifying the signal. An active mic mixer allows amplification control of each audio source and usually includes other processing features as well.

- Consoles today are available in various configurations, use different technologies, and are designed for particular production purposes. A console may be analog or digital; appropriate for on-air broadcast, production, or postproduction; software-based and used as a virtual console with a hard-disk recorder; or it may be a control surface.

- In an analog console, audio signals flow in and out of physical modules through inboard wires and circuits. In a digital console, incoming analog audio signals are converted to digital information at the inputs, and interfaces handle the routing and the signal processing.

- On-air broadcast consoles, particularly for radio, do not have to be as elaborate as production consoles because most of the audio they handle has been produced already. But modern consoles for radio have sophisticated features, such as digital signal processing (DSP), computer-assisted operations, and routing flexibility.

- The features of production consoles generally include the input/output (I/O) section consisting of an I/O channel strip; input selector control; phantom power; microphone preamplifier input module; microphone preamplifier; trim or gain; pad; overload, or peak, indicator; polarity (phase) reversal; channel assignment and routing; direct switch; pan pot; equalizer and filter; dynamics section; channel/monitor control; cue and effects (F/X or EFX) sends (pre- or postfader); solo and prefader listen (PFL); mute (channel on/off); channel and monitor faders; and meters.

- The volume-unit (VU) meter is a voltage meter that measures the amount of electric energy flowing through the console. The meter has two scales: percentage of modulation and volume units. Percentage of modulation is the percentage of an applied signal in relation to the maximum signal a sound system can handle.

- Peak meters, which today are preferred over the VU meter, track peak program levels, thereby making them a more accurate indicator of signal levels passing through a console.

- Peak meters read out in bar graphs using light-emitting diodes (LEDs) or plasma displays.

- With the peak program meter (ppm), as signal levels increase there is a warning of impending overload distortion. The level indicator makes this easier to notice because its rise time is rapid and its fallback is slow.

- One goal in processing audio through the signal chain is to make sure the levels at each stage are optimal. Given the several stages in the sound chain, from microphone to console to recording to mixing to mastering, this is easier said than done.

- Meters in digital audio consoles are calibrated in decibel full-scale (dBFS), a unit of measure for the amplitude of digital audio signals. Zero dBFS occurs when all the binary bits that make up the digital signal are on.

- The master section includes master buses, the master fader, the master effects sends and returns, level and mute controls, meters, and other functions.

- The monitor section includes: recorder select, send, mix, and speaker select switches. It may also have a pan pot, mutes, and a phase coherence switch.

- Other common features of production consoles include talkback, slate/talkback, an oscillator, and, in analog consoles, a patch bay.

- A channel strip refers to one channel (usually input) of a console. It can be ordered separately from the console manufacturer and rigged to a power supply and I/O connections for stand-alone use.

- A patch bay is a central routing terminal that facilitates the routing of sound through pathways not provided in the normal console design. The patch bay makes multiple signal paths possible. Patch cords plugged into jacks connect the routing circuits.

- The signal paths used most often are wired together at the terminals of the patch bay. This normals these routes and makes it unnecessary to use patch cords to connect them. It is possible to break normal and create other signal paths by patching.

- Plugs at the end of patch cords are either unbalanced, comprising a tip and a sleeve, or balanced, comprising a tip, ring, and sleeve.

- Instead of hardware-based patch panels, many modern consoles in general and all digital consoles in particular handle patching using computer programming.

- Console automation makes it possible to automate fader functions, decoding positional information as adjustments in level are made. The data are stored in and retrieved from computer memory.

- Console automation systems have at least the three basic operating modes: write, read, and update.

- Digital consoles use the assignable concept in three configurations: in an analog console that is digitally controlled, in an all-digital console, and in a virtual console which is not a console per se but an integrated system that combines a hard-disk computer and specialized software to record and process audio directly to disk.

- With digital consoles, instead of individual controls for channel-to-track routing on each channel strip, these functions have been centralized into single sets so they can be assigned to any channel. Once assigned, the commands are stored in the console's computer, so different functions can be assigned to other channels. There is no physical connection between the controls on the console surface and the audio circuit elements.

- A control surface, or work surface, provides external control of a virtual audio environment. There are two main types of control surfaces: general-purpose controllers that can work with a wide range of gear and dedicated controllers that work with specific software.

9 Recording

Recording today almost always means operating in the digital domain. Therefore, it is first necessary to understand the basics of digital audio.

Digital Audio

Recording audio in the digital format uses a numerical representation of the audio signal's actual frequency, or time component, and amplitude, or level component. The time component is called *sampling*; the level component is called *quantization*. In analog recording, the waveform of the signal processed resembles the waveform of the original sound—they are analogous.

Sampling

Sampling takes periodic samples (voltages) of the original analog signal at fixed intervals and converts them to digital data. The rate at which the fixed intervals sample the original signal each second is called the **sampling frequency**, or **sampling rate**. For example, a sampling frequency of 48 kHz means samples are taken 48,000 times per second, or each sample period is 1/48,000 second. Because sampling and the component of time are directly related, a system's sampling rate determines its upper frequency limits. Theoretically, the higher the sampling rate, the greater a system's frequency range.

In the development of digital technology, it was determined that if the highest frequency in a signal were to be digitally encoded successfully, it would have to be sampled at a rate at least twice its frequency. In other words, if high-frequency response in digital recording is to reach 20 kHz, the sampling frequency must be at least 40 kHz. Too low a sampling rate would cause loss of too much information (see Figure 9-1).

Think of a movie camera that takes 24 still pictures per second. A sampling rate of 1/24 second seems adequate to record most visual activities. Although the camera shutter closes after each 1/24 second and nothing is recorded, not enough information is lost to impair perception of the event. A person running, for example, does not run far enough in the split second the shutter is closed to alter the naturalness of the movement. If the sampling rates were slowed to 1 frame per second, the running movement would be

179

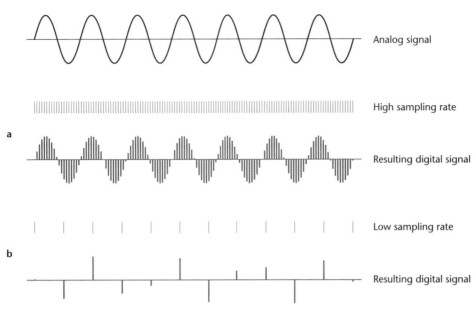

Figure 9-1 Sampling. (a) A signal sampled frequently enough contains sufficient information for proper decoding. (b) Too low a sampling rate loses too much information for proper decoding.

quick and abrupt; if it were slowed to 1 frame per minute, the running would be difficult to follow.

A number of sampling rates are used in digital audio. The most common are 32 kHz, 44.1 kHz, 48 kHz, and 96 kHz. For the Internet, sampling rates below 32 kHz are often used (see Chapter 14). To store more audio data on computer disks, submultiples of 44.1 kHz usually are used, such as 22.05 and 11.025. Multiples of 44.1 kHz (88.2 kHz and 176.4 kHz) and 48 kHz (96 kHz and 192 kHz) are used for greater increases in frequency response.

The international sampling rate—32 kHz—is used for broadcast digital audio. Because the maximum bandwidth in broadcast transmission is 15 kHz, the 32 kHz sampling rate is sufficient. For compact disc and digital tape recording, 44.1, and 48 kHz are used. Generally, standards for the digital versatile disc (DVD) are 48 and 96 kHz. DVD consists of several formats, however, some of which use higher sampling rates (see Figure 9-2; see also "Digital Versatile Disc" later in this chapter).

Depending on the comparative sampling frequencies, there may or may not be a significant difference in frequency response. For example, 44.1 kHz and 48 kHz sound almost alike, as do 88.2 kHz and 96 kHz. But the difference between 48 kHz and 96 kHz is dramatic. Among other things, 44.1 kHz and 48 kHz do not have the transparent response of the higher sampling rates. *Transparent sound* has a wide and flat frequency response, a sharp time response, clarity, detail, and very low noise and distortion.

Quantization

While sampling rate affects high frequency response, the number of bits taken per sample affects dynamic range, noise, and distortion. As samples of the waveform are taken, these voltages are converted into discrete quantities and assigned values, a process

KHz	Applications
16	Used in some telephone applications and data reduction
18.9	CD-ROM/XA (extended architecture) and CD-interactive (CD-I) standard for low- to moderate-quality audio
32	Used in some broadcast systems and the R-DAT (digital audiocassette recorder) long-play mode
37.9	CD-ROM/XA and CD-I intermediate-quality audio using ADPCM (adaptive differential pulse-code modulation)
44.1	Widely used in many formats, including the CD
48	Used in several formats, including R-DAT and digital video recorders
88.2, 96, 176.4, and 192	Double and quadruple sampling rates standardized as options in the DVD-Audio format and used in some high-end equipment
2.8224	Used in the Super Audio Compact Disc (SACD) format

Figure 9-2 Selected sampling frequencies and their applications.

known as *quantization.* The assigned value is in the form of *bits*, from *b*inary dig*its*. Most of us learned math using the decimal, or base 10, system, which consists of 10 numerals—0 through 9. The binary, or base 2, system uses two numbers—0 and 1. In converting the analog signal to digital, when the voltage is off, the assigned value is 0; when the voltage is on, the assigned value is 1.

A quantity expressed as a binary number is called a *digital word*: 10 is a two-bit word, 101 is a three-bit word, 10101 is a five-bit word, and so on. Each *n*-bit binary word produces 2*n* discrete levels. Therefore, a one-bit word produces two discrete levels—0, 1; a two-bit word produces four discrete levels—00, 01, 10, and 11; a three-bit word produces eight discrete levels—000, 001, 010, 011, 100, 101, 110, and 111; and so on. So the more quantizing levels there are, the longer the digital word or *word length* must be. (Word length is also referred to as *bit depth* and *resolution*.)

The longer the digital word, the better the dynamic range. For example, the number of discrete voltage steps possible in an 8-bit word is 256; in a 16-bit word, it is 65,536; in a 20-bit word, it is 1,048,576; and in a 24-bit word, it is 16,777,216. The greater the number of these quantizing levels, the more accurate the representation of the analog signal and the wider the dynamic range (see Figures 9-3 and 9-4).[1]

---

1. In quantizing the analog signal into discrete binary numbers (voltages), noise, known as quantizing noise, is generated. The signal-to-noise ratio in an analog-to-digital conversion system is 6 dB for each bit. A 16-bit system is sufficient to deal with quantizing noise. This gives digital sound a signal-to-noise ratio of 96 dB (6 dB × 16-bit system), which is pretty good by analog standards; but by digital standards, 20-bit systems are better at 120 dB, and 24-bit systems are dramatically better at 144 dB.

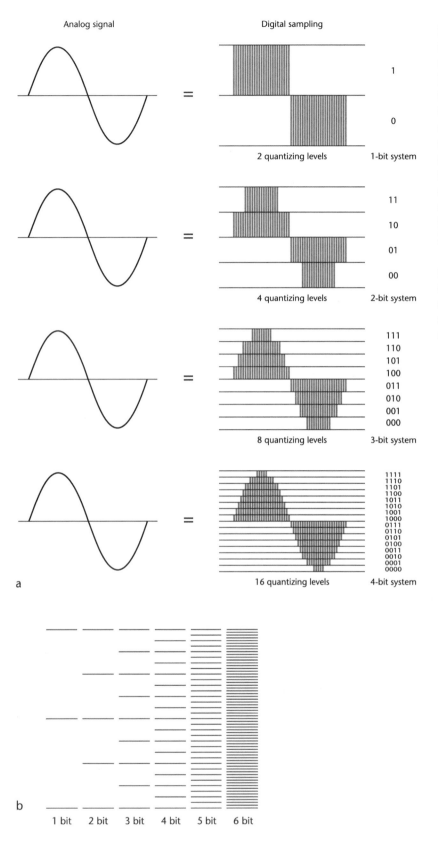

Figure 9-3 Quantizing.
(a) As the number of quantizing levels increases, the digital sample of the analog signal becomes more accurate. In 16-bit systems the audio spectrum is divided into 65,536 values in a single sample. A 20-bit system captures 1,048,576 values in a single sample. A 24-bit system captures 16,777,216 values in a single sample. (b) The addition of a single bit doubles the data that a digital device can capture.

Bit Depth	Dynamic Range	Application
8	44 dB	Older PCs and multimedia applications yielding low-quality audio.
16	92 dB	Many professional recorders and multimedia PCs. The standard for CD and R-DAT. Widely used in consumer-grade media.
20	116 dB	High-quality professional audio and mastering.
24	140 dB	Very high-quality recording, including DVD-Audio.

Figure 9-4 Quantizing resolutions and applications.

This raises a question: How can a representation of the original signal be better than the original signal itself? Assume the original analog signal is an ounce of water with an infinite number of values (molecules). The amount and the "character" of the water changes with the number of molecules; it has one "value" with 500 molecules, another with 501, still another with 2,975, and so forth. But all together, the values are infinite. Moreover, changes in the original quantity of water are inevitable: Some of it may evaporate, some may be lost if poured, and some may be contaminated or absorbed by dust or dirt.

But what if the water molecules are sampled and then converted to a stronger, more durable form? In so doing, a representation of the water would be obtained in a facsimile from which nothing would be lost. But sufficient samples would have to be obtained to ensure that the character of the original water is maintained.

For example, suppose the molecule samples were converted to ball bearings and a quantity of 1 million ball bearings was a sufficient sample. In this form, the original water is not vulnerable to evaporation or contamination from dust or dirt. Even if a ball bearing is lost, they are all the same; therefore, losing one ball bearing does not affect the content or quality of the others.

Audio Data Rate

A higher sampling rate does not necessarily ensure better frequency response if the word length is short and vice versa. Uncompressed digital audio is expressed by two measurements, word length (or bit depth) and sampling frequency, such as 16-bit/44.1 kHz. The two numbers are used to compute data rate.

Bit depth defines the digital word length used to represent a given sample and is equivalent to dynamic range. Larger bit depths theoretically yield greater dynamic range. The *sampling frequency* determines the audio bandwidth. Higher sampling frequencies theoretically yield wider audio bandwidth. The relationship between sampling frequency and quantization is called the *audio data rate.*

Recording Systems

Today, the vast majority of digital audio recording systems used in audio production are removable-media and fixed disk-based. Of these systems, the most commonly employed are the memory recorder, hard-disk recorder, digital audio workstation, CD, DVD, and high-density optical disc. (That said, with changes in digital audio technology occurring almost daily it seems, the systems discussed below could be obsolescent by tomorrow and obsolete by next week.)

Memory Recorders

A *memory recorder* is a portable digital recorder that has no moving parts and therefore requires no maintenance. The storage medium is a *memory card,* a nonvolatile memory card that can be electrically recorded onto, erased, and reprogrammed. *Nonvolatile* means the card does not need power to maintain the stored information.

Several models of memory recorders are available. Depending on the design, the storage medium, recording configurations, recording times, bit depths, and sampling frequencies vary. An example of a memory recorder and its features is displayed in Figure 9-5.

Memory cards have taken portability in digital recording to a new level. They are quite small and lightweight, and some models easily fit into the palm of a hand. They hold a

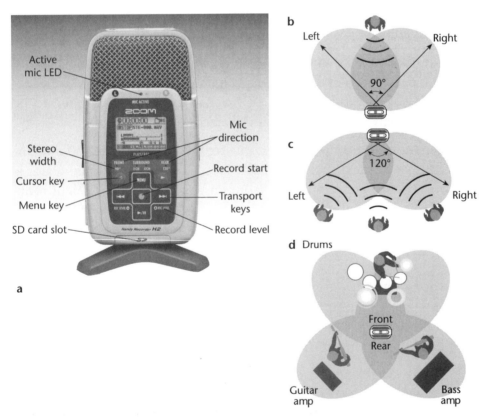

Figure 9-5 Zoom H2. (a) This model includes four cardioid microphone capsules, which allow (b) front 90-degree, (c) rear 120-degree, and (d) 360-degree pickup. The 360-degree pickup facilitates conversion of a recording to 5.1 surround sound. It comes with a 512 MB Secure Digital card but can accommodate up to a 16 GB card, allowing for as much as 24 hours of recording time using the 16-bit/44.1 kHz WAV format. The data formats include WAV (44.1 kHz, 48 kHz, and 96 kHz at 16- or 24-bit), MP3 to 320 Kbps, and variable bit rate (bit rate is not constant). Other features include a metronome, a guitar/bass tuner, a low-pass filter, voice-activated recording, and a USB interface. It weighs 4 ounces.

substantial quantity of data for their size, which facilitate long recording times, and memory cards have fast read access times. They are a robust recording medium, as are the recorders, which makes the technology highly suitable for production on location. Most memory recorders provide flexibility in recording formats and supported audio formats; selectable sampling rates and bit depths; wide frequency response; and USB connectivity. Many models include a built-in stereo microphone or two microphones for separate mono or stereo pickup; some models also include editing features.

Examples of memory cards include flash cards such as CompactFlash, flash memory sticks (a family of formats so named because the original cards were about the size and the thickness of a stick of chewing gum), Secure Digital (SD) memory cards, and SmartMedia. The PCMCIA card (named for the Personal Computer Memory Card International Association) is yet another recording medium used in memory recorders. Depending on the recorder, the flash card may be removable or fixed.

Hard-Disk Recorders

Digital recorders also use fixed and removable hard disks. Compared with memory recorders, they usually provide better sound quality and greater recording flexibility (see Figure 9-6). They are available in portable and rack-mountable models.

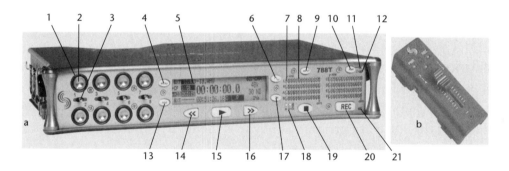

1. **Input activity ring LEDs** (indicates input activity for each input)
2. **Input gain control** (controls analog and digital input gain)
3. **Input selector/solo switch** (pushed left selects odd-numbered inputs; pushed right selects even-numbered inputs)
4. **Menu key**
5. **LCD display**
6. **Tone key** (activates tone oscillation)
7. **Track arm LEDs** (indicates that the respective track is armed to record)
8. **Level meter LEDs** (indicates level in dBFS)
9. **Input key** (accesses track setup menu)
10. **Power key**
11. **Power/charge LED**
12. **Headphone output peak LED** (indicates overload of headphone amp)
13. **HDD key** (enters the take list and the drive directory)
14. **Rewind key**
15. **Play key**
16. **Fast-forward key**
17. **LCD backlight key**
18. **Media activity key LEDs** (indicates storage media activity)
19. **Stop/pause key**
20. **Record key**
21. **Record LED**

Figure 9-6 Sound Devices 788T and its control features. (a) This model is about the size of a small paperback book and weighs about 3.6 pounds without the battery. It includes eight mic/line inputs, a selectable sampling rate up to 98 kHz with selectable sampling rate converters on each digital input, peak/VU meters, a word clock, time code, and internal hard drive and a Flash slot, FireWire and USB connections, and a separate USB keyboard input for control. (b) Remote fader controller includes two 2-position toggle switches; programmable to control record, start/stop, and other functions; and LEDs to indicate record and power status. It can be mounted to a boom pole.

Storage Capacity of Memory and Hard-Disk Recorders

The amount of data that memory and hard-disk recorders can encode is impressive given their size. But all technology has its limitations. When using these recorders, especially in the field, it is essential to know their storage capacities in advance so that you do not get caught shorthanded (see Figure 9-7).

Number of Tracks	Bit Depth	Sampling Rate	Storage Needed
2	16	44.1 kHz	606 MB
2	24	44.1 kHz	909 MB
2	24	96 kHz	1.9 GB
8	16	44.1 kHz	2.4 GB
8	24	44.1 kHz	3.6 GB
8	24	96 kHz	7.7 GB
16	16	44.1 kHz	4.8 GB
16	24	44.1 kHz	7.1 GB
16	24	96 kHz	15.4 GB
24	16	44.1 kHz	7.1 GB
24	24	44.1 kHz	10.7 GB
24	24	96 kHz	23.3 GB

Figure 9-7 Required storage capacity for a one-hour recording.

Digital Audio Workstation

Like many digital audio recorders, a *digital audio workstation (DAW)* records, edits, and plays back. But unlike digital audio recorders, DAWs have considerably greater processing power because of the software programs they use. Generally, there are two types of DAW systems: computer-based and integrated.

Computer-Based Digital Audio Workstation

A computer-based DAW is a stand-alone unit with all processing handled by the computer. A software program facilitates recording and editing. Most programs also provide some degree of digital signal processing (DSP), or additional DSP may be available as an add-on so long as the computer has sufficient storage capacity.

For recording, typical computer-based DAWs support either two-track or multitrack production and include a virtual mixer and record transport controls (play, record, rewind, and so on). The relationships of channels to inputs, outputs, and tracks are not directly linked. Once the computer-based audio data is recorded and stored, it can be assigned to any output(s) and moved in time.

For example, a DAW may have four inputs, eight outputs, 16 channels, and 256 virtual tracks. This means that up to four inputs can be used to record up to four channels at one time; up to eight channels at one time can be used for internal mixing or routing; up to 16 channels (real tracks) are simultaneously available during playback; and up to

256 separate *soundfiles*[2] can be maintained and assigned to a virtual track. ***Virtual tracks*** provide all the functionality of an actual track but cannot be played back simultaneously. For example, in a 16-channel system with 256 virtual tracks, only 16 tracks can play back at once. Think of 16 stacks of index cards totaling 256 cards. Assume each stack is a channel. A card can be moved from anywhere in a stack to the top of the same stack or to the top of another stack. There are 256 cards, but only 16 of them can be on top at the same time. In other words, any virtual track can be assigned to any channel and slipped along that channel or across channels.

It is difficult to discuss recording operations generically because terms, configurations, and visual displays differ from system to system. Layout and control functions, however, are similar to those in recording consoles (see Chapter 8). Depending on the DAW, a system may have more or fewer signal processing capabilities in its recording software.

Sound Card

A computer must have a ***sound card*** to input, manipulate, and output audio. It either comes with the computer or must be purchased separately and installed. In either case, it is important to make sure the card is compatible with the computer's platform—PC, Macintosh, or other proprietary system. Also, because the sound card interfaces with other audio equipment, it is necessary to know your input/output requirements, such as the types of balanced or unbalanced connectors and the number of recording channels the card has to handle. Signal-to-noise ratio is another consideration. A sound card capable of −70 dB and below is necessary for producing professional-quality audio.

Integrated Digital Audio Workstation

An ***integrated DAW*** not only consists of the computer and its related software but may also include a console; a control surface—either universal or one specially designed for use with a particular software program; a ***server*** for integration with and networking to a collection of devices such as other audio, video, and musical instrument digital interface (MIDI) sources within or among facilities in the same or different locations; and a ***storage area network (SAN)*** for transfer and storage of data between computer systems and other storage elements such as disk controllers and servers. A DAW's system-wide communication with other external devices and communication between devices in general is facilitated through the distribution of digital interfaces. Those in common use are ***AES/EBU, S/PDIF, SCSI, iSCSI, MADI,*** and ***FireWire*** (see Figure 9-8).

Although a server and storage area network greatly facilitate operations in broadcast and production facilities, their programming and management are the provinces of computer and other technical personnel. Therefore, the following two sections only briefly address their functions.

---

2. Audio encoded onto the disk takes the form of a ***soundfile.*** The soundfile contains information about the sound such as amplitude and duration. When the soundfile is opened, most systems display that information.

Figure 9-8 Digital interfaces.

AES/EBU is a professional digital audio connection interface standard specified jointly by the Audio Engineering Society (AES) and the European Broadcast Union (EBU). Its standard calls for two audio channels to be encoded in a serial data stream and transmitted through a balanced line using XLR connectors.

S/PDIF (Sony/Philips Digital Interface) is the consumer version of the AES/EBU standard. It calls for an unbalanced line using phono connectors. S/PDIF is implemented on consumer audio equipment such as CD players.

SCSI (Small Computer Systems Interface) is the standard for hardware and software command language. Pronounced "scuzzy," it allows two-way communication between, primarily, hard-disk and CD-ROM drives to exchange digital data at fast speeds. SCSI can also be used with other components, such as scanners.

iSCSI (Internet SCSI) is a standard based on the Internet Protocol (IP) for linking data storage devices over a network and transferring data by carrying SCSI commands over IP networks.

MADI (Multichannel Audio Digital Interface) is the standard used when interfacing multichannel digital audio. It allows up to 56 channels of digital audio to be sent down one coaxial cable.

FireWire is a low-cost networking scheme that is a more formidable cable interface than SCSI. Powering is flexible, modes are asynchronous/isosynchronous within the same network, and compatibility is backward and forward with continuous transmission in either direction. Because it can interface with just about anything electronic, with fewer problems of compatibility than with other interfaces, in the appropriate applications FireWire has become the interface of choice.

Figure 9-8 Digital interfaces.

Server

A *server* is a computer dedicated to providing one or more services over a computer network, typically through a request-response routine. These services are furnished by specialized server applications, which are computer programs designed to handle multiple concurrent requests.[3]

In relation to a broadcast or audio production facility, a server's large-capacity disk arrays record, store, and play hours of such materials as entire programs, program segments, news clips, music recordings, and sound effects and music libraries. In other words, just about any recordable program material. A server can run a number of programs simultaneously. For example, a director can access a sound bite for an on-air

---

3. From *Wikipedia.*

newscast while a producer in another studio accesses an interview for a documentary still in production and an editor in still another studio accesses music and sound effects cues for a commercial.

Storage Area Network (SAN)

A *storage area network (SAN)* can be likened to the common flow of data in a personal computer shared by different kinds of storage devices such as a hard disk, a CD, DVD, or Blu-ray player. It is designed to serve a large network of users and handle sizeable data transfers among different interconnected data storage devices. The computer storage devices are attached to servers and remotely-controlled.

Recordable, Rewritable, and Interactive Compact Discs

The *recordable compact disc (CD-R)* has unlimited playback, but it can be recorded on only once. The CD-R conforms to the standards document known as **Orange Book**. According to this standard, data encoded on a CD-R does not have to be recorded all at once but can be added to whenever the user wishes, making it more convenient to produce sequential audio material. But CD-Rs conforming to the Orange Book standard will not play on any CD player.

To be playable on a standard CD player, the CD-R must conform to the **Red Book** standard, which requires that a table of contents (TOC) file be encoded onto the disc.[4] A TOC file includes information related to subcode and copy prohibition data, index numbering, and timing information. The TOC, which is written onto the disc after audio assembly, tells the CD player where each cut starts and ends. Once it is encoded, any audio added to the disc will not be playable on standard CD players due to the write-once limitation of CD-R. It is therefore important to know the "color book" standards with which a CD recorder is compatible. Details of these standards are beyond the scope of this book but are available on the Internet.

Compact-disc recorders are available in different recording speeds. For example, single- (1x), double-(2x), quad-(4x)—up to 16x speed. Single-speed machines record in real time; that is, at the CD's playback speed, 2x machines record at twice the playback speed, reducing by half the time it takes to create a CD, and so on. For the higher recording speeds, the computer and the hard drive must be fast enough.

---

4. In addition to the Orange and Red Book standards, there are Yellow, Green, White, Blue, and Scarlet Book standards. The **Yellow Book** format describes the basic specifications for computer-based CD-ROM (compact disc–read-only memory). The **Green Book** format describes the basic specifications for CD-I (compact disc–interactive) and CD-ROM XA (the XA is short for extended architecture). It is aimed at multimedia applications that combine audio, graphic images, animation, and full-motion video. The **White Book** describes basic specifications for full-motion, compressed videodiscs. The **Blue Book** provides specifications for the HDCD (high-definition compact disc) format, such as Digital Versatile Disc–Audio (DVD-A). The **Scarlet Book** includes the protocol for the Super Audio Compact Disc (SACD).

Playing times vary with the CD format. CDs for *consumer format* use a 63-minute blank disc. Disc length for the *professional format* is 63 minutes (550 MB), 74 minutes (650 MB), or 80 minutes (700 MB).

The *rewritable CD (CD-RW)* is steps better than the CD-R because it can be recorded on, erased, and used many times again for other recordings. If the driver program supports it, erase can even be random. Like the CD recorders, CD-RW drives operate at different speeds to shorten recording times.

After the Orange Book, any user with a CD recorder drive can create a CD from a computer. CD-RW drives can write both CD-R and CD-RW discs and can read any type of CD.

CDVU+ (pronounced "CD view plus") is a compact disc with interactive content. It was created by the Walt Disney Company to reverse the decline in music CD sales. In addition to the music, it includes multimedia material such as band photos, interviews, and articles relevant to the band or the music, or both.

Digital Versatile Disc

The *digital versatile disc (DVD)* is the same diameter and thickness as the compact disc, but it can encode a much greater amount of data. The storage capacity of the current CD is 650 MB, or about 74 minutes of stereo audio. The storage capacity of the DVD can be on a number of levels, each one far exceeding that of the CD. For example, the single-side, single-layer DVD has a capacity of 4.7 billion bytes, equivalent to the capacity of seven CD-ROMs; the double-side, dual-layer DVD with 17 billion bytes is equivalent to the capacity of 26 CD-ROMs.

The CD has a fixed bit depth of 16 bits and a sampling rate of 44.1 kHz. DVD formats can accommodate various bit depths and sampling rates. The CD is a two-channel format and can encode 5.1 (six channels) surround-sound but only with data reduction. *DVD-Audio (DVD-A)* can encode up to eight audio tracks without data compression.

In addition to DVD-Audio, other DVD formats include: DVD-Video (DVD-V), DVD-Recordable (DVD-R), authoring and general, DVD-Rewritable (DVD-RW), and another rewritable format, DVD+RW, DVD-ROM, and DVD-RAM. Of these formats, only DVD-V has met commercial expectations. Moreover, with the advent of the high-density optical format, the DVD is being supplanted.

High-Density Optical Disc Formats

High-density disc technology is another entrant into the competition to meet the demands of high-definition media. The most familiar format at this writing is the *Blu-ray Disc. (BD)*. Another high-density optical disc format, *HD DVD*, was developed to compete with the Blu-ray Disc but lost out and is no longer marketed.

Blu-Ray Disc

The **Blu-ray Disc (BD)** format enables recording, playback, and rewriting of high-definition media. It was designed to supercede the DVD. It produces not only superior picture quality but superior audio quality as well. The name derives from the blue-violet laser used to read and write data. Blu-ray has or will have formats that include BD-ROM, a read-only format developed for prerecorded content; BD-R, a recordable format for PC data storage; BD-RW, a rewritable format for PC data storage; and BD-RE, a rewritable format for HDTV recording.

Single-sided, single-layer 4.7-inch discs have a recording capacity of 25 GB; dual-layer discs can hold 50 GB. Double-sided 4.7-inch discs, single-layer and dual-layer, have a capacity of 50 GB and 100 GB, respectively. The recording capacity of single-sided 3.1-inch discs is 7.8 MB for single-layer and 15.6 GB for dual-layer. The double-sided, single-layer 3.1-inch disc holds 15.6 MB of data; the dual-layer disc holds 31.2 GB. These recording capacities are far greater than those of DVDs (see Figure 9-9).

The 25 GB disc can record more than two hours of HDTV and about 13 hours of **standard television (STV)**. About nine hours of HDTV can be stored on a 50 GB disc and about 23 hours of STV. Write times vary with drive speed and disc format (see Figure 9-10).

Parameters	BD	BD	DVD	DVD
Recording capacity	25 GB	50 GB	4.7 GB	9.4 GB
Number of layers	Single-layer	Dual-layer	Single-layer	Dual-layer
Data transfer rate	36 Mbps	36 Mbps	11.08 Mbps	11.08 Mbps
Compression protocol	MPEG-2* MPEG-4* AVC* VC-1*	MPEG-2 MPEG-4 AVC VC-1	MPEG-2	MPEG-2

*MPEG-2 is the compression standard for broadcast-quality video and audio. MPEG-4 also supports high-quality video and audio and 3D content. *Advanced Video Coding (AVC)* is part of the MPEG-4 protocols. It is the compression standard for high-definition video and audio and achieves very high data compression. *VC-1* is a specification standardized by the Society of Motion Picture and Television Engineers (SMPTE) and implemented by Microsoft as Windows Media Video 9. It relates specifically to the decoding of compressed content.

Figure 9-9 Differences between Blu-ray Disc and DVD.

Drive Speed	Data Rate		Single- layer	Dual- layer
	Mbps	MB/s		
1×	36	4.5	90	180
2×	72	9	45	90
4×	144	18	23	45
6×	216	27	15	30
8×	288	36	12	23
12×	432	54	8	15

Figure 9-10 Drive speed, data rate, and write times (in minutes) for Blu-ray Discs.

Blu-ray supports most audio compression schemes. They include, as mandatory, lossless pulse code modulation (PCM), Meridian Lossless Packing (MLP), and TRUE HD two-channel; as optional, it supports DTS HD. The mandatory lossy compression protocols are Dolby Digital, Dolby Digital Plus (developed especially for HDTV and Blu-ray), DTS, and MPEG audio.

Other Blu-ray formats now available or in development are the *Mini Blu-ray Disc* that can store about 7.5 GB of data; the *BD5* and *BD9 discs* with lower storage capacities, 4482 MB and 8152 MB respectively; the *Blu-ray recordable* (*BD-R*) and *rewritable* (*BD-RE*) *discs*; and the *Blu-ray Live* (*BD Live*) *disc,* which addresses Internet recording and interactivity.

Musical Instrument Digital Interface

Conventional production usually depends on at least a few people to produce the various stages of an audio project. But with *MIDI* (pronounced mi-dee) one person can perform most, if not all of the functions, including the capability to produce virtually any sonic effect, musical sound, or combination of sounds, in any musical genre, for any size and type of ensemble without the need for a studio.

What MIDI Is

In MIDI, *digital* refers to a set of instructions in the form of digital (binary) data that must be interpreted by an electronic sound-generating, or sound-modifying, device such as a synthesizer or computer that can respond to the directions. MIDI does not create or communicate sound, it communicates instructions. Instructions to a device or program may include creation, playback, or alteration of sound or control function parameters. In other words, the process is not unlike that of a piano roll and a player-piano. The roll itself does not make any sound. When inserted into a player-piano, it instructs the piano to play the programmed sound.

Interface is the link permitting the control signals generated by commands from one synthesizer or controller to trigger other synthesizers and equipment. Thus, one person can "play" several "instruments," thereby having the capability to create an infinite variety of combined sounds that would otherwise be unachievable.

With MIDI, different voicings from various MIDI devices can be layered to reproduce virtually any sonic structure; multiple hardware and software electronic instruments, performance controllers, computers, and other related devices can communicate and be synchronized with each other over a connected network. Moreover, most MIDI synthesizers are compatible with most others because the entire electronic industry adopted the MIDI specification (see "How MIDI Works" in the next section).

MIDI software is available in a number of categories: (1) performance—software that allows composition, orchestration, arranging, and performing music; (2) productivity—programs that transcribe, data base, and print music using any MIDI setup; (3) editing—

for editing digital samples; (4) patching librarians—for storing settings or "patches"; and (5) instruction—software for learning MIDI operations.

A detailed discussion of all of these elements is beyond the scope of this book. It is useful, however, to have some idea of how MIDI works and what a typical MIDI setup includes.

How MIDI Works

MIDI enables hard- and software-based synthesizers, computers, rhythm machines, sequencers, and other signal-processing devices to be interconnected through an interface. The interface is based on a standard convention, or protocol, called *General MIDI*, devised by the International MIDI Association (IMA) and agreed to by manufacturers of MIDI hardware and software. General MIDI defines a set of minimum standards among MIDI devices. These standards have been expanded in the General MIDI 2 protocol.

MIDI data is communicated digitally throughout a production system as a string of MIDI messages. MIDI messages may be grouped into two categories: channel messages and system messages. A channel message applies to the specific MIDI channel named in the message. A system message addresses all the channels.

Channel Messages

MIDI has the ability to send and receive messages on any of 16 discrete channels. *Channel messages* give information on whether an instrument should send or receive and on which channel. They also indicate when a note event begins or ends and control information such as velocity, attack, and program change. Channel messages are grouped into channel mode messages and channel voice messages.

Channel Mode Messages

Channel mode messages facilitate MIDI response appropriate to monophonic, polyphonic, or polytimbral processing. These modes have been specified as: *Mode 1—Omni On/Poly*; *Mode 2—Omni On/Mono*; *Mode 3—Omni Off/Poly*; *Mode 4—Omni Off/Mono*.

In the **Omni On modes**, a MIDI device responds to all channel messages transmitted over all MIDI channels. In the **Omni Off modes**, a MIDI device responds to a single channel or group of assigned channels. In the **Poly On mode**, an instrument can produce more than one note at a time and can respond to data from any MIDI channel. In **Poly Off**, an instrument can produce more than one note at a time and can respond to data from one or more channels. A mono mode is for devices that can generate only one note at a time.

Channel Voice Messages

To transmit performance data throughout the MIDI system, *channel voice messages* are generated whenever the controller of a MIDI instrument is played. There are seven types of channel messages: *Note On, Note Off, Channel Pressure, Polyphonic Key Pressure, Program Change, Control Change,* and *Pitch Bend.*

System Messages

System messages affect an entire device or every device in a MIDI system regardless of the MIDI channel. They give timing information such as what the current bar of the song is and when to start and stop, as well as clocking functions that keep a MIDI sequencer system in sync (see "Sequencer" later in this chapter). There are three system message types: System Common Messages, System Real-Time Messages, and System Exclusive Messages.

System Common Messages transmit MIDI time code, tune request, song select, song position point, and end of exclusive cues.

System Real-Time Messages coordinate and synchronize the timing of clock-based MIDI devices such as drum machines, synthesizers, and sequencers. System real-time messages are Timing Clock, Start, Stop, Continue, Active Sensing, and System Reset.

System Exclusive (SysEx) Messages customize MIDI messages between MIDI devices. It communicates device-specific data that are not part of standard MIDI messages.

Basic Components and MIDI System Signal Flow

A basic MIDI facility typically includes a MIDI controller, sequencer, hard and/or soft synthesizer(s), computer, MIDI computer interface, sampler and sample CDs, loudspeakers, and appropriate audio and MIDI cables. Other equipment may include a mixer, recorder, and drum machine.

MIDI instruments are connected using a standardized cable with five-pin DIN connectors at each end. (A DIN connector is a connector originally standardized by the Deutsches Institut für Normung [DIN], the German national standards organization.) There is also a five-pin connector that provides MIDI phantom power.

While MIDI devices share the same type of jack, there are three types of MIDI connectors on electronic devices: MIDI IN accepts MIDI signals from another device; MIDI OUT sends signals generated within a device to the MIDI IN of other devices; MIDI THRU is like MIDI OUT, but it passes information arriving at a device's MIDI IN connector to other devices without regard for internally generated MIDI data. Figure 9-11 displays an example of signal flow in a MIDI setup.

The following is a typical MIDI signal flow, assuming the use of a software-based synthesizer: MIDI controller; MIDI cable from the controller's MIDI OUT to the interface's MIDI IN; MIDI interface; FireWire, USB, or sound card (PCI [Personal Computer

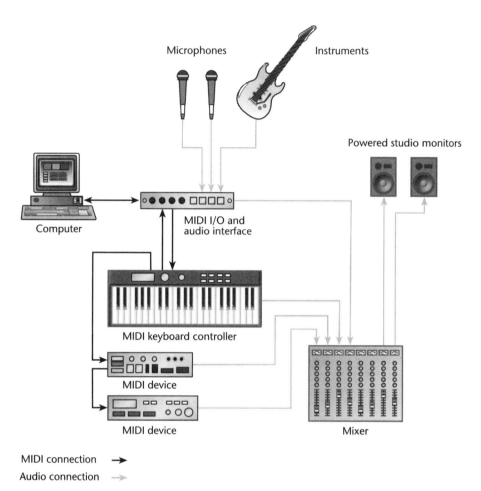

Figure 9-11 Example of signal flow in a MIDI setup.

Interface]); MIDI driver that facilitates the recording software to transfer data to the interface; sequencer; synthesizer; FireWire, USB, or PCI connection; MIDI interface; and loudspeakers.

Sequencer

The *sequencer* is the brain of a MIDI setup. It can be a stand-alone unit, a computer that runs a sequencer program, or a circuit built into a keyboard instrument. A sequencer resembles a multitrack recorder for MIDI data. It does not record audio, it receives information from MIDI devices and stores it in memory as separate "tracks." Once information is in a sequencer's memory, it can be edited and transmitted to other MIDI instruments for playback.

The advantages of MIDI sequencing over conventional recording are (1) performance and orchestration are completely shapeable in MIDI form, (2) there is no generational loss in copying or manipulating MIDI data, and (3) the amount of data needed to represent MIDI performance is comparatively inconsequential compared to that of digital audio.

Connectors

Several types of connectors are used to interface audio equipment such as recorders and MIDI devices. The five-pin DIN connector was discussed in the previous section. Other types of connectors are displayed in Figure 9-12.

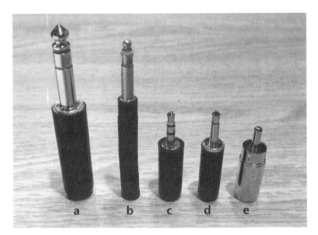

Figure 9-12 Common connectors for audio. Left to right: (a) 1/4-inch balanced (tip/ring/sleeve) stereo phone plug. (b) Bantam balanced stereo phone plug—phone plugs are used for microphone- or line-level audio signals and as a headphone connector; phone plugs are also unbalanced (tip/sleeve). (c) Mini stereo plug. (d) Mini mono plug—mini plugs are used for mic inputs, headphones, iPods, and other consumer gear; they are unbalanced. (e) RCA or phono plug—RCA/phono plugs are used for line-level inputs and outputs and are unbalanced; they are used as connectors on many compact mixers and consumer equipment and usually come in left (white) and (red) pairs.

Digital Audio Networking

Through telephone lines, a recording can be produced in real time between studios across town or across the country with little or no loss in audio quality and at a relatively low cost. Computer technology has also facilitated long-distance audio production via the Internet. This aspect of digital audio networking—online collaborative recording—is discussed in Chapter 14.

Integrated services digital network (ISDN) is a public telephone service that allows inexpensive use of a flexible, wide-area, all-digital network (see Figures 9-13 and 9-14). With ISDN it is possible to have a vocalist in New York, wearing headphones for the foldback feed, singing into a microphone whose signal is routed to a studio in Los Angeles. In L.A., the singer's audio is fed through a console, along with the accompaniment from, say, the San Francisco studio, and recorded. When necessary, the singer in New York, the accompanying musicians in San Francisco, and the recordist in L.A. can communicate with one another through a talkback system. Commercials are done with the announcer in a studio in one city and the recordist adding the effects in another city. And unlike much of today's advanced technology, ISDN is a relatively uncomplicated service to use.

Until now, ISDN recording, while locked to picture, has been difficult because standard ISDN lines do not carry images; therefore, while recording audio remotely, the talent is unable to see the picture. A technique has been developed that overcomes this problem, however.[5]

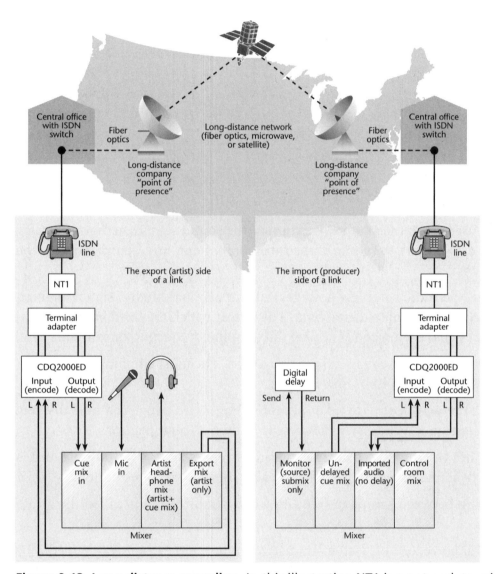

Figure 9-13 Long-distance recording. In this illustration NT1 is a network terminator that protects the network from electrical malfunctions. CDQ2000ED code enables you to send a cue mix to an artist in another location, delay the mix sent to your monitors, not delay the received artist's solo signal, mix the two, give direction, and make production judgments in real time.

5. See "Audio Know-How," by Ron DiCesare, *Post Magazine,* March 2008, p. 28.

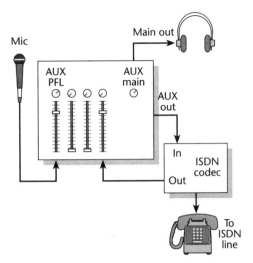

Figure 9-14 Simplified setup for long-distance recording. A codec is a device that encodes a signal at one end of a transmission and decodes it at the other end.

From Jeffrey P. Fisher and Harlan Hogan, *The Voice Actor's Guide to Home Recording* (Boston: Thomson Course Technology, 2005), p. 73.

Main Points

- Digital audio uses a numerical representation of the sound signal's actual frequency and amplitude. In digital, sampling is the time component, and quantization is the level component.

- Sampling takes periodic samples (voltages) of the original analog signal at fixed intervals and converts them to digital data. The rate at which the fixed intervals sample the original signal each second is called the sampling frequency, or sampling rate.

- A number of sampling rates are used in digital audio. The most common are 32 kHz, 44.056 kHz, 44.1 kHz, 48 kHz, and 96 kHz.

- As samples of the waveform are taken, these voltages are converted into discrete quantities and assigned values. This process is known as quantization.

- Bit depth defines the digital word length used to represent a given sample and is equivalent to dynamic range. Word length is also referred to as resolution.

- The relationship between sampling frequency and quantization is called the audio data rate.

- Most digital audio recording systems in use today use either removable media or fixed hard disks; some use both. Of these systems, the most commonly employed are the memory recorder, hard-disk recorder, digital audio workstation, CD, DVD, and high-density optical disc.

- A memory recorder is a portable digital recorder that has no moving parts and therefore requires no maintenance. Its storage medium is a memory card, a nonvolatile memory card that can be electrically recorded onto, erased, and reprogrammed. The card does not need power to maintain the stored information.

- Digital recorders also use fixed and removable hard disks. Compared with memory recorders, they usually provide better sound quality and greater recording flexibility.

- When using memory and hard-disk recorders, especially in the field, it is essential to know their storage capacities in advance so you do not get caught short.

- A digital audio workstation (DAW) records, edits, and plays back. DAWs have considerable processing power because of the software programs they use. Generally, there are two types of DAW systems: computer-based and integrated.

- A computer-based DAW is a stand-alone unit with all processing handled by the computer.

- A computer must have a sound card to input, manipulate, and output audio. A sound card with a signal-to-noise ratio of −70 dB and below usually ensures that it can produce professional-quality audio.

- An integrated DAW not only consists of the computer and its related software but may also include a console, a control surface, a server, and a storage area network (SAN).

- A DAW's system-wide communication with other external devices, and communication between devices in general, is facilitated through the distribution of digital interfaces such as AES/EBU, S/PDIF, SCSI, iSCSI, MADI, and FireWire.

- A server is a computer dedicated to providing one or more services over a computer network, typically through a request-response routine.

- A storage area network (SAN) can be likened to the common flow of data in a personal computer shared by different kinds of storage devices such as a hard disk and CD, DVD or optical disc player.

- The recordable compact disc (CD-R) is a write-once medium with unlimited playback. The rewritable CD (CD-RW) can be recorded on, erased, and used again for other recordings. The CDVU+ (CD view plus) is a compact disc with interactive content.

- The digital versatile disc (DVD) is the same diameter and thickness as the compact disc, but it can hold a much greater amount of data. DVDs come in a variety of formats: DVD-Video (DVD-V), DVD-Audio (DVD-A), DVD-Recordable (DVD-R) authoring and general, and two rewritable formats—DVD-RW and DVD+RW.

- DVD-Audio differs from DVD-Video in that there is much more storage room for audio data. DVD-A can provide a greater number of extremely high-quality audio channels.

- Recordable and rewritable DVDs are high-density versions of the CD-R and the CD-RW. Two formats are used to record DVDs. They are designated DVD+R and DVD-R and are incompatible with one another. There are two categories of DVD-R: general and authoring. The general category was developed for business and consumer applications such as data archiving and onetime recording.

- High-density optical disc formats are designed to meet the demands of high-definition (HD) media. The most popular format at this writing is the Blu-ray Disc (BD).

- In musical instrument digital interface (MIDI), digital refers to a set of instructions in the form of digital (binary) data that must be interpreted by an electronic sound-generating, or sound-modifying, device such as a synthesizer or computer that can respond to the directions. Interface is the link permitting the control signals generated by commands from one synthesizer or controller to trigger other synthesizers and equipment.

- MIDI software is available in a number of categories: (1) performance—software that allows composition, orchestration, arranging, and performing music; (2) productivity—programs that transcribe, data base, and print music using any MIDI setup; (3) editing—for editing digital samples; (4) patching librarians—for storing settings or "patches;" and (5) instruction—software for learning MIDI operations.

- MIDI messages may be grouped into two categories: channel messages and system messages. A channel message applies to the specific MIDI channel named in the message. Channel messages give information on whether an instrument should send or receive and on which channel. A system message addresses all the channels. System messages affect an entire device or every device in a MIDI system regardless of the MIDI channel.

- Channel messages are grouped into channel mode messages and channel voice messages.

- There are three system message types: System Common Messages, System Real-Time Messages, and System Exclusive Messages.

- A basic MIDI facility typically includes: a MIDI controller, sequencer, hard and/or soft synthesizer(s), computer, MIDI computer interface, sampler and sample CDs, loudspeakers, and appropriate audio and MIDI cables. Other equipment may include a mixer, recorder, and drum machine.

- MIDI instruments are connected using a standardized cable with five-pin DIN connectors at each end. There is also a five-pin connector that provides MIDI phantom power.

- There are three types of MIDI connectors on electronic devices: MIDI IN, MIDI OUT, and MIDI THRU.

- A typical MIDI signal flow, assuming the use of a software-based synthesizer is: MIDI controller; MIDI cable from the controller's MIDI OUT to the interface's MIDI IN; MIDI interface; FireWire, USB, or sound card (PCI [Personal Computer Interface]); MIDI driver that facilitates the recording software to transfer data to the interface; sequencer; synthesizer; FireWire, USB, or PCI connection; MIDI interface; and loudspeakers.

- The sequencer is the brain of a MIDI setup. It resembles a multitrack recorder for MIDI data. It receives information from MIDI devices and stores it in memory as separate "tracks."

- Several types of connectors are used to interface audio equipment, such as recorders and MIDI devices.

- Digital audio networking using the Integrated Services Digital Network (ISDN) makes it possible to produce a recording in real time between studios across town or across the country with little or no loss in audio quality and at a relatively low cost.

10 | Synchronization and Transfers

Little in production and postproduction can be accomplished without *synchronization*—the ability to lock two or more signals or devices that have microprocessor intelligence so that they operate at precisely the same rate. That includes almost any combination of audio, video, and film equipment, from a simple audio-to-audio or audio-to-video recorder interface—analog or digital, tape or disk—to a complete studio system that interfaces a digital audio workstation, console, synthesizer, effects processor, and other equipment throughout a facility.

Accurate synchronization requires a system to code and coordinate the recording media and the controlling mechanisms to ensure that signals remain in sync.

Time Codes

Of the various time codes available, two are mainly used today: SMPTE time code, which is the most employed, and MIDI time code.

SMPTE Time Code

SMPTE (Society of Motion Picture and Television Engineers) (pronounced "sempty") *time code* was originally developed to make videotape editing more efficient; its identifying code numbers are broken down into hours, minutes, seconds, and frames. The code number 01:22:48:15 is read as 1 hour, 22 minutes, 48 seconds, and 15 frames. Videotape has 30 *frames per second* (*fps*), or 29.97, to be exact. Each 1/30 second of each video frame is tagged with a unique identifying number called a *time code address*. The advantages of time coding became immediately apparent and were applied to coding audiotape.

Even though tape is rarely used now, and DAWs have internal databases to keep multiple audio (and video) tracks in sync, time coding is used as a reference. It is a convenient and precise way of identifying segments to the split second and, more importantly, time codes are necessary to standardize references and/or sync tracks when transferred to external devices.

MIDI Time Code

MIDI time code (MTC) was developed as a way to translate SMPTE time code into MIDI messages. An absolute timing reference, SMPTE time code remains constant throughout a program. In MIDI recording, timing references are relative and vary with both tempo and tempo changes. Because most studios use SMPTE time code addresses (as opposed to beats in a musical bar) as references, trying to convert between the two timing systems to cue or trigger an event would be tedious and time-consuming. MIDI time code allows MIDI-based devices to operate on the SMPTE timing reference independent of tempo.

Using MTC with a computer requires a MIDI interface to convert a MIDI signal into computer data and vice versa. Many computer recording/editing software programs have MIDI capability, so synchronizing a project to MTC or SMPTE time code is just a matter of accessing the program's appropriate synchronization page.

Time Formats with Computer-Based Recorder/Editors

Computer-based recorder/editors incorporate at least SMPTE time code for reference; many systems also include other time formats for internal use such as real time, music time, and film time. These format names differ among programs, but their functions are essentially comparable.

Real time displays the time scale in actual minutes and seconds. Many systems are able to refine real time to tenths, hundredths, and thousandths of a second.

Music time is in bars and beats and usually requires tempo data on which to base it. It can be adjusted to preserve relative timing to a variety of values such as quarter-note, quarter-triplet, eighth-note, eighth-triplet, and so on.

Film time displays the time scale in feet and frames.

MIDI time code is included in hard-disk recorder/editor systems with MIDI capability. MTC is accurate to a quarter of a frame.

As noted earlier, the need for time coding in digital recorder/editors is sometimes questioned because of their internal databases that keep tracks in sync wherever they are moved and placed in the computer. So long as the entire audio production is done on a computer, coding does not matter. If the audio is exported to other devices, however, coding becomes essential for synchronization.

Synchronizing Digital Equipment

Synchronizing digital equipment requires keeping the digital data synchronized in the digital domain. For example, computers process data at a much faster rate than the real-time devices that may be connected to it. Time code alone cannot keep the digital interconnectivity of data compatible. Every digital audio system has a signal generated inside the device that controls sampling frequency. This signal is commonly known as a word clock. The *word clock,* sometimes also referred to as a *sample clock* or *digital clock,* is an extremely stable synchronization signal used to control the rate at which digital audio data is converted or transmitted. It is responsible for the timing associated with moving audio data from one digital device to another. If the word clocks of different audio devices are not in sync, resulting problems in the data transfer process can seriously degrade the audio signal.

Jitter

A word-clock signal cues every audio device in the system to record, play back, or transfer each sample at the same time. It is important to note that with digital audio, the determining sync factor is the sampling frequency, not the time code rate. A degradation in the word-clock signals among the digital devices being interfaced can create *jitter*—a variation in time from sample to sample that causes changes in the shape of the audio waveform. Jitter creates such adverse sonic effects as reduced detail, harsher sound, and ghost imaging. The best way to avoid jitter in syncing digital devices is to use a dedicated low-jitter master clock generator (see Figure 10-1).

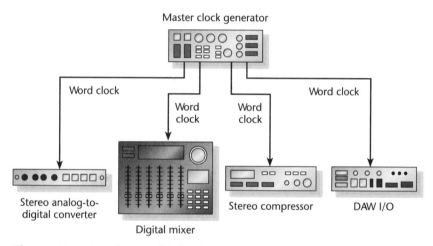

Figure 10-1 Syncing multiple digital devices to a master clock generator.

It is important to underscore that in digital studios, there can be only one master clock to control the clocks of the other digital devices. Uncompressed digital audio plays at a fixed rate. Although two or more devices in the signal chain can be set to run at the same sampling frequency, it is unlikely that the word clocks in each of these devices will run at the same time, which creates discontinuities in the audio streams.

Other ways to avoid jitter are to use balanced, well-shielded digital cables of the correct impedance; use short cables (longer cables are more subject to interference and data delays); keep digital and analog cables separate; and use the most accurate clock source as the master time reference if a master clock generator is not employed.

Driver Support and Latency

An audio *driver* is a program that allows the transfer of audio signals to and from an audio interface. Aside from its functionality in meeting needs, it is critical to select a driver with low latency (less than about 5 ms). *Latency* is the period of time it takes for data to get from one designated point to another. In audio, latency is the signal delay through the driver and the interface to the output. Some drivers have low latency; others have a moderate amount.

Latency does not in and of itself affect sound quality. The problem is with synchronization. Little or no latency in a digital system synchronizes the input and playback signals. The problem of latency can be avoided with audio interfaces that include the ability to mix incoming signals with already-recorded audio coming from the computer and then send the signal back out in sync.

Frame Rates

Five frame rate standards are used within SMPTE time code: 23.976, 24, 25, 29.97, and 30 frames per second. *Frame rate* refers to the number of film or video frames displayed in 1 second of real time.

23.976 fps

This is the frame rate used in high-definition video where the HD camera is substituting for film. The format is called *24p*. The *24* refers to the standard frames-per-second rate used for film applications in the United States. The *p* stands for progressive, which refers to the scanning method used in producing a video picture. The audio recorder used with 24p, and with most audio production recording, runs at 30 fps. The discrepancy in the two different frame rates is resolved when picture and sound are transferred for post-production editing.

Some newer digital audio and video recorder/editors allow for 23.976 and 24p time code display and synchronization. Hence, there is no need for a conversion to 30 fps unless material is output to a television standard.

24 fps

This is the frame rate used for pure film applications in the United States. Once a film is shot and transferred to a DAW for postproduction, 24 fps is not used.

25 fps

This is the frame rate used in Europe for film and video shot for television.

29.97 fps and 30 fps

To consider these two frame rates, it is first necessary to understand the implications of drop frame and non-drop frame.

Drop Frame and Non-Drop Frame

In the days before color television, the frame rate of U.S. black-and-white TV was 30 fps. With color TV, the rate was reduced to 29.97 fps to allow easier color syncing of new programs and reproduction of black-and-white programs. Today, American television and videotape recorders run at 29.97 fps.

The problem with 30 fps time code running at 29.97 fps is that it comes up 108 frames short every hour. To correct this problem, a time code format called *drop frame* was developed. Drop frame skips the first two frame counts in each minute, except for each tenth minute (00, 10, 20, etc.), to force the time code to match the clock time.

Solving one problem, however, created another. A frame rate of 29.97 fps for, say, a 1-minute commercial will show as exactly 1 minute on a clock but will read 00:00:59:28 on a time code display. One hour of real time will read out as 00:59:56:12. In editing, not working with whole numbers can be bothersome, to say nothing of trying to get an exact program time in broadcasting. To resolve this problem, the 30 fps and 29.97 fps frame rates can be adjusted between drop frame and *non-drop frame*.

Drop frame is necessary when precise timing is critical and when synchronizing audio to video. But in most other production—audio and video—non-drop frame is used because it is easier to work with. It is worth remembering that recordings used in any given production must employ one mode or the other; the two modes are not interchangeable.

For the uses of the 29.97 fps and 30 fps codes in their drop frame and non-drop frame modes, see Figure 10-2. Given the array of frame rates in use and whether they are drop frame or non-drop frame, it is not uncommon during complex productions either to lose track of what was used and when or to misunderstand the requirements of a particular stage in the production chain. Some frame rates and counts are incompatible, such as 29.97 fps drop frame and non-drop frame. Others may be compatible in certain ways, such as 30 fps drop frame that can be converted to 29.97 fps drop frame in the process of transferring film and audio to a DAW. If possible, avoid mix-ups by using the frame rate and the frame count needed for the final delivery master throughout production and postproduction.

Some digital recorder/editors differentiate between the drop frame and non-drop frame time code displays. Non-drop frame uses colons between the numbers—00:00:00:00, whereas drop frame uses semicolons—00;00;00;00. An easy way to remember is that dropping off the lower dot indicates the drop frame format.

Frame Rate (fps)	Frame Count	Primary Uses
29.97	Non-drop frame	Postproduction editorial, original video production, and delivery masters for some nonbroadcast uses such as DVD-V
29.97	Drop frame	Delivery masters for broadcast and original video production on episodic television
30	Non-drop frame	Shooting film for music video or commercials for television at 24 fps or 30 fps
30	Drop frame	Used with 24 fps film origination of episodic or long-form television when the delivery master requirement is 29.97 drop frame

Figure 10-2 29.97 and 30 fps frame rates, counts, and their primary uses.
From Tomlinson Holman, *Sound for Film and Television*, 2nd ed. (Boston: Focal Press, 2002), p. 144.

Transfers

Copying sound (or picture) from one audio (film or video) device to another is commonly called a *transfer*. The term *dub*, in popular use for decades and still in the audio lexicon, means essentially the same thing.

Analog-to-Analog Audio Transfers

Analog-to-analog transfers are rarely done these days unless it is to preserve the sonic authenticity of a recording for archival purposes. In dubbing an analog recording from vinyl record to analog tape, each transfer of material loses a generation, worsening the signal-to-noise ratio (see Figure 10-3). Using only top-notch equipment and noise-reduction software that can act on such sounds as clicks, scratches, hum, rumble, hiss, and surface noise can minimize loss of audio quality. The loss in signal-to-noise ratio is more acute when transferring from vinyl record to analog tape than from analog tape to analog tape because the sound on a vinyl record is already several generations down due to the multigenerational steps in the mastering process.

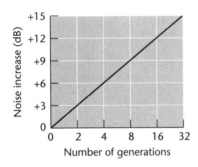

Figure 10-3 The effect that transferring an analog-to-analog recording has on sound quality.

In transferring material to open-reel analog tape, it is best to begin recording the sound a few seconds after the tape has started spinning to prevent the sound from *wowing in*—gradually reaching full speed. Even the finest analog open-reel audiotape recorders take at least one second to reach full speed. If the tape recorder has automated cueing, startup time is more precise and dependable.

Analog-to-Digital Audio Transfers

Two primary considerations in transferring analog audio to digital audio are maintaining levels and not reducing dynamic range. Remember that if a signal goes "into the red" in analog recording, there is usually some headroom before distortion occurs. Once a signal is "in the red" with digital sound, it is already distorted. Therefore, in doing an analog-to-digital transfer, the first step is to do equipment *calibration*—adjust all levels to a standard so that their measurements are similar. For example, a reading of, say, 0 VU on the console should produce an equivalent reading of 0 VU or –20 dBFS digital signal level on the recorder(s).

In setting levels to avoid distortion and maintain dynamic range, one obvious approach is to set the level of the digital recorder at 0 VU during the loudest passages in the analog recording. This helps ensure that all levels will be 0 VU or below. In quiet passages, however, the level may be too low. For the sake of audibility, it may be necessary to use gentle compression to slightly raise the lower-level signal (see Chapters 11 and 13). Of course, any technique has to take into account the program material. Transferring classical music requires a different aesthetic than transferring rock music; dealing with dialog may not require as many sonic adjustments as dealing with the dynamics of sound effects.

Unless it is necessary, most signal processing is avoided in the transfer, or kept to a minimum, so as not to alter the original sound. This usually does not include transfers that are done to correct obvious audio deficiencies such as using EQ and compression to enhance the clarity of the original analog recording, especially if it is down a generation or more. Nor does it include taking advantage of the powerful noise-reduction capabilities of digital signal processing, which "clean" the sound without altering it (see Chapter 11).

Digital-to-Digital Audio Transfers

Making a digital-to-digital transfer can be a straightforward process or—given the differences in quality among recording systems, the platforms they use, and susceptibility to digital errors—it can require some care. In any transfer of a digital signal from one digital device to another, the sampling frequency must be the same. If the sampling rate of the original recording is 48 kHz, for example, the mixer through which the signal is sent for transferring must also be set at 48 kHz.

In practice, though, when importing digital sources to a DAW, it is possible that the sampling rates of the various sources may be different. For example, the sample rate of a CD is 44.1 kHz; digital videotape is usually 48 kHz; Internet and multimedia audio might be 32 kHz or 22.050 kHz. By taking a few precautions, the havoc of sampling errors can be avoided. Try to use as few sampling-rate conversions as possible. Determine the final sampling rate and set the DAW to this rate. If the final sampling rate is 44.1 or 48 kHz, most DAWs can convert between these rates internally.

The number of bits (word length) transferred is not as important as the matching of sampling rates so long as the master (source) and the slave (destination) devices are using the same digital formats such as AES/EBU, S/PDIF, FireWire, and so on. That said, keeping the word length as long as possible during transfer helps reduce distortion: 24-bits is better than 16 bits. Moreover, feeding a 16-bit signal to a 24-bit device is more desirable than feeding a 24-bit signal to a 16-bit device. In the former instance, the 24-bit device will usually add zeros to fill out the digital word. In the latter instance, the last 8 bits are cut off, thereby introducing some distortion.

Other procedures worth noting in making digital transfers are as follows:

■ Digital audio data cables and word-clock lines need to be the same length. Cable length affects timing, which affects the phase relationship of the word clock to the digital audio data.

- Make sure all signals—time code, digital audio, and word clock—are flowing from the source recording to the destination recording. Check signal flow and make sure there are no pops or clicks.

- Avoid using *wild time code* during formatting. Wild time code occurs when the time code generator used for the original recording was not locked to the device that made the recording.

- With tape, make sure that there is plenty of preroll and keep the transfer start point consistent.

- Use high-quality digital audio cables.

- Transferring a WAV, AIFF (Audio Interchange File Format), or Sound Designer II file, for example, rather than a digital audio signal, ensures a virtually perfect copy because it is an exact duplicate of the original file.

- With FireWire, which has become the interface of choice, audio transfers over a computer connection are virtually trouble-free. This standardized high-speed connection not only can be used with audio, including multichannel, but with devices such as computers, hard drives, CD burners, digital video, and scanners. With FireWire, it now is possible to connect up to 63 devices. When a new bus bridge becomes available, it will be possible to connect more than 60,000 devices together on a common bus.

There are two standards of FireWire, 400 and 800. FireWire 400 has a maximum speed of 400 Mbits per second; 800 has a maximum speed of 800 Mbits per second. Three types of connectors are associated with FireWire: the four-pin found on devices such as video recorders and Windows PCs; the six-pin for Apples; and the nine-pin for FireWire 800. Maximum cable length is about 15 feet.

When a disk recorder is involved in a transfer either from within the computer from one hard-drive location to another or from one computer to another, the copy is exactly like the original. Digital tape-to-tape transfers or transfers to or from CD-Rs, CD-RWs, DVD-Rs, and the rewritable DVDs may or may not be exactly like the original due to digital errors and problems with error correction that may occur in the transfer process.

Transfers into a disk recorder usually involve either a file transfer or a streaming audio transfer. A *file transfer* is nonlinear and digital to digital. A *streaming transfer* is linear and may involve either analog or digital sources.

File transfers are done at higher than normal audio speeds. This cuts down the wait time compared with streaming audio transfers, which are in real time. Streaming audio transfers are also susceptible to digital bit errors; and if the error coding breaks down, interpolated data may be substituted into the missing portions, creating noticeable audio problems after several generations (see Figures 10-4 and 10-5).

Formats	Applications and Characteristics
AIFF (Audio Interchange File Format)	Created for use on Macintosh computers, but most professional PC programs can read and write AIFF files. Supports bit resolutions in multiples of 8, but most AIFF files are 16- to 24-bit.
BWF (Broadcast Wave Format)	PC and Mac compatible. An enhanced WAV file that supports metadata. Files may be linear or lossy coded using MPEG-1 or MPEG-2. Adopted by the AES/EBU as a standard interchange.
SDII (Sound Designer II)	Developed by Digidesign for use on Mac computers. Supports sampling frequencies up to 48 kHz by Digidesign and up to 96 kHz through MOTU (Mark of the Unicorn).
WAV (Waveform)	Developed by Microsoft and accepted by most DAWs. Supports a variety of sampling rates and bit resolutions and a number of audio channels.

Figure 10-4 Audio file formats.

Formats	Applications and Characteristics
AAF (Advanced Authoring Format)	File interchange format designed for video postproduction and authoring. Transfers audio and video files. AAF is expected to replace OMF. Unlike MXF, AAF is designed to be used with works-in-progress.
AES31 (Audio Engineering Society)	Supported by most DAWs but not Digidesign. Audio-only interchange.
OMF 1 and 2 (Open Media Format)	Produced by Digidesign but interchanges with most DAWs. Transfers audio and picture files.
MXF (Material Exchange Format)	Based on the AAF data model. Transfers audio and video files in a streamable format. MXF is used to transfer completed projects on a networked DAW.

Figure 10-5 Project exchange formats.

Main Points

- Synchronization provides the ability to lock two or more signals or devices so they operate at precisely the same rate.

- Accurate synchronization requires a system to code the recording media and the controlling mechanisms to ensure signals remain in sync.

- Of the various time codes available, two are mainly used today. SMPTE time code, which is the most employed, and MIDI time code.

- SMPTE time code's identifying code numbers are broken down into hours, minutes, seconds, and frames. Each encoded value is called a time code address.

- MIDI time code (MTC) translates SMPTE time code into MIDI messages.

- Computer-based recording/editing systems include one or more of the following time formats: real time, music time, film time, and MIDI time code.

- Every digital audio system has a signal, known as a word clock (also called a sample clock or digital clock), generated inside the device that controls sampling frequency. It is an extremely stable synchronization signal used to control the rate at which digital audio data is converted or transmitted. With digital audio, sampling rate is the determining sync factor.

- A degradation in the word-clock signals among the digital devices interfaced can create jitter—a variation in time from sample to sample that causes changes in the shape of the audio waveform.

- An audio driver is a program that allows the transfer of audio signals to and from an audio interface.

- It is critical to select a driver with low latency (less than about 5 ms). Latency is the period of time it takes for data to get from one designated point to another. In audio, latency is the signal delay through the driver and the interface to the output.

- The problem of latency can be avoided with audio interfaces that include the ability to mix incoming signals with already-recorded audio coming from the computer and then to send the signal back out in sync.

- Frame rate refers to the number of film or video frames displayed in 1 second of real time.

- Five frame rate standards are used within SMPTE time code: 23.976, 24, 25, 29.97, and 30 frames per second (fps).

- Frame rates are in either drop frame or non-drop frame format. Drop frame time code is time-accurate because it makes up for the error that results from the difference between the 29.97 fps and the 30 fps rate of video. Non-drop frame is the original video time code calculated at 30 fps. The two modes are not interchangeable.

- Copying sound (or picture) from one audio (film or video) device to another is called a transfer or a dub.

- Common audio transfers are analog to analog, analog to digital, and digital to digital.

11 Signal Processors

Signal processors are devices used to alter some characteristic of a sound. Generally, they can be grouped into four categories: spectrum processors, time processors, amplitude processors, and noise processors. A *spectrum processor*, such as the equalizer, affects the spectral balances in a signal. A *time processor*, such as a reverberation or delay device, affects the time interval between a signal and its repetition(s). An *amplitude processor* (or *dynamic processor*), such as the compressor-limiter, affects a signal's dynamic range. A *noise processor* does not alter a signal so much as it makes the signal clearer by reducing various types of noise.

Some signal processors can belong to more than one category. For example, the equalizer also alters a signal's amplitude and therefore can be classified as an amplitude processor as well. The flanger, which affects the time of a signal, also affects its frequency response. A de-esser alters amplitude and frequency. Compression and expansion also affect the time of an event. In other words, many effects are variations of the same principle.

A signal processor may be dedicated to a single function—that is, an equalizer just equalizes, a reverberation unit only produces reverb, and so on—or it may be a multieffects unit. The processing engine in a multieffects unit can be configured in a variety of ways. For example, one model may limit, compress, and pitch-shift, and another model may provide reverb as well as equalize, limit, compress, and noise gate.

Signal processors may be inboard, incorporated into production consoles (see Chapter 8); outboard stand-alone units; or a *plug-in*—an add-on software tool that gives a digital recording/editing system signal-processing alternatives beyond what the original system provides.

In the interest of organization, the signal processors covered in this chapter are arranged by category in relation to their primary discrete function and are then discussed relative to multieffects processors. Examples in each category include outboard units, plug-ins, or both.

Spectrum Processors

Spectrum processors include equalizers, filters, and psychoacoustic processors.

Equalizers

The best-known and most common signal processor is the *equalizer*—an electronic device that alters frequency response by increasing or decreasing the level of a signal at a specific portion of the spectrum. This alteration can be done in two ways: by *boost* or *cut* (also known as *peak* or *dip*) or by *shelving*.

Boost and cut, respectively, increase and decrease the level of a band of frequencies around a *center frequency*—the frequency at which maximum boost or cut occurs. This type of *equalization* (*EQ*) is often referred to as *bell curve* or *haystack* due to the shape of the response curve (see Figure 11-1).

Shelving also increases or decreases amplitude by a fixed amount, gradually flattening out or shelving, at the maximum level when the chosen (called *turnover* or *cutoff*) frequency is reached. Level then remains constant at all frequencies beyond that point (see Figure 11-2).

In other words, with boost/cut EQ, when a frequency is selected for boost or cut by a certain amplitude, that frequency is the one most affected. Adjacent frequencies are also

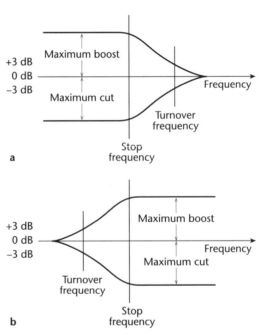

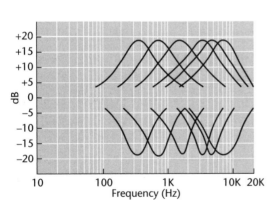

Figure 11-1 Bell curve or haystack showing 18 dB boost or cut at 350 Hz, 700 Hz, 1,600 Hz, 3,200 Hz, 4,800 Hz, and 7,200 Hz.

Figure 11-2 Low-frequency shelving equalization and (b) high-frequency shelving equalization. The turnover frequency shown is where the gain is 3 dB above (or below) the shelving level—in other words, the frequency where the equalizer begins to flatten out. The stop frequency is the point at which the gain stops increasing or decreasing.

affected but by gradually lesser changes in level. With shelving EQ, all frequencies above (high-frequency shelving) or below (low-frequency shelving) the selected frequency are equally increased or decreased by the level selected.

The number of frequencies on equalizers varies. Generally, the frequencies are in full-, half-, and third-octave intervals. If the lowest frequency on a full-octave equalizer is, say, 50 Hz, the other frequencies ascend in octaves: 100 Hz, 200 Hz, 400 Hz, 800 Hz, and so on, usually to 12,800 Hz. A half-octave equalizer ascends in half octaves. If the lowest frequency is 50 Hz, the intervals are at or near 75 Hz, 100 Hz, 150 Hz, 200 Hz, 300 Hz, 400 Hz, 600 Hz, and so on. A third-octave equalizer would have intervals at or near 50 Hz, 60 Hz, 80 Hz, 100 Hz, 120 Hz, 160 Hz, 200 Hz, 240 Hz, 320 Hz, 400 Hz, 480 Hz, 640 Hz, and so on. Obviously, the more settings, the better the sound control—but at some cost. The more settings there are on an equalizer (or any device, for that matter), the more difficult it is to use correctly because problems such as added noise and phasing may be introduced, to say nothing of having to keep track of more control settings.

Two types of equalizers are in general use: fixed-frequency and parametric.

Fixed-Frequency Equalizer

The *fixed-frequency equalizer* is so called because it operates at fixed frequencies usually selected from two (high and low), three (high, middle, and low), or four (high, upper-middle, lower-middle, and low) ranges of the frequency spectrum (see Figures 8-1 and 8-5). Typically, the high and low fixed-frequency equalizers on consoles are shelving equalizers. The midrange EQs are center-frequency boost/cut equalizers. Each group of frequencies is located at a separate control, but only one center frequency at a time per control may be selected. At or near each frequency selector is a level control that boosts or cuts the selected center and band frequencies. A fixed-frequency equalizer has a pre-set *bandwidth*—a range of frequencies on either side of the center frequency selected for equalizing that is also affected. The degrees of amplitude to which these frequencies are modified form the *bandwidth curve*. If you boost, say, 350 Hz a total of 18 dB, the bandwidth of frequencies also affected may go to as low as 80 Hz on one side and up to 2,000 Hz on the other. The peak of the curve is 350 Hz—the frequency that is boosted the full 18 dB. The adjacent frequencies are also boosted but to a lesser extent, depending on the bandwidth. Because each fixed-frequency equalizer can have a different fixed bandwidth and bandwidth curve, it is a good idea to study the manufacturer's specifications before you use one. A measure of the bandwidth of frequencies an equalizer affects is known as the *Q*.

Graphic Equalizer

The *graphic equalizer* is a type of fixed-frequency equalizer. It consists of sliding, instead of rotating, controls that boost or attenuate selected frequencies. It is called "graphic" because the positioning of these controls gives a graphic representation of the frequency curve set. (The display does not include the bandwidth of each frequency, however.)

Figure 11-3 Graphic equalizer. This model is digital stereo, with 31 EQ bands at one-third octave intervals from 20 Hz to 20 kHz. Equalization gain is switchable between 0–24 dB to ±6 dB and ±12 dB. It also includes high- and low-cut filters.

Because each frequency on a graphic equalizer has a separate sliding control, it is possible to use as many as you wish simultaneously (see Figure 11-3).

Parametric Equalizer

The main difference between a *parametric equalizer* (see Figure 11-4) and a fixed-frequency equalizer is that the parametric has continuously variable frequencies and bandwidths, making it possible to change a bandwidth curve by making it wider or narrower, thereby altering the affected frequencies and their levels. This provides greater flexibility and more precision in controlling equalization. In other words, in parametric EQ, it is possible to vary the Q from anywhere between high-Q settings, which produce narrow bands of frequencies, to low-Q settings, which affect wider bands of frequencies (see Figure 11-5).

Paragraphic Equalizer

A *paragraphic equalizer* combines the sliding controls of a graphic equalizer with the flexibility of parametric equalization (see Figure 11-6).

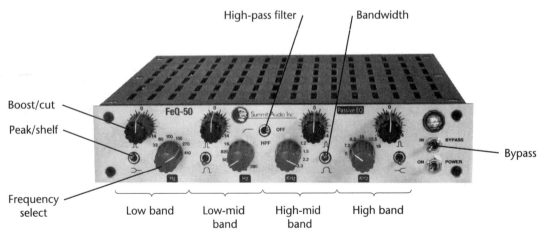

Figure 11-4 Parametric equalizer. This model includes four EQ bands, each with six switch-selectable frequencies and 14 dB of fully sweepable level increase or attenuation. The low-middle and high-middle are the parametric bands and can switch between narrow and wide bandwidths. The low- and high-frequency bands can switch between boost/cut and shelving EQ. Also included is a switchable high-pass filter at 30 Hz to reduce rumble.

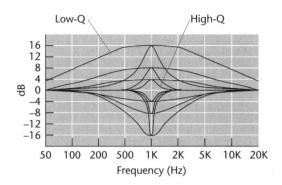

Figure 11-5 Selectable bandwidths of a parametric equalizer showing the effects of low-Q and high-Q settings.

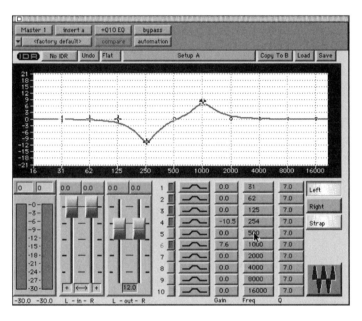

Figure 11-6 Paragraphic equalizer plug-in.

Filters

A *filter* is a device that attenuates certain bands of frequencies. It is a component of an equalizer. There are differences between attenuating with an equalizer and with a filter, however. First, with an equalizer, attenuation affects only the selected frequency and the frequencies on either side of it, whereas with a filter all frequencies above or below the selected frequency are affected. Second, an equalizer allows you to vary the amount of drop in loudness; with a filter, the drop is usually preset and relatively steep.

Among the most common filters are high-pass, low-pass, band-pass, and notch.

High- and Low-Pass Filters

A *high-pass (low-cut) filter* attenuates all frequencies below a preset point; a *low-pass (high-cut)* **filter** attenuates all frequencies above a preset point (see Figure 11-7).

Suppose in a recording there is a bothersome rumble between 35 Hz and 50 Hz. By setting a high-pass filter at 50 Hz, all frequencies below that point are cut and the band of frequencies above it continues to pass—hence the name *high-pass (low-cut) filter*.

The low-pass (high-cut) filter works on the same principle but affects the higher frequencies. If there is hiss in a recording, you can get rid of it by setting a low-pass filter

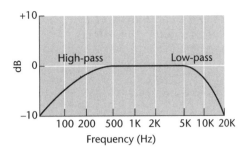

Figure 11-7 High-pass (low-cut) and low-pass (high-cut) filter curves.

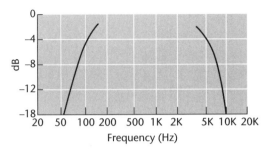

Figure 11-8 Band-pass filtering. The frequencies below 120 Hz and above 5,000 Hz are sharply attenuated, thereby allowing the frequencies in the band between to pass.

at, say, 10,000 Hz. This cuts the frequencies above that point and allows the band of frequencies below 10,000 Hz to pass through. But keep in mind that all sound above 10 kHz—the program material, if there is any, along with the hiss—will be filtered.

Band-Pass Filter

A *band-pass filter* is a device that sets high- and low-frequency cutoff points and permits the band of frequencies in between to pass (see Figure 11-8). Band-pass filters are used more for corrective rather than creative purposes.

Notch Filter

A *notch filter* is also used mainly for corrective purposes. It can cut out an extremely narrow band, allowing the frequencies on either side of the notch to pass. For example, a constant problem in audio is AC (alternating current) hum, which has a frequency of 60 Hz. A notch filter can remove it without appreciably affecting the adjacent frequencies.

Psychoacoustic Processors

A *psychoacoustic processor* is designed to add clarity, definition, overall presence, and life, or "sizzle," to program material. Some units add tone-generated odd and even harmonics[1] to the audio; others are fixed or program-adaptive, high-frequency equalizers. A psychoacoustic processor might also achieve its effect by adding comb filtering and by introducing narrow-band phase shifts between stereo channels. One well-known psychoacoustic processor is the Aphex Aural Exciter.

---

1. Each harmonic or set of harmonics adds a characteristic tonal color to sound, although they have less effect on changes in timbre as they rise in pitch above the fundamental. In general, even-numbered harmonics—second, fourth, and sixth—create an open, warm, filled-out sound. The first two even harmonics are one and two octaves above the fundamental, so the tones blend. Odd-numbered harmonics—third and fifth—produce a closed, harsh, stopped-down sound. The first two odd harmonics are an octave plus a fifth and two octaves plus a major third above the fundamental, which bring their own tonality to the music.

Time Processors

Time processors are devices that affect the time relationships of signals. These effects include reverberation and delay.

Reverberation

Reverberation, you will recall, is created by random, multiple, blended repetitions of a sound or signal. As these repetitions decrease in intensity, they increase in number. Reverberant sound increases average signal level and adds depth, spatial dimension, and additional excitement to the listening experience.

A reverberation effect has two main elements: the initial reflections and the decay of those reflections (see Chapter 1). Therefore, reverb results when the first reflections hit surfaces and continue to bounce around until they decay. In creating reverb electronically, using the parlance of audio, a signal is sent to the reverb processor as *dry sound*—without reverb—and is returned as *wet sound*—with reverb.

The types of reverb in current use are digital, convolution, plate, and acoustic chamber. Reverb plug-in software may be considered a fifth type. There is also *spring reverberation*, which is rarely employed today because of its mediocre sound quality. It is sometimes used, however, in guitar amplifiers because of its low cost, small size, and when the musician is going for the particular sound quality spring reverbs produce.

Digital Reverberation

Digital reverberation is the most common today. Most digital reverb devices are capable of producing a variety of different acoustic environments. Generally, when fed into the circuitry and digitized, the signal is delayed for several milliseconds. The delayed signal is then recycled to produce the reverb effect. The process is repeated many times per second, with amplitude reduced to achieve decay.

Specifically, in digital reverb, numerous delay times create discrete echoes, followed by multiple repetitions of these initial delays to create the ambience, which continues with decreasing clarity and amplitude. High-quality digital reverb units are capable of an extremely wide range of effects, produce high-quality sound, and take up relatively little room.

Digital reverb systems can simulate a variety of acoustical and mechanical reverberant sounds such as small and large concert halls, bright- and dark-sounding halls, small and large rooms, and small and large reverb plates (see "Plate Reverberation" later in this chapter). With each effect, it is also possible to control individually the attack; decay; diffusion (density); high-, middle-, and low-frequency decay times; and other sonic colorings.

One important feature of most digital reverb units is *predelay*—the amount of time between the onset of the direct sound and the appearance of the first reflections. Predelay is essential for creating a believable room ambience because early reflections arrive before reverberation. It also helps create the perception of a room's size: Shorter predelay times give the sense of a smaller room and vice versa.

Most digital reverb systems are programmed and programmable. They come with pre-programmed effects but also permit new ones to be programmed in and stored for reuse (see Figure 11-9).

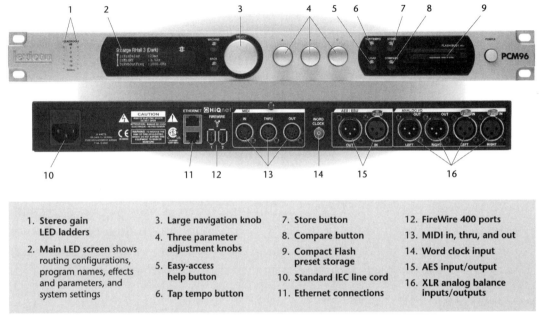

1. Stereo gain LED ladders	3. Large navigation knob	7. Store button	12. FireWire 400 ports
2. Main LED screen shows routing configurations, program names, effects and parameters, and system settings	4. Three parameter adjustment knobs	8. Compare button	13. MIDI in, thru, and out
	5. Easy-access help button	9. Compact Flash preset storage	14. Word clock input
	6. Tap tempo button	10. Standard IEC line cord	15. AES input/output
		11. Ethernet connections	16. XLR analog balance inputs/outputs

Figure 11-9 Digital reverberation processor, front and rear views. This model includes monaural and stereo reverbs for 28 effects, including chamber, hall, plate, room, chorus/flange, and delay. There are digital audio workstation automation and FireWire streaming through a plug-in format, compact Flash preset storage, and sampling rates of 44.1 kHz, 48 kHz, 88.2 kHz, and 96 kHz.

Convolution Reverb

Convolution reverb is a sample-based process that multiplies the spectrums of two audio files. One file represents the acoustic signature of an acoustic space. It is called the *impulse response* (**IR**). The other file is the source, or *carrier*. It takes on the characteristics of the acoustic space when it is multiplied by the IR. Hence, it has the quality of having been recorded in that space. By facilitating the interaction of any two arbitrary audio files, convolution reverb provides a virtually infinite range of unusual sonic possibilities.

Among the more common uses of convolution reverb is providing the actual likeness of real acoustic spaces interacting with any sound source you wish such as Boston's Symphony Hall, Nashville's Ryman Auditorium, a particular recording stage, a living room, a kitchen, or a jail cell (see Figure 11-10). The process can create effects such as exotic echoes and delays, a single clave or marimba hit, and different tempos and timbres.

Figure 11-10 Reverberation plug-in. This sampling reverberation plug-in offers one-, two-, and four-channel sampled acoustic environments ranging from real halls, to cathedrals, to bathrooms, to closets. It also provides the means for users to create their own acoustic samples.

Reverberation Plate

The *reverberation plate* is a mechanical-electronic device consisting of a thin steel plate suspended under tension in an enclosed frame (see Figure 11-11). It is large and heavy and requires isolation in a separate room. A moving-coil driver, acting like a small speaker, vibrates the plate, thus transducing the electrical signals from the console into mechanical energy. A contact microphone (two for stereo) picks up the plate's vibrations, transduces them back into electric energy, and returns them to the console. The multiple reflections from the vibrating plate create the reverb effect.

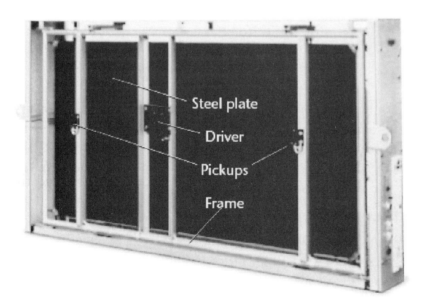

Figure 11-11 Reverberation plate.

Acoustic Chamber Reverberation

The *acoustic reverberation chamber* is a natural and realistic type of simulated reverb because it works on acoustic sound in an acoustic environment. It is a room with sound-reflective surfaces and nonparallel walls to avoid flutter echoes—multiple echoes at a rapid, even rate—and standing waves—apparently stationary waveforms created by multiple reflections between opposite, usually parallel, room surfaces. It usually contains two directional microphones (for stereo), placed off room center, and a loudspeaker, usually near a corner angled or back-to-back to the mic(s) to minimize the amount of direct sound the mic(s) pick up. The dry sound feeds from the console through the loudspeaker, reflects around the chamber, is picked up by the mic(s), and is fed back wet into the console for further processing and routing.

Reverberation and Ambience

In considering a reverberation system, it is helpful to keep in mind that reverberation and ambience, often thought of as synonymous, are different. Reverb is the remainder of sound that exists in a room after the source of the sound is stopped.[2] *Ambience* refers to the acoustical qualities of a listening space, including reverberation, echoes, background noise, and so on.[3] In general, reverb adds spaciousness to sound; ambience adds solidity and body.

Delay

Delay is the time interval between a sound or signal and its repetition. By manipulating delay times, it is possible to create a number of echo effects (see "Uses of Delay" later in this chapter). This is done most commonly with an electronic digital delay.

Digital Delay

Digital delay is generated by routing audio through an electronic buffer. The information is held for a specific period of time, which is set by the user, before it is sent to the output. A single-repeat delay processes the sound only once; multiple delays process the signal over and over. The amount and the number of delay times vary with the unit (see Figure 11-12).

Two parameters about delay that are important to understand are delay time and feedback. *Delay time* regulates how long a given sound is held and therefore the amount of time between delays. *Feedback*, also known as *regeneration*, controls how much of that delayed signal is returned to the input. Raising the amount of feedback increases the number of repeats and the length of decay. Turning it down completely generates only one repeat.

---

2. Glenn D. White and Gary J. Louie, *The Audio Dictionary*, 3rd ed. (Seattle: University of Washington Press, 2005), p. 331.
3. Ibid, p. 16.

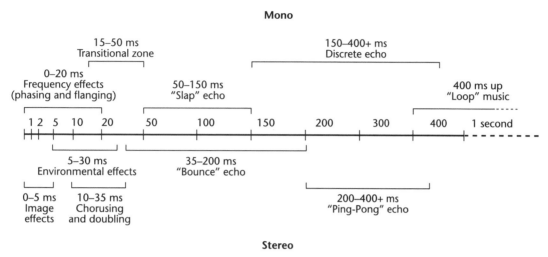

Figure 11-12 Time delay values and effects.

The better digital delays have excellent signal-to-noise ratio, low distortion, good high-frequency response with longer delay times, and an extensive array of effects. They are also excellent for prereverb delay. Lower-grade units are not as clean-sounding, and high-frequency response is noisier with longer delay times.

Uses of Delay

Delay has a number of creative applications. Among the common effects are doubling, chorus, slap back echo, and prereverb delay.

- **Doubling**—One popular use of delay is to fatten sound. The effect, which gives an instrument or voice a fuller, stronger sound, is called *doubling*. It is created by setting the delay to about 15 to 35 ms. These short delays are like early sound reflections and lend a sense of openness or ambience to dead-sounding instruments or voices.

  Doubling can also be done live by recording one track and then overdubbing the same part on a separate track in synchronization with the first. Because it is not possible to repeat a performance exactly, variations in pitch, timing, and room sounds add fullness or openness to sound. By continuing this process, it is possible to create a chorus effect.

- **Chorus**—The *chorus effect* is achieved by recirculating the doubling effect. The delay time is about the same as in doubling—15 to 35 ms—but is repeated. This effect can make a single voice sound like many and add spaciousness to a sound. Two voices singing in a relatively dead studio can be made to sound like a choir singing in a hall by chorusing the original sound.

- **Slap back echo**—A *slap back echo* is a delayed sound perceived as a distinct echo, much like the discrete Ping-Pong sound emitted by sonar devices when a contact is made. Slap back delay times are generally short, about 50 to 150 ms.

■ **Prereverb delay**—As mentioned in the discussion of digital reverb, there is a definite time lag between the arrival of direct waves from a sound source and the arrival of reflected sound in acoustic conditions. In some reverb systems, there is no delay between the dry and wet signals. By using a delay unit to delay the input signal before it gets to the reverb unit, it is possible to improve the quality of reverberation, making it sound more natural.

Flanging

Flanging is produced electronically. The signal is combined with its time-delayed replica. Delay time is relatively short, from 0 to 20 ms. Ordinarily, the ear cannot perceive time differences between direct and delayed sounds that are this short. But due to phase cancellations when the direct and delayed signals are combined, the result is a ***comb-filter effect***—a series of peaks and dips in the frequency response. This creates a filtered tone quality that sounds hollow, swishy, and outer space-like.

In addition to the various delay times, flangers typically provide feedback rate and depth controls. *Feedback rate* determines how quickly a delay time is modulated; for example, a feedback rate setting of 0.1 Hz performs one cycle sweep every 10 seconds. ***Depth controls*** adjust the spread between minimum and maximum delay times; depth is expressed as a ratio.

Many flangers provide controls to delay feedback in phase or out of phase. In-phase flanging is "positive"—the direct and delayed signals have the same polarity. Positive flanging accents even harmonics, producing a metallic sound. Out-of-phase flanging is "negative"—the two signals are opposite in polarity and accents odd harmonics. Negative flanging can create strong, sucking effects like a sound turned inside out.

Phasing

Phasing and flanging are similar in the way they are created. In fact, it is sometimes difficult to differentiate between the two. Instead of using a time-delay circuit, however, phasers use a phase shifter. Delays are very short, between 0 ms and 10 ms. The peaks and dips are more irregular and farther apart than in flanging, which results in something like a wavering vibrato that pulsates or undulates. Phasers provide a less pronounced pitched effect than flangers because their delay times are slightly shorter and the phasing effect has less depth than with flanging.

Phasers use two parameters that control modulation of the filters: rate (or speed) and depth (or intensity). Rate determines the sweep speed between the minimum and the maximum values of the frequency range. Depth defines the width of that range between the lowest and the highest frequencies.

Morphing

Morphing is the continuous, seamless transformation of one effect (aural or visual) into another. It is more than a sophisticated dissolve (the sonic counterpart of a dissolve is the ***crossfade***). Morphing is a complete restructuring of two completely different and

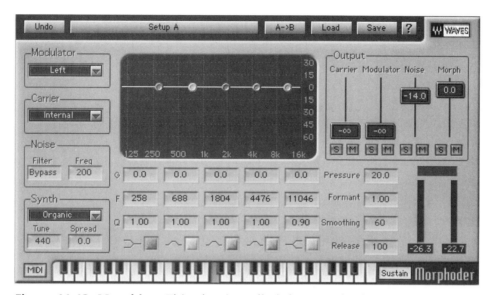

Figure 11-13 Morphing. This plug-in, called the Morphoder, is a processor of the vocoder type (see "Voice Processors" later in this chapter). It allows two audio signals to be combined using one source as a modulator input and a synthesizer as the carrier. The effect is that the synthesizer will "talk" and actually say the words spoken by the voice; or a drum track can be the modulator, resulting in a rhythmic keyboard track in sync with the drum track.

independent effects. Because most audio-morphing effects are delay-based, audio-morphing devices can be classified as time processors (see Figure 11-13).

A few examples of audio morphing include turning human speech or vocal lines into lines impossible to be spoken or sung by a human; turning sounds that exist into sounds that do not exist; spinning vowel-like sounds, varying their rate and depth, and then freezing them until they fade away; flanging cascades of sound across stereo space, adding echo, and varying the envelope control of rates; adding echoing rhythms to a multivoice chorus that become more dense as they repeat, with the effect growing stronger as the notes fade away; and taking a musical instrument and adding pitch sweeps that dive into a pool of swirling echoes that bounce from side to side or end by being sucked up.

Amplitude Processors

Amplitude, or *dynamic*, *processors* are devices that affect dynamic range. These effects include such functions as compression, limiting, de-essing, expanding, noise gating, and pitch shifting.

Compressor

The term *compressor* is customarily linked with the term *limiter*. They do basically the same signal processing but to different degrees. The *compressor* is a processor whose output level increases at a slower rate as its input level increases (see Figure 11-14). It is used to restrict dynamic range because of the peak signal limitations of an electronic system, for artistic goals, due to the surrounding acoustical requirements, or any combination of these factors.

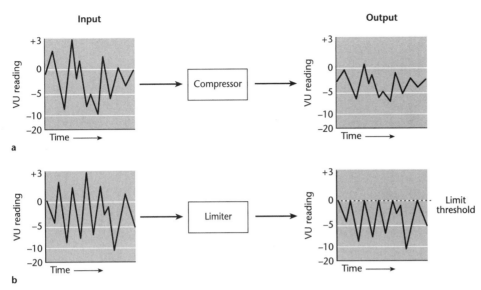

Figure 11-14 Effect of (a) compression and (b) limiting.

Compressors usually have four basic controls—for compression ratio, compression threshold, attack time, and release time—each of which can affect the others. Some compressors also include a makeup gain control. Compressor plug-ins may have additional features that act on a signal's dynamics.

The *compression ratio* establishes the proportion of change between the input and the output levels. The ratios are usually variable and, depending on the compressor, there are several selectable points between 1.1:1 and 20:1. Some recent compressor designs change ratios instantaneously, depending on the program's dynamic content and the range of control settings. If you set the compression ratio for, say, 2:1, it means that for every 2 dB increase of the input signal, the output will increase by 1 dB; at 5:1, a 5 dB increase of the input signal increases the output by 1 dB. In other words, it "reins in" excessive program dynamics. This is how sound with a dynamic range greater than what the equipment can handle is brought to usable proportions before distortion occurs.

The *compression threshold* is the level at which compression ratio takes effect. It is an adjustable setting and is usually selected based on a subjective judgment of where compression should begin. It is difficult to predetermine what settings will work best for a given sound at a certain level; it is a matter of listening and experimenting. The compressor has no effect on the signal below the threshold-level setting. For an illustration of the relationship between compression ratio and threshold, see Figure 11-15.

Once the threshold is reached, compression begins, reducing the gain according to the amount the signal exceeds the threshold level and according to the ratio set. The moment the compressor starts gain reduction is called the *knee. Hard knee compression* is abrupt; *soft knee compression* is smoother and less apparent.

Attack time is the length of time it takes the compressor to start compressing after the threshold has been reached. In a good compressor, attack times range from 500 *microseconds* (μs) to 100 ms. Depending on the setting, an attack time can enhance or

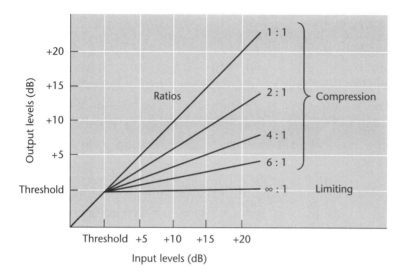

Figure 11-15 The relationship of various compression ratios to a fixed threshold point. The graph also displays the difference between the effects of limiting and compression.

detract from a sound. If the attack time is long, it can help bring out percussive attacks; but if it is too long, it can miss or overshoot the beginning of the compressed sound. If the attack time is too short, it reduces punch by attenuating the attacks, sometimes producing popping or clicking sounds. When it is controlled, a short attack time can heighten transients and add a crisp accent to sound. Generally, attack time should be set so that signals exceed the threshold level long enough to cause an increase in the average level. Otherwise, gain reduction will decrease overall level. Again, your ear is the best judge of the appropriate attack time setting.

Release time, or *recovery time*, is the time it takes a compressed signal to return to normal (*unity gain*) after the input signal has fallen below the threshold. Typical release times vary from 20 ms to several seconds. It is perhaps the most critical variable in compression because it controls the moment-to-moment changes in the level and therefore the overall loudness. One purpose of the release-time function is to make imperceptible the variations in loudness level caused by the compression. For example, longer release times are usually applied to music that is slower and more legato (that is, smoother and more tightly connected); shorter release times are usually applied to fast music.

Generally, release times should be set long enough that if signal levels repeatedly rise above the threshold, they cause gain reduction only once. If the release time is too long, a loud section of the audio could cause gain reduction that continues through a soft section.

These suggestions are not to imply rules—they are only guidelines. In fact, various release times produce different effects. Some enhance sound, others degrade it. See Chapter 13 for a list of the different effects compression produces and several of the applications that compressors (and limiters) have.

One additional important compressor control is called *makeup gain*. It allows adjustment of the output level to the desired optimum. It is used, for example, when loud parts of a signal are so reduced that the overall result sounds too quiet.

Broadband and Split-Band Compressors

Compressors fall into two categories: broadband and split-band. A *broadband compressor* acts on the dynamic range of the input signal across the entire frequency spectrum. The *split-band compressor* affects an input signal independently by splitting the audio into multiple bands, as needed, and then recombining the outputs of the bands into a single mono or stereo broadband signal. Good split-band compressors provide separate threshold, ratio control, attack and release times, and makeup gain for each compression band (see Figure 11-16).

The split-band compressor allows for finer control of dynamic range. For example, a bass can be compressed in the low end without adversely affecting the higher end. Conversely, speech can be de-essed without losing fullness in the lower end.

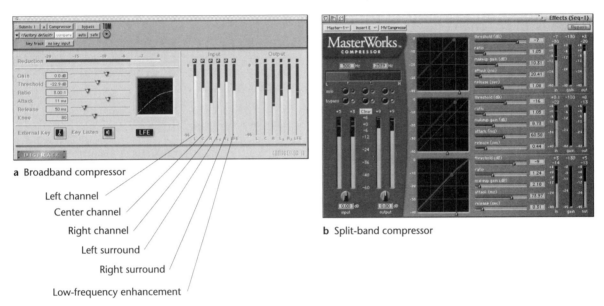

a Broadband compressor

Left channel
Center channel
Right channel
Left surround
Right surround
Low-frequency enhancement

b Split-band compressor

Figure 11-16 Compressor plug-ins. (a) A broadband compressor that can be used to control the dynamic range in recording and mixing 5.1 surround sound. (b) A split-band compressor that provides three separate bands of compression with graphic, adjustable crossover points among the three. Each band has its own settings, facilitating control over the entire spectrum of the signal being compressed, and a solo control that isolates an individual band for separate monitoring. This model has 64-bit processing and metering with numerical peak and RMS (root mean square) value displays.

Limiter

The *limiter* is a compressor whose output level stays at or below a preset point regardless of the input level. It has a compression ratio between 10:1 and infinity; it puts a ceiling on the loudness of a sound at a preset level (see Figure 11-14). Regardless of how loud the input signal is, the output will not go above this ceiling. This makes the limiter useful in situations where high sound levels are frequent or where a performer or console operator cannot prevent loud sounds from going into the red.

The limiter has a preset compression ratio but a variable threshold; the threshold sets the point where limiting begins. Attack and release times, if not preset, should be relatively short, especially the attack time. A short attack time is usually essential to a clean-sounding limit.

Unlike compression, which can have little effect on the frequency response, limiting can reduce high-frequency response. Also, if limiting is severe, the signal-to-noise ratio drops dramatically. What makes a good limiter? One that is used infrequently but effectively, that is, except in broadcasting, where limiting the signal before transmission is essential to control peak levels and hence overload distortion.

De-Esser

The *de-esser* is basically a fast-acting compressor that acts on high frequencies by attenuating them. It gets rid of the annoying hissy consonant sounds such as *s*, *z*, *ch*, and *sh* in speech and vocals. A de-esser may be a stand-alone unit or, more common, built into compressors and voice processors.

Expander

An *expander*, like a compressor, affects dynamic range (see Figure 11-17a). But whereas a compressor reduces it, an expander increases it. Like a compressor, an expander has variable ratios and is triggered when sound reaches a set threshold level. The ratios on an expander, however, are the inverse of those on a compressor but are usually gentler: 1:2, 1.5:2, and so on. At 1:2, each 1 dB of input expands to 2 dB of output; at 1:3, each 1 dB of input expands to 3 dB of output. Because an expander is triggered when a signal falls below a set threshold, it is commonly used as a noise gate.

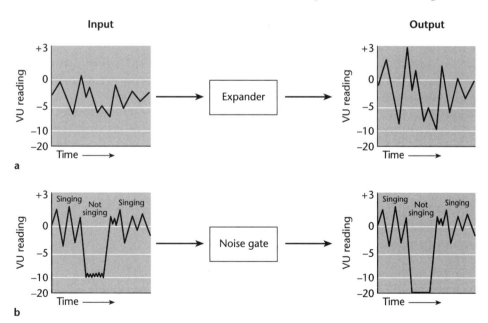

Figure 11-17 Effect of (a) expansion and (b) noise gating. Without noise gating, ambient noise is masked during singing and audible when singing is not present. Noise gating eliminates the ambient noise when there is no singing.

Noise Gate

Like the compressor, the expander/*noise gate* has the same dynamic determinants but they act inversely to those of the compressor. In addition to ratio settings, there is threshold: When the input signal level drops below the threshold, the gate closes and mutes the output. When the input signal level exceeds the threshold, the gate opens. Attack time determines how long it takes for the gate to go from full off to full on once the input level exceeds the threshold. Attack times are usually quite short—1 ms or even less. Longer attacks tend to chop off fast transients on percussive sounds. Release time sets the time required for the gate to go from full on to full off once the signal level falls below the threshold. Another control is the *key input*, sometimes called a *side chain input*, which allows a different signal to be fed in to govern the gating action such as using a bass drum as the key signal to turn another sound on and off in time with the bass drum's rhythm.

The noise gate is used primarily as a fix-it tool to reduce or eliminate unwanted low-level noise from amplifiers, ambience, rumble, noisy tracks, and leakage. It also has creative uses, however, to produce dynamic special effects. As an example of a practical application, assume you have two microphones—one for a singer and one for an accompanying piano. When the singer and the pianist are performing, the sound level will probably be loud enough to mask unwanted low-level noises. But if the pianist is playing quietly and the vocalist is not singing, or vice versa, the open, unused microphone may pick up these noises (see Figure 11-17b).

An obvious solution to this problem is to turn down the fader when a microphone is not being used, cutting it off acoustically and electronically; but this could become hectic for a console operator if several sound sources need to be coordinated. Another solution is to set the expander's threshold level at a point just above the quietest sound level that the vocalist (or piano) emits. When the vocalist stops singing, the loudness of the sound entering the mic falls below the threshold point of the expander, which shuts down, or gates, the mic. When a signal is above the threshold, there is no gating action and therefore no removal of noise.

The key to successful noise gating is in the coordination of the threshold and the ratio settings. Because there is often little difference between the low level of a sound's decay and the low level of noise, in gating noise you have to be wary that you do not cut off program material as well. Always be careful when you use a noise gate; unless it is set precisely, it can adversely affect response.

Pitch Shifter

A *pitch shifter* is a device that uses both compression and expansion to change the pitch of a signal. It is used to correct minor off-pitch problems, create special effects, or change the length of a program without changing its pitch. The latter function is called *time compression/expansion*. For example, if a singer delivers a note slightly flat or sharp, it is possible to raise or lower the pitch so that it is in tune. A pitch shifter also allows an input signal to be harmonized by mixing it with the harmonized signal at selected pitch ratios.

A pitch shifter works by compressing and expanding audio data. When the audio is compressed, it runs faster and raises pitch; it also shortens the audio segment. When the audio is expanded, it lowers pitch and lengthens the audio data. During processing, therefore, the pitch shifter is also rapidly cutting and pasting segments of data at varying intervals.

The basic parameter for pitch shifting is transposition. *Transposing* is changing the original pitch of a sound into another pitch; in music, it is changing into another key. Transposition sets the harmony-line interval, typically within a range of one or two octaves. A pitch shifter may also include a delay line with feedback and predelay controls.

Depending on the model or software, a pitch shifter may also be capable of **speed-up pitch-shifting**, which changes the timbre and pitch of natural sounds. Speed-up pitch-shifting is sometimes referred to as the "chipmunk effect."

As a time compressor, a pitch shifter can shorten recorded audio material with no editing, no deletion of content, and no alteration in pitch (see Figure 11-18).

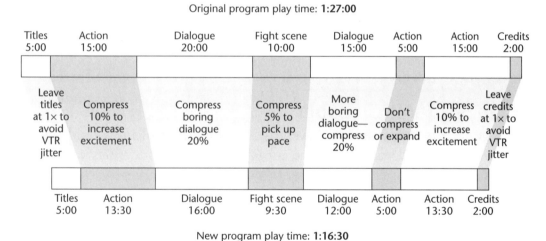

Figure 11-18 Time compression of an event sequence.

Noise Processors

Noise processors reduce or eliminate noise from an audio signal. With the advent of **digital signal processing (DSP)** plug-ins, these processors have become powerful tools in getting rid of virtually any unwanted noise. In fact, because noise reduction with digital processing is so effective, getting rid of recorded and system noise has become far less of a problem than it once was. It has also been a boon to audio restoration.

Software programs are dedicated to getting rid of different types of noise such as clicks, crackles, pops, hum, buzz, rumble, computer-generated noise, unwanted background ambience, and recovery of lost signals due, for example, to clipping. They are available in bundles with separate programs for particular types of noise reduction.

Digital noise reduction is able to remove constant, steady noises. In a vocal track with high-level background noise from lights, ventilating fans, and studio acoustics, almost all of the noise can be removed without affecting voice quality.

In digital noise reduction, there are parameters to control and balance. It is important to consider the amount of noise removed from the signal, the amount of signal removed from the program material, and the amount of new sonic colorations added to the signal. Failure to coordinate these factors can sonically detract from the program material if not exacerbate the original noise problem.

The following are other points to consider when using noise reduction[4]:

- Always preview before processing and have a backup copy.

- To maintain perspective, continue to compare the processed sound against the unprocessed sound.

- Do not rely only on automatic settings. They may not precisely produce the desired effect or may introduce unwanted artifacts, or both.

- Use the "noise only" monitoring feature to check the part of the audio removed by the software.

- In heavy noise situations, a multiband expander or an EQ boost in the frequency range of the target audio helps make the audio clearer.

- In rhythmic material, be careful that the noise reduction processing does not adversely affect the rhythmic patterns or the transient response.

Multieffects Signal Processors

A *multieffects signal processor* combines several of the functions of individual signal processing in a single unit. The variety and the parameters of these functions vary with the unit; but because most multieffects processors are digital, they are powerful audio-processing tools albeit, in some cases, dauntingly complicated. Multieffects processors are available in stand-alone units, plug-ins, and plug-in bundles, and most have wide frequency response, at least 16-bit resolution, and dozens of programmable presets.

Voice Processors

One type of popular multieffects processor used for voice work is the ***voice processor*** (also referred to as a ***vocoder***). Because of its particular application in shaping the sound of the all-important spoken and singing voice, it warrants some attention here.

A voice, or vocal, processor can enhance, modify, pitch-correct, harmonize, and change completely the sound of a voice, even to the extent of gender. Functions vary with the model, but in general a system may include some, many, or most of the following: preamp, EQ, harmonizer, compression, noise gate, reverb, delay, and chorus.

---

4. Based on Mike Levine, "Noises Off," *Electronic Musician*, August, 2008, p. 50.

Voice-modeling menus create different textures and may include any number of effects for inflections; spectral changes in frequency balance; *vibratos* (variations in the frequency of a sound generally at a rate of 2 and 15 times per second; glottals (breathiness, rasp, and growl); warp (changes in *formants*—a frequency band in a voice or musical instrument that contains more energy and loudness than the neighboring area); harmony processing that provides multivoice harmonies; and pitch shifting in *semitones*, or in *cents*—1/100 semitone. Voice processors are available in rack-mounted models and as plug-ins.

Other Types of Plug-Ins

In addition to plug-ins that perform the relatively familiar signal-processing functions, specialized plug-ins add an almost infinite amount of flexibility to sound shaping. Among the hundreds available are programs for mastering—the final stage in preparing audio material for duplication; stereo and surround-sound calibration, panning, and mixing; musical synthesis with patches included; virtual instrumentation of just about any musical sound source such as keyboards, fretted instruments, horns, drums, and full orchestras; metering, metronome, and instrument tuning; time alignment of vocals, dialogue, and musical instruments; simulation of various types of guitar amplifiers; software sampling with multiformat sound libraries; and emulation—making digital audio sound like analog.

Format Compatibility of Plug-Ins

Plug-ins come in a number of different formats. Before purchasing one, make sure it is compatible with your software production system. For example, the most popular formats for Windows are Steinberg's Virtual Studio Technology (VST) and Direct X, a group of application program interfaces. Because formats come and go, as do software programs, listing here which plug-in formats are compatible with which production systems would be unwieldy and become quickly outdated. A check of vendors' websites can provide their available plug-ins and the systems with which they are compatible.

Main Points

- Signal processors are used to alter some characteristic of a sound. They can be grouped into four categories: spectrum; time; amplitude, or dynamic; and noise.

- Signal processors may be inboard, incorporated into production consoles; outboard stand-alone units; or a plug-in—an add-on software tool that gives a digital recording/editing system signal-processing alternatives beyond what the original system provides.

- The equalizer and the filter are examples of spectrum processors because they alter the spectral balance of a signal. The equalizer increases or decreases the level of a signal at a selected frequency by boost or cut (also known as peak and dip) or by shelving. The filter attenuates certain frequencies above, below, between, or at a preset point(s).

- Common types of equalizers in use are the fixed-frequency, parametric, graphic, and paragraphic.

- The most common filters are high-pass (low-cut), low-pass (high-cut), band-pass, and notch.

- Psychoacoustic processors add clarity, definition, and overall presence to sound.

- Time processors affect the time relationships of signals. Reverberation and delay are two such effects.

- The four types of reverberation systems used for the most part today are digital, convolution, plate, and acoustic chamber; reverb plug-in software may be considered a fifth type.

- Digital reverb reproduces electronically the sound of different acoustic environments.

- Convolution reverb is a sample-based process that multiplies the spectrums of two audio files. One file represents the acoustic signature of an acoustic space. It is called the impulse response (IR). The other file, or source, takes on the characteristics of the acoustic space when it is multiplied by the IR. Hence, it has the quality of having been recorded in that space.

- The reverberation plate is a mechanical-electronic device consisting of a thin steel plate suspended under tension in an enclosed frame, a moving-coil driver, and a contact microphone(s).

- The acoustic reverberation chamber is a natural and realistic type of simulated reverb because it works on acoustic sound in an acoustic environment with sound-reflective surfaces.

- An important feature of most digital reverb units is predelay—the amount of time between the onset of the direct sound and the appearance of the first reflections.

- Delay is the time interval between a sound or signal and its repetition.

- Delay effects, such as doubling, chorus, slap back echo, and prereverb delay, are usually produced electronically with a digital delay device.

- Flanging and phasing split a signal and slightly delay one part to create controlled phase cancellations that generate a pulsating sound. Flanging uses a time delay; phasing uses a phase shifter.

- Morphing is the continuous, seamless transformation of one effect (aural or visual) into another.

- Amplitude (dynamic) processors affect a sound's dynamic range. These effects include compression, limiting, de-essing, expanding, noise gating, and pitch shifting.

■ With compression, as the input level increases, the output level also increases but at a slower rate, reducing dynamic range. With limiting, the output level stays at or below a preset point regardless of its input level. With expansion, as the input level increases, the output level also increases but at a greater rate, increasing dynamic range.

■ A broadband compressor acts on the dynamic range of the input signal across the entire frequency spectrum. The split-band compressor affects an input signal independently by splitting the audio into multiple bands, as needed, and then recombining the outputs of the bands into a single mono or stereo broadband signal.

■ A de-esser is basically a fast-acting compressor that acts on high-frequency sibilance by attenuating it.

■ An expander, like a compressor, affects dynamic range. But whereas a compressor reduces it, an expander increases it.

■ A noise gate is used primarily to reduce or eliminate unwanted low-level noise such as ambience and leakage. It is also used creatively to produce dynamic special effects.

■ A pitch shifter uses both compression and expansion to change the pitch of a signal or the running time of a program.

■ Noise processors are designed to reduce or eliminate such noises as clicks, crackles, hum, and rumble from an audio signal.

■ Multieffects signal processors combine several of the functions of individual signal processorsin a single unit.

■ A voice, or vocal, processor (also referred to as a vocoder) can enhance, modify, pitch-correct, harmonize, and change completely the sound of a voice, even to the extent of gender.

■ Highly specialized plug-ins add an almost infinite amount of flexibility to sound shaping.

■ When selecting a plug-in, it is important to know whether it is compatible with the software production system used.

12 Editing

The results of good production for picture are readily perceptible to the viewer—lighting, cinematography, composition, transitions, special effects, and so on. Not so with audio. When audio is well produced, it is complementary to the overall dramatic intent of the production and works as a subtle and powerful aspect of the whole. As producer/director George Lucas once commented, "Sound is fifty percent of the motion picture experience."[1] However, if a sound track is poorly crafted or overly produced and the dialogue, sound effects, or music dominate, it detracts from the film-viewing experience. Nowhere in audio production is "invisibility" more important than with editing.

Editing is indispensable to the production process. Program segments may need to be rearranged, shortened, or cut out altogether. Directors commonly record elements of a program out of sequence; editing makes this possible. It also makes it possible to transpose parts of words; "recompose" music; change the character of a sound effect; improve the quality of dialogue; take out noises such as clicks and pops; eliminate mistakes, long pauses, coughing, "ahs," "ers," "ums," and other awkwardness; record a segment several times and choose the best parts of each take; change the relationship of characters in a drama; create the pace; establish timing; and even redirect an entire storyline. The art of editing requires the ability to see a whole and build toward it while it is still in parts. The best editors have a first-rate ear and innate sensitivity to the aesthetics of sound.

Digital Editing

Digital editing allows the assembly of digitally sampled material in or out of sequence, taken from any part of a recording, and placed in any other part of the recording almost instantly. It is therefore also referred to as *nonlinear editing*. Nonlinear editing is not new. Film and audiotape have always been edited nonlinearly; that is, a sound (or shot) is accessed in one part of a recording and added to another part of the recording, or deleted, in whatever order the editor chooses.

---

1. In Robin Beauchamp, *Designing Sound for Animation* (Oxford: Focal Press, 2005).

In the digital domain, nonlinear editing is done using hardware and software. These tools are far beyond anything an editor could envision in the days before computers; editing audio tape involved manual splicing with a razor blade. With even a basic *nonlinear editor (NLE)*, it is possible to "see" a sound in its waveform, audition an edit at any stage in the procedure, cut, paste, and copy, adjust levels, add signal processing, and restore any change in the edited material to its original waveform at any time, quickly and seamlessly—all without endangering the master audio. A variety of programs support simple one- and two-track editing environments for mono and stereo audio, respectively, as well as multitrack layouts for more complicated productions. If needed, many editing software programs can display video in sync with the audio.

Digital editing affords the convenience of allowing any recording from almost any source to be transferred and coded or converted in the process. Once editing (and mixing, see Chapter 13) at the computer is completed, the audio may be sent on for mastering or transferred back to the distribution medium if video or online delivery is involved.

Functions of Editing Software

Many excellent audio-editing software programs are available. Although they vary in price and sophistication, they all perform functions similar to word processing or a graphics program, such as cut, paste, delete, insert, and so on. They also perform a variety of other functions, depending on the program's complexity and application—from music recording to synchronizing sound with picture.

Given the number of editing programs available, it would be unwieldy to list and explain their many features here. The following section is a distillation of the basic functions found in many NLEs.

Basic Functions in Digital Editing

With an NLE, digital audio takes the form of a *soundfile,* which contains information about the sound such as amplitude and duration. When the soundfile is opened, that information is displayed as a waveform on the monitor.

The *waveform* displays the profile of a sound's amplitude over time. By being able to see a representation of a sound, it is easy to spot its dynamics (see Figure 12-1). It is also possible to see greater detail in a waveform by zooming in, a feature that facilitates extremely precise editing. Once the soundfile is retrieved and its waveform displayed, it can be played back, or auditioned, to determine which of its sections is to be defined for editing.

As a sound is played, a *cursor* scrolls the waveform, enabling the editor to see precisely the part of the sound that is playing at any given moment. When the editor determines the part of the sound to be edited, the segment is highlighted as a *defined region.* Much like selected text in a word processing program, once a region is defined, the selected edit is performed only in that section of the waveform. The region can be cut from the waveform display or moved and/or copied to another part of the waveform or to another

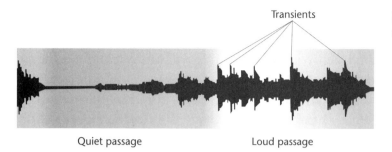

Transients

Quiet passage   Loud passage

Figure 12-1 Dynamics of a waveform.

waveform. It can also be inverted or changed in level, envelope, frequency, and so on, up to the limits of the system.

Keeping track of key events in a given region is essential and *markers* can be placed anywhere in the waveform to facilitate jumping the play cursor to the desired marker points. The marker can be a graphic identifier using a number, a letter, or text (see Figure 12-2).

Anytime in the editing process, the soundfile can be auditioned in a number of ways: from beginning to end, from the defined region, from marker to marker, looping, and at increased or decreased speed in either direction. This latter operation is called scrubbing.

Scrubbing lets you move the play cursor using a mouse through the defined region at any speed and listen to the section being scrubbed. With scrubbing, you can audibly and visibly locate with greater precision the in and out points of a defined region. Many NLEs have jogging and shuttling functions. *Jogging* facilitates an editor's ability to navigate or skip through a clip, region, or entire project quickly and with greater ease.

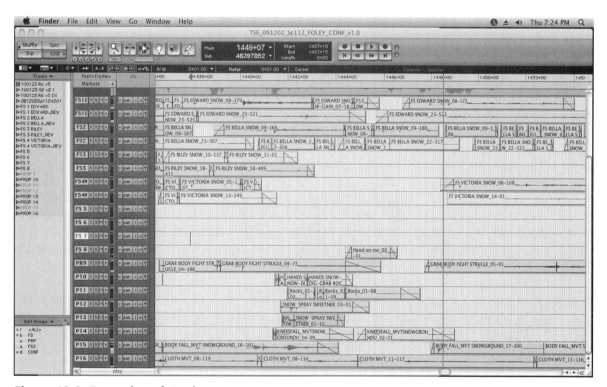

Figure 12-2 Examples of markers.

As noted earlier, the basic operations in digital editing are similar to those in word processing, for example, when you delete a word entirely or cut or copy it from one part of a sentence and paste it elsewhere, or when you move entire paragraphs around. Once a region is defined, the *Cut command* removes it from its original location and copies it to the computer's random access memory (RAM) for temporary storage. This section of computer memory is usually referred to as the *clipboard*. Using the *Copy command*, the defined region is added to the clipboard but is not cut from its original position. The *Paste command* copies the defined region from the clipboard and inserts it into the waveform immediately after the position of the play cursor. Additional paste functions facilitate how a defined region is placed in any part of the waveform. *Undo/Redo* allows reversing the previous edit or applying the edit (or change) again.

Snapping appends a defined region to another region, like a magnet with no gap or overlap between them. *Slipping* moves a defined region freely with spaces preceding or following it, or it can overlap a portion of another region. *Spotting* places a defined region into a specific location displayed in time code, minutes and seconds, bars and beats, or feet and frames.

There are also commands in digital editing similar to the insert and replace operations in word processing. *Insert* moves the audio that originally followed the play cursor to a point immediately following the newly inserted segment. *Replace* overwrites the audio immediately following the play cursor.

Scaling and *zooming* allow adjustments of the track view; that is, the waveform can be made taller or shorter, expanded to the right or left, widened to show more of its duration, or tightened to better display a more concentrated duration.

Trim or *crop* shortens or expands a defined region to a desired length. On most NLEs, it provides a quick way to remove noise or silence from the head or tail of an audio clip. There may also be a *Delete Silence* command that removes unwanted silences between words and sentences or on music tracks. A *Limit Silence* command determines the length of the silence to be removed.

Time compression and *expansion* decreases or increases the length of a sound file so that it plays for a shorter or longer period of time. With most editing programs, this is accomplished without changing the sound's pitch.

Looping allows soundfiles to be repeated exactly at the touch of a button as many times as desired. A looping program may also facilitate creation of synthetic sounds and pitch shifting.

Track grouping moves two or more tracks when they have to retain a direct time relationship; in a music recording, for example, this function is used when one track contains the vocal, another track contains the accompanying guitar, and other tracks contain the supporting rhythm instruments.

Time displays include *start display,* which gives the start point of the current selection; *end display,* which gives the end point of the current selection; *length display,* which gives the duration of the current selection; and ***current time,*** which indicates the present point of the play cursor in a track. Data indicators can be displayed in time code, minutes and seconds, bars and beats, or feet and frames.

Still another advantage of digital editing is that the edits you make can be nondestructive. ***Nondestructive editing*** changes only the pointers, not the audio data. The original soundfile is not altered regardless of what editing or signal processing you apply. ***Destructive editing,*** on the other hand, changes the data by overwriting it. This raises the question: Why employ destructive editing when you can process a soundfile in any way you wish and still preserve the original? There are three answers: The editing program itself may be destructive, that is, changes to the files are temporary until the file is saved; destructive editing may be necessary when memory is limited—it is easier to save a single soundfile than both the original and the duplicate soundfiles; and it may be necessary when the edited soundfile has to be downloaded to another system.

Editing Example

Let's go through a short editing procedure with a specific example: the guitar strums in Figure 12-3. The peaks in the waveform are where the volume goes up; the valleys are where the volume goes down. Different types of sounds produce different types of waveforms. Vowel sounds in speech and wind sounds, for example, produce waveforms with less pronounced peaks and valleys because they have softer attacks and longer decays (see Figure 12-4).

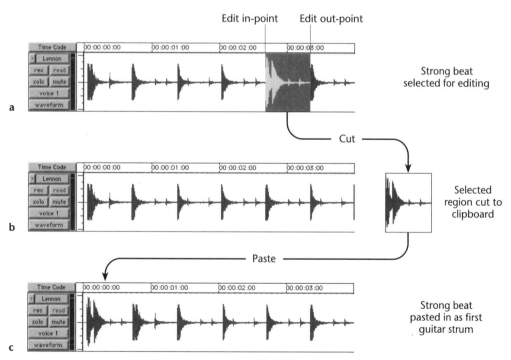

Figure 12-3 Editing example. Guitar strums must be edited to move the fifth beat to the first by (a) selecting the defined region to edit, (b) cutting it to the clipboard, and (c) pasting it to the first position.

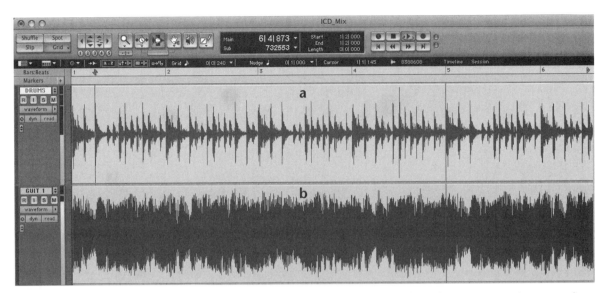

Figure 12-4 Waveforms showing percussive and sustained sounds. Editing percussive sounds (a) is easier than editing sustained sounds (b) because percussives usually have distinct breaks in the audio.

Notice that the accents in the fifth beat, which begin at roughly 02:45, are played more strongly compared with the accents in the previous four beats. The challenge is to move this stronger strum from the fifth beat to the first and still maintain the 4/4 time. Whenever possible, define a region precisely before a volume peak and end it immediately before another volume peak. In this case, that would be from the instant before the fifth beat begins, at about 02:45, to the tail end of the beat sequence at what would be about 04:00.

The editing procedure would be as follows: Scrub the region to be edited until you are sure of the in and out edit points. If necessary, use the *zoom* magnification tool for a more precise look at the in and out points. These points can be verified using the current position indicator. Click on the selector and drag the cursor from the in point to the out point, thereby defining the region to be edited. Once the region is defined, clicking on the Edit menu Cut command removes the edit and places it on the clipboard.

To replace the edited region at the beginning of the track, position the cursor there and click on the Edit menu Paste command. Another method of making the move is to select the shuffle mode, assuming the edit has to snap to another region, and use the grabber tool to actually move the defined region. If placement of the edit is critical to maintaining the beat, the grid mode may be the one to use.

This example is quite basic and generalized. Techniques specific to editing dialogue, sound effects, and music are discussed later in this chapter.

Transitions

Sequencing two sounds (or shots) involves creating a ***transition***. Transitions are the connective tissue in any project; they establish pace and provide formal unity and continuity with regard to the relationship of parts to the whole. In audio, four techniques are used to make transitions: segue or cut, crossfade, soft cut, and fade-out/fade-in.

Segue and Cut

Segue (pronounced "seg-way") is a musical term that means "follow on." In radio, it refers to the playing of two or more recordings with no live announcing in between or live announcing over the segue. In a broader sense, segue is analogous to the term *cut* used to describe transitions in TV and film. In this context, cutting from one element to another means establishing a picture or sound immediately after the previous picture or sound stops, and doing it at once, not gradually. In discussing the effects of this particular type of transition, we use the broader term **cut**. Cutting creates transitions that are sharp and well defined, picking up the rhythm of sequences.

Crossfade

The *crossfade* is another type of transition for smaller changes in time, locale, and action, although you can vary the length of these changes somewhat by increasing or decreasing its duration. The crossfade accomplishes the same thing as the fade-out/fade-in, but aesthetically it is softer, more fluid, and more graceful. It also maintains, rather than breaks, rhythmic continuity and pace.

The crossfade can be produced in a number of ways, depending on the crossfade times and the loudness levels of the sounds when they cross. Usually, it is more aesthetically satisfying to cross the sounds at the moment they are at full and equal loudness. This keeps audience attention "stage-center" with no loss of focus or gap in continuity (see Figure 12-5).

Soft Cut

A *soft cut* is a term used with picture when a shot change is brief but not quite as abrupt as a cut nor as deliberate as a dissolve. In audio, a soft cut can be used for transitions that need a quick, yet aesthetically, graceful change; to cover a minor technical apparency without appreciably affecting rhythm, tempo, pace, or dramatic intent; or to provide, as the term suggests, a somewhat gentler way to move from one audio cue to another.

Fade-Out/Fade-In

The *fade-out/fade-in* transition is used to make a clearly defined change from one time, place, and action to another. Aesthetically, it is gentler than the cut; it gives a stronger sense of finality to an ending scene and a sense of new possibilities to the beginning scene. Faster fades suggest shorter lapses of time, smaller changes of location, or fewer events in a series of actions. They still provide a definite break in the presentation, but their quicker rate implies that less has happened. You should not, however, consider these guidelines as prescriptive. There are no formulas for how long transitions should be relative to the scenes they bridge; it is a matter of what feels right.

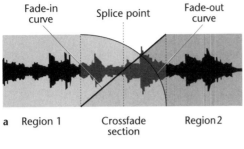

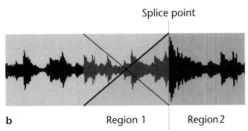

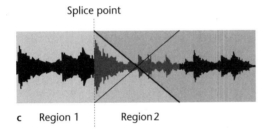

Figure 12-5 Common types of crossfades. (a) Standard, or centered, crossfade on both sides of the splice point. In this example the fade-in curve is linear and smooth, and the fade-out curve is gradual, reducing level steadily. (b) Pre-crossfade creates a crossfade before the splice point, thus maintaining the level of the beginning of region 2 instead of fading across it. Pre-crossfade is useful if there is a strong percussive downbeat or a loud sound at the beginning of region 2. (c) Post-crossfade generates the crossfade after the splice point. It is useful in maintaining the level of region 1 until it ends, to keep, for example, a strong upbeat or an exclamatory sound that occurs at the end of region 1.

General Editing Guidelines

As with any creative activity, there are about as many approaches as there are players. From the various techniques used in digital editing, the following are a few generally accepted guidelines.

- It is physically easier and sonically cleaner to select the in and out edit points at silent spots in the track.

- If there is no silent spot, listen and look for the attack of a dynamic such as a hard consonant, a percussive hit, or other transient sound. The best place to edit is just before the dynamic. The quick burst of its onset usually provides enough separation from the preceding sound (see Figure 12-6).

- If it is not possible to find a silent or well-defined point in the track, start and end the edit at zero crossings. A *zero crossing* is the point where the waveform crosses the centerline. It denotes a value of zero amplitude and divides the positive (upper) and negative (lower) parts of the waveform. By using this technique, you avoid or minimize the popping or clicking sound at the transition between two regions.

- If the zero-crossing technique still yields too much unwanted sound at the edit point, crossfading smoothes the edit. A crossfade fades out one segment while fading in another and requires sufficient material on either side of the edit point with which to work (see Figure 12-7). Crossfades can vary in length from a few seconds to a few milliseconds. The audibility of a crossfade of a few milliseconds is virtually imperceptible.

■ In performing a *fade-in,* when a signal increases in amplitude from silence to the desired level over a period of time, or a *fade-out,* when a signal gradually decreases to silence, the rates of increase or decrease can vary. The rate of a fade's curve can be linear—constant over the length of the fade; *logarithmic*—starting quickly and then slowly tapering off at the end; or *S-type*—starting quickly, slowing toward the middle, and then speeding up toward the end.

■ Avoid using time-based effects, such as reverb and delay, during recording. It makes pasting sections from different tracks difficult because they may not match. Dry, or unprocessed, tracks are far easier to edit because they provide a more uniform sound.

Figure 12-6 Editing before the dynamic. The best places to edit in this example are just before the hard consonants in the words "can," "together," and "dear."

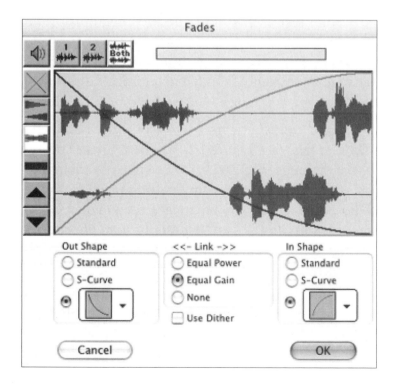

Figure 12-7 Fades dialogue box. This command allows several different fade-out/fade-in curves from which to choose in crossfading between two adjoining regions.

Organization

An essential part of organizing the editing stage of a project is the edit decision list.

Edit Decision List

The *edit decision list* (*EDL*) is a step-by-step list generated during editing. It includes the in and out edit points of a shot or an audio segment; the nature of the transitions; the duration of the edit; and, if needed, cross-references to other source media (i.e., whether the audio comes from a video track, a digital recorder, and so on).

The format of an EDL may be charted in whatever arrangement is most functional to a production and editing system. Generally, you should include clear, descriptive information that covers what, where and when. Coding is usually in time code, but with music it may be in minutes and seconds. Produce an EDL at the outset of editing to serve as the guide to subsequent editing sessions, during which it becomes a log and is revised and refined until the final edit. As an accurate record of all editing events, the EDL is indispensable both for control and as a timesaver.

Organizing Edit Tracks

The approach to organizing edit tracks obviously depends on the number of individual sound tracks involved. If only a few tracks are to be edited, which may be the case in, say, an interview, the procedure is apparent: Intercut the questions and the answers so the continuity is logical. But when numerous sound tracks are involved, which is likely in drama and music recording, it is necessary to devise a system whereby they are clearly named and organized to facilitate editing and mixing. There is no definitive way of doing this; audio editors use various approaches. The point is: Before any editing begins, name and catalog all the sounds and keep a running log throughout the editing process; otherwise mix-ups—or worse—are inevitable. List each sound and include appropriate information such as its content; time code address; film frame number; scene and take number, any special instructions for editing, signal processing, or mixing; and any problems with the sound such as noise, change in ambience, sudden dropout, a fluff in pronunciation, and so on.

In productions with dialogue, music, and sound effects, first group the sound by category—often referred to as the *DME tracks* (see Figure 12-8). Then, further group them in each category. For example, the dialogue tracks may be arranged by character and then divided into dialogue from the production recording and dialogue from the automated dialogue replacement (ADR). Sound effects can be categorized as Foley, background, ambience, location, hard (or cut), soft, and design. A *design sound effect* does not exist in nature; it has to be created. A *hard,* or *cut* sound effect, such as a car ignition, door slam, or pistol shot, begins and ends cleanly requiring little adjustment in editing to remain in sync with the picture. A *soft sound effect,* such as crowd noise, buzzing, and ocean waves does not have a defined beginning and ending and does not explicitly synchronize with the picture.

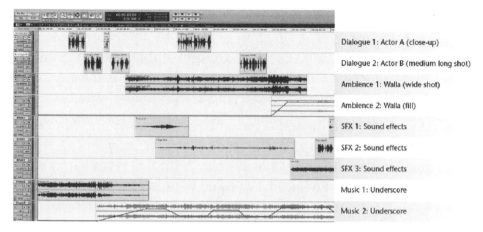

Dialogue 1: Actor A (close-up)

Dialogue 2: Actor B (medium long shot)

Ambience 1: Walla (wide shot)

Ambience 2: Walla (fill)

SFX 1: Sound effects

SFX 2: Sound effects

SFX 3: Sound effects

Music 1: Underscore

Music 2: Underscore

Figure 12-8 Edit window showing DME track layout.

Once sounds have been grouped, assign them to individual tracks, determining to the extent possible those sounds that do and do not have to overlap. This not only facilitates editing but also affects a sound's placement in a track.

Drive Management

Managing all your soundfiles is an important aspect of organization in the editing process. Just as file management is a recordkeeping essential to avoid chaos in maintaining production details, so is drive management. With the ability of drives to process and store an ever-increasing magnitude of data, it is imperative to also catalog the information they hold. Devise whatever system works for you, but keep track of which drives contain which files and what soundfiles are where. Be sure to save work in progress often and back up your project frequently to a different drive. It seems like obvious advice, but too frequently the obvious is overlooked.

Differences Between Editing Sound and Editing Picture

Editing picture is one-dimensional: One shot is cut, dissolved, or faded out and into another shot. Once the transition has been made, in terms of editing, little happens until the next transition.

Editing sound, on the other hand, is multidimensional. Sounds are layered within each shot, so editing audio becomes more than attending to transitions. In a scene, an actor may be speaking to another actor with traffic outside, a clock ticking, a bath running in another room, footsteps moving back and forth, and music underscoring the action. All these elements have to be edited so that the various sonic layers are properly matched and synchronized and the perspectives are maintained.

Editing Speech and Dialogue

Among the considerations basic to editing speech and dialogue are recognizing the sounds that make up words; cutting together similar and dissimilar sounds; handling emphasis and inflection; and matching ambience (or room tone).

Identifying Sounds That Make Up Words

Editing speech more often than not requires dealing with the sounds that make up a word rather than with the entire word. These sounds are called *phonemes*—the smallest unit of speech capable of conveying a distinction in meaning, such as the *p* and the *b* in the words "pat" and "bat" or the *m* and the *d* in the words "mark" and "dark."

In editing, some sounds are easier than others to recognize. The easiest are those consonants with striking power, such as *d*, *k*, *p*, and *t*—sounds with a pronounced attack identified sonically by a click or pop and visually by a spike in the waveform (see Figure 12-9). Consonants are either voiced or unvoiced. A voiced consonant, such as the *v* in "vary," issues from vocal tone (resonating the vocal cords) and breath. An unvoiced consonant, such as the *p* in "put," is formed only of breath.

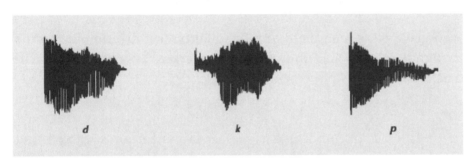

Figure 12-9 Waveforms of the consonants *d*, *k*, and *p*. These waveforms were generated by a female alto voice delivering them with emphasis. Waveforms of the same consonants will look different with other types of voices and deliveries.

The vowels *a*, *e*, *i*, *o*, and *u* are the most difficult to identify and separate because they lack any attack. Vowels usually blend with the other sounds in a word. This is particularly the case when they occur in a diphthong, such as *ay-ih* in "stay." When vowels begin or are embedded in phrases in connected speech, their sound is more readily apparent. One way to locate vowels, or any sound that is difficult to perceive, is to listen for differences in pitch or to look for a change in the waveform, however slight.

Sometimes, sounds are run together and cannot be separated in the usual way with a cut. If cutting between sounds is still a problem, try the crossfade technique (described previously).

Editing Similar and Dissimilar Sounds

Editing dissimilar sounds in speech is easier than editing similar sounds because they are usually distinct and often flow more naturally. Consider the sentence, "Sound is both challenging and creative." If we delete *both*, the edit will be made after *is* and before *challenging*. The *s* will be pasted to the *ch* and, because they are different sounds, the rhythmic transition between *is* and *challenging* is natural and distinct. Such is not the case with speech sounds that are similar or slurred together, such as "and Donna" or "Joe's soda." Editing in and out of similar sounds may require crossfading, cutting and replacing parts of key sounds to smooth transitions and retain the natural pattern of speech.

Emphasis and Inflection

Another common problem for the sound editor is dealing with emphasis and inflection. Suppose the speaker says, "How are you?" with the emphasis on "you" to express concern. For some reason, the "you" is garbled, and without this word it is not possible to use the phrase. If it is unimportant, there's no problem; but if it must be kept, there are three alternatives: Ask the person to deliver the line again, which may be impractical if not impossible; go through the recording to hear whether the person said "you" elsewhere with the same or almost the same inflection; or construct the word from similar sounds the speaker uttered.

Ambience

Ambience is background sound. Other terms used synonymously are *room tone* and *presence*. Some people draw a distinction between these terms: *ambience* is any background sound that is part of a recording or has been added in postproduction; and *room tone* or *presence* is background sound recorded during actual production to provide the sound editor with the material to assemble sonically consistent backgrounds—not only for maintaining continuity of content but also for matching the background sounds.

One technique used to make the transition from one statement/background to the other is diverting the listeners' attention. For example, if the ambience during one statement was quiet when the room was filled with people, and the ambience during the second statement was reflectant when the room was almost empty, you could try to locate in the recording a cough, a murmur, someone accidentally hitting the microphone, or some other distraction. Paste the distracter between the two statements (the distracter would also contain some room background) so attention momentarily is called to it instead of to the obvious change in background sound.

Another technique used to match backgrounds is to mix one background with another, or alternately crossfade them, to even them out. This assumes that the ambiences were recorded "in the clear" before or after the event. Always record at least a few minutes of room tone or ambience to have on hand for editing.

Still another approach frequently used to smooth a potentially awkward transition between two ambiences is to have the sound and the picture cut at slightly different places in the shot change. In this situation, the audio slightly precedes or carries into the succeeding visual edit. This is called *split editing*.

A common technique used to handle background sound is *looping*. A loop is a section of audio that is repeated, with its start and end having no perceptible edit point. When background sound, such as crowd, wind, or room tone, is continuous—particularly through lengthy scenes—running a continuous track could be unwieldy, take up unnecessary memory, or both. Using the automatic loop function in an NLE solves this problem. But remember: *To be effective, a loop must sound continuous, not repetitive.* To help eliminate a perceptible edit point, start and end the waveform on the zero crossing and avoid using material that has distinctive sonic events that may call attention to the loop.

In broadcasting, field reporting is so common that the audience has grown used to abrupt changes in levels and background sound within the same program. Nevertheless, change should be motivated and not unnecessarily jarring. With dialogue, however, audiences are more apt to be annoyed by uneven background sound. The best thing to do during the recording is to anticipate the editing.

Ambience is a concern not only in editing speech; it is also an important factor when editing sound effects and music. In all three domains, ambience—background sound—is usually not effective without foreground sound. The two together bring perspective, environment, and size to a scene.

Editing Sound Effects

Many of the techniques used in dialogue editing are also used in editing sound effects. If there is an essential difference between the two, dialogue editing mostly involves fixing, whereas sound-effect editing also involves creating. Among the typical challenges a sound effect (SFX) editor faces are building backgrounds, building effects, and matching perspective.

Building Backgrounds

In shooting picture or producing material for radio, segments are often recorded out of order. In the various takes, background sound may change. Even if the location stays the same, background sound may change over time, however slightly, so it may not match a particular shot. Or a scene may be recorded in different areas of the same location. Or a required background sound may not be easily obtained during production and has to be created in the studio. Or it may be less costly to produce a background on a computer than to hire people to perform and record it. In such cases, it is the editor's role to build the appropriate background sound.

For example, a scene requires the sound of a storm. This particular storm requires several different sonic components—wind, rain, thunder claps, and thunder rumble—and each component has to have a texture: fierce, howling wind; pelting rain; and thunder that tears and booms and then rolls into a long rumble. By processing and layering various prerecorded tracks of wind, rain, and thunder, an editor can build the appropriate storm effect. If the scene has a particular visual rhythm, the editor can cut the sound effects to complement it, adding yet another sonic dimension to the background.

Building Effects

A sound effects editor is often called on to create a specific sound effect by building it. The effect may be needed because it does not exist in the natural world, is unavailable due to poor production planning, to save the expense of paying for sound personnel and studio time to produce it, or because it is simply easier to create on a computer.

The sound of fire, for example, may require the components of crackle to convey the licking sound of its mounting threat, roar to enhance its intensity, and the whoosh of small explosions to add punctuated impacts. Soundfiles for each of these components can be created, manipulated, and processed by the sound editor to create the overall effect.

Matching Perspective

In dealing with different but related or connected sounds in the same locale, an editor has to be sure that perspectives match. For example, in editing the screech of tires to a car crash, the crash has to sound as though it came out of the screeching tires. It sometimes happens that the screech is heard close up and the crash far away, as if the sounds, though related, occurred in two different locations.

There is also the problem of making sure the sound effect is coming from the shot's environment. If the ambience of the effect sounds as though it is coming from outside the shot, or, in the parlance of audio, on top of the film, the editor has to mix the effect into the appropriate background sound.

Guidelines for Editing Sound Effects

Here are some other guidelines that may prove helpful in editing sound effects:

- Digitize sound effects at full level, even the quieter ones. When signal processing is used, it helps to prevent noise buildup and aids in masking noise. Level can always be lowered when called for.

- It is easier to edit the SFX tracks after the dialogue and music tracks are in place. That way, the editor has a better sense of determining how to adjust levels so an effect is neither too loud nor too quiet.

- A single sound effect may be composed of several different sounds. For example, opening a door may include the rattle of the doorknob, the turn of the knob, the click of the bolt, perhaps a squeak and a scrape of the door opening, the click of the knob release, and the squeak and the scrape plus the thud of the door closing.

- Cut the effect as close to the first point of sound as possible.

- Sound effects are ordinarily recorded and placed in a track in mono because most are single-source sounds. Ambience, however, is ordinarily not a single-source sound and is therefore handled in stereo or surround.

- Place a percussive, or transient, effect—such as a door slam or the crack of a punch—where the action stops. Laying it in where the action starts will result in the effect's seeming out of sync with the picture.

- Most sounds have a natural decay, or tail. A sound may start suddenly with a sharp attack but does not stop that way; even transient sounds have some trail-off. Cutting into the tail will be noticeable unless another sound comes in over it and "washes it out," or it is crossfaded with another sound.

- When editing in a sound effect that occurs off-screen, it is usually distracting to lay it over dialogue. Spot the effect between two lines of dialogue.

- Some sounds, such as a horse's hoofbeats, are difficult to sync with picture. All four hooves cannot be synched. Generally, editors follow the first front leg and then establish the horse's rhythm.

- If, when looping an effect, it is difficult to achieve a seamless loop, try a very short crossfade at the hearable loop point. It should smooth the apparent beginning point of the repetition each time the sound is repeated.

- Organize the SFX tracks so they are grouped: the mono effects on, say, tracks 1 through 8, the stereo tracks on 9 through 16, the ambience tracks on 17 through 20, tracks that require special signal processing on 21 through 24, and so on.

Editing Music

A music editor is usually a trained musician. This is particularly helpful in working with the composer. That said, editing music is difficult to discuss in any detail because it involves using one language—the printed word—to explain another language—the notes, chords, rhythms, and other features of abstract, temporal sound. Although there is some similarity between editing speech and dialogue and editing music, such as consideration of space, rhythm, loudness, and inflection (intonation), there are also differences. Music contains so many simultaneous sonic elements that matching sounds is more complex, and slight editing mistakes are more easily detected. In music editing, you have to consider cutting on the right accent to maintain rhythm, tonality, relative loudness, and style. If any of these elements is aurally incompatible, the edit will be obvious.

Generally, edits that heighten intensity cut together well, such as going from quiet to loud, slow to fast, or nonrhythmic to rhythmic. A transition from a seemingly formless or meandering phrase to one that is obviously structured and definite also tends to work.

Cutting to Resolution

Perhaps one of the most useful guidelines is to cut before an accent, a downbeat, or a resolution. Think of the final chord in a musical phrase or song. Although it resolves the music, it is the chord before it that creates the anticipation of and the need for resolution; it sets up the last chord. Edit on the anticipatory note—the one requiring some resolution, however brief—so that it leads naturally to the note being joined.

Preserving Tempo

Most Western music has a *time signature*—2/4 ("two-four"), 3/4, 4/4, 3/8, 6/8, and so forth. The first numeral indicates the number of beats in each measure; the second indicates the value of the note that receives each beat. For example, in 4/4 time, there are four beats to a measure and each quarter-note receives a whole beat; in 3/8 time, there are three beats to the measure and each eighth-note receives a beat. In editing music, you have to preserve the beat, or the edit will be noticeable as a jerk or stutter in the tempo. If you cannot read music or no sheet music exists, pay close attention to the waveform of the music to discern the tempo. Listen to the beat and look for the resulting spike in the waveform.

Repetitive Measures

One way to shorten or lengthen audio material through editing is to use repetitive measures in the music. These measures can be cut out to shorten material, which is obvious. Lengthening the audio using a digital system is relatively straightforward: Repetitive measures can be extended by digital time expansion or by copying, pasting, and sliding them.

Preserving the tempo in music editing is not an isolated consideration. There are other factors such as looping, key signature, comping, and musical style and texture.

Looping

Looping is often used in dealing with tempo in music. Unlike dealing with sound effects, where the concern is making sure the loop sounds continuous and not repetitive, with music the concerns are making sure the loop both serves the score and, if necessary, can be adjusted to changes in tempo.

When editing loops, keep in mind the following tips:

- Cut at the beginning of the first beat in the measure or bar, preferably immediately before the first cycle of the attack.

- Edit immediately before the attack begins. Cutting into the transient could alter the envelope of the voicing and change its character.

- The start and end points of the loop should start at zero crossing.

- If the edit point is perceptible, perform a very small fade-in at the beginning of a loop and a very small fade-out at the end of the loop, or do a very small crossfade. Be sure to assign a file name to a loop, and note the tempo and the number of measures in the loop's file name.[2]

Key Signature

Just as most music has a time signature to regulate its tempo, it also has a *key signature*—E major or B minor, for example—that determines its overall tonality. Some keys are compatible: When you change from one to the other, it sounds natural, or "in tune." Other keys are not, and pasting them together is jarring, or "out of tune." Unless it is for effect, or if the picture justifies the change, edited music should sound constant so as not to be noticed.

Comping

Comping takes the best part(s) of each recorded track and combines them into a composite final version. In theory, comping music seems straightforward: Edit together all the best takes of every note, phrase, section, lyric, or whatever. In practice, however, that approach often does not work because, overall, the music may lack coherence, sound too mechanical, or result in a part from one take not making sense when played next to

2. From Todd Souvigneir, "Closing the Loop," *Electronic Musician*, April 2003, p. 39

a part from another take. There could also be problems in matching pitch—the segments may not be in tune; in the timing—performances may not have quite the same tempo or phrasing; in delivery—one segment may have a more impassioned performance than another; or in recording quality—segments may not have the same sonic fidelity. Maintaining perspective is critical if comping is to be aesthetically successful. It is analogous to a painter who has to work close to a canvas on a detail but must step back to view the entire painting to determine if the detail works (see Figure 12-10).

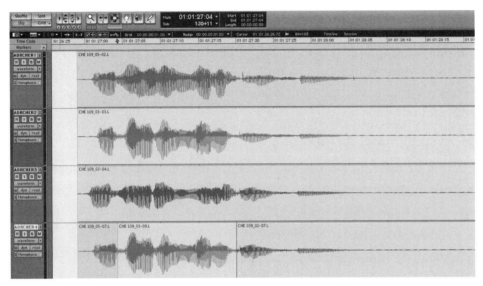

Figure 12-10 Comping. Fragments from takes 1, 2, and 3 have been combined to create the final product.

Style and Texture

Each type of music and musical group has a unique style and texture. This distinguishes the style of jazz from hip-hop, the texture of one voice from another although both may have identical registers, or one group from another although both may play the same instruments and music.

Editing from the same piece of music usually does not present a problem in matching style and texture so long as you follow the other guidelines for editing. But if the music is from different sources, matching elements can be a problem. Normally, you would not edit different styles—a piece of classical music to rock music just because they had the same tempo, or a dance band to a military band just because they were playing the same song. Unless by design, the differences in sound would make the edits conspicuous and distracting.

Listening Fatigue

Editing for long periods of time can cause *listening fatigue*—the reduced ability to perceive or remember the nuances of sound. In computer editing, the problem can be compounded by eyestrain and physical discomfort. If listening fatigue sets in during editing, it will become apparent: such features of sound as tempo, inflection, and tonality are continually mismatched, cuts are slightly off, and it is difficult to keep track of what should be edited to what.

One way to defer listening fatigue is to work in a quiet acoustic environment with no predominance of midrange frequencies because they tend to tire the listener faster. It is also important to remember to bring down playback gain after turning it up, as is often required to hear an edit point better. Finally, take regular breaks to rest the ears, stretch your muscles, and tend to anything else that brings relaxation.

Main Points

- Editing permits the rearranging, shortening, deleting, and recomposing of elements in a production. It allows elements to be recorded out of sequence and as often as necessary.

- Digital editing allows the retrieval, assembly, and reassembly of disk-based material quickly and in any order—regardless of the order in which the material was recorded and its location on the disk.

- A nonlinear editor (NLE) makes it is possible to audition an edit at any stage in the procedure, adjust levels, add signal processing, and restore any change in the edited material to its original waveform without endangering the master audio.

- Audio encoded on a NLE takes the form of a soundfile, which is displayed in a waveform. A waveform displays the profile of a sound's amplitude over time.

- Basic functions in digital editing include scrubbing; cut, copy, paste, delete, insert, and typeover; undo/redo; snapping, slipping, and spotting; scaling and zooming; trim or crop; time compression and expansion; looping; track grouping; time displays; and crossfades.

- Nondestructive editing does not alter the original soundfile regardless of what editing or signal processing you apply. Destructive editing permanently alters the original soundfile by overwriting it.

- Transitions used in audio editing include the segue or cut, the crossfade, soft cut, and the fade-out/fade-in.

- An essential part of editing is the edit decision list, a step-by-step list generated during editing of the in and out edit points of a shot or an audio segment, the nature of the transitions, the duration of the edit, and, if needed, the source reel numbers or time code addresses.

- Before editing begins, organize the edit tracks by cataloging all of the sounds and keep a running log throughout the editing process.

- As part of the organization, name each file.

- Employ drive management: Keep track of which disk drives contain which files and what soundfiles are where.

■ Editing picture is one-dimensional: one shot is cut, dissolved, or faded out and in to another shot; little happens until the next transition. Editing sound is multidimensional: Sounds are layered within each shot, so editing audio becomes more than attending to transitions.

■ Among the considerations basic to editing speech are recognizing the sounds that make up words; cutting together similar and dissimilar sounds; handling emphasis and inflection; and matching ambience.

■ Among the challenges a sound-effect editor deals with are building backgrounds, building effects, and matching perspective.

■ When editing music, attention must be paid to cutting to resolution, preserving tempo, repetitive measures, looping, key signature, comping, and style and texture.

■ Comping takes the best part(s) of each recorded track and combines them into a composite final version.

■ Editing for long periods of time can cause listening fatigue. Take regular breaks.

13 Mixing

M*ixing* is the stage in audio production when the recorded and edited tracks are readied for mastering, duplication, and distribution by combining them into a natural and integrated whole. Generally, the term *mixing* is used in radio, television, and music recording. In theatrical productions for film and television, the stages are *premixing* and *rerecording*. Premixing involves preparing the dialogue, music, and sound effects tracks for rerecording when they are combined into their final form—stereo and/or surround sound. For ease of reference, *mixing* is used as an umbrella term throughout this chapter.

Basic Purposes of Mixing

Regardless of terminology, mixing, premixing, and rerecording have the same purposes:

- To enhance the sound quality and the style of the existing audio tracks through signal processing and other means

- To balance levels

- To create the acoustic space, artificially if necessary

- To establish aural perspective

- To position the sounds within the aural frame

- To preserve the intelligibility of each sound or group of sounds

- To add special effects

- To maintain the sonic integrity of the audio overall, regardless of how many sounds are heard simultaneously

Maintaining Aesthetic Perspective

The general purposes of mixing notwithstanding, an overriding challenge is to maintain aesthetic perspective. The ears have an uncanny ability to focus on a single sound in the midst of many sounds. You may have noticed that in a room with several people talking in separate conversations at once, you can focus on hearing one conversation to the exclusion of the others. This capability is known as the *cocktail party effect*. In mixing and rerecording, it can be both a blessing and a curse.

255

Mixing requires that as you pay attention to the details in a recording, you never lose aesthetic perspective of the overall sound balance and imaging. This is easier said than done. Aural perception changes over time. What sounds one way at the outset of a mixing session often sounds quite another way an hour or so later, to say nothing of the listening fatigue that inevitably sets in during a long session. To make matters worse, the ear tends to get used to sounds heard continuously over relatively short periods of time. Then there is "the desire to make things sound better [that] is so strong that one does not actually need it to sound better in order for it to sound better."[1]

These effects are manifested in several ways. In what sensory researchers call *accommodation*, the ear may fill in, or resolve, sounds that are not actually there. The ear may also tune out certain sounds and therefore not hear them. This is particularly the case when the focus is on another sound. Because all the sounds are competing for your attention as a mixer, it becomes necessary to concentrate on those that require processing at any given time. While attending to the details, it is possible to lose the perspective of how those details fit into the overall mix. The more you listen to the fine tunings, the greater the danger of drifting from the big picture. What to do?

- Begin mixing sessions rested, including the ears. Do not listen to anything but the quiet for several hours before a mix.

- Do not take anything that can impair perception and judgment.

- Keep the problem of perspective always in mind.

- Take a checks-and-balances approach: After attending to a detail, listen to it within the context of the overall mix.

- Seek another opinion.

- As with any lengthy audio session, take regular and frequent "ears" breaks. When no union regulations are in place that prescribe break times and if a client balks, tactfully explain the problem of listening fatigue: that trying to use every second of studio time just because it is paid for will reach a point of diminishing aesthetic returns.

Mixing Versus Layering

Not to quibble about semantics, but mixing suggests a blend in which the ingredients lose their uniqueness in becoming part of the whole. Although such blending is important, in relation to a mix the term *layering* may be more to the point.

When sounds are combined, there are four essential objectives to keep in mind:

- Establish the main and supporting sounds to create focus or point of view.

- Position the sounds to create relationships of space and distance, and in music, cohesion.

---

1. Alexander U. Case, *Sound FX* (Boston: Focal Press, 2007), p. 85.

- Maintain spectral balance so that the aural space is properly weighted.

- Maintain the definition of each sound without losing definition overall.

These considerations come closer to the definition of layering than they do of mixing. The following discussion notwithstanding, *mixing* is the term used to refer to the process.

Layering involves some of the most important aspects of aural communication: balance, perspective, and intelligibility. When many sounds occur at once, unless they are layered properly, it could result in a loud sound drowning out a quiet sound; sounds with similar frequencies muddying one another; sounds in the same spatial position interfering with focus; and sounds that are too loud competing for attention—in short, a mishmash. Usually, when elements in a mix are muddled, it is because too many of them are sonically alike in pitch, tempo, loudness, intensity, envelope, timbre, style, positioning in the aural frame, or there are just too many sounds playing at once.

Layering: Sound with Picture

Imagine the soundtrack for a Gothic mystery thriller. The scene: a sinister castle on a lonely mountaintop high above a black forest, silhouetted against the dark, starless sky by flashes of lightning. You can almost hear the sound: rumbling, rolling thunder; ominous bass chords from an organ, cellos, and double basses; and the low-pitched moan of the wind.

The layering seems straightforward, depending on the focus: music over wind and thunder to establish the overall scariness; wind over thunder and music to focus on the forlorn emptiness; and thunder over wind and music to center attention on the storm about to break above the haunting bleakness. But with this particular mix, setting the appropriate levels may be insufficient to communicate the effect. The sounds are so much alike—low pitched and sustained—that they may cover one another, creating a combined sound that is thick and muddy and that lacks clarity and definition. The frequency range, rhythm, and envelope of the sounds are too similar: low pitched, continuous, weak in attack, and long in sustain.

One way to layer them more effectively is to make the wind a bit wilder, thereby sharpening its pitch. Instead of rolling thunder, start it with a sharp crack and shorten the sustain of the rumble to separate it from any similar sustain in the music. Perhaps compress the thunder to give it more punch and better locate it in the aural space. These minor changes make each sound more distinctive, with little or no loss in the overall effect on the scene.

This technique also works in complex mixes. Take a far-flung battle scene: soldiers shouting and screaming, cannons booming, rifles and machine guns clattering, jet fighter planes diving to the attack, explosions, and intense orchestral music dramatically underscoring the action. Although there are several different elements, they are distinctive enough to be layered without losing their intelligibility.

The pitch of the cannons is lower than that of the rifles and the machine guns; their firing rhythms and sound envelopes are also different. The rifles and the machine guns are distinct because their pitches, rhythms, and envelopes are not the same, either. The explosions can be pitched lower or higher than the cannons; they also have a different sound envelope. The pitch of the jets may be within the same range as the rifles and the machine guns, but their sustained, whining roar is the only sound of its kind in the mix. The shouting and the screaming of the soldiers have varied rhythms, pitches, and tone colors. As for the music, its timbres, blend, and intensity are different from those of the other sounds. Remember too that the differences in loudness levels and positioning in a stereo or surround-sound frame will help contribute to the clarity of this mix. Appropriate signal processing is employed as well.

In relation to loudness and the frequency spectrum, two useful devices in maintaining intelligibility are the compressor and the equalizer. Compressing certain sounds increases flexibility in placing them because it facilitates tailoring their dynamic ranges. This is a more convenient and sonically better way to place sounds than by simply using the fader. Through modest and deft equalization, attenuating, or boosting, sounds can cut or fill holes in the aural frame, thereby also facilitating placement without affecting intelligibility.

Some scenes are so complex, however, that there are simply too many sonic elements in the sound effects (SFX) and music to deal with separately. In such instances, try grouping them and playing no more than three or four groups at the same time, varying the levels as you go. For example, in the previous battle scene, the different elements (other than the voices) could be put into four groups: mortars, guns, planes, and music. By varying the levels and positioning the groups in the foreground, background, side-to-side, and front-to-rear and moving them in, out, or through the scene, you avoid the soundtrack collapsing into a big ball of noise. (The movements cannot be too sudden or frequent, however, or they will call attention to themselves and distract the listener-viewer.) In dealing with several layers of sound, the trick is to use only a few layers at a time and to balance their densities and clarity.

Another approach to scenes densely packed with audio effects is to use only the sounds that are needed—perhaps basing their inclusion on how the character perceives them or to counterpoint intense visual action with relatively spare sound. For example, it is opening night at the theater: there is the hubbub of the gathering audience, the last-minute preparations and hysteria backstage, and the orchestra tuning up; the star is frightfully nervous, pacing the dressing room. By dropping away all the sounds except the pacing, the star's anxiety becomes greatly heightened.

Focusing sonically on what the audience sees at the moment also works. In the battle scene described earlier, in a tight shot of, say, the cannons booming, play to that sound. When the shot is off the cannons, back off their sound. In a wider shot with the soldiers firing their rifles in the foreground and explosions bursting in the background, raise the levels of the soldiers' actions to be louder than the explosions.

Another reason not to play too many sounds at once, particularly loud sounds, is that if they stay constant, the effect is lost; they lose their interest. Contrast and perspective are the keys to keeping complex scenes sonically interesting.

It is also unwise to play too many loud sounds at the same time because it is annoying. In a hectic scene with thunderclaps, heavy rain, a growling monster rampaging through a city, people screaming, and cars crashing, there is no sonic relief. It is loud sound on loud sound; every moment is hard. The mix can be used to create holes in the din without diminishing intensity or fright and can provide relief from time to time throughout the sequence. For example, the rain could be used as a buffer between two loud sounds. After a crash or a scream, bring up the rain before the next loud sound hits. Or use the growl, which has low-frequency relief, to buffer two loud sounds.

Be wary of sounds that "eat up" certain frequencies. Water sounds in general and rain in particular are so high-frequency-intense that they are difficult to blend into a mix, and the presence of other high-frequency sounds only exacerbates the problem. Deep, rumbly sounds like thunder present the same problem at the low end of the frequency spectrum. One means of handling such sounds is to look for ways to change their perspectives. Have the rain fall on cars, vegetation, and pavement and in puddles. Make the thunder louder or quieter as the perspective of the storm cloud changes in relation to the people in the scene.

Layering: Music

With music, an ensemble often has a variety of instruments playing at once. Their blend is important to the music's structure but not to the extent that violins become indistinguishable from cellos, or the brass drowns out the woodwinds, or a screaming electric guitar makes it difficult to hear the vocalist. Layering also affects blend—positioning the voicings front-to-rear, side-to-side, or (with surround sound) front-to-back-side (or back).

For example, in an ensemble with, say, a vocalist, lead and rhythm guitars, keyboard, and drums, one approach to layering in stereo could place the vocalist in front of the accompanying instruments, the guitars behind and somewhat to the vocalist's left and right, the keyboard behind the guitars panned left to right, and the drums behind the keyboard panned left to right of center.

With an orchestra in surround, the frontal layering would position the ensemble as it usually is front-to-rear and left-to-right—violins left to center and right to center, basses right, behind the violins, and so on. Ambience would be layered in the surround channels to define the size of the space. A jazz ensemble with piano, bass, and drums might be layered in surround to place the listener as part of the group. One approach could be positioning the piano in the middle of the surround space, the bass toward the front, and the drums across the rear.

With music, however the voicings are layered, it is fundamental that the sounds coalesce. If the blend is lacking, even layering well done will not produce an aesthetically satisfying sound.

Perspective

In layering, some sounds are more important than others; the predominant one usually establishes the focus or point of view. In a commercial, the announcer's voice is usually louder than any accompanying music or effects because the main message is likely to be in the copy. In an auto-racing scene, with the sounds of speeding cars, a cheering crowd, and dramatic music defining the excitement, the dominating sound of the cars focuses on the race. The crowd and the music may be in the middleground or background, with the music under to provide the dramatic support. To establish the overall dramatic excitement of the event, the music may convey that point of view best, in which case the speeding cars and the cheering crowd might be layered under the music as supporting elements.

In a song, it is obvious that a vocalist should stand out from the accompaniment or that an ensemble should not overwhelm a solo instrument. When an ensemble plays all at once, there are foreground instruments—lead guitar in a rock group, violins in an orchestra, or a piano in a jazz trio—and background instruments—rhythm guitar, bass, woodwinds, and drums.

Whatever the combination of effects, establishing the main and supporting sounds is fundamental to good mixing, indeed, to good dramatic technique and musical balances. *Foreground does not mean much without background.*

But because of the psychological relationship between sound and picture, perspectives between what is heard and what is seen do not necessarily have to match but rather complement one another. In other words, you can cheat in handling perspective.

For example, take a scene in which two people are talking as they walk in the countryside and stop by a tree. The shot as they are walking is a long shot (LS), which changes to a medium close-up (MCU) at the tree. Reducing the loudness in the LS to match the visual perspective could interfere with comprehension and be annoying because the audience would have to strain to hear, and the lip movements would be difficult to see.

When people speak at a distance, the difficulty in seeing lip movements and the reduced volume inhibit comprehension. It may be better to ride the levels at almost full loudness and roll off low-end frequencies because the farther away the voice, the thinner the sound. Let the picture also help establish the distance and the perspective.

Psychologically, the picture establishes the context of the sound. This also works in reverse. In the close-up, there must be some sonic change to be consistent with the shot change. Because the close-up does not show the countryside but does show the faces better, establish the environment by increasing ambience in the sound track. In this case, the ambience establishes the unseen space in the picture. Furthermore, by adding the ambience, the dialogue will seem more diffused. This creates a sense of change without interfering with comprehension because the sound is louder and the actors' lip movements are easier to see.

Signal Processing

Signal processing is so much a part of audio production that sound shaping seems impossible without it. Yet overdependency on signal processing has created the myth that just about anything can be done with it to ensure the sonic success of a recording. These notions are misleading. Signal processing ineptly or inappropriately applied can ruin a good recording. In production, it serves to remember that usually *less is more.*

Among the most commonly employed types of signal processing are equalization, compression, reverberation, and delay.[2] It is worth noting at the outset of the following discussion that the effects of some signal processing are subtle and take experience to handle. Bear in mind too that no single effect in mixing should be evaluated in isolation: The outcome of EQ, compression, reverberation, delay, spatial placement, and so on are all interrelated.

Equalization

One question often asked of a mixer is, "What kind of a sound will I get on this track if I equalize so many decibels at such and such a frequency?" The question suggests that there are ways to predetermine equalization. There are not! Consider the different things that can affect sound. For example, with an actress you might ask: Is the voice higher-pitched or lower-pitched? Thin or dense sounding? Is the delivery strong or weak? Is there ambience and, if so, is it appropriate? What type of microphone was used for the recording? Is the mic-to-source distance appropriate? If other actors are interacting, are the perspectives correct? These influences do not even include the director's personal preference, perhaps the most variable factor of all.

EQ: How Much, Where, and When?

The best way to approach equalization is to know the frequency ranges of the voicings involved, know what each octave in the audible frequency spectrum contributes to the overall sound, listen to the sound in context, have a good idea of what you want to achieve before starting the mixdown, and decide whether EQ is even needed on a particular sound.

Also, remember the following:

- Equalization alters a sound's harmonic structure.

- Very few people, even under ideal conditions, can hear a change of 1 dB or less, and many people cannot hear changes of 2 or 3 dB.

- Large increases or decreases in equalization should be avoided.

- Equalization should not be used as a substitute for better microphone selection and mic placement.

---

2. It may be a useful reminder that the techniques discussed in this and most of the following sections in this chapter can be achieved in the virtual domain and by using outboard equipment.

- Equalization often involves boosting frequencies, and that can mean more noise, among other problems. Be careful with digital sound when increasing some of the unpleasant frequencies in the midrange and the high end.

- Beware of *cumulative equalization*. Only a certain number of tracks in the same frequency range should be increased or decreased. For example, on one channel you may increase by 4 dB at 5,000 Hz a sound effect to make it snappier; then on another channel, you increase by 2 dB at 5,000 Hz to give a voice a shade more presence; on a third channel, you increase by 3 dB at 5,000 Hz to bring out a string section. If you consider each channel separately, there has been little equalization at 5,000 Hz, but the cumulative boost at the same frequency, which in this example is 9 dB, could unbalance the overall blend.

- Because boosting frequencies on one track often necessitates attenuating frequencies somewhere else, consider *subtractive equalization* first. For example, if a sound is overly bright, instead of trying to mellow it by boosting the appropriate lower frequencies, reduce some of the higher frequencies responsible for the excessive brightness.

- Be aware of the effects of additive and subtractive equalization (see Figure 13-1).

- Frequencies above and below the ranges of different sound sources may be filtered to reduce unwanted sound and improve definition. However, be careful not to reduce frequencies essential to the natural timbre of a sound source.

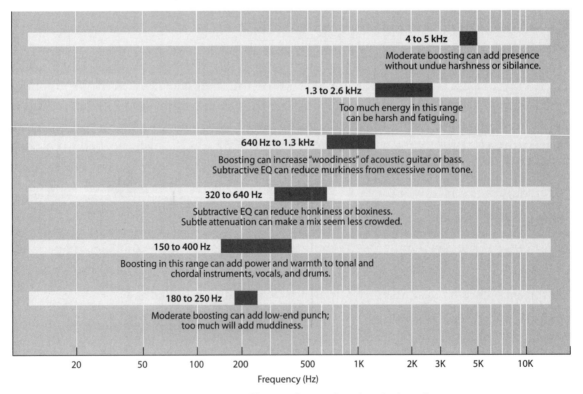

4 to 5 kHz
Moderate boosting can add presence without undue harshness or sibilance.

1.3 to 2.6 kHz
Too much energy in this range can be harsh and fatiguing.

640 Hz to 1.3 kHz
Boosting can increase "woodiness" of acoustic guitar or bass. Subtractive EQ can reduce murkiness from excessive room tone.

320 to 640 Hz
Subtractive EQ can reduce honkiness or boxiness. Subtle attenuation can make a mix seem less crowded.

150 to 400 Hz
Boosting in this range can add power and warmth to tonal and chordal instruments, vocals, and drums.

180 to 250 Hz
Moderate boosting can add low-end punch; too much will add muddiness.

20   50   100   200   500   1K   2K 3K   5K   10K

Frequency (Hz)

Figure 13-1 Additive and subtractive effects of equalization in key frequency ranges.

- To achieve a satisfactory blend, the sounds of individual elements may have to be changed in ways that could make them unpleasant to listen to by themselves. For example, the range from 1,600 to 2,500 Hz contributes most to the intelligibility of speech. If it is necessary to boost some of the frequencies in this range to improve the clarity of dialogue and to make it stand out from, say, the music underscoring, it may also be necessary to attenuate competing frequencies in the music. By doing so, the speech and the music by themselves may not sound particularly good; the speech may be somewhat harsh and the music may lack crispness or presence. But played together, the two sonic elements should sound natural.

- Use *complementary equalization* to help define sound sources in comparable frequency ranges and keep masking to a minimum. Many sounds have comparable frequency ranges such as the bass drum and the bass guitar, or thunder and low-throated explosions, or the guitar and female vocal, or high-pitched wind and a siren. Because physical law states that no two things can occupy the same space at the same time, it makes sense to equalize voicings that share frequency ranges so that they complement, rather than interfere with, one another (see Figures 13-2 and 13-3).

- An absence of frequencies above 600 Hz adversely affects the intelligibility of consonants; an absence of frequencies below 600 Hz adversely affects the intelligibility of vowels.

- Equal degrees of EQ between 400 Hz and 2,000 Hz are more noticeable than equalizing above or below that range, especially in digital sound (remember the equal loudness principle; see Chapter 3).

- Each sound has a naturally occurring peak at a frequency or band of frequencies that contains more energy than the surrounding frequencies and which, by being boosted or cut, enhances or mars the sound. In other words, the naturally occurring peak can become a sweet spot or a sore spot. The peaks are caused by natural harmonics and overtones or by a *formant*—an individual frequency or range of frequencies that is consistently emphasized because it contains more amplitude than adjacent frequencies.

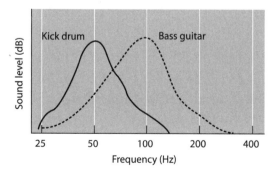

Figure 13-2 Complementary EQ for bass instruments.

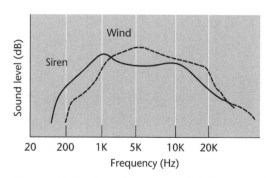

Figure 13-3 Complementary EQ for sound effects in the upper midrange.

To find the resonance area, turn up the gain on the appropriate section of the equalizer and sweep the frequency control until the voicing sounds noticeably better or worse. Once you find the sweet or sore spot, return the equalizer's gain to zero and boost or cut the enhancing or offending frequencies to taste.

Equalization and Semantics

A major problem in equalization is describing what it sounds like. What does it mean, for example, when a producer or director wants "sizzle," "fatness," "brightness," or "edge" in a sound? Not only is there a problem of semantics, but you must identify the adjustments needed to achieve the desired effect. Then, too, one person's "sizzle" and "fatness" may be another person's "bite" and "boom." The following may be of some help in translating the verbal into the sonic.

- Twenty to 50 Hz is considered the "rumble zone," and a subwoofer or full-range loudspeaker is required to reproduce it accurately. Even so, it does not take much of a boost in this range to add unwanted boom to the sound, which also eats up headroom.

- The range from about 60 to 80 Hz adds punch to sound. It can also give sound impact, size, power, and warmth, without clouding, depending on the sound source and the amount of EQ. The range is also bassy enough to eat up headroom with too much of a boost.

- A boost between 200 Hz and 300 Hz can add warmth and body to a thin mix, but too much of an increase makes sound woody or tubby. It can also cloud sound, making the low end, in particular, indistinct.

- Generally, boosting below 500 Hz can make sound fat, thick, warm, or robust. Too much can make it muddy, boomy, thumpy, or barrel-like.

- Flat, extended low frequencies add fullness, richness, or solidity to sound. They can also make sound rumbly.

- Low-frequency roll-off thins sound. This can enhance audio by making it seem clearer and cleaner, or it can detract by making it seem colder, tinnier, or weaker.

- With music, mid-frequency boost between 500 Hz and 7 kHz (5 kHz area for most instruments, 1.5 to 2.5 kHz for bass instruments) can add presence, punch, edge, clarity, or definition to sound. It can also make sound muddy (hornlike), tinny (telephonelike), nasal or honky (500 Hz to 3 kHz), hard (2 to 4 kHz), strident or piercing (2 to 5 kHz), twangy (3 kHz), metallic (3 to 5 kHz), or sibilant (4 to 7 kHz). Between 500 Hz and 800 Hz, too much boost can cause a mix to sound hard or stiff.

- Flat mid-frequencies sound natural or smooth. They may also lack punch or color.

- Mid-frequency boost (1 to 2 kHz) improves intelligibility without increasing sibilance. Too much boost in this range adds unpleasant tinniness.

- Mid-frequency dip makes sound mellow. It can also hollow (500 to 1,000 Hz), muffle (5 kHz), or muddy (5 kHz) sound.

- The 2 to 4 kHz range contains the frequencies to which humans are most sensitive. If a sound has to cut through the mix, this is the range to work with; but too much boosting across these frequencies adds a harshness that brings on listening fatigue sooner rather than later.

- High-frequency boost above 7 kHz can enhance sound by making it bright, crisp, etched, or sizzly. It can also detract from sound by making it edgy, glassy, sibilant, biting, or too sizzly.

- Extended high frequencies in the range of roughly 10 kHz and higher tend to open sound, making it airy, transparent, natural, or detailed. Too much boost makes a mix sound brittle or icy.

- High-frequency roll-off mellows, rounds, or smoothes sound. It can also dull, muffle, veil, or distance sound.[3]

Compression

Compression is mainly used to deal with the dynamic ranges of certain sounds so that they better integrate into the overall mix and to make program materials suitable for their intended reproducing medium (see "Dynamic Range" later in this chapter). Like any other signal processing, compression is not a panacea for corrective action; it is more a sound-shaping tool and, as such, should be used only when aesthetically justified.

Compressors (and limiters) have many applications; some are listed here:

- Compression minimizes the wide changes in loudness levels caused when a performer fails to maintain a consistent mic-to-source distance.

- Compression smoothes the variations in attack and loudness of sounds with wide ranges or wide sound-pressure levels such as the guitar, bass, trumpet, French horn, and drums. It can also smooth percussive sound effects such as jangling keys, breaking glass, crashes, and explosions.

- Compression can improve the intelligibility of speech in an analog tape recording that has been rerecorded, or dubbed, several times.

- Compressing speech or singing brings it forward and helps it jump out of the overall mix.

- Compression reduces apparent noise if the compression ratios are low. Higher ratios add more noise.

- Limiting prevents loud sound levels, either constant or momentary, from saturating the recording.

- The combination of compression and limiting can add more power or apparent loudness to sound.

3. Some of this material is adapted from Bruce Bartlett, "Modern Recording and Music," *Modern Recording and Music Magazine*, November 1982. Used with permission.

- The combination of compression and limiting is often used by AM radio stations to prevent distortion from loud music and to bring out the bass sounds. This adds more power to the sound, making the station more obvious to someone sweeping the dial.

- Compression in commercials is used to raise average output level and thus sonically capture audience attention.

An important aspect of managing compression is in controlling release times. Various release times produce different effects. Some enhance sound, others degrade it, as the following list of potential effects suggests.

- A fast release time combined with a low compression ratio makes a signal seem louder than it actually is.

- Too short a release time with too high a ratio causes the compressor to pump or breathe. You actually hear it working when a signal rapidly returns to normal after it has been compressed and quickly released.

- A longer release time smoothes a fluctuating signal.

- A longer release time combined with a short attack time gives the signal some of the characteristics of a sound going backward. This effect is particularly noticeable with transients.

- Too long a release time creates a muddy sound and can cause the gain reduction triggered by a loud signal to continue through a soft one that follows.

Reverberation

Due to the common practice of miking each sound component separately (for greater control) and closely (to reduce leakage) and to avoid contaminating voice and sound effect tracks with any defining ambience, original multitrack recordings often lack, by design, a complementary acoustic environment. In such cases, the acoustics are added in the mix by artificial means using signal-processing devices such as reverb and digital delay (see Chapter 11).

When acoustics are added to the mix, it is better to do it after equalizing (because it is difficult to get a true sense of the effects of frequency changes in a reverberant space) and after panning (to get a better idea of how reverb affects positioning). Unless it is justified by the dramatic situation or the intention of the musical arrangement, avoid giving widely different reverb times to various components or it will sound as though they are not in the same space.

The particular quality of reverberation depends, of course, on the situation, such as camera-to-source distance, room size and furnishings, or whether a particular musical style requires a more closed or open acoustic environment.

In determining reverb balances, it helps to adjust one track at a time (on the tracks to which reverb is added). Reverb can be located in the mix by panning; it does not have to envelop an entire recording. Reverb in stereo mixes should achieve a sense of depth and breadth. In surround sound, it should not overwhelm or swallow the mix, nor if there is reverb from the front loudspeakers should it be the same as it is from the rear-side (or rear) loudspeakers. In acoustic conditions, the listeners sitting closer to an ensemble hear less reverb than the listeners sitting farther away.

With reverberation some equalization may be necessary. Because plates and chambers tend to generate lower frequencies that muddy sound, attenuating the reverb between 60 Hz and 100 Hz may be necessary to clean up the sound. If muddiness is not a problem, boosting lower frequencies gives the reverb a larger and more distant sound. Boosting higher frequencies gives the reverb a brighter, closer, more present sound.

Less-expensive reverberation devices and plug-ins tend to lack good treble response. By slightly boosting the high end, the reverb will sound somewhat more natural and lifelike.

Be wary of the reverb's midrange interfering with the midrange of a speaker or singer. Attenuating or notching out the reverb's competing midrange frequencies can better define the voice and help make it stand out.

Other effects, such as *chorusing* and *accented reverb*, can be used after reverberation is applied. By setting the chorus for a delay between 20 ms and 30 ms and adding it to the reverb, sound gains a shimmering, fuller quality.

Before making a final decision about the reverb you employ, do an A-B comparison. Check reverb proportions using large and small loudspeakers to make sure the reverb neither envelops sound nor is so subtle that it defies definition.

Digital Delay

Sound reaches listeners at different times, depending on where a listener is located relative to the sound source. The closer to the sound source you are, the sooner the sound reaches you and vice versa. Hence, a major component of reverberation is *delay*—the time interval between a sound or signal and each of its repeats. To provide more realistic reverberation, therefore, many digital reverbs include *predelay*, which is the amount of time between the onset of the direct sound and the appearance of the first reflections. If a reverb unit or plug-in does not include predelay, the same effect can be generated by using digital delay before reverb.

Predelay adds a feeling of space to the reverberation. In either case, predelay should be short—15 to 20 ms usually suffices. (A millisecond is equivalent to about 1 foot in space.) With some outboard delays, the longer the delay time, the poorer the signal-to-noise ratio.

Post-delay—adding delay after reverb—is another way to add dimension to sound, particularly to a voice. In the case of the voice, it may be necessary to boost the high end to brighten the sound, to avoid muddying it, or both.

In using delay, there is one precaution: Make sure the device or plug-in has a bandwidth of at least 12 kHz. Given the quality of sound produced today, however, 15 kHz and higher is recommended.

Two features of digital delay—feedback and modulation—can be employed in various ways to help create a wide array of effects with flanging, chorusing, doubling, and slap back echo. *Feedback*, or *regeneration*, as the terms suggest, feeds a proportion of the delayed signal back into the delay line, in essence, "echoing the echo."

Modulation is controlled by two parameters: width and speed. Width dictates how wide a range above and below the chosen delay time the modulator will be allowed to swing. You can vary the delay by any number of milliseconds above and below the designated time. Speed dictates how rapidly the time delay will oscillate.

Dynamic Range

An essential part of mixing is to make sure the audio material is within the dynamic range of the medium for which it is intended. If dynamic range is not wide enough, the full impact of the audio is not realized and sound quality suffers. If the dynamic range is too wide for a medium to handle, the audio distorts.

The following are general guidelines for the dynamic ranges of various media:

> AM radio—48 dB
>
> FM radio—70 dB
>
> HD (Hybrid Digital) radio—96 dB
>
> Standard television (STV)—60 dB
>
> High-definition television (HDTV)—85 dB (minimum)
>
> Film—85 dB (minimum)
>
> CD—85 dB (minimum)

Mixing for Radio

The foremost considerations in doing a mix for radio are the frequency response of the medium (AM or FM), dynamic range, whether the broadcast is in analog or digital sound, and the wide range of receivers the listening audience uses, from the car radio to the high-end component system.

Although conventional AM radio may transmit in stereo and play music from compact discs, its frequency response is mediocre—roughly 100 to 5,000 Hz. The frequency response of FM is considerably wider, from 20 to 20,000 Hz. Dynamic range for AM is 48 dB; for FM, it is 70 dB. Therefore, it would seem that mixing for AM requires care to ensure that the essential sonic information is within its narrower frequency band and dynamic range and that in mixing for FM there is no such problem. Both statements would be true were it not for the broad assortment of radio receivers that vary so greatly in size and sound quality and for the variety of listening conditions under which radio is heard.

There is also the additional problem of how the levels of music CDs have changed over the years. Compact discs produced 25 years ago had an average (root mean square) level of −18 dB. In 1990, as the pop music industry entered the "level wars," it was −12 dB. In 1995, average level was raised to −6 dB. Since 2000, the average level of many CDs is between zero-level (0 dBFS) and −3 dB. As the average level is raised using compression, the music gets louder and has more punch, but dynamic range is reduced and there is a greater loss in clarity.

There is no way to do an optimum mix, for either AM or FM, to satisfy listeners with a boom box, a transistor radio, and car stereos that run the gamut from mediocre to excellent and are played against engine, road, and air-conditioner noise. To be sure, car stereo systems have improved dramatically and surround systems are increasingly available, but unless the car itself is built to lower the noise floor against sonic intrusions, the quality of the sound system is almost moot.

The best approach is to mix using loudspeakers that are average in terms of frequency response, dynamic range, size, and cost and to keep the essential sonic information—speech, sound effects, and music—within the 150 to 5,000 Hz band, which most radio receivers can handle. With AM radio's limited frequency response, it often helps to compress the sound to give it more power in the low end and more presence in the midrange. For FM mixes, a sound check on high-quality loudspeakers is wise to ensure that the harmonics and the overtones beyond 5,000 Hz are audible to the listener using a high-quality receiver.

But be careful here. Extremes in equalization should be avoided because of FM broadcast pre-emphasis. *Pre-emphasis* boosts the treble range by 6 dB per octave, starting at 2.1 kHz (in the United States) or 3.2 kHz (in Europe). In receivers, there is a complementary de-emphasis to compensate for the treble boost. The result of all this is a flat response and a reduction of high-frequency noise but also a considerable reduction in high-frequency headroom. Therefore, if a mix is too bright, the broadcast processing will clamp down on the signal.

As for dynamic range, given the wide variety of sound systems used to hear radio and under different listening conditions, music with a wide dynamic range is usually a problem for most of the audience. To handle dynamic range, broadcast stations employ processing that controls the dynamics of the signal before transmission, thereby bringing it within the usable proportions of a receiver.

Another factor that may influence a music mix, if not during the mixdown session then in the way it is handled for broadcast, is a *tight board*—radio parlance for having no dead air and playing everything at a consistent level. Because most radio stations compress and limit their output, running a tight board tends to raise the level of music with soft intros, back it off as the song builds, and then let compression and limiting do the rest. Songs ending in a fade are increased in level as the fade begins, until the music segues evenly into the next song or spot announcement.

Because of this, it is a good idea to keep a mix for radio on the dry side. Compression can increase the audibility of reverb. In broadcast signal processing, quieter elements, such as reverb tails, are increased in level so they are closer to that of the louder elements.

Also, avoid limiting and compression in the mix for the sake of loudness because the broadcast processing will reduce the music level to where the station's engineers want it to be anyway.

Monaural compatibility, that is, how a stereo mix sounds in mono, is yet another factor to consider.

Hybrid Digital (HD) *radio* not only provides the capability of offering multiple programs on a single channel but also produces CD-quality sound and reduced interference and static. Frequency response is 20 to 20,000 Hz and dynamic range is 96 dB. These parameters greatly improve the sonic fidelity of programs compared with conventional AM and FM broadcasts. This is particularly advantageous to both producers and listeners of music. But again, the only way to get the full benefit of HD radio is to have the receiver capable of reproducing its full-frequency and wide-dynamic-range signal. (Note that with television, *HD* refers to **high definition**, whereas with radio, *HD* is a brand name for a method of digital audio transmission developed by iBiquity Digital Corporation.)

Mixing stereo in radio usually means positioning speech in the center and music across the stereo field without its interfering with the intelligibility of the speech. If there are sound effects, they can be positioned relative to their dramatic placement so long as they do not distract from the focus of the material. Because there is no picture to ground sound effects, and because radio is a "theater of the mind" medium, there is more freedom in positioning effects than there is in TV and film. A lot of movement of SFX across the stereo field, however, should be done only as a special effect and if it is compatible with the production style and the message.

Spatial Imaging for Picture

Mixing not only involves signal processing and consideration of dynamic range but for television and film the spatial positioning of the dialogue, music, and sound effect (DME) tracks in the stereo or surround-sound aural frame. For music, spatial positioning calls for placement of the various instruments in the stereo and surround-sound frame (see "Spatial Imaging for Music" later in this chapter).

Stereo

Natural assumptions in placing elements in a stereo mix for television and film are that dialogue and SFX are positioned in relation to their on-screen locations and that music, if it is not coming from an on-screen source, fills the aural frame from the left to the right. For the most part, these assumptions are imprecise. Placement depends on the screen format, the reproduction system, and the type of material produced.

The aesthetic demands of television and film differ because of the differences between their screen sizes and the size and the number of loudspeakers—their sonic and pictorial dimensions—and the environments in which TV and film are viewed. Clearly, film has more space than television in which to place and maneuver the aural and visual elements.

In most film theaters, the loudspeakers are positioned to reproduce surround sound, so they are placed from left to right behind the screen and down the sides to the rear of the theater. But film mixes also have to take into account DVD and high-density optical disc distribution, which means that the mix will be played back on a TV receiver with a stereo or surround-sound, and maybe a mono, loudspeaker system. Therefore the mix for theaters has to be suitable for that acoustic environment and for the frequency response and the dynamic range that the loudspeaker system can reproduce. The mix for DVD has to sound decent when played back on the array of home systems out there. However, when it comes to *localization*—the placement of dialogue, music, and SFX in the stereo frame—there are two aesthetic considerations in TV and film: scale and perspective.

Scale

Until the advent of stereo TV, the television loudspeaker was smaller than the screen, but together the scales of picture and sound images have seemed proportional. No doubt, conditioning has had something to do with this perception.

With stereo TV, loudspeakers are either attached or built in to the left and right sides of the set or detachable. With small-screen TVs, permanently attached speakers can be no farther apart than the width of the TV set. This is a limiting factor in creating a stereo image because the aural space is so narrow. Detachable speakers can be situated an optimal distance apart—6 feet is usually recommended to reproduce a more realistic stereo image. Speakers in wide-screen TVs are usually mounted far enough apart to reproduce a decent stereo image. In fact, when sound is more spacious because of stereo, the picture seems bigger: *What we hear affects what we see.*

With film, the acceptance of proportion between picture and sound is more understandable. Both the size of the screen and the "size" of the sound system are perceived as similarly large.

Perspective

Despite the trend toward much larger screens, compared to film, television is still a small-screen medium. Regardless of a TV's screen size, the aspect ratios of the medium are not as sizeable as film. *Aspect ratio* is the ratio of image width to height. The aspect ratio for the standard video screen is 4×3 (1.33:1); for HDTV, it is 16×9 (1.78:1). For wide motion picture screens, aspect ratios are between 5.55×3 (1.85:1) and 7×3 (2.35:1). This means that with a 19-inch or 66-inch video screen, the shot is the same—there is no more information included in the width or height of the larger screen compared to the smaller screen. This is why television relies on close-up (CU) shots to enhance impact and to show detail that otherwise would be lost. Speech (and song lyrics) is therefore concentrated in the center.

Screen size and the left, center, right frontal loudspeaker array gives mixers a bit more leeway in film—but not much more. The three channels are necessary because of the screen width and the size of the audience area. Without a center channel, people sitting at the left and the right would hear only the loudspeaker closest to them and receive no stereo effect. The center channel anchors the sound. Trying to match sound with shot changes would be chaotic.

Localization of Talk and Dialogue

In television, talk and dialogue are usually kept at or near the center of the stereo frame. Unless the shot remains the same, trying to match a performer's sonic location to that person's on-screen position can disorient the listener-viewer.

For example, if in a variety show a wide shot shows (from the viewer's perspective) the host in the center, the announcer to the left, and the band leader and the band to the right and the shot does not change, the audio can come from these locations in the stereo space. If the host and the announcer exchange remarks and the shot cuts to the host on the right and the announcer to the left in a two-shot, and the shot stays that way, the host's sound can be panned toward the right and the announcer's sound can be panned toward the left. If during their interchange, however, the shots cut back and forth between close-ups of the host and the announcer, the left and right stereo imaging becomes disconcerting because the image of either the host or the announcer is in the center of the frame when the sound is toward the left or right. When frequent shot changes occur, the best approach is to keep the overall speech toward or at the center (see Figure 13-4).

When a performer is moving in a shot, say, from left to right, and the camera-to-source distance remains the same, the stereo image can be panned to follow the performer's movement without audience disorientation. If the performer's camera-to-source distance changes, however, due to cutting from wider shots to closer shots or vice versa, or due to intercutting another actor into the frame even though the first performer's momentum is clearly left to right, the dialogue has to be centered to avoid dislocation (see Figure 13-5).

In film, as a general rule, on-screen dialogue is also placed in the center. If a character moves about and there are several cuts, as in television it can become annoying to have

Announcer's sound   Host's sound

a

Announcer's sound

b

Host's sound

Announcer's and host's sound

c

Figure 13-4 Speech localization in a two-shot. (a) In this example, so long as the announcer and the host remain positioned left and right in a medium shot and the shot does not change, their sounds can be panned toward the left and the right, respectively, with no dislocation. (b) If the shot changes, say, to a medium close-up of the announcer followed by an MCU of the host and the stereo imaging remains the same, it will create a Ping-Pong effect. (c) If close-ups of the announcer and the host are planned, the sound in the original two-shot should be centered for both of them and carried through that way throughout the sequence. Panning the sound with the shot changes is even more sonically awkward than the Ping-Pong effect.

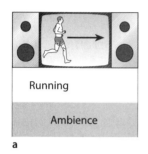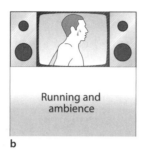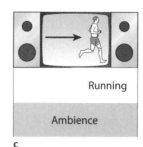

a   b   c

Figure 13-5 Sound localization in a moving shot. (a) If a subject is, say, running across the screen from left to right and the shot does not change, the stereo imaging can also move from left to right without dislocation. (b) If the shot cuts to show perspiration on the runner's face, in which case the across-screen movement would be reflected in the moving background, the subject's sound would have to be centered. If the sound continued moving left to right in the CU, the difference between the visual and the aural perspectives would be disorienting. (c) When cutting from the CU back to the wide shot, the sound once again can move across the screen with the runner without disorientation because the perspectives match. If throughout the runner's across-screen movement there were a few cuts from the wide shot to the CU, however, the sound in the wide shots would have to be more centered to avoid the Ping-Pong effect.

the sound jump around, particularly if more than one character is involved. On the other hand, if characters maintain their positions in a scene, even though shots change, say, from wide to medium close-up or vice versa, so long as they are shown together stereo imaging can be effected without disorienting the audience.

Sound Effects

The handling of SFX is usually conservative in mixing for TV. Obvious motion should be selective and occur mostly with effects that make pronounced crossing movements. The extent of the movement has to be carefully controlled so that it is not greater than the physical dimension of the screen (unless it is surround sound).

Ambiences in stereo television certainly can be fuller than they are in mono TV. Obviously, the significant perceptible difference between mono and stereo TV is in the fullness and the depth of the ambience.

Sound effects also tend to be concentrated toward the middle in film. If they are stationary or move across a wide distance, they may be located and panned without distraction. But too much movement muddles the sound to say nothing of disorienting, if not annoying, the audience. To create the sense that an effect is positioned relative to the action, the effect may be reverberated. Most of the dry effect is placed at or near screen-center, and the wet part is used to convey its placement in the frame. Background sounds and ambience may be mixed toward the left and the right of center to create overall tone and to add dimension.

Music

Generally, in the DME mix for TV and film, underscored music is the one element that is usually in stereo. It is typically mixed across the stereo field with the left and the right sides framing dialogue and sound effects.

Surround Sound

Before discussing mixing for surround sound, it may help to cover a few surround-sound basics.[4]

Surround-Sound Basics

Sound is omnidirectional; our natural acoustic environment is 360 degrees. Surround sound provides the opportunity to come far closer to reproducing that experience than stereo by enabling the sounds and the listener to somewhat occupy the same space. With stereo, the audio is localized wide and deep in front of the listener, whereas *surround sound* increases the depth of the front-to-rear and side-to-side sound images, placing the listener more inside the aural event. In stereo, two discrete channel signals are reproduced separately through two loudspeakers, creating phantom images between them. In surround sound, discrete multichannel signals are reproduced separately, each through a dedicated loudspeaker.

When referring to the various surround-sound systems—5.1, 6.1, 7.1, 10.2, and so on—the first number refers to the discrete production channels of full-bandwidth audio—20 Hz to 20 kHz. These channels play back through the array of loudspeakers used to reproduce them.

The second number refers to a separate, discrete channel(s) for *low-frequency enhancement (LFE)*. (The *E* can also stand for *effects*.) The LFE production channel has a frequency response rated from 5 to 125 Hz. A subwoofer is used to play back the LFE channel. Because few subwoofers can produce sounds lower than 15 to 20 Hz, their range more realistically begins around 30 to 35 Hz.

In the 5.1 surround-sound format, audio from the five channels is sent to loudspeakers positioned frontally—left, center, and right—and to the left and right surround loudspeakers. LFE audio feeds to the subwoofer, which may be positioned between the left and center or the center and right frontal loudspeakers (see Chapter 5). Sometimes two subwoofers are used to reproduce the mono LFE signal, ordinarily positioned behind and outside the front-left and front-right speakers or to the sides of the recordist/listener.

Track Assignment

Although there is no agreed-upon protocol for assigning surround-sound tracks, the International Telecommunication Union (ITU) has suggested that the track assignments be as follows: track 1, front-left; track 2, front-right; track 3, front-center; track 4, subwoofer; track 5, rear-left surround; and track 6, rear-right surround. Other groupings are also used (see Figure 13-6). Whichever mode of assignment you use, make sure the mix file is clearly labeled as to which tracks are assigned where.

---

4. Discussion of surround sound in this chapter assumes the 5.1 format, which is most widely used. However, the *7.1* format has begun to make inroads; it features seven channels of full-frequency sound in the left, center, right, left surround, right surround, rear-left, and rear-right plus the LFE channel.

Track	1	2	3	4	5	6	7	8
Mode 1	L	R	Ls	Rs	C	LFE	Lt	Rt
Mode 2	L	C	R	Ls	Rs	LFE	Lt	Rt
Mode 3	L	Ls	C	Rs	R	LFE	Lt	Rt
Mode 4	L	R	C	LFE	Ls	Rs	Lt	Rt
Mode 5	L	C	Rs	R	Ls	LFE	Lt	Rt
Mode 6	C	L	R	Ls	Rs	LFE	Lt	Rt

Figure 13-6 Six common modes of assigning surround-sound channels. Tracks 7 and 8 are the left and right stereo downmix.

Imaging Surround Sound

Mixing surround sound for picture differs from mixing it for music (see "Spatial Imaging for Music" later in this chapter). With music, there is no screen to focus on, so listener attention can be directed in whatever way is consistent with the musicians' vision and the aesthetics of the music. With picture, the primary information is coming from the screen in front of the audience, so it is necessary that audience attention be focused there and not drawn away by the surround sounds, a distraction known as the *exit sign effect*—sounds in the surround imaging that cause the audience to turn toward them.

How sonic elements are placed in a surround-sound mix for television depends to a considerable extent on the program, except for speech (and lyrics) and compensating for the home loudspeaker setup. In TV, the word, spoken or sung, is typically delegated to the center channel. Sometimes to give the sound source some spread, to avoid too much center-channel buildup, or to adjust for the absence of a center-channel loudspeaker in signal reception, speech is panned toward the left and the right of center. Surround sound notwithstanding, the two main objectives of mixing speech are still to make sure it is clear and to avoid dislocation.

As for sounds and music, taste and the program type affect placement. For example, in a talk show, the audience sound may be panned to the left, right, and surround loudspeakers. In sports, the crowd may be handled in the same way or the action sounds may be mixed into the left and right imaging, with the crowd in the surrounds. Music underscoring for a drama may be handled by sending it to the left, right, and surround speakers, or just to the left and right speakers and using the surrounds for ambience. In music programs, delegating the audio is often related to the type of music played. With classical music, the mix is primarily left, center, and right, with the surrounds used for ambience. Pop music may approach the mix by taking more advantage of the surrounds to place voicings. Or because it is television, with the picture showing an ensemble front and centered, the surrounds may be used for audience sound, if there is one, and ambience.

Then, too, with any surround-sound mix, you must consider how it will translate on a stereo or mono TV receiver, so back-and-forth monitoring is essential throughout the mixdown or rerecording session.

The traditional approach to surround sound for film has been to delegate the principal audio—dialogue, music, and sound effects—to the left, center, and right channels and the nonessential sound, such as ambience and background effects, to the surround channels. Specifically, the addition of the center and the surround channels to conventional stereo reproduction creates a stable center and background imaging. The center loudspeaker provides more precise localization, particularly of dialogue. This is more important with television sound than it is with film sound because the TV image takes up a smaller space in the field of view. Hence, the center loudspeaker helps localize dialogue toward the center of the screen.

Because audio producers have become more accustomed to working with surround sound, and audiences—film audiences in particular—have become more used to it as part of the overall viewing experience, the surround channels are employed for more than just ambience and additional environmental effects, when the situation warrants. The thinking is that sound is omnidirectional and our natural acoustic environment puts it all around us all the time, so why not do the same thing with surround sound, the caveats being so long as it contributes to or furthers the story and does not call attention to itself, distracting the audience.

In these types of surround mixes, the dialogue of a character walking into a scene may be heard first from the side or rear and panned to the front-center as he appears on-screen. Music from a band playing behind a character seated in a venue with lots of people and hubbub may be heard in the surround speakers, with the dialogue frontally centered and the hubbub panned from the front speakers to the surrounds. A battle scene may have the sound of explosions and firing weaponry and the shouts of soldiers coming from the front and the surround speakers, placing the audience in the middle of the action.

The advantages of multidimensional manipulation of sound include:

- Dialogue and sound effects can be accurately localized across a wide or small screen for almost any audience position.

- Specific sound effects can be localized to the surround-sound loudspeakers.

- Ambience and environmental sounds can be designed to reach the audience from all directions.

- Panning of sound can occur across the front sound stage and between front and surround locations.

Spatial Imaging for Music

In multitrack recording, each element is recorded at an optimal level and on a separate track. If all the elements were played back in the same way, it would sound as though they were coming from precisely the same location, to say nothing about how imbalanced the voicings would be. In reality, of course, this is not the case. Each musical component must be positioned in an aural frame by setting the levels of loudness to create front-to-rear perspective, or depth, and panning to establish left-to-right perspective, or breadth. In setting levels, the louder a sound, the closer it seems to be; and, conversely, the quieter a sound, the farther away it seems. Frequency and reverb also affect positioning.

Stereo

In mixing stereo, there are five main areas in which to position sounds laterally: left, left-center, center, right-center, and right. This is done through panning. Differences in loudness affect front-to-rear positioning; the louder the sound, the closer it is perceived to be, the quieter the sound, the farther away it is perceived to be.

There are many options in positioning various elements of an ensemble in an aural frame, but three factors enter into the decision: the aural balance, how the ensemble arranges itself when playing before a live audience, and the type of music played. Keep in mind that each musical style has its own values.

Pop music is usually emotional and contains a strong beat. Drums and bass therefore are usually focused in the mix. Country music is generally vocal-centered with the accompaniment important, but subordinate. Jazz and classical music are more varied and require different approaches. The mixer must have a clear idea of what the music sounds like in a natural acoustic setting before attempting a studio mix, unless the sonic manipulations are such that they can be produced only in a studio.

Sounds and where they are placed in aural space have different effects on perception. In a stereo field, these effects include the following: The sound closest to the center and nearest to the listener is the most predominant; a sound farther back but still in the center creates depth and a balance or counterweight to the sound that is front and center; sound placed to one side usually requires a similarly weighted sound on the opposite side or else the left-to-right aural space will seem unbalanced and skew listener attention; and the more you spread sound across the aural space, the wider the sound sources will seem.

This is not to suggest that all parts of aural space must be sonically balanced or filled at all times; that depends on the ensemble and the music. A symphony orchestra usually positions first violins to the left of the conductor, second violins to the left-center, violas to the right-center, and cellos to the right. If the music calls for just the first violins to play, it is natural for the sound to come mainly from the left. To pan the first violins left to right would establish a stereo balance but would be poor aesthetic judgment and would disorient the listener, especially when the full orchestra returned and the first violins jumped back to their original orchestral position.

To illustrate aural framing in a stereo field, Figures 13-7 to 13-9 provide a few examples.

Surround Sound

Compared with stereo, mixing for surround sound opens up a new world of aesthetic options in dealing with the relationship of the listener to the music (see Figures 13-10 and 13-11). But by so doing, it also creates new challenges in dealing with those options. Among them are handling the center and surround channels, reverberation, and bass management.

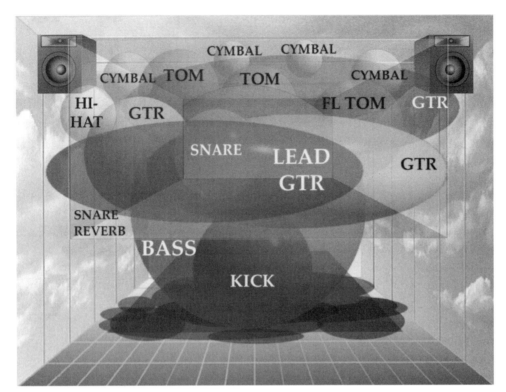

Figure 13-7 Rock mix. Quite full with lots of fattening and overlapping sounds. The lead guitar is spread in stereo with a rhythm guitar behind it and another stereo guitar in the background. The low end is clean, with a strong kick drum and bass. (In this figure and in Figures 13-8 and 13-9, the size of the globes indicates the relative loudness of the voicings.)

Figure 13-8 Jazz mix. Overall, a clean, clear mix, with the guitar, piano, and hi-hat in front and the kick drum atypically loud for a jazz mix.

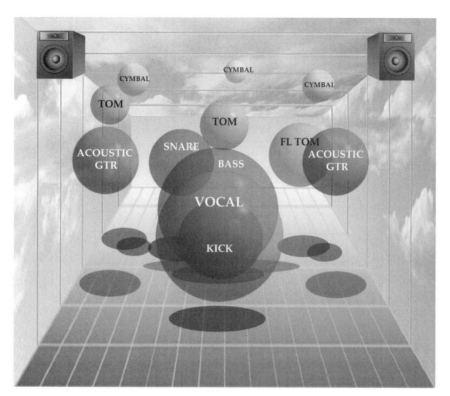

Figure 13-9 Country mix. A loud vocal in front of a clean, clear, spacious mix of the ensemble.

Figure 13-10 Surround-sound mix of an a capella choir.

Figure 13-11 Surround-sound reverb panned in the rear with a predelay on the original sound.

Center Channel

Because there is no center channel or loudspeaker in stereo, the center image is a psychoacoustic illusion; in surround sound, it is not. There is a discrete center channel and speaker in surround sound, so if you are not careful about delegating the signal (or signals) there, it could unbalance the entire frontal imaging. This is particularly important in a music mix.

There is no single recommended way of handling the center channel; it depends on producer preference and the music. Generally, dealing with the center channel can be divided into two broad approaches: delegating little—if anything—to it, or using it selectively.

Those who use the center channel little or not at all believe that handling the center image is better done by applying the stereo model: letting the left and right loudspeakers create a phantom center. When too much audio is sent to the center channel, there is a greater build in the middle of the frontal sound image. This makes the voicings coming from the center speaker more dominant than they should be, thereby focusing attention there to the detriment of the overall musical balance.

Another consideration is that many home surround systems do not come with a center loudspeaker; when they do, it is often positioned incorrectly or not set up at all, so there is no way of reproducing any center-channel audio.

Producers who prefer to use the center channel take various approaches. One technique creates a phantom center between the left and right loudspeakers, along with a duplicated discrete center channel several decibels down. This adds depth and perspective to the center voicings without overly intensifying their image.

In a typical pop song, the bass guitar and the kick drum are positioned rear-center to anchor the mix. If they are delegated to the center channel, it may be necessary to diffuse their center-channel impact. Their signal can be reduced in level and fed to the left and right loudspeakers, then panned toward the center.

Regardless of the aesthetic involved in using or not using the center channel, one caveat is important to remember: If a voicing is delegated only to the center channel and to no other channels, a playback system with no center loudspeaker will not reproduce that voicing.

Surround Channels

How the surround channels are used comes down to what the music calls for, producer preference, or both. It is an artistic decision—there are no rules.

Some music mixes, such as classical and live concerts, may take a more objective approach. The presentation is mainly frontal, with the surrounds used for ambience to place the listener in the venue's audience. Other types of more studio-based music, such as pop and perhaps jazz, may take a more subjective approach and place the listener more inside the music. For example, a jazz combo with lead piano may be mixed to center the listener at or near the piano, with the rest of the ensemble and the ambience surrounding the listener. Or an approach may be a combination of the objective and the subjective.

Reverberation

The presence of the center channel calls for some precautions when using reverb. Just as putting too much of any voicing in the center channel focuses the ear on it, the same is true with reverberation. There are also the added concerns of phasing problems with the reverb in other channels, particularly the left and the right, and if the music is played back on systems without a center loudspeaker or with a center loudspeaker positioned incorrectly.

The current wisdom is to leave the center channel dry and put reverb in the left and right channels, continuing it in the surrounds. Any reverb placed in the center is minor and is usually different from what is in the other channels.

Bass Management

Bass management refers to the redirection of low-frequency content from each of the full-bandwidth production channels to the subwoofer, where it is combined with the LFE channel. The advantage of the LFE channel is that it provides more headroom below 125 Hz, where the ear is less sensitive and requires more boost to perceive equal loudness with the midrange. By providing this headroom, bass enhancement can be used without eating up other frequencies. Generally, the LFE channel is for low-end effects used in theatrical film and television such as rumbles, explosions, thunder, and gunshots. If it is used in mixing music, it is for the very lowest notes of the lowest bass instruments. Generally, however, in music mixes, low-end instruments are usually assigned to the full-frequency-range channels, not the LFE, for two main reasons: The LFE channel has limited frequency response and most bass instruments have ranges that go beyond 125 Hz, and because of the potential of bass enhancement to imbalance or overwhelm the mix.

Approaches to Mixing Music in Surround Sound

Two basic approaches have emerged to mixing music in surround sound: the traditional approach and the perspective approach. The *traditional approach* positions the listener in front of the musicians, with the room (or the artificial reverberation) adding the ambience. The added dimension of the ambience is what surrounds the listener. The *perspective approach* positions the listener inside the ensemble, creating the experience of being surrounded by the musical ingredients. Due to conditioning, this is not the natural way most people experience music (unless you are a musician). These approaches raise the question: Because technology has made possible a different perspective in designing a musical experience, should we take advantage of that opportunity? The answer of course rests with the musicians and the music.

It is generally agreed among most recordists, however, that regardless of the mixing approach and for a number of reasons, surround sound is a far superior sonic experience compared with stereo.

Recordkeeping and Cue Sheets

Obvious though the importance of documenting the various stages in the production process may be, it is an often underestimated or, worse, overlooked part of the mixing (and recording). Keeping good records is essential to the success of the final product because it helps avoid confusion, disorder, wasted time, and added expense.

Recordkeeping

The number of details in a production can be daunting. A mix alone often takes several sessions to complete, and any adjustments previously made must be reset precisely. Automated, computer-assisted mixers, and DAWs store much essential internally configured data automatically. Such systems may include software functions that facilitate keeping a record of each track's processing and a field for comments. They may or may not provide the flexibility needed for all the necessary documentation such as impressions of takes, individual performances, recommendations for corrections and improvements, results of various approaches to signal processing, and so on. Therefore, it would be necessary to devise a form either in hard copy or computerized. In such cases, each studio makes up its own forms. Choose the template that works best for you.

Whether or not the means for recordkeeping is provided by the software program, generally agreed on information should be at hand and easy to reference. Such information includes:

- Session particulars on a so-called *track sheet*, such as the production's name, and cue information about dialogue, SFX, and music. Or for a music recording, song title, session date(s), producer, engineer, assistant engineer, and instrument on each track. Additional information also helps such as recording medium, sampling frequency, bit depth, frame rate (if necessary), and microphones used and their positioning during recording

- Pertinent information about each take such as what worked and did not work in the performance and what the mix did or did not accomplish in relation to those factors.

- EQ settings and levels; compression and reverb send/return settings; pan positions; submaster assignments; special effects; tempo changes; song key; time code settings; a lyric sheet with notations about interpretation, dynamics, vocal noises, or fluctuations in level on a particular phrase or word that need attention; any other signal processing data necessary for reference; and perceptions of the results of each mix.

Cue Sheets

Cue sheets are essential throughout any production in any medium, and they are no less indispensable during the mix of DME tracks. They are the road maps that facilitate finding sounds on a track(s). The forms vary from studio to studio; they may be handwritten or computer-generated, but they should contain at least the following information.

- **A grid with each track forming a column and time cues laid out in a row**—Time cues may be designated in time code, real time, or footage, depending on the medium and the format. By using one column to serve all tracks, it is easy to see at a glance the relationships among the time cues on a track-by-track basis.

- **What the sound is**—Each cue must be identified. Identification should be both brief to avoid clutter and precise to give the mixer certainty about the cue.

- **When a sound starts**—The word or words identifying a sound are written at the precise point it begins. With dialogue or narration, in-points may be indicated by a line or the first two or three words.

- **How a sound starts**—Unless otherwise indicated, it is assumed that a sound starts clean; that is, the level has been preset before the sound's entry. If a cue is faded in, faded in slowly, crossfaded with another sound, or the like, that must be indicated on the cue sheet.

- **The duration of a sound**—The point at which a cue begins to the point at which it ends is its duration. The simplest way to indicate this is with a straight line between the two points. Avoid using different-colored markers, double and triple lines, or other graphic highlights. The cue sheet or screen should be clean and uncluttered. If the cues are handwritten, pencil is better than ink in case changes must be made.

- **When a sound ends**—This can be indicated by the same word(s) used at the entry cue accompanied by the word out or auto (for automatically). This tells the mixer that the end cue is clean and has been handled in the premix.

- **How a sound ends**—If a sound fades, crossfades, or the like, this should be indicated at the point where the sound must be out or crossfaded. The mixer then has to decide when to begin the out-cue so that it has been effected by the time indicated.

- **Simple symbology**—Where appropriate, accompany cues with symbols such as < for a fade-in, > for a fade-out, + to raise level, – to lower level, and Ø for crossfade.

Metering

A word about the importance of using meters to help identify and avoid sonic problems. In producing audio, our ears should always be the final arbiters. There are instances, however, when a problem may be evident but its cause is difficult to identify. In such cases, the ear may be better served by the eye.

Metering tools can perform many different types of analyses and are readily available in stand-alone models and plug-ins. They can display in real-time waveforms, spectrograms, and scopes with attendant alphanumeric information and keep a history of an event. The array of metering programs available can deal with just about any problem—loudness, distortion threshold, frequency, signal and interchannel phasing, monitoring anomalies, stereo and surround-sound imaging and balances, transfer function, and signal correlation, to name a few.

Keep in mind that the useful data that meters provide are just that: data. Meters are not intuitive about sound. Rely on the information they provide, but do not be seduced by it, especially when an aesthetic value is involved. As producer/engineer Bruce Swedien said, "I will always sacrifice a technical value for a production value."

Evaluating the Finished Product

What makes good sound? Ask 100 audio specialists to evaluate the same sonic material and undoubtedly you will get 100 different responses. That is one of the beauties of sound: It is so personal. Who is to tell you that your taste is wrong? If it satisfies you as a listener, that is all that matters. When sound is produced for an audience, however, professional "ears" must temper personal taste. To this end, there are generally accepted standards that audio pros agree are reasonable bases for artistic judgment.

Before discussing these standards, a word about the monitor loudspeakers is in order. Remember that the sound you evaluate is influenced by the loudspeaker reproducing it.

You must therefore be thoroughly familiar with its frequency response and how it otherwise affects sonic reproduction. If a sound is overly bright or unduly dull, you have to know whether that is the result of the recording or the loudspeaker. Remember, a good way to familiarize yourself with a loudspeaker's response is to take a few test discs and well-produced commercial recordings with which you are thoroughly familiar and listen to them on the monitor system until you are confident about its response characteristics.

Intelligibility

It makes sense that if there is narration, dialogue, or song lyrics, the words must be intelligible. If they are not, meaning is lost. But when working with material over a long period of time, the words become so familiar that it might not be apparent that they are muffled, masked, or otherwise difficult to distinguish. In evaluating intelligibility, it is therefore a good idea to do it with fresh ears—as though you were hearing the words for the first time. If that does not give you the needed distance from the material, ask someone else if the words or lyrics are clear.

Tonal Balance

Bass, midrange, and treble frequencies should be balanced; no single octave or range of octaves should stand out. Be particularly aware of too much low end that muddies and masks sound; overly bright upper midrange and treble that brings out sibilance and noise; absence of brilliance that dulls sound; and too much midrange that causes the harshness, shrillness, or edge that annoys and fatigues.

The timbre of the voice, sound effects, and acoustic instruments should sound natural and realistic. Music and sounds generated by electric and electronic instruments do not necessarily have to sound so, unless they are supposed to.

Ensemble sound should blend as a whole. As such, solos and lead voicings should be sonically proportional in relation to the accompaniment.

Spatial Balance and Perspective

All sonic elements in aural space should be unambiguously localized; it should be clear where various sounds are coming from. Their relationships—front-to-back and side-to-side—should be in proper perspective: Dialogue spoken from the rear of a room should sound somewhat distant and reverberant; an oboe solo should be distinct yet come from its relative position in the orchestra; a vocal should not be too far in front of an ensemble or buried in it; background music should not overwhelm the announcer; and crowd noise should not be more prominent than the sportscaster's voice.

Positional and loudness changes should be subtle and sound natural. They should not jar or distract by jumping out, falling back, or bouncing side-to-side (unless the change is justified in relation to the picture).

Definition

Each element should be clearly defined—identifiable, separate, and distinct—yet, if grouped, blended so that no single element stands out or crowds or masks another. Each element should have its position in, and yet be a natural part of, the sound's overall spectral range and spatial arrangement.

Dynamic Range

The range of levels from softest to loudest should be as wide as the medium allows, making sure that the softest sounds are easily audible and the loudest sounds are undistorted. If compressed, sound should not seem squeezed together, nor should it surge from quiet to loud and vice versa.

Clarity

A clear recording is as noise- and distortion-free as possible. Hum, hiss, leakage, phasing, smearing, blurring from too much reverb and harmonic, intermodulation, and loudness distortion—all muddle sound, adversely affecting clarity.

Airiness

Sound should be airy and open. It should not sound isolated, stuffy, muffled, closed-down, dead, lifeless, overwhelming, or oppressive.

Acoustical Appropriateness

Acoustics, of course, must be good, but they must also be appropriate. The space in which a character is seen and the acoustic dimension of that space must match. Classical music and jazz sound most natural in an open, relatively spacious environment; acoustics for rock-and-roll can range from tight to open. A radio announcer belongs in an intimate acoustic environment.

Source Quality

When a recording is broadcast, downloaded, or sent on for mastering, there is usually some loss in sound quality. This occurs with both analog and digital sound. For example, what seems like an appropriate amount of reverb when listening to a scene or a song in a studio may be barely discernible after transmission or transfer. As a general guideline, be aware that a source recording should have higher resolution than its eventual release medium.

Production Values

In dealing with production and production values, director Francis Ford Coppola uses a triangle to explain what the priorities should be. The top of the triangle says "Good." The bottom-left side says "Quick." The bottom-right side says "Cheap." You can connect only two of the sides but not all three. If the production is good and quick, it will not be cheap. If is good and cheap, it will not be quick. And if the production is quick and cheap...

The degree to which you are able to develop and appraise production values is what separates the mere craftsperson from the true artist. Production values relate to the material's style, interest, color, and inventiveness. It is the most difficult part of an evaluation to define or quantify because response is qualitative and intuitive. Material with excellent production values grabs and moves you. It draws you into the production, compelling you to forget your role as objective observer; you become the audience. When this happens, it is not only the culmination of the production process, but its fulfillment.

Main Points

- Mixing is the phase of postproduction when the recorded and edited tracks are readied for mastering, duplication, and distribution by combining them into a natural and integrated whole.

- The term mixing is used generally in radio, television, and music recording to describe the process of combining individual audio tracks into two (stereo) or more (surround sound) master tracks. In theatrical film and TV, the dialogue, music, and sound effect tracks are premixed and then rerecorded. Rerecording is the process of combining the DME tracks into their final form—stereo or surround sound.

- Regardless of terminology, mixing, premixing, and rerecording have the same purposes: to enhance the sound quality and the style of the existing audio tracks through signal processing and other means; to balance levels; to create the acoustic space, artificially if necessary; to establish aural perspective; to position the sounds within the aural frame; to preserve the intelligibility of each sound or group of sounds; to add special effects; to maintain the sonic integrity of the audio, overall, regardless of how many sounds are heard simultaneously.

- The general purpose of mixing notwithstanding, the overriding challenge is to maintain aesthetic perspective.

- In layering sound, it is important to establish the main and supporting sounds to create focus or point of view; position the sounds to create relationships of space and distance; maintain spectral balance so that the aural space is properly weighted; and maintain the definition of each sound.

- To help maintain definition as well as intelligibility in a mix, the various sounds should have different sonic features. These features can be varied in pitch, tempo, loudness, intensity, envelope, timbre, style, and so on.

- In layering sounds, it is also important to establish perspective. Some sounds are more important than others; the predominant one usually establishes the focus or point of view.

- When signal processing, it is always wise to remember that a good mix cannot salvage a bad recording, but a poor mix can ruin a good one.

- When equalizing, avoid large increases or decreases in equalization (EQ), do not increase or decrease too many tracks at the same frequency, and do not use EQ as a substitute for better microphone selection and placement. Try subtractive, instead of additive, equalization and use complementary EQ to keep masking to a minimum. Equalizing between 400 Hz and 2,000 Hz is more noticeable than equalizing above and below that range. Be sure to equalize with an awareness of the frequency limits of the medium in which you are working.

- Sounds are compressed to deal with the dynamic ranges of certain tracks so that they better integrate into the overall mix. Like any other signal processing, it is not a panacea for corrective action.

- The quality of reverberation added to a recording in the mix depends on the appropriate acoustic space to be created.

- Do not add artificial reverb until after signal processing and panning because it is difficult to get a true sense of the effects of frequency and positional change in a reverberant space. Also, avoid giving widely different reverb times to the various components in a sound track or music ensemble unless they are supposed to sound as though they are in different acoustic environments.

- A major component of reverberation is delay.

- An essential part of mixing is to make sure the audio material is within the dynamic range of the medium for which it is intended.

- The foremost considerations in doing a mix for radio are the frequency response of the medium (AM or FM), dynamic range, whether the broadcast is in analog or digital sound, and the wide range of receivers the listening audience uses, from the car radio to the high-end component system.

- Localization refers to the placement of dialogue, music, and sound effects in the stereo frame.

- Scale and perspective are two basic considerations in stereo imaging for picture relative to the differences in screen size between television and film.

- Stereo placement in film and TV usually positions dialogue and sounds in the center and music to the left, in the center, and to the right. Large-screen film positions dialogue in the center with limited lateral movement, sound effects across a somewhat wider space but still toward the center, and music left, center, and right. One reason for such placement is to avoid disorienting the audience in relation to the on-screen sources of sound and image. Another reason is that in motion picture theaters the audience sitting to the left or right side of the screen will not hear a left- or right-emphasized sound image.

- Surround sound comes far closer than stereo to reproducing our natural acoustic environment by enabling the sounds and the listener to occupy the same space. It increases the depth of the front-to-rear and the side-to-side sound images.

- The 5.1 surround format uses five full-bandwidth channels and a low-frequency enhancement (LFE) channel for sounds below 125 Hz. The 7.1 surround format adds two full-bandwidth channels to feed the left- and right-side-surround loudspeakers.

- Generally, the left, center, and right channels contain the principal audio—dialogue, music, and sound effects—and are reproduced by the frontal loudspeakers. The center channel is used for dialogue. The surround-sound channels are dedicated to background sound(s) and reproduced by the side or rear loudspeakers or both. As producers and the audience grow more accustomed to surround sound, the surround channels are used for secondary audio in addition to ambience and environmental effects.

- However surround sound is mixed, the main imperative is to not pull the audience's attention from the screen.

- Factors involved in placing musical components in the stereo frame are the aural balance, the arrangement of the ensemble when performing, and the type of music played.

- In mixing music (and any group of sounds) in stereo, there are five main areas in which to position sounds laterally: left, left-center, center, right-center, and right. This is done through panning. Differences in loudness affect front-to-rear positioning; the louder the sound, the closer it is perceived to be, the quieter the sound, the farther it is perceived to be.

- In mixing for surround sound, four important elements to manage are the center channel, the surround channels, reverberation, and bass management.

- Two basic approaches have emerged to mixing surround sound: the traditional approach and the perspective approach.

- The traditional approach positions the listener in front of the musicians, with the room (or the artificial reverberation) adding the ambience. The added dimension of the ambience is what surrounds the listener. The perspective approach positions the listener inside the ensemble, creating the experience of being surrounded by the musical ingredients.

- Recordkeeping, whether handwritten or using computer software, is important in any type of mixing. The number of details in a mix can be daunting. Cue sheets are essential throughout the production process, but they are indispensable in mixing the DME tracks.

- It is important to use meters to help identify and avoid sonic problems. There are times when they can identify a problem the ear cannot perceive.

- In evaluating a final product, factors that should be considered include intelligibility, tonal balance, spatial balance and perspective, definition, dynamic range, clarity, airiness, acoustical appropriateness, and source quality.

- Production values relate to the material's style, interest, color, and inventiveness.

14 Internet Audio

Digital technology in general and the Internet in particular have provided the means to produce and disseminate audio on an unprecedented scale. Opportunities abound and include producing audio for myriad online venues and applications; recording, editing, and producing online sessions interactively; the marketing and distribution of your own work; hiring out your production services to others; podcasting; and creating audio just for the fun of it. With that said, the basic principles involved in creating a professional audio product are similar regardless of where production is carried out—in a major production facility with state-of-the-art gear or on a laptop. The goal is always to produce work of a high technical and aesthetic caliber.

Because digital technology, the Internet, and mobile media are rapidly and continually evolving, this chapter is necessarily more general in scope, touching on key technical aspects and production considerations.

Data Transfer Networks

The delivery and the playback of audio over the Internet relies on a system of computers configured and connected in a way that allows them to communicate with one another—in other words, a network. When you download a ringtone to your cell phone, stream a radio program to your laptop, share your music among an online community, or upload a podcast from your computer, the audio is transmitted from a source, generally a server, to a user or client across one or more networks. Think of the Internet as an extremely large network comprising many smaller networks.

Local-Area Networks

A *local-area network* (*LAN*) is a network configured for a small, localized area such as a home, classroom, or business. Generally, a LAN is more controllable than a wide-area network because it is small enough to be managed by only a few people. LANs often feature fast data transfer speeds because the connection types and the hardware of all computer systems on the network can be controlled. When developing audio for use on a LAN, an audio designer may take advantage of this fast connectivity to produce high-quality audio not possible on less controlled wide-area networks.

Wide-Area Networks

A *wide-area network* (*WAN*) is a network configured for a large geographical area. Often, a WAN is composed of several interconnected LANs. The Internet is the largest and best-known example of a WAN. A WAN is generally less controllable than a LAN because it comprises too many computers and individual LANs for any one person or group to manage. Some computers on a WAN may be quite fast, whereas others may be quite slow. When producing audio for the Web, a designer must take into consideration that WANs are extremely sizable and multifaceted.

Servers

A *server* is a computer configured on a network to provide information to other computers. Websites are stored on a server, which receives Web page requests from users and transmits the desired page. Any images, video, and audio associated with that page are likewise sent from a server across the network to the user.

Clients

A *client* is a computer connected to a network configured to make requests to a server. A client could be a personal home computer, an office workstation, or another server. Client computers are often the limiting factor when developing audio (or anything else) for use on the Internet. Whereas servers are fast, robust, and capable of quickly processing large amounts of data, clients come in all shapes and sizes. A video gamer might have an extremely fast computer connected to the Internet over a high-speed connection. On the other hand, a casual Internet user may use an older PC connected through a telephone modem at a very slow speed. Therefore, when designing audio for the Web, the limitations of the client computers must be considered.

Audio Fidelity

Networks, including the Internet, have a variety of limiting factors that reduce the speed at which data can be transmitted. The overall time it takes for information to move from a server to a client is known as the *connection speed*.

We are all familiar with the experience of clicking on a Web link and waiting for endless minutes as an audio file opens. Because audio files are often quite large, transmitting them from server to client can take a long time. To reach the largest audience possible, a Web sound designer must design audio for the slowest likely connection. The slower the connection speed, the poorer the sound quality.

Sound sent by a server across the Internet can and often does take longer to reach its intended client than it takes for the client to play it back. Waiting for long periods of time to download audio over a network is frustrating. A number of solutions have been developed to address this problem such as improvements in connection speed, reducing file size by manipulation, and data compression. These techniques allow information to flow faster across a network but in some cases not without a tradeoff in audio quality.

Connection Speed

The greater the connection speed, the faster a network can transmit information, including audio information. Connection speed is measured in *kilobits per second* (Kbps). For example, a connection speed of 150 Kbps can allow stereo CD-quality sound if played in real time. In contrast, if sound is transmitted or streamed in real time at a connection speed of 8 Kbps the result is a lower, telephone-quality sound (see Figure 14-1). However, most Internet audio is not transmitted in real time, so connection speed is viewed as a limitation on the speed of transmission rather than as a means of determining a transmission's sound quality.

File Manipulation

Another way to improve Internet sound is by reducing the size of audio files because size reduction facilitates file transfer between computers. This can be done through manipulation and compression. To avoid confusion, the term *compression* may refer to either audio level or volume compression or to audio data compression where the amount of information in a recorded sample of audio is reduced to facilitate faster transmission.

There are different ways to handle file size reduction by manipulation such as reducing the sampling rate; reducing the bit depth; reducing the number of channels; reducing playing time by editing; and, with music, using instrumental rather than vocal-based tracks (see Figure 14-2).

Often, these reductions in file size result in a loss of sound quality because many of them actually remove information from the file. Because the Internet is a huge, varied, and sometimes slow network, most audio distributed across the Web is reduced in file size to

Connection Speed (Kbps)	Mode	Audio Quality	Bandwidth (kHz)	Application
128–150	Stereo	CD quality	20	Intranets
96	Stereo	Near CD quality	15	ISDN, LAN
56–64	Stereo	Near FM quality	12	ISDN, LAN
24–32	Stereo	Boombox FM quality	7.5	28.8 modem
16	Mono	AM quality	4.5	28.8 modem
12	Mono	SW quality	4	14.4 modem
8	Mono	Telephone sound	2.5	Telephone

ISDN = Integrated Services Digital Network; LAN = local area network.

Figure 14-1 Changes in audio quality in relation to connection speed.

Word Length/Sampling Rate	44.1 kHz	22.05 kHz	11.025 kHz
16-bit stereo	10 MB	5 MB	2.5 MB
16-bit mono/8-bit stereo	5 MB	2.5 MB	1.26 MB
8-bit mono	2.5 MB	1.26 MB	630 KB

1,000 KB = 1 MB

Figure 14-2 Approximate file sizes for one minute of audio recorded at differing sampling rates and resolutions.

improve transmission speed, and therefore most Web audio is of reduced quality. However, if longer download times are acceptable, audio quality does not have to suffer.

Reducing the Sampling Rate

Some sounds, such as a solo instrument, a sound effect, and a straight narration, to name just a few, do not require a CD-quality sampling rate of 44.1 kHz. For these sounds, 32 kHz may suffice.

Reducing Bit Depth

Audio with a narrow dynamic range, such as speech, simple sound effects, and certain instruments, does not require greater bit depth. A resolution of 8 bits could support such sound with little difficulty. Of course, the wider dynamic range associated with music requires a higher bit rate—16-bit and higher.

Reducing the Number of Channels

Stereo audio uses twice as much data as mono. If an audio file can be handled in mono, it makes sense to do so.

Reducing Playing Time by Editing

Obviously, reducing playing time reduces file size. Of course, this is not always feasible or desirable, but when the opportunity arises, editing the file will help. In this case, *editing* refers to eliminating extraneous bits of data (as opposed to conventional editing). Three ways to handle such editing is through compression, noise reduction, and equalization.

Compression

Compression (in relation to dynamic range as opposed to data) reduces the distances between the peaks and the troughs of a signal. This raises the level of the overall signal, thereby overriding background noise.

Noise reduction is best handled by listening to the silent parts of a file to check for unwanted noise. If it is present, that section of the file can be cleaned, taking care to retain all desirable sound.

Equalization comes in handy to add the high frequencies that are usually lost in data compression.

Audio Data Compression

Audio data compression is the most common way to reduce the size of large audio files by removing psychoacoustically unimportant data. The process is facilitated by a codec, a device that computes enormous mathematical calculations (called algorithms) to make data compression possible.

Several audio compression formats are in use today; the most familiar are those developed by the *Moving Picture Experts Group (MPEG)*. The MPEG approach to compression is based on what is known as *acoustic masking*. It works by establishing what the brain perceives the ear to be hearing at different frequencies. When a tone, called a *masker*, is at a particular frequency, the human ear cannot hear audio on nearby frequencies if they are at a low level. Based on this principle, MPEG developers determined various frequencies that could be eliminated, thereby thinning out the audio data contained in a file.

MPEG Layer 3 technology is commonly known as MP3. It is considered an excellent system for speech, sound effects, and most types of music. It supports a variety of sound applications and Web authoring environments. MPEG is not the only option available to the online audio producer.

File Formats

Because programs that play digital audio need to recognize the files before they can play them, files converted into digital audio must be saved in a particular format. The process adds an *extension* (a period followed by a two- or three-letter descriptor) to the file name, identifying it as an audio file. It also adds *header information*, which tells the playback program how to interpret the data. File identifiers specify the file name, file size, duration, sampling rate, bit depth, number of channels, and type of compression used.

A large number of both *proprietary* and *open source* formats are available on the Internet, and they come and go; a few, however, have been in relatively widespread use for a while (see Figure 14-3). These include MPEG formats (.mpa, .mp2, .mp3, .mp4), Windows Media Audio (.wma), WAV or Waveform audio format (.wav), RealAudio

Lossless File Formats	Extensions
Wav	.wav
Aiff (Audio Interchange File Format)	.aif, .aiff
RealAudio	.ra
Broadcast Wave Format	.wav
Windows Media Audio	.wma
Free Lossless Audio Codec	.flac

Lossy File Formats	Extensions
MPEG Audio	.mpa, .mp2, .mp3, .mp4
ATRAC (used with mini disc)	
Flash	.swf
Sun	.au
Ogg	.ogg

Metafile Formats
(Metafile formats are designed to interchange all the information needed to reconstruct a project.)
AES-31 (AES is the Audio Engineering Society)
OMF (open media format)

Figure 14-3 Common file formats and their associated extensions.

(.ra), QuickTime (.mov), and Flash (.swf) as well as Free Lossless Audio Codec (.flac) and Audio File Format Ogg Vorbis (.ogv, .oga, .ogx, .ogg, .spx).

Nonstreaming Versus Streaming Audio

The difference between nonstreaming and streaming audio is that streaming allows audio data to be sent across a computer network so that no interruptions occur at the receiving end for what appears to be continuous audio playback. In practice, however, interruptions do occur with slower connections.

Downloadable nonstreaming formats require that the user first download the entire file to some form of media, be it a hard disk or a thumb drive. A plug-in application then plays the file. No specific server (transmitter) software is needed.

A key principle behind streaming technologies is *buffering.* As the *player,* which is built into or added onto a user's Web browser, receives encoded data, it stores it in a buffer before use. After data builds a substantial buffer, the *player* (such as RealPlayer) begins to play it. All incoming data is first stored in the buffer before playing. Thus, the player is able to maintain a continuous audio output despite the changing transmission speeds of the data. Sometimes the buffer runs empty, and the player has to wait until it receives more data.

Streaming is useful if the desire is to have audio play automatically within a Web browser or Web page. Nonstreaming files often need to be started manually by the user and often take some time to download before playback can begin.

Online Collaborative Recording

Integrated Services Digital Network (ISDN) made it possible to produce a recording session in real time between studios across town, across the country, or overseas. Various software applications allow multiple users to connect to each other in real time and record or perform together. These systems generally require very fast connection speeds and robust server and client setups.

The Internet has also made it possible for individuals to collaborate by sharing files to produce such audio materials as spot announcements, music recordings, and sound effects. An entire project can be posted to a secure server and downloaded by one or more members of the production team, who can provide additional audio and then edit and mix the project.

The possibilities of this technology seem nearly limitless. With online collaborative recording, it will be possible to assemble a team of top sound artists from across the globe without requiring travel, relocation, or adjustments to personal schedules. Musicians from different cities or states could be engaged for a recording session controlled from a central control room. These musicians could report to studios near their own homes yet still perform together as a group just as they would in a single studio.

It will also be possible to arrange a recording session in one country but monitor and mix it elsewhere. Wireless technology makes it possible to record sound effects in the field and transmit them instantly to a studio control room. As Internet technology and connection speeds improve, the sound quality in such collaborative experiences will equal that of the best studios.

Podcasting

Podcasting is a development in Internet technology that allows users to create and distribute their own audio (and video) productions over the Web. The term *podcasting* is a combination of the words *pod*, referring to the iPod sound player, and *casting*, short for broadcasting. It points to the essential idea behind podcasting: to create an audio broadcast suitable for use on a portable MP3 player like the iPod.

From a technical perspective, podcasting is more related to Internet technology than to audio production. Much attention has gone into the development and the deployment of the various Web technologies that make podcasting possible, but less attention has gone into the good use of sound in a podcast. Typical podcasts feature poor-quality audio and amateurish production values. However, some podcasts are well done, usually on large, heavily trafficked websites that feature professionally produced audio—narration, music, and sound effects. They are essentially professional radio broadcasts distributed via the Internet.

Though the current emphasis in podcasting is with Web technology and Web distribution, the podcaster is still faced with many of the same limitations as any other developer who distributes audio over the Internet. File size is still of paramount concern. Though fast connections make the download of podcasts relatively speedy, it is still advantageous for a podcaster to compress audio and reduce file sizes to reach as wide an audience as possible. It is also important for the podcaster to consider that users may not be willing to upload a large podcast to an iPod or other portable MP3 player already full of other media. A smaller file size leaves a smaller footprint on an MP3 player, making storage and playback easier for the listener.

Most audio podcasts are distributed in MP3 format, which is playable on virtually all computers and MP3 players, although some MP3 players require a specific type of encoding for certain MP3 files to be played. Despite this limitation, MP3 is still the file type of choice for podcasting.

Creating a podcast MP3 is relatively straightforward. Computer technology notwithstanding, the equipment required is the same used in conventional radio broadcasting. What accounts for differences in sound quality is whether the podcaster employs consumer-grade equipment with no signal-processing capability or any of the higher-quality podcasting equipment packages available.

Conceptually, a podcast can take any number of forms. Some are released in sequence or on a schedule—daily, weekly, or monthly. Many are simply experiments or onetime releases. It is becoming increasingly common for news outlets to create podcast versions of some broadcasts (both audio and video) so that users can listen or watch on the go.

Whatever the format, if the podcaster is serious about the product and building an audience, it pays to keep good Internet sound production practices in mind.

Audio Production for Mobile Media

Producing audio for mobile media such as iPods, MP3 players, cell and smart phones, and PDAs involves numerous considerations, especially where they intersect with multiple platforms and the parameters of Internet delivery. Unlike production for a state-of-the-art cinema experience or home entertainment center geared to the highest fidelity, producing audio for mobile media presents particular technical and aesthetic challenges that are generally without historical precedent. It is a paradox that with the opportunity to produce better sound than ever before—and to hear it through great systems—too many listeners are hearing their digital audio in compressed form, much of which reduces sound quality. To exacerbate the condition, many listen through mediocre headphones or earbuds, often in noisy ambient environments, or through a less-than-sonorous computer speaker or loudspeaker system. In relation to aesthetic satisfaction from mobile media, less is definitely not more.

You will recall that mobile devices are designed to handle compressed audio—based on the need to manage access speed and sound quality according to available bandwidth and storage capacity. Although this may seem purely a technical matter, the implications affect creative and aesthetic decision-making at every stage of production.

Playback through mobile media is often through small loudspeakers with a limited frequency response and dynamic range (such as inboard and outboard computer speakers of varying quality and cell phone speakers). The latter are designed with the human voice in mind and therefore have a correspondingly narrow frequency response. Earbuds are capable of handling a broader spectrum, but they too are limited in playing back acoustically rich and detailed audio because of their size and unnatural positioning as a sound source at the outer edge of the ear canal. Headphones, particularly those with noise-canceling capability, offer the better sound option for individual listening.

Editing and mixing audio for mobile media generally require careful and selective equalization in the upper and lower ranges of the program material; highs and lows are rolled off, and the midrange is emphasized. Dynamics usually must be compressed so that program material is heard clearly through tiny loudspeakers.

Apart from the technical challenges, the conditions for listening to mobile media for those on the go are not necessarily conducive to focused, attentive listening. People are more likely to listen to an iPod on the bus, while riding a bicycle, or while walking down a city street than in the solitude of a quiet room. These environments are often acoustically competitive and many sounds are masked by ambient din. To compound the situation, a listener may be engaged in any number of other activities—reading, texting, exercising, and so on. In a word: multitasking. The listening experience is therefore compromised on many levels and exists in a multisensory continuum of stimulation.

There is also the incongruous problem of the audio being too good compared to the video. That is, in some reproducing systems, it is bigger in "size" than the video and its sonic impact imbalances the sound-picture relationship.

As more and more content is created specifically for mobile media, from short-form webisodes to audio/video blogs, podcasts, and games, a new aesthetic is emerging. For the audio producer working with mobile media, the sonic palette remains somewhat restricted and the production parameters limited, at least until the technical means afford greater possibilities with respect to aesthetic ends.

Main Points

- Computer technology in general and the Internet in particular have provided the means to produce and disseminate audio on an unprecedented scale.

- The delivery and the playback of audio over the Internet relies on a system of computers configured and connected in a way that allows them to communicate with one another—in other words, a network.

- A local-area network (LAN) is a network configured for a small, localized area such as a home or business. A wide-area network (WAN) is a network configured for a large geographical area.

- A server is a computer configured on a network to provide information to other computers. A client is a computer connected to a network configured to make requests to a server.

- Among the factors relevant to high-quality audio are the connection speed and the file size.

- Reducing file size can be done by file manipulation or data compression.

- File manipulation includes reducing sampling rate, bit depth, number of channels, and playing time.

- Playing time can be reduced by editing through compression of the dynamic range, noise reduction, and equalization.

- File formats facilitate the saving of digital audio files.

- The difference between nonstreaming and streaming is that streaming allows audio data to be sent across a computer network with no interruptions at the receiving end, although in practice, interruptions do occur with slower connections.

- The principle behind streaming technologies is buffering.

- With streaming technology, the transmission process passes through the encoder, the server, the Internet, and the player.

- Downloading nonstreaming data is usually slow and therefore limited to small files.

- It is possible to do collaborative audio production online by uploading and downloading such audio materials as music, voiceovers, and sound effects. An entire project can be posted to a server and then downloaded by one or more members of the production team, who can provide additional audio and then edit and mix the project.

- Podcasting is a development in Internet technology that allows users to create and distribute their own audio (and video) productions over the Web.

- File size is of paramount concern to the podcaster. Though fast connections make the download of podcasts relatively speedy, it is still advantageous to compress audio and reduce file sizes to reach as wide an audience as possible.

- Most audio podcasts are distributed in MP3 format, which is playable on virtually all computers and MP3 players.

- Sound quality in podcasts varies widely for several reasons: The emphasis is more on achieving widespread distribution than on audio production values; equipment runs from consumer-grade to professional; and many podcasters have little or no experience with audio production techniques.

- Unlike production for a state-of-the-art cinema experience or home entertainment center geared to high fidelity, producing audio for mobile media presents particular technical and aesthetic challenges that are generally without historical precedent.

- Playback through mobile media is often through small loudspeakers with a limited frequency response and dynamic range.

- Editing and mixing audio for mobile media generally requires careful and selective equalization in the upper and lower ranges of the program material; highs and lows are rolled off, and the midrange is emphasized. Dynamics usually must be compressed so that program material is heard clearly through tiny loudspeakers.

- The conditions for listening to mobile media for those on the go are not necessarily conducive to focused, attentive listening.

- There is the incongruous problem of the audio being too good compared to the video; in some reproducing systems, it is bigger in "size" than the video, and its sonic impact imbalances the sound-picture relationship.

- For the audio producer working with mobile media, the sonic palette remains somewhat restricted and the production parameters limited, at least until the technical means afford greater possibilities with respect to aesthetic ends.

15 Influences of Sound on Meaning

Sound influences how we create meaning. While language and the spoken word are in some respects most obvious, nonverbal speech, sound effects, and music also inform our capacity to interpret and understand dramatic intention. The subtleties and nuances of the human voice can communicate more about characters and their motivation than what the words alone might signify. Well-crafted and appropriate sound effects lend realism and convincing illusion to a production while music adds emotional depth and dimension to our experience as an audience.

Characteristics of Sound

All sound—speech, sound effects, and music—is made up of the same basic elements: pitch, loudness, timbre, tempo, and rhythm. Furthermore, every sound has its own "life cycle" or sound envelope comprising an attack, duration, and decay. During audio production, everyone involved is dealing with these elements, consciously or subconsciously, and assessing their effects on perception. Because each element contains certain characteristics that affect our response to sound, understanding those effects is fundamental to the art and craft of sound design. The following outlines some of the associations and responses that the different parameters of sound may elicit.

- *Pitch* refers to the highness or lowness of a sound—its frequency. High-pitched sound often suggests something delicate, bright, or elevated; low-pitched sound may indicate something sinister, strong, or peaceful.

- *Loudness,* or dynamic range, describes the relative volume of sound—how loud or soft it is. Loud sound can suggest closeness, strength, or importance; soft sound may convey distance, weakness, or tranquility.

- *Timbre* is the characteristic tonal quality of a sound. It not only identifies a sound source—reedy or brassy—but also sonic qualities such as rich, thin, edgy, or metallic. Reedy tonal qualities produced by a clarinet or an oboe, for example, can suggest something wistful, lonely, or sweet. A brassy sound can imply something cold, harsh, fierce, bitter, forceful, martial, or big.

- *Tempo* refers to the speed or pace of a sound. Fast tempos agitate, excite, or accelerate; slow tempos may suggest monotony, dignity, or control.

- *Rhythm* relates to a sonic time pattern. It may be simple, constant, complex, or changing. A simple rhythm can convey deliberateness, regularity, or lack of complication. A constant rhythm can imply dullness, depression, or uniformity. Rhythmic complexity suggests intricacy or elaborateness. Changing rhythms can create a sense of uncertainty, vigor, or the erratic.

- *Attack*—the way a sound begins—can be hard, soft, crisp, or gradual. Hard or crisp attacks can suggest sharpness, excitement, or danger. Soft or gradual attacks can imply something gentle, muted, or blasé.

- *Duration* refers to how long a sound lasts. Sound short in duration can convey restlessness, nervousness, or excitation; more sustained sounds can create a sense of peace, persistence, or fatigue.

- *Decay*—how fast a sound fades out—can be quick, gradual, or slow. Quick decays can create a sense of confinement, closeness, or definiteness; slow decays can convey distance, smoothness, or uncertainty.

Of course, these elements are not heard individually but in combination. Other aspects of sound, such as changing pitch, changing loudness, and acoustic interactions, also affect response. That these characteristics are elemental in sonic structure is not to suggest that sound design is prescriptive or developed by applying formulas; the basic components of sound structure do not occur separately but together in myriad forms. Rather, it is to introduce and define the building blocks of sound from which the sound designer shapes aural structure and meaning.

Nonverbal Speech

For an actor, effectively delivering the words from a page—whether they are in a commercial, documentary, or drama—involves more than just reciting them. It is often not *what* is said but *how* it is said that shapes the meaning. Examples of how nonverbal speech influences meaning include emphasis, inflection, speech patterns, pace, mood, and accent.

Emphasis

Emphasis—stressing a syllable or a word—is important to all speech, whether voiceover, narration, or dialogue. It often conveys the gist of what is said. Consider the question, "What were you thinking?" With no particular emphasis, the question is straightforward and might mean, "What is on your mind?" If, however, any word in the phrase is emphasized, a simple question may become an admonition or an accusation. The words remain the same; the aural emphasis alters the message.

Inflection

Inflection—altering the pitch or tone of the voice—can also influence verbal meaning. By raising the pitch of the voice at the end of a sentence, a declarative statement becomes a question. Put stress on it, and it becomes an exclamation.

Speech Patterns

Speech patterns, cadence, or rhythm are important to natural-sounding speech and creating a believable character. A writer must be equally aware of *what* words mean and *how* they should sound. If the speaker is formal, vocabulary and sentence structure should be precise, and speech rhythms should sound even and businesslike. Informality would sound looser, more relaxed, and more personal.

Pace

The *pace* or tempo of spoken words can communicate nonverbal information about a character and the emotional tenor of a given situation. Halting, hesitant dialogue conveys a very different sensibility than lines delivered smoothly and slowly or those that are breathless and quick.

Mood

Sound can be evocative and affects the *mood* or feeling of words and sentences. Consider the following line from Keats' *Ode to a Nightingale,* "The murmurous haunt of flies on summer eves."[1] The sounds of the words themselves evoke the din of insects on a summer night.

Accent

An *accent* can tell you if a speaker is cultured or crude, a Jamaican from Kingston, or an American from Brooklyn, or someone from China, Spain, or India.

Sound Effects

Sound effects (SFX) can be classified as anything sonic that is not speech or music. They are essential to storytelling, bringing realism and added dimension to a production. It is worth noting that the art of sound effects design is about creating not only something big or bizarre but also crafting subtle, low-key moments. Good effects are about conveying a compelling illusion. In general, sound effects can be contextual or narrative. These functions are not mutually exclusive; they allow for a range of possibilities in the sonic continuum between what we listen for in dialogue—namely, sound and words to convey meaning—and what we experience more viscerally and emotionally in music.

Contextual Sound

Contextual sound emanates from and duplicates a sound source as it is. It is often illustrative and also referred to as *diegetic sound.* The term derives from the Greek, *diegesis,* meaning to tell or recount and, in the context of film, has come to describe what comes from within the story space. If a gun fires, a car drives by, or leaves rustle in the wind, what you see is what you hear; the sound is naturalistic in structure and perspective.

---

1. Sir Arthur Thomas Quiller-Couch, *The Oxford Book of English Verse* (Oxford: Clarendon, 1919, [c1901]); Bartleby.com, www.bartleby.com, 1999.

Narrative Sound

Narrative sound adds more to a scene than what is apparent and so performs an informational function. It can be descriptive or commentative.

Descriptive Sound

As the term suggests, *descriptive sound* describes sonic aspects of a scene, usually those not directly connected with the main action—but key in adding to the compelling nature of the illusion. Descriptive sound for a village scene set in the Middle Ages might include oxcarts lumbering by, the sounds of a tinker repairing a pot, a distant church bell tolling, and the indistinguishable hubbub of human activity in a market square.

Commentative Sound

Commentative sound also describes, but it makes an additional statement, one that usually has something to do with the story line. For example: An aging veteran wanders through the uniform rows of white crosses in a cemetery. A wind comes up as he pauses before individual markers. The wind is infused with the faint sound of battle, snippets of conversations, laughter, and music as he remembers his fallen comrades.

Functions of Sound Effects

Sound effects have specific functions in how they influence meaning within the general contextual and narrative categories. They break the screen plane, define space, focus attention, establish locale, create environment, emphasize and intensify action, depict identity, set pace, provide counterpoint, create humor, symbolize meaning, and create metaphor. Paradoxical as it may seem, silence is also a functional sound effect.

Breaking the Screen Plane

A film or video without sounds, natural or produced, detaches an audience from the on-screen action. The audience becomes an observer, looking at the scene from outside rather than made to feel a part of the action—at the center of an acoustic space. The presence of sound changes the audience relationship to what is happening on screen; it becomes part of the action in a sense. The audience becomes a participant in that there is no longer a separation between the listener-viewer and the screen plane. Therefore, it can also be said that sound effects add realism to the picture.

Defining Space

Sound defines space by establishing distance, direction of movement, position, openness, and dimension. Distance—how close or far a sound seems to be—is created mainly by relative loudness, or *sound perspective*. The louder a sound, the closer to the listener-viewer it is. Thunder at a low sound level tells you that a storm is some distance away; as the storm moves closer, the thunder grows louder.

Focusing Attention

In shots, other than close-ups, in which a number of elements are seen at the same time, how do you know where to focus attention? Of course directors compose shots to direct the eye, but the eye can wander. Sound, however, draws attention and provides the viewer with a focus. In a shot of a large room filled with people, the eye takes it all in, but if a person shouts or begins choking, the sound directs the eye to that individual.

Establishing Locale

Sounds can establish locale. A cawing seagull places you at the ocean; honking car horns and screeching brakes place you in city traffic; the squeak of athletic shoes, the rhythmic slap of a bouncing ball, and the roar of a crowd place you at a basketball game.

Creating Environment

Establishing locale begins to create an environment, but more brush strokes and textures are often needed to complete the picture. Honky-tonk saloon music may establish the Old West, but sounds of a blacksmith hammering, horses whinnying, wagon wheels rolling, and six-guns firing create environment.

Emphasizing Action

Sounds can emphasize or highlight action. A person falling down a flight of stairs tumbles all the harder if each bump is accented.

Intensifying Action

Whereas emphasizing action highlights or calls attention to something important, intensifying action increases or heightens dramatic impact. A car's twisted metal settling in the aftermath of a collision emits an agonized groaning sound. In animation, sound (and music) intensifies the extent of a character's running, falling, crashing, skidding, chomping, and chasing.

Depicting Identity

Depicting identity is perhaps one of the most obvious uses of sound. Barking identifies a dog, slurred speech identifies a drunk, and so on. But on a more informational level, sound can also give a character or an object its own distinctive sound signature: the rattle sound of a rattlesnake to identify a slippery villain with a venomous intent; thin, clear, hard sounds to convey a cold character devoid of compassion and so on.

Setting Pace

Sounds, or the lack of them, help set pace. The incessant, even rhythm of a machine creates a steady pace to underscore monotony. The controlled professionalism of two detectives discussing crucial evidence becomes more vital if the activity around them includes such sonic elements as footsteps moving quickly, telephones ringing, papers shuffled, and a general hubbub of voices.

Providing Counterpoint

Sounds provide counterpoint when they are different from what is expected, thereby making an additional comment on the action. A wounded soldier lying on a bed and looking at a ceiling fan's rotating blades that sound like those of a helicopter suggest the battlefield he has just left.

Creating Humor

Sounds can be funny. Think of boings, boinks, and plops; the swirling swoops of a pennywhistle; the chuga-chugaburp-cough-chuga of a steam engine trying to get started. Comic sounds are indispensable in cartoons in highlighting the shenanigans of their characters.

Symbolizing Meaning

Sound can be used symbolically. The sound of water swirling down a drain is heard as a murder victim slumps to the floor of a bathtub.

Creating Metaphor

Sound can create a metaphorical relationship between what is heard and what is seen. A wife leaving her husband after enduring the last straw in a deeply troubled marriage walks out of their house, slamming the door. The sound of the slam has the palpable impact of finality and with it there is a slowly decaying reverberation that reflects a married life that has faded into nothingness.

Silence

Silence is not generally thought of as sound *per se*—that seems like a contradiction in terms. But it is the pauses or silences between words, sounds, and musical notes that help create rhythm, contrast, and power—elements important to sonic communication.

In situations where we anticipate sound, silence is a particularly powerful element. A horrifying sight compels a scream—but with the mouth wide open there is only silence, suggesting an unspeakable horror. The silence preceding sound is equally effective. A pistol shot breaks the quiet of winter night. Similarly, silence can be dramatic following sound. An explosive device is set to go off in a crowded city square. The ticking of the bomb gets louder as it reaches detonation time. Then, silence.

Music

Music is elemental. Its sonic combinations are infinite, and its aesthetic values fulfill basic human needs. Therein lies its power in *underscoring*—adding background music that enhances the content of a scene by evoking a particular idea, emotion, point of view, or atmosphere. Music is generally thought of as an art form that evokes emotion. That is true, of course. It provides *affective information*—information related to feeling and mood. But it also provides *cognitive information*—information related to mental processes of knowledge, reasoning, memory, judgment, and perception.

Underscore music is original or library music. Unlike sound effects, underscoring is *nondiegetic sound* in that it comes from outside the story space. Underscoring serves picture in a number of ways. As composer Aaron Copland observed many years ago, and which still holds true today: Underscoring creates a more convincing atmosphere of time and place; it underlines psychological refinements—the unspoken thoughts of a character or situation; it serves to fill pauses between conversation; it builds a sense of continuity; it underpins dramatic buildup and gives finality to a scene.[2]

Music Characteristics

Music has the same basic structural elements common to all sound, such as pitch, loudness, tempo, tone color, and envelope. It also contains other characteristics that broaden its perceptual and aesthetic meaning such as melody and tonality; harmony and its qualities of consonance, dissonance, and texture; tempo; dynamic range that is quite wide compared with speech and sounds; and style in limitless variety. The characteristics of music are both more and less complex than those of verbal language. Unlike speech (and sound effects), musical structure is both horizontal and vertical and therefore at once linear and simultaneous. That is, linear sound provides melody and rhythm; simultaneous sound provides harmony and texture. The entire audible spectrum of sound can be used in an infinite variety of combinations.

Melody

Melody is a succession of pitched musical tones of varied durations. Because each tone has duration, melody also establishes rhythm. Hence, melody has both a tone quality and a time quality and cannot be separated from rhythm. Generally, if a melody moves in narrowly pitched steps and ranges, it tends to be expressive and emotional. If it moves in widely pitched steps and ranges, it tends to be conservative and unexpressive. Melodies are usually written in keys or tonalities, designated as major and minor. Subjectively, keys in the major mode usually sound positive, happy, bright, and vigorous; keys in the minor mode usually sound darker, tentative, wistful, and melancholy.

Harmony

Harmony is a simultaneous sounding of two or more tones, although three or more tones are usually necessary to be classified as a chord. *Chords* are categorized as consonant or dissonant, and they are important to musical texture. *Consonance* in music is produced by agreeable, settled, balanced, stable-sounding chords. *Dissonance* is produced by unsettled, unstable, unresolved, tense-sounding chords. *Texture*, as the term suggests, is the result of materials interwoven to create a fabric. In music, melody and harmony are those interwoven materials. Undoubtedly, the infinite variety of musical textures that can be designed is a major reason for music's universal appeal and role in human communication.

Tempo

Tempo provides the pulse and the drive in music. A quick tempo tends to intensify stimulation; a slow tempo tends to allay it.

---

2. Aaron Copland, *Our New Music* (New York: McGraw-Hill, 1941).

Dynamic Range

Because the *dynamic range* of music can be much wider than the dynamic ranges of speech and sounds, it is possible to create a greater variety of loudness-related effects with an equal breadth of emotional impact and response.

Style

Style is a fixed, identifiable musical quality uniquely expressed, executed, or performed. It is that combination of characteristics that distinguishes chamber music from jazz and hip-hop from rock. Like texture, style is a source of infinite musical variety.

Functions of Music Underscoring

Music underscoring performs many of the same functions in audio design as sound effects but more broadly and diversely. One essential difference between sound effects and music is that *sound effects are generally associated with action and music with reaction*. This can be argued, of course, but it serves to provide insight into their different roles and effects. The unique language, vast vocabulary, and universal resonance of music also make it so powerful and so widely applicable in aural communication.

Establishing Locale

Many musical styles and themes are indigenous to particular regions. By recalling these styles and themes or by simulating a reasonable sonic facsimile, music can establish a locale, such as an Indian village or Rio de Janeiro during Carnival.

Emphasizing Action

Music emphasizes action by defining or underscoring an event. For example, a dramatic chord underscores shock or a moment of decision or tempo increasing from slow to fast emphasizes impending danger.

Intensifying Action

Music intensifies action, usually with crescendo or repetition. The scariness of sinister music builds to a climax behind a scene of sheer terror and crashes in a final, frightening chord. The repetition of a short melody, phrase, or rhythm intensifies boredom, the threat of danger, or an imminent action.

Depicting Identity

Music can identify characters, events, and programs. Think of John Williams's score for *Jaws* with its distinct musical phrase associated with the menacing shark. A particular theme played during an event identifies the event each time it is heard. Themes also have long served to identify radio and television programs, films, and personalities.

Setting Pace

Music sets pace mainly through tempo and rhythm. Slow tempo suggests dignity, importance, or dullness; fast tempo suggests gaiety, agility, or triviality. Changing tempo from slow to fast accelerates pace and escalates action; changing from fast to slow decelerates pace and winds down or concludes action. Regular rhythm suggests stability, monotony, or simplicity; irregular (syncopated) rhythm suggests complexity, excitement, or instability. Using up-tempo music for a slow-moving scene accelerates the movements within the scene and vice versa.

Providing Counterpoint

Music that provides counterpoint adds an idea or a feeling that would not otherwise be obvious. Football players shown blocking, passing, and running are counterpointed with ballet music to underscore their grace and coordination.

Creating Humor

A sliding trombone, clanking percussion, or a galumphing bassoon can define a comic highlight or underscore its humor.

Fixing Time

Among the many uses for musical style is fixing time. Depending on the harmonic structure, the voicings in the playing ensemble, or both, it is possible to suggest ancient Greece, medieval France, the Roaring Twenties, 1960s San Francisco, the future, times of day, and so on.

Recalling or Foretelling Events

If music can be used to fix a period in time, it can also be used to recall a past event or foretell a future occurrence. For example, a theme used to underscore a tragic crash is repeated at dramatically appropriate times to recall the incident.

Evoking Atmosphere, Feeling, or Mood

Perhaps no other form of human communication is as effective as music in providing atmosphere, feeling, or mood. There is a musical analog for virtually every condition and emotion. Music can evoke atmospheres that are thick, unsavory, cold, sultry, and ethereal. It can evoke feelings that are obvious and easy to suggest, such as love, hate, and awe, as well as subtle feelings such as friendship, estrangement, pity, and kindness. Music can convey the most obvious and the subtlest of moods: ecstasy, depression, melancholy, and amiability.

Influences of Sound Design on Meaning

The following example demonstrates how *sound design* can affect the meaning of the picture.

FADE IN

INTERIOR. BEDROOM. NIGHT. A LITTLE GIRL IS LYING ON A BED LOOKING AT THE CEILING. A SHAFT OF MOONLIGHT COMES IN THROUGH AN OPEN WINDOW ILLUMINATING ONLY PART OF HER FACE. THE CAMERA SLOWLY ZOOMS IN.

Clearly, the script's story and the director's choices would govern the sound design for this shot. But the intent of this example is to demonstrate sound's significant influence on picture. Consider the shot with the following sound patterns and how each pattern influences its meaning and feel.

- The sounds of conversation and revelry coming from another room
- The sounds of a man and a woman arguing in an adjacent room and a sudden crash
- Two men are heard whispering offscreen
- An old woman's voiceover describes childhood memories
- The girl breathing, humming softly—almost imperceptibly—to herself
- The thrum of an air conditioner and the polyrhythmic din of insects
- Gentle breaking of waves and a distant foghorn
- The whine of air raid sirens, the rumble of airplanes, and the dull thudding of distant bombs
- A single dog howling, building to a scattered chorus of baying hounds in the distance
- The creaking of floorboards and the sound of a door latch opening
- The distant sounds of a playground with children laughing and singing
- Street traffic, the occasional car horn, and the booming bass of music from a passing car

This example has other thematic possibilities, of course.

The choices of dialogue and narration open up numerous avenues for the audience to interpret the scene differently. In addition to what is said, aspects of emphasis, inflection, patterns of speech, pace, mood, and accent also suggest a wide range of dramatic possibilities.

An audience hearing the muffled argument between a man and a woman through the walls may not hear specific words, but the nonverbal dimension of their conversation communicates the tension between them. Their voices rise and lower in intensity, the tempo of the exchange varies, and punctuated silences maintain a level of suspense.

If we think of the scene and hear the voiceover of an old woman reminiscing about her youth haltingly and deliberately with a Russian accent and a twinge of melancholy, it tells us one story. Change the voice to an American from the rural South who speaks quickly with a pronounced drawl and laughs to herself as she pauses between sentences, the scene changes—even though both are talking about childhood memories.

The various ambient soundscapes and sound effects palettes contribute to our understanding of the scene and how we make sense of characters' actions and intentions. The arguing couple heard against the rhythms of a hot summer night in the country carries a different sensibility than that of the inner city—what we hear tells us about time, place, and circumstance.

The Russian woman's reminiscences juxtaposed against the sounds of distant battle as opposed to ocean surf and foghorn convey a different backdrop for the narration. In these examples, what we hear beyond the content of the dialogue in terms of ambience and sound effects informs our capacity to interpret and shape meaning.

Now consider what music underscoring does to the scene, with or without the sound effects and any number of variables with regard to dialogue and/or narration. With music that is, say, celestial, mysterious, sinister, playful, comedic, romantic, melancholy, blissful, animated, or threatening, notice how the idea and the feel of the scene changes yet again. In the same vein as these musical suggestions, consider the wide range of musical styles and how these might influence our interpretation of the scene.

For the man and woman engaged in a heated argument, music can heighten the conflict—whether we are hearing hip-hop, bebop, or a piece of atonal music from a string quartet. With the Russian woman, the plaintive sound of a solo *balalaika* might lend an intimacy to her voiceover, while the strains of an orchestra or choir may give us a sense of pathos. Each choice brings with it a shading of nuance and information that pulls the audience more deeply into the drama of the moment.

The effective interplay of dialogue and narration—quite apart from what the words might signify—along with sound effects and music all contribute to how we create and interpret meaning and dramatic intent.

Main Points

- All sound is made up of the same basic components: pitch, loudness, timbre, tempo, rhythm, attack, duration, and decay.

- Influences of nonverbal speech on meaning include emphasis, inflection, speech patterns, pace, mood, and accent.

- Sound effects (SFX) can be classified as anything sonic that is not speech or music. They help amplify the reality created in a production.

- Sound effects perform two general functions: contextual and narrative. Contextual sound emanates from and duplicates a sound source as it is. It is also known as diegetic sound—coming from within the story space. Narrative sound adds more to a scene than what is apparent.

- Narrative sound can be descriptive or commentative.

- Sound effects can break the screen plane, define space, focus attention, establish locale, create environment, emphasize and intensify action, depict identity, set pace, provide counterpoint, create humor, symbolize meaning, and create metaphor.

- Silence can be used to enhance sonic effect.

- Music underscoring consists of adding background music that enhances the content of a scene by evoking a particular idea, emotion, point of view, or atmosphere.

- Underscore music is original or library music added to enhance a scene's content.

- Music has the same basic structural elements common to all sound such as pitch, loudness, tempo, tone color, and envelope. It also contains other characteristics that broaden its perceptual and aesthetic meaning such as melody and tonality; harmony and its qualities of consonance, dissonance, and texture; tempo; dynamic range that is quite wide compared with speech and sounds; and style in limitless variety.

- Melody is a succession of pitched musical tones of varied durations.

- Harmony is a simultaneous sounding of two or more tones, although three or more tones are usually necessary to define a chord.

- Tempo provides the pulse and the drive in music.

- The dynamic range of music can be much wider than the dynamic ranges of speech and sounds.

- Style is a fixed, identifiable musical quality uniquely expressed, executed, or performed.

- Music underscoring provides such functions as establishing locale, emphasizing action, intensifying action, depicting identity, setting pace, providing counterpoint, creating humor, fixing time, recalling or foretelling events, and evoking atmosphere, feeling, and mood.

- Sound design can significantly influence the meaning and feel of a picture.

GLOSSARY

λ—See **wavelength**.

5.1—The surround-sound format incorporating five discrete full-frequency audio channels and one discrete channel for low-frequency enhancement. See also **7.1** and **surround sound**.

7.1—The surround-sound format incorporating seven discrete full-frequency audio channels and one discrete channel for low-frequency enhancement. See also **5.1** and **surround sound**.

24p—The format used in high-definition video where the camera is substituting for film. The *24* refers to the standard frames-per-second rate; the *p* stands for *progressive*.

60 percent/60-minute rule—Limit listening through headphones to no more than one hour per day at levels below 60 percent of maximum volume.

accent miking—Used to pick up instruments in an ensemble when they solo. It is, in effect, a relatively close-miking technique but used when distant microphones are picking up the ensemble's overall sound and a solo passage needs to stand out. Also known as *off-miking*. See also **ambience miking, close miking,** and **distant miking**.

ACN—See **active combining network**.

acoustic masking—See **MPEG**.

acoustic pickup mic—See **contact microphone**.

acoustical phase—The time relationship between two or more sound waves at a given point in their cycles.

acoustics—The science that deals with the behavior of sound and sound control, including its generation, transmission, reception, and effects. The properties of a room that affect the quality of sound.

active combining network (ACN)—An amplifier at which the outputs of two or more signal paths are mixed together before being routed to their destination.

active microphone mixer—Allows amplification control of each audio source and usually includes other processing features as well. See also **passive microphone mixer**.

active ribbon microphone—A ribbon microphone that uses an amplifier system requiring phantom power.

ADSR—See **sound envelope**.

AES/EBU—Internationally accepted professional digital audio interface transmitted via a balanced-line connection using XLR connectors, specified jointly by the Audio Engineering Society (AES) and the European Broadcast Union (EBU). See also **Sony/Philips Digital Interface (S/PDIF)**.

ambience—Sounds such as reverberation, noise, and atmosphere that form a background to the main sound. Also called *room tone* and *presence* and, in Great Britain, *atmos*.

ambience miking—Used along with distant miking, attempts to reproduce the aural experience audiences receive in a live venue by recording in an acoustically suitable studio or concert hall. Microphones are positioned far enough from the ensemble where the later reflections are more prominent than the direct sound. See also **accent miking, close miking,** and **distant miking**.

amplifier—A device that increases the amplitude of an electric signal.

amplitude—The magnitude of a sound wave or electric signal, measured in decibels.

amplitude processor—A signal processor that affects a signal's loudness. The effects include compression, limiting, de-essing, expanding, noise gating, and pitch shifting. Also called *dynamic processor*.

anechoic chamber—A room that prevents all reflected sound through the dissipation or the absorption of sound waves.

aspect ratio—The width-to-height proportions of a video image. For the standard video screen, it is 4×3 (1.33:1); for HDTV it is 16×9 (1.78:1). For wide motion picture screens, aspect ratios are between 5.55×3 (1.85:1) and 7×3 (2.35:1).

atmos—Short for *atmosphere*, the British term for ambience. See **ambience**.

attack—(1) The way a sound begins—that is, by plucking, bowing, striking, blowing, and so on. (2) The first part of the sound envelope—how a sound starts after a sound source has been vibrated.

attack time—The length of time it takes a compressor to respond to the input signal.

attenuator—See **fader**.

audio data rate—The relationship between sampling frequency and quantization. When audio is converted to digital, it becomes data. The data rate is computed by multiplying bit depth times sampling frequency.

auditory fatigue—See **temporary threshold shift (TTS)**.

aural exciter—See **psychoacoustic processor**.

balanced line—A pair of ungrounded conductors whose voltages are opposite in polarity but equal in magnitude.

band-pass filter—A filter that attenuates above and below a selected bandwidth, allowing the frequencies in between to pass.

bandwidth—The difference between the upper and lower frequency limits of an audio component. The upper and lower frequency limits of AM radio are 535 kHz and 1,605 kHz; therefore, the bandwidth of AM radio is 1,070 kHz.

bandwidth curve—The curve shaped by the number of frequencies in a bandwidth and their relative increase or decrease in level. A bandwidth of 100 to 150 Hz with 125 Hz boosted 15 dB forms a sharp, narrow bandwidth curve; a bandwidth of 100 to 6,400 Hz with a 15 dB boost at 1,200 Hz forms a more sloping, wider bandwidth curve.

bass—The low range of the audible frequency spectrum; usually from 20 to 320 Hz.

bass management—In surround sound, the redirection of low-frequency content from each of the full-bandwidth production channels to the low-frequency enhancement channel.

bass roll-off—Attenuating bass frequencies. The control—for example, on a microphone—used to roll off bass frequencies.

bass tip-up—See **proximity effect**.

bass trap—See **diaphragmatic absorber**.

bidirectional microphone—A microphone that picks up sound to its front and back and has minimal pickup at its sides.

binaural microphone system—Two omnidirectional capacitor microphones set into the ear cavities of an artificial head, complete with pinnae. This arrangement preserves binaural localization cues during recording and reproduces sound as humans hear it—three-dimensionally. Also called *artificial head* or *dummy head (Kunstkopf) stereo*.

bit depth—See **word length**.

blast filter—See **pop filter**.

Blu-ray Disc (BD)—High-density optical disc format developed to enable recording, playback, and rewriting of high-definition media.

board—Audio mixing console.

boundary microphone—A microphone whose capsule is mounted flush with or close to, but a precise distance from, a reflective surface so that there is no phase cancellation of reflected sound at audible frequencies.

broadband compressor—A compressor that acts on the dynamic range of the input signal across the entire frequency spectrum. See also **split-band compressor**.

bus—A mixing network that combines the outputs of other channels.

calibration—Adjusting equipment—for example, a console and a recorder—according to a standard so that their measurements are similar.

capacitor microphone—A microphone that transduces acoustic energy into electric energy electrostatically. Also called *condenser microphone.*

cardioid microphone—A unidirectional microphone with a heart-shaped pickup pattern.

CD-R—See **recordable compact disc.**

CD-RW—See **rewritable compact disc.**

center frequency—In peak/dip equalizing, the frequency at which maximum boost or attenuation occurs.

channel message—In MIDI recording, the message that gives information on whether an instrument should send or receive and on which channel. It also indicates when a note event begins or ends and control information such as velocity, attack, and program change.

channel mode message—In MIDI recording, the message that facilitates response appropriate to monophonic, polyphonic, or polytimbral processing.

channel voice message—Transmits performance data throughout the MIDI system that are generated whenever the controller of a MIDI instrument is played.

chipmunk effect—See **speed-up pitch shifting.**

chorus effect—Recirculating the doubling effect to make one sound source sound like several. See also **doubling.**

clipping—Audible distortion that occurs when a signal's level exceeds the limits of a particular device or circuit.

close miking—Placing a microphone close to a sound source to pick up mostly direct sound and reduce ambience and leakage. See also **accent miking, ambience miking,** and **distant miking.**

cocktail party effect—A psychoacoustic effect that allows humans to localize the sources of sounds around them.

coincident miking—Employing two matched microphones, usually unidirectional, crossed one above the other on a vertical axis with their diaphragms. See also **X-Y miking.**

comb-filter effect—The effect produced when a signal is time-delayed and added to itself, reinforcing some frequencies and canceling others, giving sound an unnatural, hollow coloration.

commentative sound—Descriptive sound that makes a comment or an interpretation. See also **descriptive sound** and **narrative sound.**

companding—A contraction of the words *com*pressing and exp*anding* that refers to wireless mics' increasing dynamic range and reducing noise inherent in a transmission system.

comping—Taking the best part(s) of each recorded track and combining them into a composite final version.

complementary equalization—Equalizing sounds that share similar frequency ranges so that they complement, rather than interfere with, one another. See also **cumulative equalization** and **subtractive equalization**.

compression—(1) Reducing a signal's output level in relation to its input level to reduce dynamic range. (2) The drawing together of vibrating molecules, producing a high-pressure area. See also **rarefaction**.

compression ratio—The ratio of the input and output signals in a compressor.

compression threshold—The level at which a compressor acts on an input signal and the compression ratio takes effect.

compressor—A signal processor with an output level that increases at a slower rate as its input level increases.

condenser microphone—See **capacitor microphone**.

conductive hearing loss—A condition that occurs when there is damage to the eardrum or middle ear from disease; infection; excessive ear wax; foreign objects that block the eardrum; trauma to the head or neck; systemic disorders such as high- or low-blood pressure, vascular disorders, and thyroid dysfunction; and high doses of certain medications such as sedatives, antidepressants, and anti-inflammatory drugs.

console—An electronic device that amplifies, balances, processes, and combines input signals and routes them to broadcast or recording. Also called *board, mixer*, or, in Europe, *mixing desk*. See also **mixer**.

constructive interference—When sound waves are partially out of phase and partially additive, increasing amplitude where compression and rarefaction occur at the same time.

contact microphone—A microphone that attaches to a sound source and transduces the vibrations that pass through it. Also called *acoustic pickup mic*.

control surface—Provides tactual means of controlling various console-related functions. Generally there are no actual audio signals present inside a simple control surface—only control circuitry that sends digital instructions to the device doing the actual audio signal processing. Also called *work surface*.

convolution reverb—A sample-based process that multiplies the spectrums of two audio files, providing a virtually infinite range of acoustic spaces.

cordless microphone—See **wireless microphone system**.

coverage angle—The off-axis angle or point at which the loudspeaker level is down 6 dB compared with the on-axis output level.

cps—Cycles per second. See **hertz**.

crossfade—Fading in one sound source as another sound source fades out. At some point, the sounds cross at an equal level of loudness.

cumulative equalization—Too much boost of the same frequency in various tracks in a multitrack recording, which could unbalance the overall blend of a mix. See also **complementary equalization** and **subtractive equalization**.

cut—(1) An instantaneous transition from one sound or picture to another. (2) To make a disc recording. (3) A decrease in level.

cut sound effect—See **hard sound effect**.

cycles per second (cps)—See **hertz**.

DAW—See **digital audio workstation**.

dB—See **decibel**.

dBFS—See **decibel full-scale**.

dB-SPL—See **sound-pressure level**.

decay—How fast a sound fades from a certain loudness.

decay time—See **reverberation time**.

decibel (dB)—A relative and dimensionless unit to measure the ratio of two quantities.

decibel full-scale (dBFS)—A unit of measure for the amplitude of digital audio signals.

de-emphasis—Reduces the high-frequency noise at the receiver in a wireless microphone system. *See also* **pre-emphasis**.

de-esser—A compressor that reduces sibilance.

delay—The time interval between a sound or signal and each of its repeats.

delay time—The amount of time between delays. In a digital delay, delay time regulates how long a given sound is held.

descriptive sound—Describes sonic aspects of a scene not connected to the main action. See also **commentative sound** and **narrative sound**.

design sound effect—Has to be created because it does not exist in nature.

destructive editing—Permanently alters the original sound or soundfile. See also **nondestructive editing**.

destructive interference—When sound waves are partially out of phase and partially subtractive, decreasing amplitude where compression and rarefaction occur at different times.

diaphragmatic absorber—A flexible panel mounted over an air space that resonates at a frequency (or frequencies) determined by the stiffness of the panel and the size of the air space. Also called *bass trap*.

diegetic sound—Sound that comes from within the story space, such as dialogue and sound effects. See also **nondiegetic sound**.

diffraction—The spreading of sound waves as they pass around an object, depending on the wavelength and distances involved.

diffusion—The scattering of sound waves to a uniform intensity.

digital audio workstation (DAW)—A multifunctional hard-disk production system, controlled from a central location, that is integrated with and capable of being networked to other devices, such as audio, video, and MIDI sources, within or among facilities. Generally, there are two types of DAW systems: computer-based and integrated.

digital editing—The assembly of disk-based material in or out of sequence, taken from any part of a recording and placed in any other part of the recording almost instantly. Also known as *nonlinear editing (NLE)*.

digital microphone—A microphone that converts an analog signal into a digital signal at the mic capsule.

digital signal processing (DSP)—Provides various manipulations of sound in a digital format. The term is generally used to refer to signal processing using computer software.

digital versatile disc (DVD)—A compact disc providing massive data storage of digital-quality audio, video, and text.

direct sound—Sound waves that reach the listener before reflecting off any surface. See also **early reflections**.

direct surround-sound miking—A surround-sound miking approach that uses a microphone array especially designed for surround-sound pickup. See also **direct/ambient surround-sound miking**.

direct/ambient surround-sound miking—A surround-sound miking technique using a stereo microphone array for the left-right frontal pickups, plus a center mic for the center channel and a stereo microphone array for the left- and right-rear surround pickup. See also **direct surround-sound miking**.

directional microphone—See **unidirectional microphone**.

distant miking—Placing a microphone far enough from the sound source to pick up most or all of an ensemble's blended sound, including room reflections. See also **accent miking, ambience miking,** and **close miking**.

distortion—The appearance of a signal in the reproduced sound that was not in the original sound. See also **harmonic distortion, intermodulation distortion, loudness distortion,** and **transient distortion.**

diversity reception—Multiple-antenna receiving system for use with wireless microphones.

doubling—Mixing slightly delayed signals (15 to 35 ms) with the original signal to create a fuller, stronger, more ambient sound. See also **chorus effect.**

dropout—(1) A sudden attenuation of sound or loss of picture. (2) Sudden attenuation in a wireless microphone signal due to an obstruction or some other interference.

driver—A program that allows the transfer of audio signals to and from an audio interface.

dry sound—A sound devoid of reverberation or signal processing. See also **wet sound.**

DSP—See **digital signal processing.**

dub—Transferring sound from tape or disk to another tape or disk. Also called *transfer.*

duration—How long a sound lasts.

DVD—See **digital versatile disc.**

DVD-A—*See* **DVD-Audio.**

DVD-Audio (DVD-A)—A digital versatile disc format with extremely high-quality audio.

dynamic microphone—A microphone that transduces energy electromagnetically. Moving-coil and ribbon microphones are dynamic.

dynamic processor—See **amplitude processor.**

dynamic range—The range between the quietest and the loudest sounds that a sound source can produce without distortion.

early reflections—Reflections of the original sound that reach the listener within about 40 to 50 ms of the direct sound. Also called *early sound.* See also **direct sound.**

early sound—See **early reflections.**

earset microphone—Consists only of an earpiece with no headband cable-connected to a microphone.

echo—Sound reflections delayed by 35 ms or more that are perceived as discrete repetitions of the direct sound.

echo threshold—The point in time at which an echo is perceived, generally between 1–30 ms following the direct sound.

edit decision list (EDL)—A list of edits, computer-generated or handwritten, used to assemble a production.

EDL—See **edit decision list**.

eigentones—The resonance of sound at particular frequencies in an acoustic space. May add unwanted coloration to sound. More commonly known as *room modes*.

elasticity—The capacity to return to the original shape or place after deflection or displacement.

electret microphone—A capacitor microphone which, instead of requiring an external high-voltage power source, uses a permanently charged element and requires only a low-voltage power supply for the internal preamp.

electroacoustics—The electrical manipulation of acoustics.

EQ—Equalization. See **equalizer**.

equal loudness principle—The principle that confirms the human ear's nonlinear sensitivity to all audible frequencies: that midrange frequencies are perceived with greatest intensity and that bass and treble frequencies are perceived with lesser intensity.

equalizer—A signal-processing device that can boost, attenuate, or shelve frequencies in a sound source or sound system.

equivalent noise level—See **self-noise**.

ergonomics—Designing an engineering system with human comfort and convenience in mind.

expander—An amplifier whose gain decreases as its input level decreases. It increases dynamic range.

fade-in—When a signal increases in amplitude from silence to the desired level over a period of time.

fade-out—When a signal decreases to silence over a period of time.

fade-out/fade-in—A transition usually indicating a marked change in time, locale, continuity of action, and other features. It is effected by gradually decreasing the loudness of a signal level to silence (or to "black" in video) and then gradually increasing the loudness of a signal level from silence (or from "black").

fader—A device containing a resistor that is used to vary the output voltage of a circuit or component. Also known as an *attenuator*, a *gain* or *volume control*, or a *pot* or *potentiometer*.

far-field monitoring—Monitoring sound at the listening position from large, powerful frontal loudspeakers several feet away and usually built into the mixing-room wall. See also **near-field monitoring**.

feedback—When part or all of a system's output signal is returned into its own input. Feedback can be acoustic or electronic. A common example of acoustic feedback is the loud squeal or howl caused when the sound from a loudspeaker is picked up by a nearby microphone and reamplified. Electronic feedback is created in digital delay devices by feeding a proportion of the delayed signal back into the delay line. Also called *regeneration.*

filter—A device that removes unwanted frequencies or noise from a signal.

FireWire—A technology that enables isosynchronous service while providing the bandwidth needed for audio, imaging, video, and other streaming data. Isosynchronous service means it guarantees *latency*—the length of time between a requested action and when the resulting action occurs. FireWire offers a standard, simple connection to all types of electronics, including digital audio devices, digital VCRs, and digital video cameras as well as to traditional computer peripherals such as optical drives and hard-disk drives. FireWire can support up to 63 devices on a single bus.

first harmonic—See **fundamental.**

fixed-frequency equalizer—An equalizer with several fixed frequencies usually grouped in two (high and low), three (high, middle, and low), or four (high, high-middle, low-middle, and low) ranges of the frequency spectrum.

fixed-frequency wireless microphone system—A wireless system assigned to one frequency. See also **variable-frequency wireless microphone system.**

flanging—Combining a direct signal and the same signal slightly delayed and continuously varying their time relationships, using a time delay.

flat—Frequency response in an audio system that reproduces a signal between 20 Hz and 20,000 Hz (or between any two specified frequencies) that varies no more than ±3 dB.

flutter echoes—Echoes between parallel walls that occur in rapid, even series.

FM microphone—See **wireless microphone system.**

foldback—The system in a multichannel console that permits the routing of sound through a headphone monitor feed to performers in the studio.

formant—A frequency band in a voice or musical instrument that contains more energy and loudness than the neighboring area.

fps—Frames per second.

frame rate—The number of film frames that pass in 1 second of real time—frames per second (fps).

frequency—The number of times per second that a sound source vibrates, expressed in hertz (Hz); formerly expressed in *cycles per second (cps).*

frequency response—A measure of an audio system's ability to reproduce a range of frequencies with the same relative loudness; usually represented by a graph.

fundamental—The lowest frequency a sound source can produce. Also called *first harmonic* and *primary frequency*.

gain control—See **fader**.

graphic equalizer—An equalizer with sliding controls that gives a graphic representation of the response curve chosen.

Haas effect—A sound reflection arriving up to 30 ms after the direct sound must be about 10 dB louder to be audible, resulting in the direct and reflected sounds' being perceived as one. See also **precedence effect**.

hard knee compression—Abrupt gain reduction at the start of compression. See also **knee** and **soft knee compression**.

hard sound effect—Begins and ends cleanly requiring little adjustment in editing to remain in sync with the picture. Also known as a *cut sound effect*. See also **soft sound effect**.

harmonic distortion—Nonlinear distortion caused when an audio system introduces harmonics to a signal at the output that were not present at the input.

harmonics—Frequencies that are exact multiples of the fundamental.

head-related transfer function—The filtering capacities of the head, outer ears, and torso in locating a sound in three-dimensional space. See **diffraction** and **reflected sound**.

headroom—The amount of increase in loudness level that a tape, amplifier, or other piece of equipment can take, above working level, before overload distortion.

headset microphone—Microphone attached to a pair of headphones; one headphone channel feeds the program and the other headphone channel feeds the director's cues.

Helmholtz absorber—A resonator designed to absorb specific frequencies depending on size, shape, and enclosed volume of air. The enclosed volume of air is connected to the air in the room by a narrow opening, or neck. When resonant frequencies reach the neck of the enclosure, the air inside cancels those frequencies. Also called *Helmholtz resonator*.

hertz (Hz)—Unit of measurement of frequency; numerically equal to cycles per second (cps).

high-definition microphone—In general, a very high-quality microphone. In particular, a trademark of Earthworks, Inc. referring to its line of these types of mics and its proprietary technology.

high end—The treble range of the frequency spectrum.

high-pass (low-cut) filter—A filter that attenuates frequencies below a selected frequency and allows those above that point to pass.

HTRF—See **head-related transfer function.**

human interface device (HID)—A hands-on device, such as a mouse, keyboard, joystick, or touchscreen, that facilitates control of computer functions.

humbuck coil—A circuit built into a microphone to reduce hum pickup.

Hz—See **hertz.**

IID—See **interaural intensity difference.**

impedance—The measure of the total resistance to the current flow in an AC circuit; expressed in ohms.

in the mud—Sound level so quiet that it barely "kicks" the VU or peak meter.

in the red—Sound level so loud that the VU meter "rides" over 100 percent of modulation.

indirect sound—Sound waves that reflect from one or more surfaces before reaching the listener.

infinitely variable pattern microphone—A microphone that allows fine adjustments to any on-axis response from omnidirectional through bi- and unidirectional pickup patterns.

infrasonic—The range below the frequencies audible to human hearing.

inharmonic overtones—Pitches that are not exact multiples of the fundamental. See also **overtones.**

initial decay—In the sound envelope, the point at which the attack begins to lose amplitude.

inner ear—The part of the ear that contains the auditory nerve, which transmits sound waves to the brain.

input/output (I/O) channel—On an in-line console, a module containing input, output, and monitor controls for a single channel.

input section—On a console, the section into which signals from a sound source, such as a microphone, feed and are then routed to the output section.

Integrated Services Digital Network (ISDN)—A public telephone service that allows inexpensive use of a flexible, wide-area, all-digital network for, among other things, recording simultaneously from various locations.

interaural intensity difference (IID)—The difference between signal intensity levels at each ear. Also known as *interaural level difference (ILD).*

interaural level difference—See **interaural intensity difference.**

interaural time difference (ITD)—The difference between signal arrival times at each ear.

intermodulation distortion (IM)—Nonlinear distortion that occurs when different frequencies pass through an amplifier at the same time and interact to create combinations of tones unrelated to the original sounds.

Internet SCSI (iSCSI)—A standard based on the Internet Protocol (IP) for linking data storage devices over a network and transferring data by carrying SCSI commands over IP networks. See also **Small Computer Systems Interface (SCSI)** and **Internet Protocol**.

inverse square law—The acoustic situation in which the sound level changes in inverse proportion to the square of the distance from the sound source.

I/O module—See **input/output (I/O) module**.

iSCSI—See **Internet SCSI**.

ISDN—See **Integrated Services Digital Network**.

ITD—See **interaural time difference**.

jack—Receptacle or plug connector leading to the input or output circuit of a patch bay, a recorder, or other electronic component.

jitter—A variation in time from sample to sample that causes changes in the shape of the audio waveform and creates adverse sonic effects such as reduced detail, harsher sound, and ghost imaging.

jogging—In digital editing, moving the mouse from side to side to direct control of an audio track. See also **shuttling**.

kHz—See **kilohertz**.

kilohertz (kHz)—A measure of frequency equivalent to 1,000 hertz, or 1,000 cycles per second.

knee—The point at which a compressor starts gain reduction. See also **hard knee compression** and **soft knee compression**.

K-system—Measuring system developed by Bob Katz that integrates measures of metering and monitoring to standardize reference loudness.

latency—The period of time it takes for data to get from one designated point to another. In audio, the signal delay through the driver and the interface to the output.

lavaliere microphone—Microphone that used to be worn around the neck but is now worn attached to the clothing. Also called *mini-mic*.

layering—When many sounds occur at once, layering involves making sure sounds remain balanced, in perspective, and intelligible in the mix.

LFE—See **low-frequency enhancement**.

limiter—A compressor with an output level that does not exceed a preset ceiling regardless of the input level.

linearity—Having an output that varies in direct proportion to the input.

listening fatigue—Usually in lengthy listening sessions, a pronounced dulling of the auditory senses, inhibiting perceptual judgment.

localization—(1) Placement of a sound source in the stereo or surround-sound frame. (2) The direction from which a sound source seems to emanate in a stereo or surround-sound field. (3) The ability to tell the direction from which a sound is coming.

looping—Repeating a sound continuously.

lossless compression—A data compression process during which no data is discarded. See also **lossy compression**.

lossy compression—A data compression process during which data that is not critical is discarded during compression. See also **lossless compression**.

loudness—The relative volume of a sound.

loudness distortion—Distortion that occurs when the loudness of a signal is greater than the sound system can handle. Also called *overload distortion*.

low bass—Frequency range between roughly 20 Hz and 80 Hz, the lowest two octaves in the audible frequency spectrum.

low end—The bass range of the frequency spectrum.

low-frequency enhancement (LFE)—In a surround-sound system, using a separate channel and a subwoofer loudspeaker to reproduce low-frequency sounds.

low-pass (high-cut) filter—A filter that attenuates frequencies above a selected frequency and allows those below that point to pass.

MADI—See **Multichannel Audio Digital Interface**.

makeup gain—A compression control that allows adjustment of the output level to the desired optimum. Used, for example, when loud parts of a signal are so reduced that the overall result sounds too quiet.

masking—The hiding of some sounds by other sounds when each is a different frequency and they are presented together.

master section—In a multichannel production console, the section that routes the final mix to its recording destination. It usually houses, at least, the master controls for the mixing bus outputs, reverb send and reverb return, and master fader.

mastering—The final preparation of audio material for duplication and distribution.

megabyte (MB)—1,048,576 bytes (2^{20} bytes); sometimes interpreted as 1 million bytes.

megahertz (MHz)—Measure of frequency equivalent to 1 million cycles per second.

memory card—A nonvolatile memory, such as Flash memory, that can be electrically recorded onto, erased, and reprogrammed. It does not need power to maintain the stored information.

memory recorder—A digital recorder that has no moving parts and therefore requires no maintenance. Uses a memory card as the storage medium.

MHz—See **megahertz**.

mic—See **microphone**.

microphone—A transducer that converts acoustic energy into electric energy. Also called *mic*.

microphone modeler—A device or plug-in that emulates the sound of various microphones.

middle ear—The part of the ear that transfers sound waves from the eardrum to the inner ear.

middle-side (M-S) microphone—Consists of two mic capsules housed in a single casing. One capsule, usually cardioid, is the midposition microphone. The other capsule, usually bidirectional, has each lobe oriented 90 degrees laterally.

MIDI—See **Musical Instrument Digital Interface**.

MIDI time code (MTC)—Translates SMPTE time code into MIDI messages that allow MIDI-based devices to operate on the SMPTE timing reference.

midrange—The part of the frequency spectrum to which humans are most sensitive; the frequencies between roughly 320 and 2,560 Hz.

milking the audience—Boosting the level of an audience's sound during laughter or applause and/or reinforcing it with recorded laughter or applause.

millimeter (mm)—A unit of length equal to one thousandth (10^{-3}) of a meter, or 0.0394 inch.

millisecond (ms)—One-thousandth of a second.

mini-mic—Short for *miniature microphone*. Any extremely small lavaliere mic designed to be unobtrusive on-camera and which can be easily hidden in or under clothing or on a set.

mixdown—The point, usually in postproduction, when all the separately recorded audio tracks are sweetened, positioned, and combined into stereo or surround sound.

mixer—A small, highly portable device that mixes various elements of sound, typically coming from multiple microphones, and performs limited processing functions. See also **console**.

mixing desk—See **console**.

mm—See **millimeter**.

mobile media—Any of a number of different portable devices capable of storing and playing digital audio, video, and images, such as cell and smart phones, iPods, cameras, PDAs, and laptop computers.

monitor section—The section in a console that enables the signals to be heard. The monitor section in multichannel production consoles, among other things, allows monitoring of the line or recorder input, selects various inputs to the control room and studio monitors, and controls their levels.

morphing—The continuous, seamless transformation of one effect (aural or visual) into another. It is a complete restructuring of two completely different and independent effects.

moving-coil microphone—A mic with a moving-coil element. The coil is connected to a diaphragm suspended in a magnetic field.

MPEG—Stands for *Moving Picture Experts Group*. A compression format for film established by the film industry and the International Standards Organization (ISO). Uses an analytical approach to compression called *acoustic masking*.

ms—See **millisecond**.

M-S microphone—See **middle-side microphone**.

MTC—See **MIDI time code**.

mult—See **multiple**.

Multichannel Audio Digital Interface (MADI)—The standard used when interfacing multichannel digital audio.

multidirectional microphone—Microphone with more than one pickup pattern. Also called *polydirectional microphone*.

multipath—In wireless microphones, when more than one radio frequency (RF) signal from the same source arrives at the receiver's front end, creating phase mismatching.

multiple—(1) On a patch bay, jacks interconnected to each other and to no other circuit. They can be used to feed signals to and from sound sources. Also called *mults*. (2) An amplifier with several mic-level outputs to provide individual feeds, thereby eliminating the need for many. Also called a *press bridge* or a *presidential patch*.

multiple-entry-port microphone—A mic that has more than one opening for sound waves to reach the transducer. Most of these openings are used to reject sound from the sides or back of the microphone through phase cancellation. Each port returns a different frequency range to the mic capsule out of phase with sounds reaching the front of the mic. Also called *variable-D*.

Musical Instrument Digital Interface (MIDI)—A protocol that allows synthesizers, drum machines, sequencers, and other signal-processing devices to communicate with or control one another or both.

narrative sound—Sound effects that add more to a scene than what is apparent and so perform an informational function. See also **commentative sound** and **descriptive sound**.

NC—See **noise criteria**.

near-coincident miking—A stereo microphone array in which the mics are separated horizontally but the angle or space between their capsules is not more than several inches, depending on the ensemble's width. See also **X-Y miking**.

near-field monitoring—Monitoring with loudspeakers placed close to the operator, usually on or just behind the console's meter bridge, to reduce interference from control room acoustics at the monitoring position. See also **far-field monitoring**.

noise—Any unwanted sound or signal.

noise-canceling headphone—Headphone that detects ambient noise before it reaches the ears and nullifies it by synthesizing the sound waves.

noise-canceling microphone—A microphone designed for use close to the mouth and with excellent rejection of ambient sound.

noise criteria (NC)—Contours of the levels of background noise that can be tolerated within an audio studio.

noise gate—An expander with a threshold that can be set to reduce or eliminate unwanted low-level sounds, such as room ambience, rumble, and leakage, without affecting the wanted sounds.

noise reduction coefficient (NRC)—See **sound absorption coefficient**.

nondestructive editing—Editing that does not alter the original sound or soundfile, regardless of what editing or signal processing is affected. See also **destructive editing**.

nondiegetic sound—Sound outside the story space such as music underscoring. See also **diegetic sound**.

nondirectional microphone—See **omnidirectional microphone**.

nonlinear—The property of not being linear—not having an output that varies in direct proportion to the input.

nonlinear editing (NLE)—See **digital editing**.

notch filter—A filter capable of attenuating an extremely narrow bandwidth of frequencies.

NRC—See **sound absorption coefficient**.

octave—The interval between two sounds that have a frequency ratio of 2:1.

off-mic—Not being within the optimal pickup pattern of a microphone; off-axis.

off-miking—See **accent miking.**

omnidirectional microphone—Microphone that picks up sound from all directions. Also called *nondirectional microphone.*

on-mic—Being within the optimal pickup pattern of a microphone; on-axis.

oscillator—A device that generates pure tones or sine waves.

outer ear—The portion of the ear that picks up and directs sound waves through the auditory canal to the middle ear.

output section—In a mixer and console, the section that routes the signals to a recorder or broadcast or both.

overload—Feeding a component or system more amplitude than it can handle and thereby causing loudness distortion.

overload distortion—See **loudness distortion.**

overload indicator—On a console, a light-emitting diode (LED) that flashes when the input signal is approaching or has reached overload and is clipping. Also called *peak indicator.*

pad—An attenuator inserted into a component or system to reduce level.

pan pot—Short for *panoramic potentiometer.* A volume control that shifts the proportion of sound from left to right between two output buses and, hence, between the two loudspeakers necessary for reproducing a stereo image, or among the six (or more) surround-sound channels, and loudspeakers, necessary for reproducing a surround-sound image.

parabolic microphone system—A system that uses a concave dish to focus reflected sound into a microphone pointed at the center of the dish.

paragraphic equalizer—An equalizer that combines the features of a parametric and a graphic equalizer.

parametric equalizer—An equalizer in which the bandwidth of a selected frequency is continuously variable.

passive microphone—A microphone that does not require phantom power.

passive microphone mixer—Combines individual inputs into one output without amplifying the signal. See also **active microphone mixer.**

patch bay—An assembly of jacks to which are wired the inputs and the outputs of the audio components in a console and/or sound studio. Also called *patch panel.*

patch cord—A short cord or cable with a plug at each end, used to route signals in a patch bay.

patch panel—See **patch bay.**

peak indicator—See **overload indicator.**

peak meter—A meter designed to indicate peak loudness levels in a signal.

peak program meter (ppm)—A meter designed to indicate transient peaks in the level of a signal.

percentage of modulation—The percentage of an applied signal in relation to the maximum signal a sound system can handle.

perspective miking—Establishing through mic-to-source distance the audio viewpoint in relation to the performers and their environment in screen space.

PFL—See **solo**.

phantom power—Operating voltage supplied to a capacitor microphone by an external power source or mixer, thereby eliminating the need to use batteries.

phase—The time relationship between two or more sounds reaching a microphone or signals in a circuit. When this time relationship is coincident, the sounds or signals are in phase and their amplitudes are additive. When this time relationship is not coincident, the sounds or signals are out of phase and their amplitudes are subtractive.

phase reversal—See **polarity reversal**.

phase shift—The phase relationship of two signals at a given time, or the phase change of a signal over an interval of time.

phasing—An effect created by splitting a signal in two and time-delaying one of the signal portions, using a phase shifter.

pickup pattern—See **polar response pattern**.

pitch—The subjective perception of frequency—the highness or lowness of a sound.

pitch shifter—A signal processor that varies the pitch of a signal. The basic parameter for pitch shifting is transposition.

plug-in—An add-on software tool that gives a hard-disk recording/editing system signal processing alternatives beyond what the original system provides. Available separately or in bundles.

polarity—The relative position of two signal leads—the high (+) and the low (−)—in the same circuit.

polarity reversal—The control on a console that inverts the polarity of an input signal 180 degrees. Sometimes called *phase reversal*.

polar response—The indication of how a loudspeaker focuses sound at the monitoring position(s).

polar response pattern—The graph of a microphone's directional characteristics as seen from above. The graph indicates response over a 360-degree circumference in a series of concentric circles, each representing a 5 dB loss in level as the circles move inward toward the center. Also called *pickup pattern*.

polydirectional microphone—See **multidirectional microphone.**

pop filter—Foam rubber windscreen placed inside the microphone head. Particularly effective in reducing sound from plosives and blowing. Also called *blast filter*. See also **windscreen.**

porous absorber—A sound absorber made up of porous material whose tiny air spaces are most effective at absorbing high frequencies.

pot—Short for potentiometer. See **fader.**

potentiometer—See **fader.**

ppm—See **peak program meter.**

precedence effect—The tendency to perceive the direct and immediate repetitions of a sound as coming from the same position or direction even if the immediate repetitions coming from another direction are louder. See also **Haas effect.**

predelay—The amount of time between the onset of the direct sound and the appearance of the first reflections.

prefader listen (PFL)—See **solo.**

pre-emphasis—(1) Boosts the high frequencies in wireless microphone transmission. See also **de-emphasis.** (2) Boosts the treble range in radio broadcast transmission by 6 dB per octave, starting at 2.1 kHz (in the United States) or 3.2 kHz (in Europe).

premix—(1) Mixing groups of similar voicings, such as strings, backup vocals, and the components of a drum set before routing them to a master channel(s). (2) The stage in postproduction when dialogue, music, and sound effects are prepared for final mixing.

presence—(1) Perception of a sound as being close and realistic. (2) Also used as a synonym for ambience and room tone. See **ambience.**

primary frequency—See **fundamental.**

proximity effect—Increase in the bass response of some mics as the distance between the mic and its sound source is decreased. Also known as *bass tip-up*.

proximity-prone mini-mic—Used for body miking; tends to add presence to close dialogue and reject background sound. See also **transparent mini-mic.**

psychoacoustic processor—Signal processor that adds clarity, definition, overall presence, and life, or "sizzle," to recorded sound.

psychoacoustics—The study of human perception of and subjective response to sound stimuli.

pure tone—A single frequency devoid of harmonics and overtones.

Q—A measure of the bandwidth of frequencies an equalizer affects.

quantization—Converting a waveform that is infinitely variable into a finite series of discrete levels.

radio microphone—See **wireless microphone system**.

rarefaction—Temporary drawing apart of vibrating molecules, causing a partial vacuum to occur. See also **compression** (2).

read mode—Mode of operation in an automated mixdown when the console controls are operated automatically by the data previously encoded in the computer. Also called *safe mode*. See also **update mode** and **write mode**.

recordable compact disc (CD-R)—A CD format allowing users to record one time but to play back the recorded information repeatedly.

recovery time—See **release time**.

reflected sound—Reflections of the direct sound that bounce off one or more surfaces before reaching the listener.

regeneration—See **feedback**.

release—In the sound envelope, the time and the manner in which a sound diminishes to inaudibility.

release time—The length of time it takes a compressor to return to its normal level (unity gain) after the signal has been attenuated or withdrawn. Also called *recovery time*.

rerecording—The final stage in postproduction, when the premixed tracks or stems—dialogue, music, and sound effects—are combined into stereo and surround sound and sent to the edit master.

resolution—See **word length**.

resonance—Transmitting a vibration from one body to another when the frequency of the first body is exactly, or almost exactly, the natural frequency of the second body.

reverberation—Multiple blended, random reflections of a sound wave after the sound source has ceased vibrating. The types of reverberation in current use are digital, convolution, plate, and acoustic chamber. Also called *reverb* and *reverberant sound*.

reverberation time—The length of time it takes a sound to die away—the time it takes a sound to decrease to one-millionth of its original intensity, or 60 dB-SPL. Also called *decay time*.

rewritable compact disc (CD-RW)—A compact disc format that can be recorded on, erased, and used again for another recording.

rhythm—The sonic time pattern.

ribbon microphone—A microphone with a ribbon diaphragm suspended in a magnetic field.

ride the gain—Continually adjusting controls on a console or other audio equipment to maintain a more or less constant level.

room modes—See **eigentones**.

room tone—Another term used for ambience. Also called *presence*. See **ambience**.

SAC—See **sound absorption coefficient**.

safe mode—See **read mode**.

sample clock—See **word clock**.

sampling—(1) Examining an analog signal at regular intervals defined by the sampling frequency. (2) A process whereby a section of digital audio representing a sonic event, acoustic or electroacoustic, is stored on disk or into electronic memory.

sampling frequency—The frequency (or rate) at which an analog signal is sampled. Also called *sampling rate*.

scrubbing—In hard-disk editing, moving the play cursor through the defined region at any speed to listen to a sound being readied for editing.

SCSI—See **Small Computer Systems Interface**.

segue—(1) Cutting from one effect to another with nothing in between. (2) Playing two recordings one after the other, with no announcement in between.

self-noise—The electrical noise, or hiss, an electronic device produces. Also called *equivalent noise level*.

sensitivity—(1) Measurement of the voltage (dBV) a microphone produces, which indicates its efficiency. (2) The sound-pressure level directly in front of the loudspeaker, on-axis, at a given distance and produced by a given amount of power.

sensorineural hearing loss—A nerve-based condition that occurs when the microscopic hair cells of the inner ear are compromised or damaged.

sequencer—An electronic device that can be programmed to store and automatically play back a repeating series of notes on an electronic musical instrument such as a synthesizer.

SFX—See **sound effects**.

shelving—Maximum boost or cut of a signal at a particular frequency that remains constant at all points beyond that frequency so the response curve resembles a shelf.

shock mount—A device that isolates a microphone from mechanical vibrations. It can be attached externally or built into a microphone.

shotgun microphone—A highly directional microphone with a tube that resembles the barrel of a rifle.

signal processors—Devices used to alter some characteristic of a sound. See also **amplitude processor, spectrum processor**, and **time processor**.

signal-to-noise ratio (S/N)—The ratio, expressed in decibels, of an electronic device's nominal output to its noise floor. The wider the S/N ratio, the better.

sine wave—A fundamental frequency with no harmonics or overtones. Also called **pure tone**.

single-entry-port microphone—A directional microphone that uses a single port to bring sounds from the rear of the mic to the capsule. Because these sounds from the rear reach the capsule out of phase with those that reach the front of the capsule, they are canceled. Also called *single-D microphone*.

slap back echo—The effect created when an original signal repeats as distinct echoes that decrease in level with each repetition.

slate—The part of a talkback system that feeds sound to a recording. It is used for verbal identification of the material recorded, the take number, and other information just before each recording.

Small Computer Systems Interface (SCSI)—The standard for hardware and software command language that allows two-way communication between, primarily, hard-disk and CD-ROM drives. Pronounced "scuzzy."

SMPTE time code—A reference in hours, minutes, seconds, and frames used for coding to facilitate editing and synchronization. Pronounced "sempty."

S/N—See **signal-to-noise ratio**.

soft cut—Term used with picture when a shot change is brief but not quite as abrupt as a cut nor as deliberate as a dissolve. The effect can be used in audio for transitions that need a quick, yet aesthetically, graceful change.

soft knee compression—Smooth gain reduction at the start of compression. See also **knee** and **hard knee compression**.

soft sound effect—Does not have a defined beginning and ending and does not explicitly synchronize with the picture. See also **hard sound effect**.

solo—A control on a multichannel console that automatically cuts off all signals feeding the monitor system except those signals feeding through the channel that the solo control activates. Sometimes called *prefader listen* (PFL).

Sony/Philips Digital Interface (S/PDIF)—The consumer version of the AES/EBU interface calling for an unbalanced line using phono connectors. See also **AES/EBU**.

sound absorption coefficient—A measure of the sound-absorbing ability of a surface. This coefficient is defined as the fraction of incident sound absorbed by a surface. Values range from 0.01 for marble to 1.00 for the materials used in an almost acoustically dead enclosure. Also known as *noise reduction coefficient* (NRC).

sound card—Computer hardware necessary to input, manipulate, and output audio.

sound chain—The audio components that carry a signal from its sound source to its destination.

sound design—The process of creating the overall sonic character of a production (usually in relation to picture).

sound effects (SFX)—Anything sonic that is not speech or music.

sound envelope—Changes in the loudness of a sound over time, described as occurring in four stages: attack, initial decay, sustain, and release (ADSR).

soundfile—A sound stored in the memory of a hard-disk recorder/editor.

sound frequency spectrum—The range of frequencies audible to human hearing: about 20 Hz to 20,000 Hz.

sound-pressure level (dB-SPL)—A measure of the pressure of a sound wave, or sound-pressure level (SPL), expressed in decibels (dB).

sound transmission class (STC)—A rating that evaluates the effectiveness of barriers in isolating sound.

sound wave—A vibrational disturbance that involves mechanical motion of molecules transmitting energy from one place to another.

source music—Background music from an on-screen source such as a stereo, radio, or jukebox. It is added during postproduction.

spaced miking—Two, sometimes three, microphones spaced from several inches to several feet apart, depending on the width of the sound source and the acoustics, for stereo recording.

S/PDIF—See **Sony/Philips Digital Interface**.

spectrum editing—Using a sonogram view of an audio file to facilitate ultra-fine surgical editing.

spectrum processor—A signal processor that affects a sound's spectral range such as equalizers, filters, and psychoacoustic processors.

speed-up pitch shifting—Changes the timbre and pitch of natural sounds. Sometimes referred to as the *chipmunk effect.*

SPL—See **sound-pressure level.**

split-band compressor—A compressor that affects an input signal independently by splitting the audio into multiple bands and then recombining the outputs of the bands into a single mono or stereo broadband signal. See also **broadband compressor.**

squelch—In a wireless microphone system, a process of signal reception at the receiver that silences or mutes the receiver's audio output when there is no radio signal.

STC—See **sound transmission class.**

stereo—One-dimensional sound that creates the illusion of two-dimensional sound.

stereophonic microphone—Two directional microphone capsules, one above the other, with separate outputs, encased in one housing.

subtractive equalization—Attenuating, rather than boosting, frequencies to achieve equalization. See also **complementary equalization** and **cumulative equalization**.

surround sound—Multichannel sound, typically employing six or more channels, each one feeding to a separate loudspeaker that expands the dimensions of depth, thereby placing the listener more in the center of the aural image than in front of it. See also **5.1** and **7.1**.

surround-sound microphone system—Separate microphones, or microphone capsules, housed in a single casing, for each pickup in a given surround-sound format and a controller to adjust spatial imaging.

sustain—In the sound envelope, the period during which the sound's relative dynamics are maintained after its initial decay.

sweet spot—In control room monitoring, the designated listening position, which is the optimal distance away from and between the loudspeakers.

sweetening—Enhancing the sound of a recording in postproduction through signal processing and mixing.

synchronization—Locking two or more devices that have microprocessor intelligence so that they operate at precisely the same rate.

system message—In a MIDI system, the message that affects an entire device or every device regardless of the MIDI channel. It gives timing information, such as what the current bar of the song is and when to start and stop, as well as clocking functions that keep a MIDI sequencer system in sync.

system microphone—Interchangeable microphone capsules of various directional patterns that attach to a common base. The base contains a power supply and a preamplifier.

talkback—Studio-address intercom system that permits communication from a control room microphone to a loudspeaker or headphones in the studio.

tempo—The speed of a sound.

temporary threshold shift (TTS)—A reversible desensitization in hearing that disappears in anywhere from a few hours to several days. Also called *auditory fatigue*.

terabyte (TB)—1,024 gigabytes (2^{40} bytes).

THD—Stands for *total harmonic distortion*.

three-to-one rule—A guideline used to reduce the phasing caused when a sound reaches two microphones at slightly different times. It states that no two mics should be closer to each other than three times the distance between one of them and its sound source.

threshold of feeling—120 dB-SPL.

threshold of hearing—The lowest sound-pressure level at which sound becomes audible to the human ear. It is the zero reference of 0 dB-SPL.

threshold of pain—The sound-pressure level at which the ear begins to feel pain, about 140 dB-SPL, although levels of around 120 dB-SPL cause discomfort.

tie line—Facilitates the interconnecting of outboard devices and patch bays in a control room or between studios.

timbre—The unique tone quality or color of a sound.

time compression—Shortening the time (length) of material without changing its pitch.

time expansion—Increasing the time (length) of material without changing its pitch.

time processor—A signal processor that affects the time interval between a signal and its repetition. The effects include reverberation and delay.

tinnitus—After prolonged exposure to loud sounds, the ringing, whistling, or buzzing in the ears, even though no loud sounds are present.

TL—See **transmission loss.**

transducer—A device that converts one form of energy into another.

transfer—See **dub.**

transient—A sound that begins with a sharp attack followed by a quick decay.

transient distortion—Distortion that occurs when a sound system cannot reproduce sounds that begin with sudden, explosive attacks.

transmission loss (TL)—The amount of sound reduction provided by a barrier such as a wall, floor, or ceiling.

transmitter microphone—See **wireless microphone system.**

transparent mini-mic—Used for body miking; tends to add an open, natural sound and pick up more ambience. See also **proximity-prone mini-mic.**

treble—Frequency range between roughly 5,120 Hz and 20,000 Hz, the highest two octaves in the audible frequency spectrum.

trim—(1) To attenuate the loudness level in a component or circuit. (2) The device on a console that attenuates the loudness level at the microphone/line input.

TTS—See **temporary threshold shift.**

tube microphone—A capacitor microphone using a tube circuit in the preamp.

ultrasonic—Frequencies above the range of human hearing.

unbalanced line—A line (or circuit) with two conductors of unequal voltage.

underscore music—Nondiegetic music added to enhance the informational or emotional content of a scene.

unidirectional microphone—A microphone that picks up sound from one direction. Also called *directional microphone*.

update mode—Mode of operation in an automated mixdown when an encoded control can be recorded without affecting the coding of the other controls. See also **read mode** and **write mode**.

upper bass—Frequency range between roughly 80 Hz and 320 Hz.

upper midrange—Frequency range between roughly 2,560 Hz and 5,120 Hz.

USB microphone—A digital microphone developed for those who want to record directly into a computer without an audio interface such as a console, control surface, or mixer. USB stands for *Universal Serial Bus*.

USB microphone adapter—See **USB microphone converter**.

USB microphone converter—Device that makes it possible to connect any dynamic or capacitor XLR microphone into a computer via USB. Also known as a *USB microphone adapter*.

variable-frequency wireless microphone system—A wireless microphone system that can use more than one channel. Also known as *frequency-agile system*. See also **fixed-frequency wireless microphone system**.

velocity—The speed of a sound wave: 1,130 feet per second at sea level and 70°F.

virtual track—In hard-disk recording, a track that provides all the functionality of an actual track but cannot be played simultaneously with another virtual track.

Voice over Internet Protocol (VoIP)—Technology that allows interactive video game users who have a headset and a microphone to speak with each other, give and receive instructions, and play in a team environment against others using the same technology.

voice processor—A device that can enhance, modify, pitch-correct, harmonize, and change completely the sound of a voice. Also called *vocal processor*.

VoIP—See **Voice over Internet Protocol**.

volume contro—See **fader**.

volume-unit (VU) meter—A meter that responds to the average voltage on the line, not true volume levels. It is calibrated in volume units and percentage of modulation.

VU—See **volume-unit meter**.

waveform—A graphic representation of a sound's characteristic shape displayed, for example, on test equipment and hard-disk editing systems.

wavelength—The length of one cycle of a sound wave. Wavelength is inversely proportional to the frequency of a sound; the higher the frequency, the shorter the wavelength.

wet sound—A sound with reverberation or signal processing. See also **dry sound**.

windscreen—Foam rubber covering specially designed to fit over the outside of a microphone head. Used to reduce plosive and blowing sounds. See also **pop filter**.

wireless microphone system—System consisting of a transmitter that sends a microphone signal to a receiver connected to a console or recorder. Also called *cordless*, *FM*, *radio*, and *transmitter microphone*.

word clock—A synchronization signal used to control the rate at which digital audio data is converted or transmitted. Also called *sample clock* or *digital clock*.

word length—Describes the potential accuracy of a particular piece of hardware or software that processes audio data. In general, the more bits available, the more accurate the resulting output from the data being processed. Also called *bit depth* and *resolution*.

work surface—See **control surface**.

write mode—The mode of operation in an automated mixdown during which controls are adjusted conventionally and the adjustments are encoded in the computer for retrieval in read mode. See also **read mode** and **update mode**.

XLR connector—Common male and female microphone plugs with a three-pin connector.

X-Y miking—Coincident or near-coincident miking that places the microphones' diaphragms over or horizontal to one another. See also **coincident miking** and **near-coincident miking**.

zero crossing—The point in a waveform denoting a value of zero amplitude. It divides the positive (upper) and negative (lower) parts of the waveform.

CREDITS

Acoustical Solutions, Inc.: 4-10b

ADC Telecommunications, Inc.: 6-27, 8-17a, 8-17b

Alesis, LLC: 8-02

Atlas Sound: 6-43b, 6-41, 6-43a

Audio Ease: 11-10

Audio Engineering Associates; 6-03b

Avid: 11-16a

Behringer USA, Inc.: 11-3

beyerdynamic Inc. USA: 5-16a, 5-16b, 6-03b, 6-15a, 6-46a

Countryman Associates, Inc.: 6-13, 6-15c, 6-16a, 6-16b

Dorrough Electronics: 8-10

Douglas Quin: 3-04, 8-20, 12-7, 12-8

DPA Microphones,Inc.: 6-35c

Electro-Voice: 6-07, 6-36, 6-38c, 6-38d, 6-46b

Elektron Instruments Ltd. (Sifam Instruments Ltd.): 8-08, 8-11

Elizabeth M. Keithley, Ph.D.: 2-03a, 2-03b

E.A.R. Inc. / Insta-Mold West: 2-08b

EMT Studiotechnik GmbH: 11-11

Esto Photographics: 7-8

Globe Institute of Recording and Production: 13-7, 13-8, 13-9, 13-10, 13-11

Harman International Industries, Inc.: 6-15b, 6-17, 6-19a, 6-19b, 6-21b, 6-22a, 6-22b, 6-22c, 6-22d, 6-22e, 6-29, 6-35d, 6-38a, 6-49d, 6-49e, 11-9a, 11-9b

Herbert Zettl: 6-45, 6-47, 6-48

K-Tek: 7-15

Latch Lake Music: 6-44

Loud Technologies Inc.: 8-01, 8-21, 8-22

Metric Halo: 5-13, 8-14

MOTU Inc.: 11-16b

Royer Labs: 6-23

Rupert Neve Designs: 8-13

Sabra-Som: 6-49f

Samson Technologies Corp: 9-5

Schalltechnik Dr.-Ing. Schoeps GmbH: 6-25

sE Electronics: 7-49

Sennheiser Electronic Corporation: 6-21a, 6-28a, 6-28b, 6-30, 6-35e, 6-38b

Shure Incorporated: 6-06, 6-26, 6-49a, 6-39b

Sound Devices, LLC: 8-06, 9-6

Studio Projects US: 6-24

Summit Audio Inc: 11-4

Waves Inc: 11-13, 11-6

Whirlwind: 7-45

William Storm: 6-35a, 6-40

Wireworks Corporation: 6-39

INDEX